MADAGASCAR IN HISTORY

Essays from the 1970's

Edited by
Raymond K. Kent

The Foundation for Malagasy Studies
906 Washington Street, Albany, CA 94706

Library of Congress Catalog Card Number: 79-92715

ISBN 0-936000-00-7

Printed in the United States of America at Golden Horn
Typesetting & Publishing House, Berkeley California.

Contents

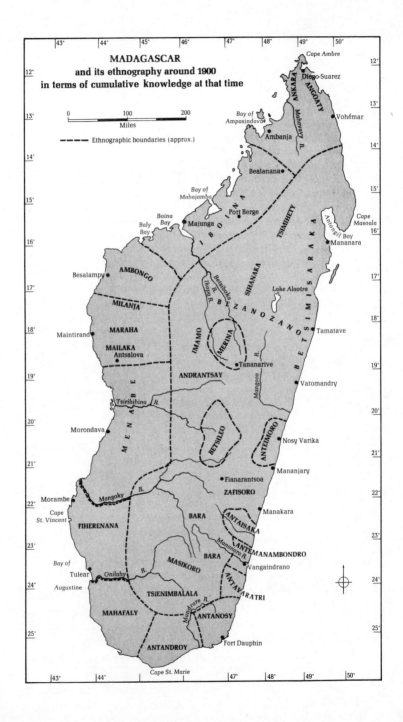

MADAGASCAR
and its ethnography around 1900
in terms of cumulative knowledge at that time

```
0        100        200
Miles
```

- - - - Ethnographic boundaries (approx.)

Cape Ambre

ANKARA

ANGOATY

Diego-Suarez

Bay of
Ampasindava

Mahavavy R.

Vohémar

Ambanja

Bealanana

IBOINA

TSIMIHETY

Bay of
Mahajamba

Port Berge

Cape
Masoala

Boina
Bay

Baly
Bay

Majunga

Antongil Bay

Mananara

SIHANAKA

Besalampy

AMBONGO

Betsiboka R.

Ikopa R.

BEZANOZANO

Lake Alaotra

BETSIMISARAKA

MILANJA

Maintirand

MARAHA

IMAMO

MERINA

Tamatave

MAILAKA
Antsalova

Tananarive

Mangoro R.

ANDRANTSAY

Vatomandry

Tsiribihina R.

MENABE

Morondava

BETSILEO

ANTEIMORO

Nosy Varika

Fianarantsoa

Mananjary

ZAFISORO

Morambe

Mangoky R.

BARA

ANTAISAKA

Manakara

Cape
St. Vincent

FIHERENANA

ANTEMANAMBONDRO

Mananara R.

BARA

MASIKORO

Vangaindrano

ANTAVARATRI

Bay of
Tulear

Onilahy R.

TSIENIMBALALA

Mandrare R.

Augustine

MAHAFALY

ANTANOSY

ANTANDROY

Fort Dauphin

Cape St. Marie

Introduction

Not very long ago Madagascar was generally excluded from the studies of Africa on the grounds of "race, language and culture" neither of which should ever have been mixed with the other two. The proximity of Madagascar to Africa could not be altered physically but earlier students of the larger and smaller continents separated only by the Mozambique Channel remained unimpressed by the sheer geographic fact. As scholarship flourished within the "Great African Island," at the end of the 1800's and throughout the colonial period, it managed to erect an edifice asserting the primacy of distant Asia at the very doorstep of Africa. It also remained self-centered and self-contained, without seeking to export what could be learned about and from man, his collective wisdom and folly, Malagasy-style. At the same time, students of Africa could not make the intellectual leap across the Mozambique Channel either. With its "Mongoloid race," its Malayo-Polynesian "language *and* culture," the Island was "different" from the mainland; its social evolution, its institutions, its problems and solutions, ultimately its past, had no bearing upon their African analogues. If a handful of French Africanists did maintain an interest in the *Ile Rouge* it was determined by colonial rule and, because Madagascar was a colony of France, very few Anglophone scholars took the trouble to become well-informed about an island in the western Indian Ocean noted mainly because of its plants and animal species.

The massive *History of Africa* in the Cambridge and UNESCO series provides a clearcut statement that the international community of scholars no longer will sanction the separation of Madagascar from Africa. When Madagascar emerged from isolation, in the 1960's, its national university also began to study Africa, an act that would have been unthinkable in earlier times. While Malagasy students were picking-up English as their third language, scholars in the English-speaking countries grew increasingly interested in Madagascar as is reflected in publications and at the level of doctoral dissertations in History and Anthropology. Nonetheless, there remain two particular forums using the English language at which Madagascar is either under-represented or, at times, represented in ways unworthy of the subject and its richness: *international journals* and *collective works* which are either thematic, methodological or anthological in nature. Thus, while the old barrier of separation has been lifted, it is still necessary to advance the factor of proximity beyond its current position. The present volume is a step in the direction of acute need. Although Africa is mentioned in some of the contributions, the volume does not deal with connections between Africa and Madagascar. Its central theme is, instead, historical reconstruction in the face of problems, obstacles and challenges that link Madagascar at once with Africa and which the Africanists and scholars working in other areas of the globe will readily recognize as their own. The anthological format of *Madagascar in History* hardly diminishes the central theme's unity and an exclusive focus on Madagascar (and within it mostly on Imerina) reduces in no way the universality of methodological and analytical concerns apparent in some contributions and subdued in others. As the subtitle suggests, this is also a deliberate attempt to leave a record of what students of Madagascar's past wanted to know and to understand in the current decade, students with very divergent backgrounds, living in and outside of Madagascar. Indeed, the team here is for the first time *really* international, with Malagasy, French, American, English and West-Indian contributors. Seven of the thirteen essays have been translated from French rendering *Madagascar in History* also into the first collective work in English. The book's largest instituitional contingent comes, as it should, from the University of Madagascar.

Stressing the *preliminary* nature of their reports and using the relatively novel "regional-survey" and the older "prehistoric-dig" techniques in two very different parts of Madagascar, Henry Wright and Susan Kus, followed by Jean-Pierre Emphoux, head the contributions with their respective archaeological essays. It remains a surprising fact of life that Archaeology is just beginning to be employed in Madagascar in serious and structured ways given that it is the *sole* discipline capable of throwing light on the *earliest* periods of Malagasy history as well as a major auxiliary for the understanding of social and economic changes in more recent times. Wisely, as they worked in Central Imerina, Wright and Kus went to the *Tantara* (popular   term for oral traditions) before selecting where to look but did *not* follow their content deliberately, preferring to let the archaeoloical record speak for itself through the "Phases" developed at the Museum of Archaeology (Antananarivo) on the basis of potters'-craft assemblages. Some of their preliminary conclusions are most timely. The earliest settlements in Imerina tended to be precisely where the simplest techniques could be employed to grow wet rice and edible tubers. Contrary to the still-surviving image of pre-literate "static societies," change was *continuous,* as ascertained by material objects, but far from having the same rate or pace in time and space. A simple unitary view of Imerina cannot be deduced from archaeological evidence while no one can as yet define the point at which state organization becomes apparent. Although population in general tended to grow, population pressure as a possible prime mover in state-formation must, for the time being, settle into the more modest role of one variable within a broader cotext of evolution. Last but hardly the least important, defensive fortifications of Central Imerina reveal discrete transformations rather than gradual change. In contrast to Central Imerina and the Muslim entrepôts in northwestern coastal Madagascar, the rest of veritable small continent has hardly been touched by the archaeologist's spade. This is what makes the dig of Jean-Pierre Emphoux particularly interesting. Working in the deep south of Madagascar, moreover, he found it necessary to amplify the preliminary archaeological findings through what he could learn about the sites from near-by present-day occupants without subordinating the verdict of material culture to that of the spoken word. Emphoux found both the pottery and metalurgical sites. Of these, Bekoropitika was the most investigated and it yielded hand-made pottery without decoration, some with handles as well. pressed out by the potter and containing what might well be the oldest fingerprints in Madagascar. The most obvious significance of the "Bekoropitika sequence" is that it represents pottery unlike any other found within Madagascar so far. Emphoux also came across some well-arranged broken-stone mounds, highly suggestive of rather ancient tombs (subject to further probings), in a pottery-site with some false *celadon* which allows a tentative placing of the site into a period within the 1400's and 1500's. There is also an extremely intriguing dry-stone circular enclosure some 600-800 meters in diameter. The metalurgical sites are all within recent times, the last couple of hundred years, most interesting finding in its own right.

The Anjoaty, called in older sources Onjatsy, Undzatse and even "Henesouastes," are of considerable historical interest. Reported in European accounts since the late 1650's and mentioned in the Arabico-Malagasy writings somewhat later, they appear at Boina Bay in the northwest, at Vohemar in the northeast and all along the eastern littoral of Madagascar as descrete sub-groups, "class" in society (in one case guardians of royal tombs), itinerant individuals possessing magical powers, and as a people. Yet, even scholars with a commanding knowledge of obscure sources would be hard-put to find solid accounts of the Anjoaty in any of the reported settings. After two years of fieldwork among the Anjoaty of Vohemar (1974-1975) David Hurvitz is concluding the first sustained and rigorous study of their society and history. In his present contribution, Hurvitz is using the vehicle of their cattle ear marks as a method of study pioneered over fifty years ago in western Madagascar by Emil Birkeli who perceived quite accurately the marks as simultaneously ethnographic and historical documents. In so doing, he confirms the method as continuously valid but one that must be refined theoretically before it can have an island-wide application. His most original feature is the addition of a factor not considered by Birkeli, one which is crucial, namely the relationship of cattle-owners to land, Hurvitz also collected oral traditions and studied both archival sources and works in print. The result is a detailed and complex study of incisions, nomenclature, lateral cattle-ear symbolism, categories of cattle and classes of people, origin of local cattle and local cattle ear marks, their subsequent modifications connected intimately with the descending ancestry of cattle and people, the matrilineal and patrilineal principles, and land-divisions in the course of time.

It is commonplace to hold that religion and government are inseparable in "traditional societies" and even that a study of each apart from the other may well be a hopeless undertaking. Such a view, of course, presupposes a static condition in which disassociation could neither exist in the past nor develop in the future without a dissolution of the traditional society. It blocks any historical study of religion and government at one point as separate entities if not at another and it precludes any substitutions whatsoever as long as a given society remains traditional. This view happens to accord well also with an assumption derived mainly through the study of African states in the last century, namely that their antecedents can be explained away through intrusive state-builders whose own religion merges into a perpetual union with the state. Essays by Gerald Berg and the present editor show not only that separateness and substitution are historically present but that without religious support government in societies of old Madagascar could not be effective. The governors invariably elaborated in the domain of religion to augment their own sacral power but this elaboration took place within the religions of the *tompon-tany*, the people, literally "masters of the soil." As Berg points out, Imerina's monarchs deliberately entered different local dieties/protectors into a national pantheon transformed into a "royal cult" which channelled the old regional loyalties toward the kings themselves. When a strong ruler like Radama I (1810-1828) displayed his belief in a modern and westernized army and his disbelief in the pantheon, the imperial expansion outside Imerina could not arrest social turmoil within it, contrary to the often-repeated belief that a focus on events which are external deflects internal tensions. When Protestantism triumphed as state religion in 1869, as "idols" were being tossed into fires, the Merina Queen disregarded warnings that royal authority itself rested on religious belief in the pantheon among most of the Merina people; and the ensuing disunity could not be reversed by administrators and the army irrespective of individual competence and collective firepower. Yet, Christianity already had strong roots in Imerina before and after 1869 while Merina society remained basically "traditional" despite growing literacy and westernization in certain of its sectors. Even by itself a comparison of the southeastern Antanosy and the Sakalava of western Madagascar in the 1600's, both with dominant intrusive elements, brings out with dramatic clarity the fact that the older view of fusion simply does not work. The Zafindraminia potentates could never unite their individual protector dieties with those of the southeastern Malagasy among whom they had settled while their use of fear and pronounced acquisitive impulse made certain that the southeasterners would not come under one central authority. In contrast, by using sacerdotal persons who inserted them into the cult of the *dady* (ancestors) and by becoming in time the *Ampagnito-be'* (Great Ancestors) of their subjects, the Maroserana became the family from which the Sakalava obtained their monarchs and it is hardly an accident of history that royal Maroserana ancestors are honored to this day in western Madagascar.

History itself comes into sharp relief in the contributions of Alain Delivré, Lee Haring and Simon Ayache as they concentrate respectively on oral tradition, folklore and biography of a historian. Intentionally or not, Delivré has established that long before Marx and the Marxists advocated the "reification" of history the Merina put this idea into practice within the confines of their culture, uniting oral tradition and historical consciousness to give a sense of inner value to the individual *and* the collective. History became also a "moral science" in Imerina as both the rulers and the ruled could refer to precedents through which to legitimize change without cultural upheaval giving thus a *historically-perceived* importance to history as at the same time a stabilizing and dynamic force in society. Acutely alert to the dangers of anachronisms, telescoping, contamination and informant problems, Delivré has worked out a structure-within-structure of Merina Oral Tradition through which to extract historical content, determine the advent of royal tradition itself, its customs and innovations, to see history as an explanation of culture and find objectivity within the *Tantara* given that oral texts were kept at the level of kings, nobles and commoners and could thus be cross-checked. In the process of his work the old "functionalist" premise that oral tradition is nothing more than rationalization of existing power has surely received a blow from which it cannot recover without negating the case of Imerina altogether. An editorial note at the end of Delivré's essay reports by way of a summary on a recent paper by Paul Ottino dealing specifically with succession in Imerina and showing the presence of political theory in the *Tantara.*

Arguing for the mutuality of history and folklore Lee Haring notes the advantage of Madagascar in terms of available sources "captured so early in the period of European contact." One salutary aspect of this mutuality is that some of the "events" contained within the vast literature for Madagascar turn out, upon closer examination, to be grist for the mill of comparative folklorists armed with indices which show that the would-be "unique event" is, in effect, folktale motif F 531.3 or A 901. This could prove unsettling to researchers seeking to locate important individuals of the past or to explain a topographical feature in a historical context. Haring also warns against attempting to reconstruct history from folktales alone and he is pessimistic about the derivation of historical truth from oral tradition without the help of written sources, archaeology and some other "corpus" of evidence, especially since a wide gap separates the dicta of European historians and the demands of Malagasy cosmology. Beyond the impediments of solipsism and the pull of culture Haring locates a most telling point and one that should be widely noted: he was not able to find a single *pan-Malagasy* culture hero. The implications of this negative discovery should not escape anyone who works with either the past or the present or both. It is Simon Ayache who supplies a *tour de force* in respect to history by producing a literate, almost modern *historian* when Imerina was barely on the threshold of literacy, in the first half of the Nineteenth century. Sent to study in England as a boy of eleven, Raombana returned to Antananarivo eight years later to become ultimately Secretary to Queen Ranavalona I, Imerina's first archivist, and somewhat clandestine author of the first "rationalistic and critical construct of national past, written in English but entirely Malagasy otherwise," altogether some 8,000 manuscript pages. Friend of Europe and precursor of nationalism, high Merina noble to whom no door was closed, Ramobana broke entirely with traditional methods of dealing with history and applied the critical method to his study of all the texts rigorously collected as well. As the appendices of Ayache's essay show, Raombana was equally critical of those within the royal palace, including the Queen, with whose own nationalism he was entirely in accord. It is Ayache's belief that Raombana might just be a culture hero for *all* the Malagasy of today. He was the first modern intellectual, the earliest advocate of the need to incorporate all of the Malagasy into the Merina state without resort to arms, and certainly a Malagasy who could work out within himself and his culture a synthesis of the two worlds, "modern" and "traditional."

With Jean Valette writing on King Radama I and Faranirina Esoavelomandroso on the Merina Prime Minister Rainilaiarivony biography continues to intersect with other historical aspects — with unification, modernization and political independence. Comparing Radama and his father, in reverse order, to the French monarchs Louis VI and Philippe-Auguste "since the former had amassed lands and people around Ile-de-France and the second used the forces so grouped to extend royal authority," Valette traces out Radama's deliberate drive to implant in a lasting way his own royal authority beyond Imerina. His military campaigns, his take-over and commercial use of Tamatave, the making of alliance with the British for his own sub-empire, his arrest of overseas slave trade, his faith in modern army and scepticism about religion, his basic realism punctured by an occasionally romantic notion, his very real ingenuity, patience and short temper are all there to be seen. The most obvious result is that within scant eighteen years Radama dominated three-fifths of Madagascar, something no one had done before him. Valette sees Radama I as yet another candidate for the status of national culture hero, not only through military unification but also because of the entry of Madagascar, through the Merina state, into the international order, also for the first time. Yet, as Valette sees it, all of the foregoing should take second place to Radama's equally deliberate effort to modernize Imerina through selective borrowing from Europe and more specifically from Great Britain. With the London Missionary Society at the center of this effort, with its educators and craftsmen, with Radama's sustained support, Imerina would come to have, at Radama's death in 1828, some 4,000 literate commoners and nobles plus 38 ongoing schools with 42 teachers and 2,309 pupils. As could be expected, Radama also alienated some important people in Imerina by depending too much on his close kinsmen, by downgrading the advisers of his late father and by being openly irreverent with the dieties in the national pantheon. As missionaries, too, created novel tensions in Imerina it only took the departure of Radama I to transit into a very different period altogether.

For some three decades, the Merina Prime Minister Rainilaiarivony, husband of two Queens, member of an ambitious lineage of commoners, statesman and diplomat, lion and fox, came to be regarded as the staunchest defender of Malagasy independence in the face of New Imperialism represented in Madagascar most clearly by France. A sympathetic observer called him the "Richelieu of a black monarchy exposed to the covetousness of the outside world" and his astute French enemy A. Martineau wrote as late as 1894 that the Malagasy Prime Minister "can hence claim before history the great honor of having upheld for thirty years the independence of his country." In a major reinterpretation of Rainilaiarivony and his times, without shedding the sympathy a historian must have for his subject, Faranirina Esoavelomandroso turns the tables on a verdict that cannot withstand her scrutiny. In his initial twenty years as Prime Minister, Rainilaiarivony developed certain policies and habits which may have been temporarily appropriate but which could not work in the last ten years, the most dangerous ones for Madagascar as a whole. The "paradox of Rainilaiarivony" was quite simply that the man who had been most adamant in the defence of Malagasy independence became the main instrument for its loss. The astute balancing act, for example, that came him in good stead with Britain and France before the Franco-"Hova" War of 1883-1885 was hardly suitable thereafter. A rapidly aging Prime Minister could not concentrate on foreign policy while enmeshing himself in the intrigues at the capital and in personal problems. After two decades in power, Rainilaiarivony's authoritarianism became even more pronounced. His own legitimacy derived more from his international role on behalf of the "Kingdom of Madagascar" than on his internal one. In fact, he was the representative of "class interest," of Merina oligarchy, being himself not only a large land owner but also an entrepreneur. He hardly ever left Antananarivo, did not communicate too well with the Merina, would not listen to subordinates' advice, distrusted the non-Merina Malagasy, including the coastal peoples who would have to be instrumental in the defence of Madagascar against possible French invasion. His troops started not to obey orders, desertions were rampant, banditry was reaching to the outskirts of the capital, and the old British benevolence was no longer shielding Madagascar from France in whose economic dependence Rainilaiarivony placed the Island through his very attempts to modernize and model the Kingdom on the pattern of Europe.

It has been almost an article of faith that the London Missionary Society came to Madagascar in 1818 as a result of immediate and direct political action and not through any long-range design. Its advent in Imerina was a simple outgrowth of the Anglo-Merina Treaty of 1817, promoted on one side by a British Governor of Mauritius and on the other by Radama I. If one takes the excursion with Vincent Belrose-Huyghues into the realm of ideas within the expansion of Europe it will be clear that nothing of the kind took place. The arrival of the LMS in the Great Island was the culmination of a process which began with the search for Eldorado. An illusion —quite real at the time— of "golden legend" involving Madagascar started a tradition after 1610 that would not change until 1820, tradition of heaping praise upon Madagascar irrespective of any realities. Indeed, less than 25 authors account for virtually everything printed in England about Madagascar between the two dates; and, when the golden legend could no longer be sustained, Madagascar was transformed into an island with inhabitants who were the "happiest in the world" but subjected to "oppression and barbaric exploitation of Europeans." This leitmotif found a response in the non-privileged classes that fed the missionary avocation preoccupied with the moral destiny of the "natives." Although the non-Conformist Academies were able to augment knowledge about Madagascar, especially by recovering what the French form the Mascarene Islands knew about it, Eighteenth-century popularizers in England expurgated everything in the literature that could tarnish the image of Madagascar as a dream-island. Even the pirates were laundered to become good Christians in Madagascar, having never engaged in a raid or sold a Malagasy into slavery and settling among the "natives" who welcomed them with open arms; and, if vagabonds from Europe could be treated that way, it was a foregone conclusion that the men of cloth and of the Gospel should be venerated. One could only speculate what would have taken place without Mauritius as a British base in the western Indian Ocean but there is no doubt that the LMS was on its way to Madagascar already in 1800, having selected the Bay of Saint-Augustine as the point of penetration. There definitely was a place for Madagascar in the history of *European* "ideas in action."

What happens to slaves after manumission is a topic which has received worldwide attention but one in its early stages of discussion for Madagascar. As Maurice Bloch puts it, the freeing of slaves in Madagascar (1897) did not wipe out the *implications* of slave descent which he sets out to study among the over-one-million-strong Merina, with one of the most advanced states in Madagascar and Africa, and some 15,000 Zafimaniry shifting cultivators located in a less than accessible part of the Island. While there are similarities between Madagascar and Africa in terms of how slaves were secured and how domestic slaves were treated, the case of Merina offers a striking difference. In Africa, ex-slaves tended to be incorporated sooner or later but this was impossible in Imerina as a result of kinship and endogamy. Without local kinship ties, without the ancestral lands and family tombs on them the ex-slaves "could never become full members of the society." It was not as much a matter of inferiority as being outside the "social system and its ideological representation." Manumission without free access to land ownership restricted the benefits of legal freedom, and no matter what "solutions" were worked-out later in time, the ex-slaves tended to be poor, in a rural setting, without access to connections in the wider world of the city and administration. They were unlike the former commoners who married back into their descent groups, who became more westernized, comparatively wealthier, more urban and with kin ties in many places that matter. While Radama's manpower requirements for conquests and for irrigation on a massive scale found Imerina replete with slaves in 1897, the Zafimaniry did not have more than about 300, none owned individually, and "houses in slave villages and free villages antedating manumission are very much alike." As among the Merina, the free Zafimaniry did not intermarry with the slaves among them or with their descendants. The similarity, however, ends here because slaves among the Zafimaniry were not ideologically *outside* the group. They did not become "non-persons" without ancestral homelands. While slaves in Imerina could not have permanent tombs of their own anywhere such was not the rule among the Zafimaniry. Equally, the former slaves did have —if somewhat restricted— the right to own land, all of which contrasts with the Merina case. Still, an even greater impact came through an intrusive missionary presence which turned all of the ex-slaves among the Zafimaniry into Catholics now endowed with churches and schools and gaining definite advantages over the Protestant and "pagan" Zafimaniry, including commercial and agricultural ones. Bloch suggests, in conclusion, a process of "entailment" as a possible way of looking at the uneven rates of integration.

Contemporary history, as study of recent events with a structure, usually events within one's own lifetime, is neither superior nor inferior to its non-contemporary counterparts but it does come with its own problems. In general, written and oral sources tend to be abundant, often overwhelming, forcing one to be selective beyond the degrees likely to be experienced by those working with earlier periods. Given that a contemporary historian is also a part of the subject under study it becomes extremely difficult to sever the factor of acute need for selectivity from the question of distance; temporal proximity does not only involve one with the problem of the angle of vision but also with that of "audience-response," anticipated *and* real since it is precisely the audience that is being historically studied in its own moment in time. It is safe to say that the concluding as well as most extensive essay of the present volume has managed to remain admirably on the margin of problems affecting contemporary history. Between 1947 and 1977 Madagascar underwent several major political, economic and social tremors intensely germane to the outside world but hardly noticed in the international arena. The tremors began with one of the two earliest anti-colonial revolts after the last great war, continued in the 1960's to make Madagascar one of the closest allies of France in Africa, and are now pulling this small continent in the western Indian Ocean in a very different direction yet. For anyone who wishes to understand the immediate antecedents of present-day Madagascar, the contribution of Yvan Paillard should provide essential reading.

December 1979   R. K. K.

An Archaeological Reconnaissance of Ancient Imerina*

H.T. WRIGHT and S. KUS
University of Michigan

Imerina possesses a rare record of its early development in the form of detailed oral histories collected in the course of the 19th century.[1] There are available, in addition, the observations of contemporary visitors[2] and historical traditions which are still alive. Nonetheless, abundant as this record happens to be, it is one that allows for no easy interpretations.[3] It is a rendition of predominantly social and political events and barely alludes to demographic and economic developments. These are, however, precisely the areas that can be documented with current archaeological techniques. What follows is a summary report concerning the trial application of a group of techniques generally known as "regional archaeological survey." The area of concern is one important in the historical development of the Merina kingdom and the later development of Malagasy Civilization as a whole. These surveys were conducted in 1975 by the Musée d'Art et d'Archéologie, University of Madagascar, in the vicinity of modern Antananarivo. After concluding this brief introduction, we will discuss the geographical focus of the reconnaissance, the specific

* The more technical aspects of the survey will appear in *Taloha*, annual publication of the Musée d'Art et d'Archéologie, Tananarive. This report aims at a wider audience to indicate the promise of a regional-survey approach and of the colaboration of archaeologists, historians, and ethnologists. We are grateful to many in Madagascar and especially to M. J.-A. Rakotoarisoa, M. J.-P. Domenichini, M. Ramilson, M.C. Vogel, and M.A. Ralaikoa. We are thankful to the museum for allowing us to study their pottery collections and to consult their survey results. Without the initial encouragement of Dr. P. Vérin and Dr. C. Kottak, we might never have visited Imerina. The funds of this visit were provided by the National Science Foundation Grant #GS-42337X.

techniques employed, and the chronological bases of the study. We will proceed with some tentative discussions of historically successive settlement patterns, and offer some elementary conclusions and some warnings about the use and the misuse of such studies.

The regional survey as a tool for the study of broad economic and social changes was first applied in Northern Peru.[4] As the work of archaeologists focused on the problems of the development of civilization in arid lands and on the testing of the so called "hydraulic theory,"[5] the method was refined to include techniques for the estimation of human population densities and the elucidation of specific agricultural patterns.[6] Regional survey approaches are now indispensible to any archaeological research which addresses the problems, both theoretical and empirical, of complex societal development.

The mapping, description, and dating of archaeological sites is preliminary to serious analysis. From these data, former land use can be assessed by looking at the association of sites with different types of land, different water resources, and the like, the assumption being that sites will be as near as other factors permit to the land they utilize. Former population size can also be estimated from the size and the number of settlements if it is assumed that for any architectural mode there is a more or less constant number of people living on each hectare of settlement. In addition, past social and economic complexities can be inferred by studying the spatial arrangements of different types of sites and comparing architectural features and artifacts within sites. Here the assumption is that important and repeated social activities should require defined spaces for their performances and often leave behind discarded but characteristic artifacts. Clearly, this type of research is based upon a structure of assumptions. If confidence in the results is to be had, these assumptions must be checked both with the excavation of different types of sites from each time period and with ethnographic studies of houses, artifacts, etc. This form of checking has yet to be undertaken in Central Madagascar.

There were several reasons for believing that regional survey techniques would work in Central Madagascar. First, a number of previous studies, culminating in the cataloguing of more than 16,000 sites visible on air photographs by Adrien Mille of the

Musée d'Art et D'Archéologie (1971), showed that ancient sites were well-preserved and easily located. Second, while the Museum's primary efforts during the last decade had been along the coast of Madagascar, several emergency excavations near Antananarivo (cited below) had produced a wide variety of ceramics which could very well represent chronologically different stages in the development of the potters' craft. If these developmental stages could be defined and dated, then each site in turn could be dated by the ceramics found on its surface and settlement maps could be constructed for each period. Third, a number of recent provocative studies by Malagasy students[7] revealed that oral traditions both previously recorded and others still recalled by resident families could point to specific sites and even to specific architectural features within them. At some future point, when archaeological survey and mapping approach completion, evidence of the material remains and of the traditions can be compared and collated to present us with a comprehensive understanding of cultural development.

Notes on the Cultural Geography of Central Imerina

One of the major geographic characteristics of Madagascar is a central mountainous massif running the North-South length of the island, generally referred to as the "Hautes Terres." The numerous rivers of the island flow from these central highlands which serve as a watershed for the rains from Southwest tradewinds that blow from 7 to 8 months of the year. The basic geological material of the island is a granite-gneiss complex and the various details of relief of the Hautes Terres are consequences of differential erosion with granites and quartzites affording various highpoints of the relief. Evident exaggerations of erosional patterns in the Hautes Terres have traditionally been attributed to human action such as timbering, annual burning, and manioc cultivation. Where this erosion has not exposed the bed rock, there is a deeply weathered soil mantle on the hills.

The general impression given by the Hautes Terres is one of numerous rounded hills, some larger mountains of volcanic origin, and steep sided valleys with flat rather than concave floors. In that area of the Hautes Terres which we term central Imerina, recent faulting and uplift along the west edge of the area have blocked the flow of rivers and created vast expanses of lakes and marshy plains. Of the latter, the Betsimitatatra is the most important in Imerina cultural history.

The extent of original forestation in Imerina is a topic of continuing debate. It will remain so until such time as either sediment cores are removed from the marshes and ancient pollen grains are studied, or charred plant remains are recovered from early sites and subjected to ethnobotanical study. Suffice it to say that today the marshes are drained and turned into rice paddies and the hills have been denuded of trees. Only the recently introduced eucalyptus commonly is seen.

Delineation of Central Imerina

At its period of major expansion, according to Mille (1970), Imerina proper was roughly delimited to the east by the forest of Angavo and to the south by the river Mania where it runs between the cliff of Angavo and the river Tsiribihina. The western limits run roughly between Tsiroanomandidy and Miandrivazo, and to the north the limit follows the 18th parallel. Our study, intentionally limited in scope, concerns the traditional core of Imerina around the present day capital of Antananarivo and Ambohimanga, as such it encompasses the rich rice plain of the Betsimitatatra and the immediately surrounding area.

Three major rivers run eastward through the heart of Imerina, the Mamba, the Ikopa, and the Sisaony. To the north is a virtual mountain wall broken only by a tributary of the Mamba, stretching from Ampananina to Ambatoantanina. South of these are the ridges of Ambohimanoro, which lie to the west of the Mamba, and Mangabe and Ambohimanga, which lie east of the Mamba (and south of the Mambakely). South of this complex, the lineation of ridges tends more or less North-South. The eastern border of our area of concern is the ridge above Ambohimalaza. Ambohibe sits upon the height of a lower parallel ridge, and further to the west Antananarivo sits on a small though lofty ridge of similar configuration. To the west where the Mamba and the Ikopa join there is no defining configuration of ridges; the western boundary is taken to run through their confluence. In the south one meets the northern extensions of a number of large ridges. On the southwest is the ridge with the dominant peak of Ankadibe. In the center is the complex of ridges on which sit Ambohitraino and Ifandro. To the southeast is the complex of

Masiapapango. These eminences cradle the extensive complex of marshes, lakes, and low rolling hills on which were placed many historically important towns. The largest marshes include the Betsimitatatra surrounding Antananarivo itself, the Andranomasina to the south of Ambohimanga and the Ankosy surrounding Imerimandroso. Both in the past and today these drained marshlands provide a major portion of the region's rice harvest.

Survey Areas and Survey Techniques

During 1975, four small blocks within the region surrounding the Betsimitatatra were selected for study (see figure 1).[†] Initially three were chosen to test the regional survey method. The selection was based on a preliminary reading of the *Tantaran'ny Andriana.*

(1) A southern block of 13.0 square kilometers southwest of Imerimanjaka is thought to be an area important early in Merina history. Imerimanjaka is the reputed burial site of Rafohy[*] and according to traditions, the site of the creation of the *fanjakahova,* the beginning of Andriana rule. To the northeast is Alasora, the capital of Andriamanelo.[*]

(2) A northeast block of 13.5 square kilometers surrounding Ambohidrabiby is often mentioned in later Merina history. Ambohidrabiby was the capital of Ralambo[*] which was gained by the marriage alliance effected between his father Andriamanelo and the daughter of the Vazimba chief Rabiby.

(3) A northwest block of 15.0 square kilometers south of Ambohidratrimo was chosen as an area peripheral to the political transformations effected both during the Andrianjaka-Andriamasinavolona[*] period and the Andrianampoinimerina period.

Subsequently a fourth block was added.

(4) A northern block of 38.2 square kilometers west of Ambohimanga was selected to give us better coverage in the area important during the 18th century, the period most crucial in the consolidation of the Merina state under Andrianampoinimerina.

Intensive archaeological survey directed at problems of regional geography or ecology requires special methods. In brief, the approach requires that every hectare of ground within a selected

[†]For Figures 1 through 7 see pp. 22ff.

[*]For all these rulers see essay by A. Delivré below. (Ed.)

survey area be examined by archaeologists with air photographs and maps in hand, preferably on foot. This procedure enables one to locate every site within the survey area and to mark its limits as defined by architectural remains and scatters of broken pottery and other artifacts. A ceramic sample is collected from every site discovered during such systematic searches. Each site or part of a site examined is roughly sketched in a field note-book kept for this purpose and notes are made of the various characteristics of sites thought to be significant for analytical purposes. Each site is assigned a unique number for identification, preferably based on a coordinate overlay system for the country.[8] The sites are then marked on a single copy of the regional base map. In the lab ceramic samples are cleaned, marked with the site identification number, and typologically asessed. In these sample surveys undertaken in the vicinity of Antananarivo it was not possible for the museum's teams to utilize quite such detailed methods in the field because of the limitations of time and of the availability of air photos and maps. However, experience in other parts of the world shows that it is best to survey an area minimally two or three times with the aid of airphotos to insure the locating of all important sites. Thus, this article is an assess-ment of preliminary survey results and is subject to revision based on subsequent resurvey.

Outline of the Development of the Potter's Craft in Central Imerina

If archaeologists are to define chronological changes in any aspect of material culture, they must first establish some relatively or absolutely dated points with external evidence. Sometimes this evidence is geological, as in the case of a stratified archaeological site wehere layers containing material from earlier occupants are found buried under layers containing remains from later occu-pants. Sometimes this evidence is physical, as in the case of a site dated by measuring the decay of radioactive carbon isotopes in ancient charcoal. Sometimes the evidence is itself cultural, as when a site is dated by written documents or, more usually, by the appearance of an object such as a coin or piece of pottery dated elsewhere by documents or other evidence. The sequence of developing ceramic assemblages for Central Imerina uses all three classes of evidence:

1. The most recent assemblage of archaeological ceramics available in the Museum is a group of sherds from a storage pit in the Fiadanana district of Antananarivo[9] associated with a piece of imported English "transfer-print" bone china known to have been manufactured between A.D. 1840 and 1860.

2. An earlier assemblage from an excavated midden on the site of Angavobe in Eastern Imerina[10] has a single radioactive carbon age determination of A.D. 1620 ± 80.[11] This single determination was confirmed by the discovery during the survey of the site of Ambohodratrimo of a piece of imported Chinese Celadon. As the zenith of celadon use on the coasts of Madagascar was during the 16th century,[12] the early 17th century date seems reasonable.

3. From an excavation in the midden at the site of Ambohitsitakatra in Northern Imerina[13] a stratigraphic super-positioning of ceramic assemblages was found. The lower and older assemblage is similar to that dated by physical and cultural evidences outlined in step 2 above. The upper and younger assemblage is similar to that dated by cultural evidence in step 1 above.

Thus, though one would like more evidence of dating, four assemblages can be placed in a chronological sequence. There are two other assemblages recognizable in the samples curated in the Musée d'Art et d'Archéologie. These must be placed in their relative chronological positions on the basis of their degree of similarity to the otherwise dated assemblages. One is known from soundings at Ankatso[14] and Antanambe[15] and it is a reasonable prototype for the earliest dated assemblage. Yet another is a reasonable prototype for the Ankatso assemblage. It is known only from a few sites found during the surveys and its chronological position is particularly insecure. The logic of the chronological ordering of the six assemblages is presented in more detail in an article to appear soon in *Taloha*.[16] After a conference of the staff and collaborators of the Museum, proper names for the cultural phases typified by the six assemblages were adopted. Table 1 presents the earlier phases and their characteristics. Doubtless future excavation will lead to changes in this scheme. Figures 2 and 3 show examples of the pottery vessels of these phases as reconstructed from typical sherds.

All the vessels represented in the collections of the Museum were hand-made and fired at a low temperature without benefit

Table 1 : Proposed Cultural Phases in Central Imerina and Their Ceramic Attributes

Phase Names	Site Assemblages	Approximate Ages	Jar Statistics			Bowl Statistics		
			% Sandy Clay Body	% Reduction Fired	% Low Neck	% Sandy Clay Body	% Reduction Fired	% Thick Lip
Fiekena	Antompan' Ifiekena	-	100%	25%	100%	62%	25%	0%
Early Ankatso	Antanambe	-	33%	11%	95%	42%	33%	67%
Late Ankatso	Ankatso	-	11%	11%	95%	33%	75%	87%
Angavo	Angavobé, Ambohidratrimo	Late XVI - Early XVII Centuries	29%	75%	33%	0%	100%	91%
Ambohi-dray	Ambohisitikatra lower, Ankadivory	Late XVII - Early XVIII Centuries	60%	45%	0%	0%	100%	60%
Kaloy	Ambohisitikatra upper, Kaloy	Late XVIII - Early XIX Centuries	35-80%	45%	50%	0%	100%	0%

of a kiln. Most fall into two broad categories: restricted mouth jars and open bowls. The following paragraphs describe the development of the potters' art during five successive phases, as this development is presently understood.

During the earliest Fiekena Phase most vessels have a sandy clay body, one quarter having an admixture of large quartz granules as well. About three quarters of the vessels were fired in an oxidizing atmosphere, the remainder being fired in a reducing atmosphere. The jars have low, barely everted necks about twenty centimeters in diameter (Fig. 2a). Some had incised bands on the neck, but none are sufficiently well-preserved to determine the decorative elements within these bands. The bowls have straight rims with simple rounded lips, and range from ten to thirty centimeters in diameter. Three quarters of the bowls are decorated in two characteristic patterns. The simpler pattern is a horizontal band with opposed triangular impressions (Fig. 2b). The more complex pattern is a wide horizontal band divided into vertical plats containing either opposed triangular impressions alone, or oblique bands alternately filled with triangular impressions (Fig. 2c). A rare feature of Fiekena assemblages are flat bases with a similar impressed decoration (Fig. 2d). The triangular impressions on Fiekena ceramics are usually broad-based isoceles forms.

In the Ankatso Phase, which probably succeeds Fiekena, most vessels have a sandy clay body, but as many as 15 percent having quartz granules as well. Bowls seem to have sandier bodies than jars and to be fired in a different manner. While only one tenth of the Ankatso jars were fired in a reducing atmosphere, about one third of the earlier Ankatso Phase bowls and three quarters of the latter Ankatso Phase bowls were so fired. Thus, while in Fiekena Phase assemblages all forms seem to have been made from the same clay mixtures and fired with the same range of techniques, in Ankatso Phase assemblages both the clay preparation and firing technique for bowls is different from that of jars. Ankatso jars have markedly everted necks, usually low as in Fiekena but often wider at the mouth, and ranging up to thirty centimeters in diameter. The surfaces are smoothed and just below the rim is an incised band (Fig. 2e). Among the earlier Ankatso Phase jars, one third have incised zig-zag motifs in the band, while the remainder have simple rows of impressions, usually triangular. Among later Ankatso Phase jars, four fifths have zig-zag lines, often embellished with impressions, while only one fifth have impressions alone and these are typically oval rather than triangular. Ankatso bowls are thin-walled and hemispherical in shape, which manifest the same range of sizes as those of Fiekena. There is a thickening on the inner lip in two-thirds of the earlier Ankatso cases and in seven-eights of the later Ankatso cases. Some bowls have a cylindrical pedestal base, a feature which continues through the remainder of the sequence. The decoration on these bowls is a striking combination of horizontal bands and vertical plats containing zig-zags, crosses, diamonds, and other elements, all of which are filled with triangular or oval impressions (Figs. 2f through 2h). The triangles, which are used in about half the cases, are usually short-based isosceles forms. The finished bowls were often coated with graphite giving them a metallic luster, but the technique had not been mastered and the graphite was easily worn off. It is notable that the complex decorative patterns on these bowls show little possible chronological variation, and such variation as is present perhaps has to do with social or geographical groupings. The reader can appreciate how the other minor features of the richly decorated vessels of the earlier phases can easily be used to date the occupations of individual sites. Unfortunately in the later phases impressed and incised decoration becomes rare, and the problems of dating ceramic samples become more difficult.

Angavo Phase ceramics ordinarily have a fine clay body with only fine sand inclusions which may well be natural. Only a quarter to a third of the jars contain any coarser sand, and no vessel has quartz granules. Only a quarter of the jars are fired in an oxidizing atmosphere; all other vessels have been reduction fired to a gray color. Vessel sizes are similar to those of the preceding phase. There seem to be two varieties of jars: a low-neck form often oxidized and never with graphite coating (Fig. 3a), and a high neck form sometimes coated with graphite on the exterior (Fig. 3b). Most bowls are thin and have interior lip thickening (Fig. 3c). A major portion of these bowls are graphited and for the most part such coatings are fixed with a polishing technique so that they do not easily rub off. Decoration is rare on both bowls and jars, and usually involves haphazardly-applied oval impressions. Angavo Phase ceramics seem very different from earlier assemblages, and following the past practices of archaeologists, one might assume that such ceramic variation is indicative of a change in local population; however, caution is required. The changes in clay, firing, and vessel form are all a result of trends noted in earlier phases. It is only the abrupt, though not total, change in surface treatment that is unexpected. As shall be discussed, the change from Ankatso to Angavo is a time of social upheaval, and old symbols in the decorative arts may well have been swept aside with old elites without involving major population changes.

In our Ambohidray Phase samples, there is a further differentiation in the techniques used in the making of jars and bowls. Jars have sandy clay bodies and more than half have coarse sand inclusions, while bowls have fine clay mixtures only. Jars are oxidized in half the cases and bowls are exclusively reduced. It is likely that different clays are being used for jars and bowls, not merely different clay preparation procedures. This may indicate certain communities were specialized in the making of different forms, but one must keep in mind the certainty that increased rice paddy construction around these communities would be providing more and more places where fine clays were collecting. Only chemical and mineralogical studies of clay sources and of the sherds themselves can demonstrate community specialization. Ambohidray jars have high everted necks, the low neck form having become rare. Graphite coatings are rare and of low quality. The hemispherical bowls are relatively thin, as before, but only half have interior lip thickening, the remainder having simple rounded lips. All bowls have graphite, but once again poor quality coatings are common.

During the Kaloy Phase, the last to concern us in this paper, there is much variation in the clay used in jars from the assemblages. All have coarse inclusions, but in some cases it is quartz sand while in others it is mica. As before about half are oxidized. In contrast, all the bowls have fine clay bodies and all are reduced. This variability strengthens the inference that different clay sources and different production sequences were used for the two shapes and suggests but does not demonstrate that different centers of production were involved. The jar form with a high everted neck continues, and some are very large (Fig. 3d), but a low neck form, often with graphite on the inner lip and neck, comprises about half the examples (Fig. 3e). The hemispherical bowls are always thick and always have simple rounded rims (Fig. 3f). The graphite coatings are of uniformly poor quality. At present the dating of a site with only one occupation by a single later phase is easy, but those sites with continuing Angavo to Ambohidray or Ambohidray to Kaloy occupations are difficult to assess. With future stratigraphic excavations and study of minor variations in rim shapes, more accurate dating should be possible.

The reader familiar with Merina history will note that archaeological names with minimal historical or ethnic significance were chosen for the phases in order not to prejudice future correlation with the historical traditions. For similar reasons we have not attempted to buttress or refine our chronological arguments with reference to the geneologies. Certainly broad historical correlations are possible: The Fiadanana Phase represents the period of the florescence of the Merina Empire after the reign of Radama I.* The preceding Kaloy Phase must include both the Period of Internecine Wars and the consolidation of the Merina State under Andrianampoinimerina. Earlier phases are more difficult to correlate, however; most centers whose traditional histories begin with the early Merina rulers —Alasora, Ambohidrabiby, Ambohimanga, and Ambohidratrimo, for example— have their first major occupations during the Angavo Phase. Sites with explicit associations with Vazimba rulers, for example, Ambohidrapeto and Ankatso itself, have Ankatso Phase occupations. However at this stage of research it would be foolish to equate Ankatso Phase settlement organization to the "Vazimba," whatever they were, or to associate our Angavo Phase settlement maps with the activities of Ralambo or Andrianjaka. Broad correlations aside, it is imperative that the archaeological framework be independent of the framework of the traditions. Only with such separation can we prevent circular reasoning when, in the future, the two sources of evidence are checked against each other.

Certainly, future stratigraphic excatvations on some of the promising new sites found during the survey program and absolute dating of the materials found will require changes in the sequence of phases. This in turn will require re-dating of sites found in the survey and changed conclusions about cultural development. This kind of dialectic between survey and excavation always oc-

*For Radama I see the article by J. Valette below. (Ed.)

curs in archaeology. Nevertheless the initial sequence of phases is good enough to allow some useful conclusions to be drawn from the trial surveys of 1975.

The Development of Settlement Patterns in Central Imerina

In the following necessarily brief introduction to the results of the 1975 surveys we avoid the temptation to emphasize the shared features found in most blocks during a given period. Where such communalities exist, they are noted; where variations exist, they too are noted. Some summary statistics are presented on Table 2.

There are very few communities of the earliest known phase, the Fiekena Phase. Groups of from two to three sites were found in three of the four survey blocks. It is possible that each of the groups represents the shifting movement of one community throughout the phase. However, ceramics are rare on these sites, and in no case are samples large enough to test this proposition. Most sites are on low flanking ridges, always close to the smaller marshy valleys ideal for wet rice or tuber cultivation. Where surface features are still visible, the sites have a single small oval or polygonal ditch enclosing an area of 0.4 to 0.8 hectares. Refuse is concentrated in a few discrete middens near the ditch. There is no pattern of associated tombs. A typical settlement group in the southern surveyed block is illustrated on Figure 4. One of the well-preserved sites shown on this air photograph tracing was recently completely destroyed by a quarry, a large oval earthwork enclosing 1.5 hectares, on a high flanking ridge of Mangabe in the north survey block. This higher and larger settlement may exemplify the process of nucleation, a movement to high defensible locations, which culminates in the settlement groups of the succeeding Ankatso Phase. Confirmation of the dating of this site is needed as only a few sherds of the Fiekena Phase were actually found, and their association with the ditched works is not assured.

The early Ankatso Phase is represented by larger and more complex settlement groups. Two discrete clusters of Ankatso Phase sites and perhaps part of a third were found in two of the four surveyed blocks. Each cluster has a large central settlement on a high hilltop, but still close to a raised water source. Each such center has a polygonal complex of multiple ditches (as many

Table 2: Prehistoric Settlement Densities in Surveyed Areas of Central Imerina

PERIOD		IMERIMANJAKA			AMBOHIDRABIBY			AMBOHIDRATRIMO			TOTAL HA. SETTLED IN SAMPLE BLOCKS	AMBOHIMANGA		
		sm.	med.	lg.	sm.	med.	lg.	sm.	med.	lg.		sm.	med.	lg.
Fiekena	#	2	1	-	-	2	-	-	-	-		1	2	-
	ha	.79	.55	-	-	1.58	-	-	-	-	2.92	.11	3.72	-
Early Ankatso	#	-	2	2	-	-	-	-	-	-		-	-	-
	ha	-	2.64	-	-	-	-	-	-	-	2.64	-	-	-
Late Ankatso	#	-	4	-	-	-	-	1	-	-		6	2	1
	ha	-	4.16	-	-	-	-	.20	-	-	4.36	.90	2.93	4.00
Angavo	#	-	2	-	-	2	-	-	2	-		7	4	4
	ha	-	1.78	-	-	2.14	-	-	1.53	-	5.45	1.07	2.73	18.40
TOTAL ANKATSO														
Ambohidray	#	1	1	-	2	4	-	-	3	-		19	11	5
	ha	.25	.71	-	.34	6.37	-	-	2.25	-	9.92	3.49	11.30	22.40
Kaloy	#	13	5	1	7	6	1	7	4	1		55	19	7
	ha	3.54	3.88	4.75	1.54	7.29	3.30	1.74	2.80	3.90	32.74	9.06	21.01	30.80

sm: .01 - .49 ha.   med.: .50 - 3.00 ha.   lg.: 3.0+ ha.

as four) surrounding an area of 1.0 to 1.5 hectares. These enclosed areas are terraced and dense concentrations of refuse ar ubiquitous. At the high point within the site are one or more tombs, usually a simple one stage tomb sited to take advantage of a natural rock outcrop. A few subsidiary sites, perhaps daughter communities, occur on nearby hights and flanking ridges. These usually have a single ditch enclosing 0.5 to 0.7 hectares of terraced area with perhaps a single tomb. In the north survey block there were also yet smaller sites of about 0.25 hectares situated close to the marshy valleys, most with only faint terracing rather than ditching. Such were not noted in other survey areas. These may be seasonal sites for rice cultivation, necessitated by the great height of Mangabe and consequent distance from the more extensive marsh areas. A late Ankatso Phase settlement group in the south block is presented in Figure 5. At the end of the Ankatso Phase, most settlements are abandoned, with only a few of the large centers continuing into the next phase.

Fiekena and Ankatso can be viewed as a single cycle of settlement development. This begins with a few undifferentiated settlements in locations selected, it would seem, for agriculture rather than defense. Through time, the average size of communities and the complexity of their fortifications increased and they are moved to more defensible and ritually more imposing hill tops. All this might suggest an increase in competition and perhaps changes in the symbolic use of space. Differentiation between the larger communities and smaller communities with fewer and less elaborate tombs suggests increased social complexity. At the end of the cycle, most of the communities are deserted, and there is region-wide reorganization.

In the Angavo Phase of the late 16th and early 17th Centuries there are no discrete clusters of settlement. Rather there is a continuous network of hilltop centers. Where there are smaller fortified settlements as in the north block, these occur on separate hilltops and eminences and are not clearly associated with the larger settlements. Angavo centers tend to be on the very highest hilltops, often far removed from water sources and rice fields. The newly established settlements have one large moat enclosing an area ranging from 0.8 to 1.2 hectares and containing dense concentrations of refuse and several tombs. Since many of these settlements are still occupied and the tombs have been frequently rebuilt, it is difficult to be certain that the larger two and three tiered tombs were erected at this time, but it seems likely that such differentiation of tomb types had begun. Smaller Angavo sites ranging from 0.2 to 05 hectares occur around the foot of Mangabe in the north block. Some have tombs within or just outside the moat, but most have none. Few and isolated as these smaller communities were, they represent the first steps toward the development of the hierarchical settlement orders which subsequently emerge in Central Imerina.

During the Ambohidray Phase of the late 17th and early 18th Centuries, there is further development on the same themes. Centers increase in size, and the range enclosed by the moats increased from 1.0 to 2.3 hectares. More smaller centers appear on the lower eminances between the larger ones. Smaller subsidiary forti- fied settlements similar to those of the previous phase are densely clustered north of Mangabe in the north block, though even these could have contained only a small number of people relative to the number in the larger centers. A few smaller sites are also found near Ambohidrabiby in the northeast block. In contrast to these evidences of settlement hierarchy, the Ambo- hidratrimo area to the northeast and the Imerimanjaka area to the south have only a few centers and completely lack small subsi- diary settlements (Figure 6 shows the settlements around Ambo- hidrabiby in the northeast block.)

The tentative steps toward more complex settlement networks reach a culmination in the succeeding Kaloy Phase of the Mid to Late 18th Century and early 19th Century. A few centers emerge as multiple moated towns ranging in enclosed area from 3 to 5 hectares. Clustered around these are many small fortified settlements of 0.1 to 0.5 hectares in area, some with internal tombs, some with none. Much of the population must have lived in these small settlements. Beyond these are larger border settlements defending the network of small dependencies. However the configuration of these border settlements suggests two quite different defensive strategies. In some cases there are huge fortresses with massive multiple moats and elaborate gates on high ridges overlooking the border regions. Amboatany in the north block and Ambo- hitraino in the south block are examples. The problem with such large fortresses is that they are themselves centers as large as those which they defend, and are thus capable of effective independent action, even of revolt. In other cases there is a staggered line of medium sized fortified settlements along the border. Examples are found south of Ambohidrabiby in the northeast block and west of Amboatany in the north block. (This latter area, showing both types of border arrangements, is presented in Figure 7). No single such border settlement could act independently or revolt, and two or three of them on the flanks of an invading army would be a threat sufficient to force dispersal of its resources and delay of its advance until large mobile forces could bring a counterattack against it. It would be useful if these different defensive arrays could be archaeologically dated. Such would require a chronological subdivision of the Kaloy Phase, which will only be possible after careful stratigraphic excavations.

In broad perspective, the Angavo, Ambohidray, and Kaloy Phases can be viewed as a single period of growth beginning with a network of small hilltop centers, some of which become larger and develop first a pattern of surrounding small dependent settlements and subsequently around these, specialized border settlements. All of these are subsequently incorporated in the network of administrative and market centers of the expanding Merina state. In this paper we will not summarize the copious evidence of the Mid 19th Century Fiadanana Phase. This period shows continued population growth, the emergence of a specialized urban-centered economy, and the integration of western knowledge and technologies into many aspects of life in Imerina. The reader will find a presentation of some of these data in our forthcoming papers in *Taloha*.

Concluding Notes

The surveys reported in this paper cover about 2 percent of Ancient Imerina and about 15% of the habitable portions of what we have termed Central Imerina. For reasons outlined in the introduction the surveyed blocks do not constitute a statistically representative sample. Nevertheless, the information recorded does allow certain broad conclusions and concrete suggestions for future work, both further archaeological survey and excavation, in the region crucial to Merina cultural development.

1) The earliest known settlements of Central Imerina are intimately associated with the smaller marshy valleys best suited to simple techniques for the cultivation of wet rice or of edible

tubers. Thus, there is no immediate reason to hypothesize an initial period of pure swidden agriculture and dry rice cultivation. At the moment, we do not know the specifics of the subsistence base (e.g., types, amounts, and proportions of crops grown)) and agricultural techniques (e.g., the introduction of complex irrigation techniques). Obviously, there have been changes in both, some of which are known from the historical record. Manioc, for example, is a crop of substantial importance in the Malagasy diet, but as a New World crop it could not have reached the area before the 16th Century. The Tantara speaks of large irrigation projects for draining the more formidable marshlands of Imerina executed by the later rulers, and there is reason to suspect that the *angady* (spade) is a recent introduction. Further, we do not know the specifics of the introduction of cattle into the highlands nor of their integration into the agricultural cycle.

Within most theoretical frameworks, subsistence base and associated techniques play a fundamental role as regards their relations to other factors such as population size, settlement patterning, and ritual organization. Even the more general theoretical questions regarding the functioning of and change within social systems, with rare exceptions, ultimately concern themselves with the subsistance base.

A large portion of the available information on such concerns is contained in the archaeological record. But the proper evaluation of such information depends on supplementing intensive archaeological survey with careful excavations designed to recover not only artifactual remains, but also animal bones and charred plant remains to be eventually studied by paleo-ethnozoologists and paleo-ethnobotanists respectively.

2) The development of settlement patterns from earliest times to the 19th Century shows continual change. This change, however, is neither uniform in pace for succesive time priods, nor geographically uniform for Imerina as a whole during any given historical period. Some areas seem to be more conservative in one period and precocious in another. One cannot present a simple unitary model of Merina social or economic organization. While our relatively small sample blocks may contain all or most of the settlements of a social unit of the first two phases, in subsequent phases they contain proportionally smaller and smaller parts of the growing socio-political units. Thus, on the basis of presently

available archaeological evidence, one cannot define the point at which state organization or any other socio-political fueature appears. To do this we would have to document the complete border systems. However, given —on the basis of traditions— that state organization may have arisen sometime during the Kaloy Phase, some things can be said about the processes that have been proposed as explanations of social change and eventual state emergence.

3) Those who argue that population growth is the "prime mover" of state development will be pleased with the evidence presented on Table 2. In general, site area seems to grow continuously. However, several objections must be raised to such a conclusion. First, the population growth curve would not necessarily be a smooth geometric increase. With a more refined chronology population declines will probably be demonstrable, one at the end of the Ankatso Phase and one at the end of the Ambohidray Phase. Second, it remains to be seen whether states emerge first in the area of highest ratio of people to area of available rice fields. This is a necessary consequence of the proposition that state organization is a direct response to population pressure.[17] Third, the rapidity of growth in some areas, for example, between the Ambohidray and Kaloy Phases in the south surveyed block, suggests a politically motivated movement of population rather than organic growth.[18] If population growth can thus be shown to be an obviously socio-political phenomenon in this case (leaving aside, for the moment, the strong theoretical argument that the growth of a human population can never be treated as an independent biological phenomenon) it cannot act as a prime mover for change within Merina society. A "prime mover" is by definition external to that system which it influences, and in this case population growth seems to be one variable in the social system itself. All these problems can be properly solved when there is more complete survey, and when we have devised from ethnographic evidence means of estimating actual population of archaeologial sites in Central Madagascar, and when the demographic implications of the records of population movement in the traditions have been assessed.

4) Craft specialization has been considered as a characteristic of state organization. The archaeological record of Imerina can be used to test this proposition. Careful excavations followed

by detailed analysis of the distributions and associations of artifacts in and between sites may eventually help answer a number
of relevant questions. Such questions concern the procurement of
raw materals and their processing: whether the areas of processing
were limited to certain work spaces within households, limited
to certain households or certain designated areas within villages,
or limited to certain villages within a regional network of sites.
There is also the question as to whether various stages of the
production sequence or the production of certain items were sex
or group specific. It is within the framework of these and similar
questions that archaeologists can strike up fruitful dialogues with
ethnographers and ethnohistorians.

The internal movement of goods and services as well as external
"commercial" concerns are areas of importance to students of
complex societies. In addition to the information on material
resources procurement and craft specialization gleaned from
archaeological excavations, site placement theory, initially
refined in the geographical sciences, can be applied to the analysis
of settlement patterns derived from archaeological survey to
demonstrate when centers came to be located for reasons of dis-
tributional and administrative efficiency, and thus which centers
might be expected to produce evidences of market activity when
excavated.

In Central Imerina, the question of external "commercial"
contacts is also important, but it may prove difficult to approach
for several reasons. On the one hand the goods known to have
been carried out of Imerina are archaeologically elusive (slaves
and perishable craft goods being examples) and, on the other hand,
goods known to have come in are not those which are thrown
away on village sites and thus easily recovered in excavations
(silver coins and guns being examples). However future work
may well reveal that other goods, such as ceramics, were also
exchanged, and the task may become more tractable. In any event,
the problems raised in this area can only be solved after a number
of areas of the island have been investigated intensively with
both survey and excavation techniques.

5) The reorganization and increased intensity of warfare is
characteristic of emerging states, though it is arguable whether
it is epiphenominal or integral to the transformation. Imerina,
with its remarkably preserved fortifications, is unique among the

world's cases of early state emergence in the opportunities it presents for the study of ancient conflict. However, these evidences are not as comprehensive as one might initially think. The fortifications are indicators of the expectation of defensive action. There is little direct archaeological evidence of offensive military organization; and, while there is evidence of logistics in the form of storage structures, weapons, and manufacturing centers for weapons, such logistic data must be recorded with excavation rather than survey techniques. Nevertheless, the evidence of defenses indicates certain developments. During the Ankatso, Angavo, and Ambohidray Phases, the emphasis is on the defense of the larger centers, to which the inhabitants of smaller settlements could have retreated in times of threat. Late in Ambohidray or early in Kaloy times, about 1700 A.D., the great border fortresses begin to be built; behind these borders there are proliferations of small hamlets and villages. Then, later in Kaloy times, the linear arrangements of smaller border settlements, doubtless requiring complex logistical support and political administration, arise. Thus, there seem to be several discrete transformations rather than a gradual increase in the complexity of defenses. Complete survey of Central Imerina is certain to provide a detailed documentation of these crucial military transformations.

The above five comments indicate that with archaeological survey methods alone, evidence of population change and military competition can be recovered. Limited excavation programs, designed in the problem framework provided by survey evidence, can document agriculture, craft production, and various forms of exchange. Without such evidence, the oral traditions are flesh without bones. Archaeology in Madagascar will provide information essential to the understanding of its history, and thus to the development of a theoretically-based science of history.

DESCRIPTION OF FIGURES

Fig. 1:   Central Imerina, showing many of the locations mentioned in the text.

Fig. 2:   Ceramics of the Fiekena and Ankatso Phases. Each vessel's exterior is portrayed on the left; its interior and cross section is on the right. The name, formal attributes, and provenence of each vessel are as follows:

a. Low Neck Jar. Rim diameter 19 cm.; Neck thickness 0.64 cm.; Inclusions 15% coarse sand; Color yellow-red; Antompon' Ifiekena.

b. Small Bowl with Incised and Impressed Decoration. Rim diameter 10 cm.; Body thickness 0.46 cm.; Inclusions 5% fine sand; Color light brown; Antampon' Ifiekena.

c. Small Bowl with Incised and Impressed Decoration. Rim diameter 12 cm.; Body thickness 0.65 cm.; Inclusions 5% medium sand; Color light brown; Antampon' Ifiekena.

d. Base with Incised and Impressed Decoration. Base diameter 8 cm.; Base thickness 0.60 cm.; Inclusions 10% coarse sand; Antampon' Ifiekena.

e. Low Neck Jar with Incised Band. Rim diameter 28 cm.; Neck thickness 0.70 cm.; Inclusions 15% coarse sand and granules of quartz; Color brown; Antanambe (Arnaud excavations).

f. Hemispherical Bowl with Incised and Impressed Decoration and Graphite Coating. Rim diameter 22 cm.; Body thickness 0.72 cm.; Inclusions 15% medium sand; Color dark yellow brown; Antanambe (Arnaud Excavations).

g. Hemispherical Bowl with Incised and Impressed Decoration and Graphite Coating. Rim diameter 18 cm.; Body thickness 0.70 cm.; Inclusions 15% coarse sand; Color very dark gray; Antanambe (Arnaud Excavations).

h. Hemispherical Bowl with Incised and Impressed Decoration and Graphite Coating. Rim diameter 14 cm.; Body thickness 0.75 cm.; Inclusions 15% coarse sand, mica; Color very dark gray; Antanambe (Arnaud Excavations).

Fig. 3:   Ceramics of the Angavo and Kaloy Phases.

a. Low Necked Jar. Rim diameter 18 cm.; Neck thickness 0.95 cm.; Inclusions 5% fine sand; Color light brown; Angavobe (Mille and Verin Sondage II Lower:6).

b. High Necked Jar. Rim diameter 20 cm.; Neck thickness 0.84 cm.; Inclusions 5% mica and fine sand; Color black; Angavobe (Mille and Verin Sondage II Upper:10).

c. Hemispherical Bowl with Graphite Coating. Rim diameter 30 cm.; Body thickness 0.51 cm.; Inclusions 5% fine sand; Color black. Angavobe (Mille and Verin Sondage II lower:2).

d. High Necked Jar. Rim diameter 28 cm.; Neck thickness 0.77 cm.; Inclusions 10% coarse sand; Color reddish brown; Kaloy (Verin Sondage IV:2).

e. Low Necked Pot. Rim diameter 21 cm.; Neck thickness 0.63 cm.; Inclusions 15% Medium Sand; Color reddish brown; Kaloy (Verin Sondage IV:3).

f. Hemispherical Bowl with Graphite Coating. Rim diameter 27 cm.; Body thickness 0.63 cm.; Inclusions absent; Color gray; Kaloy (Sondage III:4).

Fig. 4: Settlements of the Fiekena Phase in the area southwest of Imerimanjaka. Sites are stippled, with heavy lines marking the moats. The contour interval is 50 meters. The use of a symbol for rice paddies to mark the valley floors is arbitrary, and at this period at least may not represent the actual use of these areas.

Fig. 5: Settlements of the Late Ankatso Phase south of Imerimanjaka. The symbolization is as before with the addition that tombs inside sites are shown with black squares, and large valley floors are arbitrarily represented with a marsh symbol.

Fig. 6: Settlements of the Ambohidray Phase around Ambohidrabiby. The symbolization is unchanged.

Fig. 7: Settlements of the Kaloy Phase west of Ambohimanga. Black squares outside moats represent exterior tombs. Note that even though this period is perhaps a century long at most, the settlement plan presents an archaeological palimpsest, with the high fortress of Amboatany being an earlier foundation and the fortress of Imerimandroso and many of the large villages along the Mamba being a later border system.

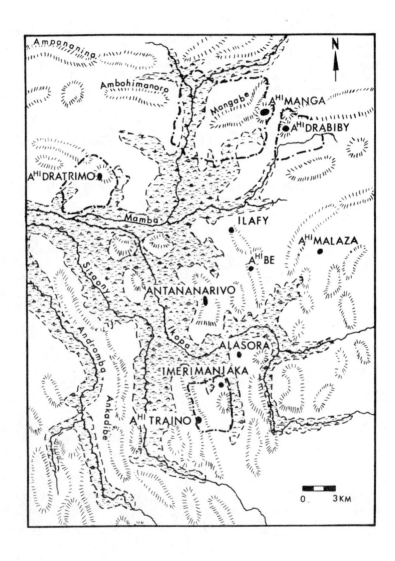

FIGURE 1

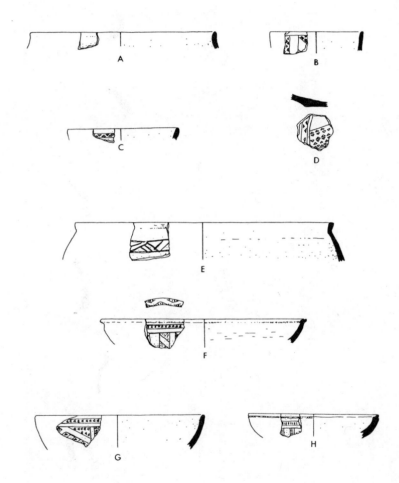

FIGURE 2

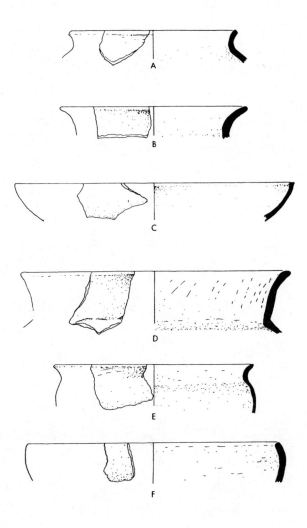

FIGURE 3

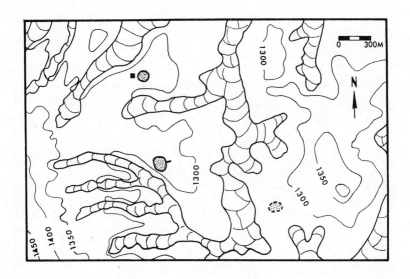

FIGURE 4

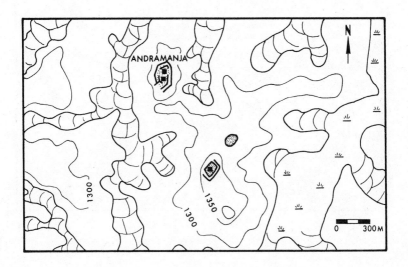

FIGURE 5

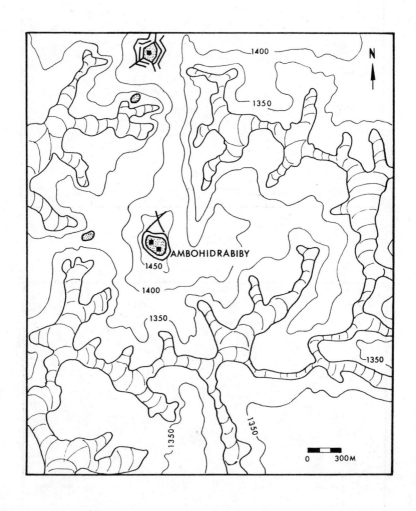

FIGURE 6

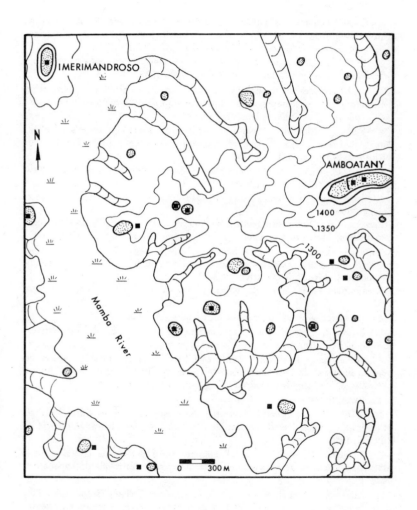

FIGURE 7

NOTES

1. Callet, Tantara, 1873-1902, transl. G.S. Chapus and E. Ratsimba as *Histoire des Rois*, 1953-1958; Savaron, "Contribution à l'Histoire d'Imerina, *Bulletin de l'Academie Malgache*, XI (1928), 61-81; XIV (1931), 57-73.

2. COACM *Collection des Ouvrages Anciens concernant Madagascar.* Grandidier, Alfred and Gulliame (eds.), Paris, 1903-1920.

3. A. Delivré presents a lengthty discussion on the difficulties of interpreting the *Tantara* in his fascinating study, *Interpretation d'une Tradition Orale.* Paris, 1967. After 1967, see Delivré's article below. (ed.)

4. Willey, Gordon R., "Prehistoric Settlement Patterns in the Viru Valley, Peru," *Bulletin of the Bureau of American Ethnology*, #155, Smithsonian Institution, Washington, D.C., 1953.

5. Wittfogel, K.A., *Oriental Despotism: A Comparative Study of Power*, New Haven, Conn.: Yale University Press, 1957.

6. McC. Adams, r., *Land Behind Baghdad*. The University of Chicago Press, Chicago, 1965.
Parsons, J.R., "Prehistoric Settlement Patterns in the Texaco Region, Mexico," *University of Michigan Museum of Anthropology Memoir*, #3, Ann Arbor, 1971.

7. Razafintsalama, A., *Les Tsimahafotsy d'Ambohimanga: Organisation Familiale et Sociale en Imerina, Madagascar.* Cahier du Centre de Sociologie et d'Antropologie Sociale, Cahier #1, Tananarive, 1973.
Razafindratovo, J., *Etude du Village d'Ilafy.* ORSTOM Tananarive, Mimeo, 1965.

8. This system was first utilized for the island by A. Mille.

9. Verin, P., "Deux Sites Archéologique de la Banlieue de Tananarive," *Annales n°5 de l'Université de Madagascar.* Letters, 1966.

10. Mille, A. et P. Vérin, "Premieres Observations sur l'Habita Ancien en Imerina suivies de la Description Archéologique de Sites d'Angavobe et d'Ambohitrinitrimo." *Bulletin de l'Académie Malgache*, Tananarive, 1967.

11. Vérin, Perre; p.c.

12. Vérin, P., *Les Echelles Anciennes du Commerce sur les Côtes Nord de Madagascar.* Tomes I et II, Service de Reproduction des Thèses, Université de Lille, III, 1975.

13. Mantaux, C. et P. Vérin, "Traditions et Archéologie de la Vallée de la Mananara," *Bulletin de Madagascar.* #183, Imprimerie Nationale de Tananarive, 1969.

14. Mille, A., "Ambohidempona et Ankatso, deux Collines Historiques a l'Est de Tananarive," *Annales de l'Université de Madagascar.* Serie Lettres en Sciences Humaine, Notes et Documents #9, 1968.

15. Arnaud, R., "Les Anciens Villages Fortifies de l'Ambohimarina," *Taloha* 3. Revue du Musée d'Art et d'Archéologie, 1970.

16. Wright, H.T., "Observations sur l'Evolution de la Ceramique Traditionelle en Imerina Centrale," *Taloha.* n.d.

17. Brumfield, E., "Regional Growth in the Eastern Valley of Mexico: A Test of the 'Population Pressure' Hypothesis," *The Early Mesoamerican Village.* K. Flannery (ed.), Academic Press, New York, 1976.

18. The *Tantara* often mentions the premeditated geographical rearrangements of population by Andrianampoinimerina.

Bibliographical Note: in addition to works cited in the notes above, the authors have consulted the following materials for the current article: R. Battistini, *L'Afrique Australe et Madagascar*, Paris, 1967; N. Heseltine, *Madagascar*, New York, 1971; S. Kus, "Une Reconnaissance Archeologique d'Ambohimanga et ses Environs," *Taloha*, n.d.; A. Mille, *Contribution a l'Etude des Villages Fortifies de l'Imerina Ancien*, 1970, University of Madagascar, Museum of Art and Archaeology, *Travaux et Documents*, II and III; G. Richard-Vindard and R. Battistini (eds.), *Biogeography and Ecology of Madagascar*, The Hague, 1972; H.T. Wright, III and S. Kus, "Une Reconnaissance Archeologique en Imerina Centrale," *Taloha*, n.d.

Archaeology and Migrations in Northern Androy: A Preliminary Report

J.-P. EMPHOUX*
University of Madagascar
Museum of Art and Archaeology

Until the present time, professional archaeological research within the Island of Madagascar has been carried out mainly in the Central Highlands and it has dealt on the whole with the relatively recent periods, from the Sixteenth to the Nineteenth centuries.[1] Elsewhere in Madagascar, a systematic archaeological investigation was conducted a few years ago by Pierre Vérin into the Muslim trading centers of the northwestern littoral.[2] Southern Madagascar has so far been more the object of paleontological than of archaeological endeavors, as only some summary descriptions of artifacts have been given; and we also have for Talaka, a coastal site just southwest of Ambovombe, a Radiocarbon 14 date of 840 ± 80 BP.

For some two years now, an archaeological team of the national University's Museum of Archaeology has been in the Androy as its chosen area for excavations. We are at this moment only at a relative beginning of detailing a past through archaeological research *in situ* which will have to go on for a number of years to come. The site selected in the Androy country[3] is located within the perimeter delineated in the north by Bekily and Beraketa, in the south by the Cape Sainte-Marie, and in the east by Ambovombe itself. Our work is on the way, more precisely, in the northern section of this area. This is a semi-desert region of the mainland occupied today by a single ethnic group, the Antandroy[4] (or Tandroy in common usage as the prefix *ant-* meaning "people-of" is normaly dropped).

* Translated from French by R. Kent.

Madagascar is a small continent for which no evidence of pre-historic human occupation has been brought to light. Virgin land until relatively recent times, Madagascar should have obtained its first human residents from the direction of Indonesia around the start of our own era.[5] The earliest Carbon 14 dates come from the coastal areas. We have mentioned Talaka's; the other comes from Irodo at 980 ± 100 BP,[6] site situated in northeastern Madagascar. In Madagascar, where archaeology has found in general the material cultures of quite recent periods, it is not possible to disassociate the archaeological dig from the successive waves of human occupation preserved and recalled by oral traditions. Thus, archaeology in Madagascar is a continuous movement to and fro between the orally transmitted history and an archaeological dig although it is understood that we assign primacy to the dig itself and the results obtained from it.

The Archaeological Sites

Within the quadrilateral (see inclusive map) of Bekily, Beraketa, Antanimora and a point just south of Bekitro, northern Androy harbors two main categories of archaeological sites or those with old pottery and those which are metallurgical. The ancient pottery sites, although numerous, are hardly of equal importance. In effect, potsherd accumulations at the lowest points of certain thalwegs are quite numerous while sites in place under sedimentary deposits are considerably rarer. The site of Beropitika, which we have excavated systematically during the summer of 1977, is a fine example of the second category.

Beropitika

This is a flat-topped outlier in the Sakkavolo River, some twenty meters long and about a dozen meters wide, delineated by an abrupt talus which reflects, in its erosion pattern, the seasonal changes in the level of waters and in the intensity of the flow. Relative to the bed of the river its altitude does not exceed 2 to 3 meters. Induration of outlier matter which we have found in the dig seems to be of human provenance and it could itself be the cause of the outlier's conservation.

Much more compact than matter from the river banks, the outlier walls have undergone fairly regular erosion from the

AREA OF ARCHAEOLOGICAL RESEARCH

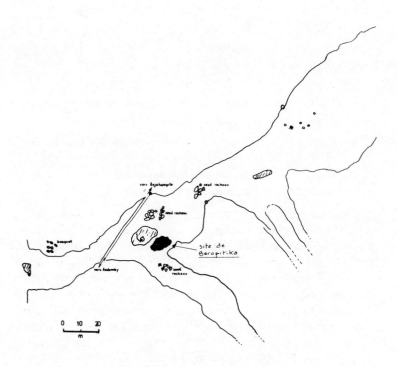

BEROPITIKA SITE MAP

Sakkavola waters, aspect which brought to light through natural profiling the potsherd sequences. We were thus able to observe visually three very distinct archaeological levels, subsequently retraced through horizontal scouring when we undertook the dig. Conducted in the manner of a prehistoric dig, ours therefore permitted the placing into evidence of three individual levels of occupation separated by considerable alluvial deposits, plus a fourth one, itself rather diffuse, with relatively recent pottery found under some 5 to 10 centimeters of the humus-bearing soil.

One could thus outline the stratigraphy as follows:

0 - 10 cm.	- humus-bearing soil with local and recent pottery fragments
10 - 20 cm.	- barren 1 - argillaceous
20 - 25 cm.	- *archaeological level 1*
25 - 40 cm.	- barren 2 - extremely compact argillaceous
40 - 45 cm.	- *archaeological level 2*
45 - 60 cm.	- barren 3 - argillaceous but less compact than barren 2
60 - 80 cm.	- *archaeological level 3*

(depending upon emplacement)

A number of formations came to surface as a result of exceedingly minute probing during the dig, among them at least two sandy levels several milimeters thick under the archaeological levels 1 and 2, and some finely-cemented slabs in the barrens 2 and 3. These formations will permit, after closer examination, the linking of certain paleoclimates with the levels of occupation. Our dig also led to the discovery of subfossil crocodile bones at the archaeological level 3 and the bones are being studied at this time. An analysis of Carbon 14 tests proposed for the archaeological level 3, where a hearth has been found, will allow us to learn if the site is indeed, as we are inclined to believe, one of the oldest in Madagascar from the point of view of human settlement.

Beropitika's Pottery

One should note some of the perceptible differences in potsherds collected within the three archaeological levels. First, at the initial level, the thickness of potsherds is least pronounced (4-5 milimeters). Next, the clay texture is also variable and the potsherds from level 2 are extremely friable. Resemblances in forms, however, lead us to believe in seasonal site-occupations. The Beropitika pottery is thus one made by hand and without decoration. Some of the vestiges do have exterior and interior slips and even traces of polishing can be observed on some of the fragments.

Lastly, the clay itself is either made homogeneous with mica or graphite as bevelling agents or else is coarse, with large quartz grains. It would be tempting to expect some special differences following the levels but none could be noted as the two basic types of potsherds are to be found in all three time-periods of occupation. The crucible itself was undoubtedly of the reductive type, with post-crucible oxidizing, all of which translates readily into fragments in which the interior is black-gray and the exterior yellow-red or brown-reddish. There are also glaring similarities in the form of objects found, some of which could be reconstituted almost in their entirety.

Undoubtedly, the most characteristic of the objects is the wide-mouthed pot, the "marmite," a receptacle with flat and thick bottom the oblique sides of which exhibit a variable height of 12 to 15 centimeters. The diameter of the mouths varies relative to the sides' height, attaining between 21 and 40 centimeters; and there are neither rim splays nor bluffness. Frequently, this "cooking" pot has two gripping handles (*cf.* sketch) all of which are located very close to the superior rim of the sides. They are either separated from it or otherwise joined to the lip of a side. The numerous samples collected revealed handles which are rectangular and rounded in shape, the rounded ones being less extensive. The rectangular ones are clearly chipped as well as detached from the side while the round counterparts are frequently nothing more than "surface outgrowths" of the sides themselves. The handles were not added to the sides but pressed out instead. Besides, one can even distinguish, at least on some of the samples, the finger-prints of the potter who had expelled the handle from the pot's belly. Other objects, currently being either assembled or under study, will enable us to detrmine the panoply of pottery sequences and cultural groups of Beropitika.

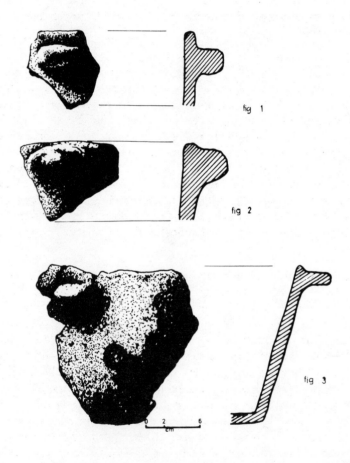

BEROPITIKA SITE
Fig. 1 & 2 - Handles in shape of "button"
Fig. 3 - Rectangular handle on the pot ("marmite") fragment

The Ambararatatoby Site
(45°28′ East - 24°16′ South; no. 6 on the inclusive map)

This site must be classed as one of the most interesting that we have uncovered in northern Androy. It is formed by a circular enclosure of large stones, one on top of another, having a diameter of 600 to 800 meters. The enclosure's wall, heavily delapidated in some places, should have measured at inception around 2 meters in height and 3 to 4 meters in width at the base. Low dry-stone walls, delinating perfectly level spaces, are to be found in the enclosure. The Menakompy River, in the north of it, provides natural protection. Informants interviewed in the northern Androy could not recall any tradition related to this site but the discovery of several fragments belonging to local pottery as well as some fragments of the "false *celadon*" permits us to put the site into the 15th to 16th centuries' span. This also explains why the Tandroy of today, who live in this area and whose ancestors could not have arrived into it earlier than about two centuries ago, have preserved no tradition regarding Ambararatatoby.

The Site of Andranosoa
(no. 4 on the inclusive map)

We have only surveyed this site and made a few probings. It is a vast one because it covers at a minimum about two square meters all along the Manambovo River. While pottery identical with the one discovered at Beropitika has been found here as well the importance of this site is in the alignment —along one of Manambovo's small affluents— of broken stone mounds and the stones are rather well arranged. There can be no doubt that these are very old constructions. We may well be dealing with ancient tombs but only a methodical dig can confirm this. We have taken samples from a "garbage dump" on the steep banks of the Manambovo; and they are awaiting Carbon 14 analysis.

There are many other pottery sites, less important than the ones reported on briefly; the entire region of northern Androy can be said to be rich in archaeological vestiges. What is of major interest, we are in the presence of a totally new pottery, new in form, different from the types known to-date.

Metallurgical Sites

With the exception of the single site of Analamahery, found in the forest, a few kilometers south of the village itself, metallurgical sites are at the same time small and numerous. Most of them are reduced to a few slagheaps and some tuyeres in stone or in clay. We have uncovered a host of these sites in the northern-most section, between Bekily and Beraketa, as well as south of Bekitro. All are certainly recent, going back in time not more than a couple of centuries. Here, it is the oral tradition that brings invaluable information to the digs. Our Tandroy informants attribute all knowledge of iron-working to one of their sub-groups, the Tebekitro (Tandroy of Bekitro), and to the Antanosy, the Tanala and even to the Bara. It is worth reporting that some of the informants have told us that while the Tandroy became specialized in the fabrication of weapons —mainly spear and axe— the Tanosy brought with them the technique for making the *vera* or spade.[7] Further research in ancient metallurgy is necessary in order to learn wheather groups of smiths were independent, each bringing its own technique from a home elsewhere, or wheather a single me-talurgy was created, with each òf the smithing groups contributing its own bit of knowledge.

The Migrations

The perimeters of the contemporary human groups in the south are far from being either fixed or well-known. There is a dynamism marking the present-day Tandroy, one that tends to expand their living space in all directions, either through the occupation of new lands or through the settling among the other human groups, like the Bara of northern Androy. With this background in mind, it seemed indispensable to complement and parallel our archaeolo-gical investigation with research concerning the origin of current settlements. The results are interesting, although, again, we are also at the beginning of work on oral traditions which come from the zone limited to northern Androy.

The most striking fact about this section of northern Androy is the never ending movement of people over the centuries.[8] Ancestors of the present-day Karimbola[9] came from the south and populated the Bekitro-Bekily-Beraketa triangle. The Beraketa region, once an exclusive Bara domain, now has a Tandroy majority. We also learned that the inhabitants of the Bekitro area derive from a junior branch of an Antanosy group originating at Ambondro, east of Ambovombe, in Anosy, since 14 genera-tions before our time. In a preliminary way, the traditions which we were able to collect lead us to think that the current Tandroy's ancestors came from the south (Karimbola) and from the southeast (Antanosy). In its progression northward, however, the Tandroy advance ran into the already-established Tanala and Bara groups; and in the extreme north of this zone, now dominated by the Tandroy, the Tanala continue to be considered as the *tompon-tany* (possessors-of-the-land, original inhabitants).

NOTES

1. *Cf.* J.-P. Domenichini, *Histoire des palladium d'Imerina d'apres des manuscripts anciens*, Tananarive, 1971.

2. *Les Echelles Anciennes du Commerce sur les Côtes nord de Madagascar*, Université de Lille III, 1975 (Thesis reproduction); *Histoire Ancienne du Nord-Ouest de Madagascar, Taloha,* 5, 1972 (Tananarive).

3. Located in the extreme south of Madagascar, Androy-land is often given as extending roughly from the Menarandra River in the west to the Mandrare River in the east, with uneven extensions northward into the interior of Madagascar. For a discussion of geographical aspects of Androy see R. Decary, *L'Androy* vol. I (Human and Physical Geography), Paris, 1930. (Ed.)

4. The Antandroy in contemporary setting appear in Suzanne Frere's illustrated study *Madagascar - Panorama de l'Androy*, Paris, 1958. Raymond Decary discusses aspects of Antandroy past in the second volume of his *L'Androy*, Paris, 1933 (his 1930 volume has a bibliography for the Antandroy, pp. 211-221). An interesting if difficult account of the Tandroy traditions will be found in (Captain) Defoort, E. "L'Androy," *Bulletin Economique de Madagascar*, XIII/2 (1913), 127-246. (Ed.)

5. This is a period arrived at by common agreement of many scholars but it remains to be confirmed; for a discussion of this problem see, H. Deschamps, *Histoire de Madagascar*, Paris, 1965, pp. 13-59. (Ed.)

6. R. Battistini and P. Vérin, "La Datation à Madagascar par la methode du R.C. 14," *Comptes Rendus, Semaine Géologique*, Tananarive, 1966.

7. This is ecologically sound since the Antanosy had been an agricultural people in earlier times. (Ed.)

8. See also H. Deschamps, *Les Migrations Interieures à Madagascar*, Paris, 1959; and Vacher, "Etudes Ethnographiques," *Revue de Madagascar*, vols. V and VI, 1903 and 1904. (Ed.)

9. Some claims have been made that the Karimbola represent the earliest inhabitants of the south. (Ed.)

Anjoaty Cattle Ear Marks

D. HURVITZ
Princeton University

The Anjoaty are a people of the coasts of Madagascar. They have been reported, at different times since 1658, from Anosy, Matitana, Boena, Ampasindava, Bobaomby, and Vohemar (as shown on map one, page 45).[1] This essay concerns the Anjoaty who live on the northeastern coast between the bay of Andravina and the Ampanobe river, centered on the town of Vohemar (as shown on map two, page 46). The Anjoaty of Vohemar raise cattle and cut cattle ear marks (*sofin'omby*) on them to signify ancestral ownership of their herds. The purpose of this essay is to explain how Anjoaty cattle ear marking works. The first section introduces the history of the Anjoaty people and of Anjoaty cattle in Vohemar. The second reviews Emil Birkeli's "*Marques de Boeufs et Traditions de Race*" to situate the study of Anjoaty marks in the context of an Island-wide theory. The review is followed by sections on the particular incisions cut on Anjoaty cattle ear marks, on the make-up of the marks as a whole, on the lateral symbolism of cattle ears, on the classes of cattle distinguished by cattle ear marks, and on the classes of people so distinguished. The second half of the essay is a history of Anjoaty cattle ear marks in Vohemar. It begins with the origin of the first Anjoaty cattle ear mark and shows the progressive modifications which have been made in it as the Anjoaty ancestry has descended over the generations while dividing up the land of Vohemar. It concludes with a comparison of the variants and with a preliminary statement on the rules underlying their variation. The conclusion of the essay will relate the Anjoaty material to Madagascar as a whole.

Anjoaty People and Anjoaty Cattle

The people of northern Madagascar are traditionally divided into Antandrano (people-of-the-water), residents of the coast who lived by sea-turtle hunting and fishing, and who bury their dead in cemeteries in the sand, and Antety (people-of-the-interior), residents of the interior who bury their dead in mountain caves.[2] The Anjoaty of Vohemar are Antandrano. Traditions report that they are the descendants of à family of ancestors who migrated to Vohemar from the northwestern coast by way of Bobaomby a dozen generations ago (around 1700).* They moved in on the Antandrano peoples who already inhabited the region, claiming the land by saying prayers at the mouths. of the major rivers and bays. They also established cemeteries at the embouchoures and thereafter were recognized as the owners or masters-of-the-land (*tompon-tany*) by the peoples of the region.

Some Anjoaty married people who were living in Vohemar when they arrived; others married people of neighboring regions; and still others married within the ancestry itself. As the Anjoaty grew in number, they split into distinct families, occupying distinct regions of Vohemar. By 1775 when Mayeur and Corby, agents of the colonist Benyowsky of Antongil, crossed Vohemar by land, the Anjoaty had already established villages on the banks of each river from Ampanobe to Andravina, and each village belonged to a separate family.[3] During this period, the Zafinivolafotsy (descendant-of-silver), a branch of the Maroserana dynastic family, were overlords of northern Madagascar.[4] They were defeated in 1823 by the Merina of the central plateau and this brought an influx of outsiders to Vohemar. By the 1860's the town of Vohemar had a normal population of several hundred[5] while the population of the region was 1,150, and included 500-600 Sakalava (people of western Madagascar ruled by the Zafinivolamena (descendants-of-gold) branches of the Maroserana in which the Anjoaty were classified), 300-400 Betsimisaraka (people of the east coast), and 100-150 Merina.[6] At the turn of the century, A. Grandidier estimated the Anjoaty population at 7,000 to 8,000.[7] In the meantime, French colonial rule (established in 1896) brought a continued influx of foreigners. By 1911 the population of the

*The traditions are not reviewed here. They will be discussed in part in the history of Anjoaty cattle ear marks. The Anjoaty themselves say that they are not descendants of the early (pre-1700) inhabitants of Vohemar, in contrast to what has previously been supposed.

town of Vohemar was 1,200 and included French, Indians, Chinese, Comorians, Makoa, Merina, Sakalava, Betsimisaraka, Tsimihety, Antaimoro, and Creoles.[8] Today the town has a population of 5,000 while the Anjoaty population for the whole region is estimated at 10,000 to 12,000.[9] The Anjoaty are thus only one element of the total population, and every Anjoaty can point to ancestors among other peoples. Nevertheless, the Anjoaty have maintained their ancestral identity and their status as masters-of-the-land, by descent from the first Anjoaty settlers, by residence in the land claimed by these settlers, and by the fact that they continue to be buried in the cemeteries established by their Anjoaty ancestors. This makes the Anjoaty of Vohemar a descent group and a residence group (a unity represented in their cemeteries). In Malagasy terminology they are a "kind" *(karazana)* of people.*

Vohemar is located between the rainy, rice growing region of the east coast of Madagascar and the dry, cattle country of northern Madagascar. When the Anjoaty arrived their primary occupation was sea-turtle hunting from the sand.** Once they came into possession of the land, they began to grow rice, now their staple food, and back-up crops such as manioc. Most importantly, they began to amass huge herds of hump backed cattle or zebu. Mayeur and Corby received zebu as presents in each of the Anjoaty villages they visited in 1775. During the period before 1823 "... the smallest village chief had thousands of

Karazana (kind) and the related word, *firazanana* ("...the manner of belonging to a race or species..."[Randriamandimby, 1973:12]), derive from *razana* (usually glossed as ancestor, but more precisely a dead member of the ancestry buried in a cemetery in the land of an ancestry). The definition of these social units seems to vary with regional and historical context, but the unique feature about them is the synthesis of descent and land. Among the Merina, *karazana* or "demes" are "bilateral in-marrying kinship groups" which "were once local groups and still have an association with their territory" (M. Bloch, *Placing the Dead*, London, 1971, p. 46). Among the Bemihisatra division of Maroserana from the northwestern coast, *firazanana* have the dual sense of categories in a political hierarchy and of cognatic clans. They are "dispersed territorially," but are "associated with the reality of residential groupings" (cf. Bare, J.F. *Pouvoir des Vivants Langage des Morts*, Paris, 1977, pp. 33-35).

**There were two types of sea-turtle hunters: those who hunted in canoes (called Vezo) and those who hunted from the sand (like the Anjoaty), *cf.* Charles Bernier, *Rapport sur une Mission sur la Côte nord-est de Madagascar*, 1834, mss. at the Archives Nationales - Section d'Outre-Mer, Paris, dossier 15³⁰/8B; Florent Guinet, "Population du Nord," in (ed.) Baron P. de Richemont, *Documents sur la Compagnie de Madagascar* (preceded by a "Notice Historique"), Paris, 1867; and G. Grandidier, "Les Tortues de mer à Madagascar," *Revue de Madagascar*, XII (July 1910), pp. 298-308.

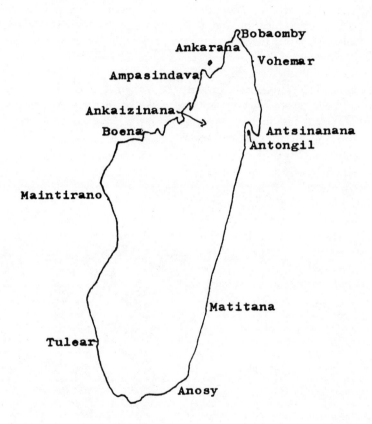

MAP ONE: MADAGASCAR

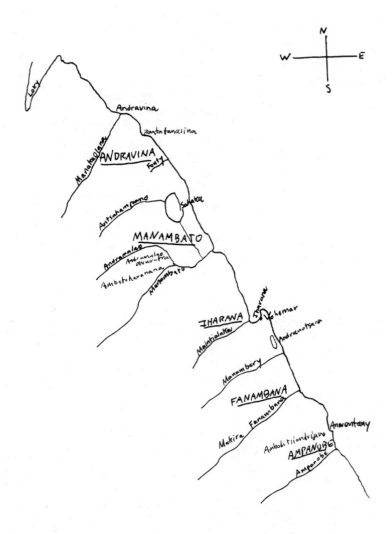

MAP TWO: VOHEMAR COUNTRY

cattle..." and there was a large commerce in cattle with the Mascarenes.[10] The Anjoaty had to protect their herds from raids and taxation by the Volafotsy. The Merina invasion changed the situation. They replaced the Volafotsy in taxing the Anjoaty and replaced the French as middlemen in the cattle trade. In the 1860's 200-300 head were exported to Mauritius each year. This trade expanded with the French protectorate and some Anjoaty amassed truly gigantic herds. Jaonatana of the Sahaka region of Manambato was said to own 10,000 zebu for example. By 1908, 20,000 head were exported to Mauritius[11] and this trade continued throughout the period of French rule. Recently exportation was stopped depressing the price of cattle, and as a result cattle owners are reluctant to sell their animals and there is a struggle for meat in the Vohemar market whenever a steer is butchered. Still, nearly every Anjoaty owns at least a few head, many own over a hundred zebu, and a few are "thousandaries" (*mpanarivo*).

The Anjoaty have burned off the vegetative cover of Vohemar for generations so that now it is grassland. They graze their cattle alongside those of their relatives and neighbors. The cattle mate freely and newborn cavles belong to their mother's owners. The zebu are usually grazed in the small area where they were born and where the herd they are born into has been grazing for generations. Despite the huge number of meandering animals, the Anjoaty recognize each of them individually (including those of their neighbors as well as their own) by patterns of coat colors, by horn shape, by age, by size, by sex, and by number of off-spring*. For example, Bakarimanilahila, an Anjoaty of Fanambana who owns over a hundred zebu, told me that he could not only recognize each of his zebu individually, but could recite for all of them a coat color genealogy in the female line for six genera-tions.**

I stress this to show that while Anjoaty cattle are all cut with

---

*For a detailed discussion of cattle coats and horns see L. Molet, "Le Boeuf dans l'Ankaizinana," *Mémoires de l'Institut Scientifique de Madagascar*, Tome II, Serie C (1953).

**To give other examples of this knowledge, I saw a man who had come 15 kilo-meters to search for a lost zebu ask some Anjoaty whether they had seen it, and though they hadn't, they knew which one he meant. I also heard of a man, named Jaojodany of Andravina, who was said to be able to recognize cattle by their bellows alone. (And the same uncanny power is reported concerning the Onjatsy of the Matitana. See G. Ferrand, *Les Musulmans à Madagascar et aux Iles Comores*, Vol. I, Paris, 1893.)

cattle ear marks, the ear marks are not used to identify individual zebu. They are not used to identify individual owners either (with exceptions).* Yearlings are cut with cattle ear marks in the dry season with no ceremony and left to heal themselves. As a general rule they are cut with marks to signify the family who originally acquired them and the area of land originally used as a means to acquire them (as explained below). Calves born into the family herd are cut with the marks of their mothers, thus perpetuating the system, and memorializing the original acquisition. Cattle ear marks are transmitted (with the cattle on which they are cut) by inheritance. Heirs who continue to live in the particular area of land settled by their ancestors, continue to cut the cattle ear mark cut by their ancestors. But as an ancestry divides into distinct family and land units, forcing some people to reside in areas outside the original settlements (but within the domain of the ancestry as a whole), modifications are introduced into cattle ear marks. In the case of the Anjoaty, this has produced a set of variants which provides a record for their descent in Vohemar.

Birkeli's Theory of Cattle Ear Marks

As early as 1902 Van Gennep noted that a "tableau" of the cattle ear marks of a well defined region in Madagascar could serve to draw up Malagasy genealogical trees and might clarify the mode of inheritance and segmentation of Malagasy peoples.[12] But the only major essay devoted to this research was written in 1926 by Emil Birkeli, a Norwegian missionary.** Birkeli understood cattle ear marks as marks of property which began as tokens of individual ownership (at an early stage of civilization) and evolved, with the generation of families, clans, tribes, and races, to represent social units. He calls the first marks "primitive forms." His working hypothesis was that the primitive forms were modified by the segmentation of tribes and by their agglomeration into ethnic groups, such that the perception of primitive forms on the cattle ear marks of a population could aid in the reconstruction of the genesis of that population. However, Birkeli

---

*Since colonial times those people who wish to assure that there is no dispute within a family over cattle ownership, brand their zebu in addition to cutting ear marks on them.

**Louis Molet has also studied the cattle ear marks of Ankaizinana in north central Madagascar (1953).

was concerned with "clans" and "tribes" (not with "kinds") and did not integrate the importance of land into his analysis.

Birkeli applied his method to ninety-two examples of cattle ear marks which he collected on the west coast of Madagascar between Maintirano and Tuléar. He divided the specimens into four categories according to a comparison of their forms. Each category derived in theory form a single primitive form (though in fact primitive forms were only provided for the first and third categories). The categories corresponded to four historical populations with particular economies, and the relations between the categories demonstrated an evolution in the economy of western Madagascar as a whole.

The cattle ear marks of the first category were called "fishtail marks." They derived from similar primitive forms called *Ohimalane* (*ohi*:tail; *malane*:a kind of fish) and *ohintsotro* (*ohi*:handle; *sotro*:spoon) (as shown in diagram one).

OHIMALANE   OHINTSOTRO

Diagram One: The primitive forms *ohimalane* (fishtail) and *ohintsoro* (spoon-handle). (Birkeli, 1926:10)

"Fishtails" were thought to be ideograms of fishtails as the name implies. "Spoon-handles" were thought to derive from them (but Birkeli could not quite see ideograms in them) (see figure one).

Figure One: A spoon handle. (Birkeli, 1926:9)

The fact that the ear marks of this category were ideograms, or at least named after objects, indicated to Birkeli that the peoples of the category possessed a simple economy of hunting and gathering. The category included the Antevaratse or Antandzoro (people-of-the-north), a tribe of immigrants from *Maka* (Mecca)

and *Ondgodza* (Grand Comoro) who landed in *Anora* (?) on
the northwestern coast of Madagascar[13] the Mikea, who were
forest dwellers; and the Vezo, who were coastal fishermen.
According to Birkeli's reconstruction, the category was composed
when some of the Antevaratse migrated south to the coast of
western Madagascar with an ear mark modeled on a fishtail.
The Mikea, who didn't possess cattle until that time, adopted
it with the name "spoon-handle." Finally, the Vezo, last to arrive
adopted it in this way:[14]

> ...The newcomer element joins the existing conglomerate
> and adopts by alliance its cattle ear marks, and is in this
> way grafted onto the old stock, without properly speaking
> belonging to the race...

The second category was labeled "...*marques d'oreille dentelées
et échancrées*..." Birkeli did not determine a common primitive
form for these examples. He grouped them together "...so as not
to have too many divisions...,"[15] but found that his classification
was verified by historical traditions. These ear marks were composed of small and large incisions. Some were ideograms and
named after objects in nature; others were numerical (in which
the number of incisions was the key to their meaning). The
category included two types of Vazimba, immigrants from
Kasomby, and residents of the interior; and numerous other
peoples such as the Antanandro (said to have an "affinity" with
the Vazimba), all said to possess a "simple" economy.

Birkeli named the third category "spearhead marks." The
primitive form was *tsimirango* ("always large")[16], and described
as "pointed-on-both-sides *(mandranidroe)*[17](as shown in diagram
two).

TSIMIRANGO
Diagram Two: The primitive form *tsimirango.*

The ear marks of this category were not considered to be ideograms,
but ones whose names, like charms, indicated the "means by
which the owner desired to see cattle raising develop."[18] A

typical name from this category is *mampohehi* (to make laugh), to which Birkeli adds in explanation "...in seeing the number and quality of animals.[19]" Thus the peoples of this category were said to possess an economy based on "economic egoism."[20] They included the Maroserana dynastic family, who came from the south, and established "Sakalava" kingdoms in western Madagascar in the 17th century.

Birkeli called the fourth category "rectangle marks." Again no primitive form was discerned, but Birkeli related the examples by the rectangular shapes of their incisions. The peoples of this category included the Andrivola dynastc family, considered related to the Maroserana. They also came from the south to establish kingdoms in western Madagascar and also had a cattle raising economy. Birkeli's general conclusion was that the impostion of the dynastic families on the pre-existing peoples resulted in an evolutionary change in the economy of western Madagascar from one based on hunting and gathering to one based on cattle raising.

Birkeli's pioneering essay contains certain problems which derive, in my opinion, from a failure to consider Malagasy peoples in terms of land, and which will be discussed as this essay proceeds. Nevertheless his reconstruction is directly relevant to an interpretation of Anjoaty cattle ear marks. For one thing, the Anjoaty, like the Antevaratse, have traditions of migration from Mecca and traditions of landing in Madagascar on the northwestern coast. In addition it appears that their migration from the northwestern coast to Vohemar was precipitated by the Maroserana expansion into northern Madagascar. Most of all the Anjoaty have an ear mark modeled on a fishtail and so clearly belong to Birkeli's fishtail category. However, in order to evaluate the meaning of a fishtail mark and the nature of a fishtail category of marks, it is necessary to study in detail the mechanics of cattle ear marking.

The Incisions on Anjoaty Cattle Ear Marks

Cattle ear marks are made of patterns of incisions cut into cattle ears with a knife. The incisions include nicks, slices, and cut-outs of different shapes, made in the sides of an ear, and perforations made in the center of an ear. Sometimes the incisions or cut-outs are named; sometimes the remaining flabs of ear are named.

Some incisions must be made on the same portion of the side of an ear in every case, while others can be cut anywhere on the sides of an ear.* Finally, sometimes the same small incision is cut more than once and is named according to the number of times it is cut. Diagram three shows all the incisions just described found on Anjoaty cattle ear marks. Most of them are found in Birkeli's catalogue for western Madagascar and Molet's catalogue for Ankaizinana.[21]

The foregoing incisions may be compared to the letters of a word since they have no meaning except when combined on the ear of a zebu. But their presence or absence from a cattle ear mark or their position on it relative to other incisions is crucial to the identity of that cattle ear mark. In theory, adding them to a cattle ear mark, taking them off an ear mark, or changing their place on an ear mark, changes the name and meaning of that cattle ear mark. In practice however, just as there is variation in the orthography of Malagasy words, such changes do not always effect the identity of a cattle ear mark. In other words, it happens that cattle ear marks with the same name can be composed of a slightly different arrangement of incisions. It seems that every ancestry has a certain stock of this sort of incision. Anjoaty employ especially the first four mentioned above. It appears that the others have been added to Anjoaty cattle ear marks through contact between ancestries (as will be described below in the tableau of Anjoaty cattle ear marks).

So far, what might be called ordinary incisions have been considered. But there is also a more complex sort of incision which consists of either a single slice or cutout, or a pattern of such incisions, with one name, restricted to one ear of a zebu. Such complex incisions have been called simply "ear marks" in the literature. It appears that this is what Birkeli means by primitive forms. In a local context they signify ancestries. But from Birkeli's evidence it appears that the same "ear mark" can signify more than one ancestry, so on a large scale, they signify classes of ancestries. Thus *ohimalane* (fishtail), for example, signifies both the Antevaratse and the Vezo of western Madagascar.

The Anjoaty cut two such "ear marks" in their cattle ear marks.

*Birkeli distinguished three sorts of incisions: those cut on the tip of the ear, those cut on the middle portion of the sides of an ear, and those cut on the base of an ear (1926:5).

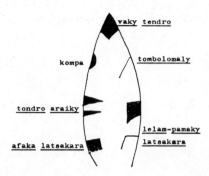

Vaky tendro (*vaky*: broken; *tendro*: top). This incision is always cut on the tip of an ear. On Anjoaty cattle ear marks it is always a triangular cut-out. However Birkeli has found three sorts of *vaky tendro*: triangular ones, convex ones, and concave ones. On Molet's catalogue they are called *sohana*, defined as *"extremite de navette de tisserand* (1953:20)."

Latsakara (*latsaka*: fallen [Molet, 1953:20]). This incision is made with an inward and a downward slice on the base of either side of either ear. This makes a flap of ear which is left hanging, and this is probably how the incision gets its name.

Afaka latsakara (*afaka*: liberated). "Freed fallen" incisions are cut-outs which begin as latsakara, but in which the flap of ear normally left hanging is removed. This makes it a square shaped cut-out.

Lelam-pamaky (*lela*: blade; *famaky*: axe). "Axe-blade" is the name for an axe-blade shaped piece of ear fashioned between cut-outs or incisions. The piece of ear is named, not the incisions themselves. On Anjoaty cattle ear marks the bottom incision of the axe-blade is always *latsakara*. But in Ankaizinana axe-blade serrations are usually formed between two rectangular cut-outs (Molet, 1953:20).

Tondro araiky (*tondro*: finger; *araiky*: one). "One finger" is the name for a finger-shaped piece of ear made between two deep triangular cut-outs. It can be cut anywhere on the sides of an ear. It is apparently an example of what Birkeli called "numerical" incisions since if three triangular cut-outs are made, making two finger-shaped serrations, it would be named "two fingers." There is only one Anjoaty cattle ear mark which contains this incision.

Kompa. Kompa are small curved cut-outs made anywhere on either side of either ear. They are found on only one Anjoaty cattle ear mark. One Anjoaty said that they were more current on Tsimihety cattle ear marks from north central Madagascar.

Tombolomaly. Tombolomaly is a simple slice cut into an ear at a downward angle. It is found only on one Anjoaty cattle ear mark.

Diagram Three: A catalogue of incisions found
on Anjoaty cattle ear marks.

The first is called *ramogogo*. In Vohemar it signifies the Anjoaty ancestry. It consists of two angular cut-outs on opposing sides of an ear (though some people diagrammed them as curved) and a *vaky tendro* on the tip (as shown in diagram four).

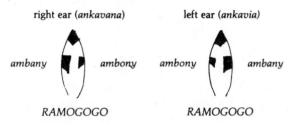

RAMOGOGO   RAMOGOGO

Note: Cattle hold their ears sideways more than up and down. The lower (*ambany*) or outer side of an ear allows for deeper incisions than the upper (*ambony*) or inner side of an ear. So identical incisions cut on both ears will be mirror images and not replicas, and to describe a cattle ear mark it is necessary to name all the component incisions, the side of the ear on which they are cut, and the ear on which they are cut.

The Anjoaty cut cattle ear marks into ear-shaped leaves to diagram them. When they held them up for inspection in front of me, it appeared that they looked at them from behind to identify them, and this may be the way they perceive cattle ear marks on cattle themselves. Nevertheless I could only orient myself among all the parts of ears by looking at them from the front, so they are presented here with the right ear to the reader's left. It appears that this is the way the ear marks in Birkeli's essay are drawn as well, but in his versions, no allowance is made for deeper incisions on the lower sides.

Diagram Four: *Ramogogo* on a right ear and *ramogogo* on a left ear.

Ramogogo was the way I heard this word spoken. I never learned its meaning. Nevertheless, Anjoaty said that it was modeled on a fishtail (as shown in figure two).

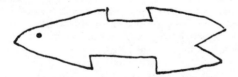

Figure Two: *Ramogogo* as a fishtail.

However Louis Molet recorded a similar "ear mark" (what he called a "mark which has a name") from Ankaizinana in north central Madagascar (shown on diagram five). Though Molet did not learn the ancestry to which it applied, he records it with the name *rambon-gogo* (*rambo*:tail; *gogo*:catfish), which translates as "catfish tail." Clearly both *ramogogo* in Vohemar and *rambon-gogo* in Ankaizinana fit Birkeli's fishtail category.

RAMBON-GOGO

Louis Molet learned that the cut-outs from the opposing sides of the ears were themselves named *kitsoany* and that they were curved. In Ankaizinana *rambon-gogo* is composed of *kitsoany* and *sohana*.

Diagram Five: *Rambon-gogo* from Ankaizinana. (Molet, 1953:21).

The second "ear mark" cut in Anjoaty cattle ear marks is called *mangaladrangitra* (*mangala*:take: *rangitra*:pointed). It means 'to-take-away-one-side-of-the-point,' and is seemingly a modification of the Maroserana "ear mark" called *tsimigango* by Birkeli and *marangitra* by Molet (as shown in diagram six). In northern Madagascar it signifies the Volafotsy branch of the Maroserana dynastic family.

MANGALADRANGITRA (on a left ear)   *MARANITRA* recorded by Molet (1953:21).

Diagram Six: The "ear marks" *mangaladrangitra* and *maranitra*.

Birkeli recorded an identical version which he called a *"miforme"* and attributed to a *"mélange de races."* This is entirely consistent with Anjoaty traditions concerning *mangaladrangitra* discussed below.

The Make-Up of Anjoaty Cattle Ear Marks as a Whole

Cattle ear marks properly speaking are composed of the totality of incisions, including ordinary ones and complex ones or "ear marks", cut on both ears of a zebu.* It is essential to distinguish

*In addition to the incisions already described, there are tiny v-shaped nicks called *famantarana*. They are cut on finished cattle ear marks as signs of individual ownership but can be inherited and thus come to represent families. These nicks

between "ear marks" restricted to one ear and cattle ear marks
concerned with both ears. This is not always easy since the name
of an "ear mark" can double as the name of the cattle ear mark
of which it is a part.** While an "ear mark" signifies an ancestry
or a class of ancestries, a cattle ear mark generally signifies an
ancestry or part of an ancestry attached to a particular area of
land. Betsimiry, an Anjoaty of Manambato, stated the general
rule for interpreting cattle ear marks: the right ear indicates the
ancestry which is the master or owner of the zebu, while the left
ear indicates the land which was the source of that zebu (Dec.
1974).*** The definition of a cattle ear mark thus corresponds to
the definition of a *karazana* or *kind* of people as a descent group
which is also a residence group. But as will be discussed below,
cattle ear marks can also signify two ancestries, related hierarchically
as owner to outsider, in terms of a defined territory.

In Vohemar Anjoaty cattle ear marks are defined as all those
with *ramogogo* on the right ear. Individual Anjoaty may own
cattle with different cattle ear marks, but only through inheritance
from other ancestries, not as Anjoaty. Diagrams seven, eight,
and nine show three Anjoaty cattle ear marks. They are Anjoaty
marks because they all have *ramogogo* on the right ears. They
are similar on the right ear otherwise, though not identical,
and differ greatly on the left ear. This indicates that thought they
are all Anjoaty cattle ear marks, they represent separate divisions
of Anjoaty within Vohemar country. These particular examples
have been chosen because they represent three kinds of Anjoaty
cattle ear marks: those with *ramogogo* on both ears, those with
ramogogo on the right ear and no "ear mark" on the left ear,
and those with *ramogogo* on the right ear and a different "ear
mark" on the left ear.*

---

are not named individually and are the least significant sort of incision since their
presence on a cattle ear mark does not significantly affect its basic meaning or alter
its name.

**Birkeli did not make this distinction and as a result his cattle ear mark diagrams
show alternately one ear with one name, two ears with one name, and two ears
with two names. In the same way, Louis Molet was unsure whether a named cattle
ear mark applied to one ear or to two ears of a zebu ("Le Boeuf," 1953; 22).

***The date here and dates hereafter refer to fieldnotes.

*Birkeli called this last sort *"formes mixtes."*

TSIMANOVADRAZANA

Tsimanodravazana (*tsy*: not; *manova*: change; *razana*: ancestor). This cattle ear mark, which refers to people who don't change ancestral affiliation, has *ramogogo* on both ears and *latsakara ambany* on both ears. It and other cattle ear marks with *ramogogo* on both ears indicates that the zebu in question were originally acquired by Anjoaty in the area of land they settled originally when they arrived in Vohemar. This class of cattle ear marks also seems to indicate that the Anjoaty who acquired the cattle were descendants of Anjoaty in the senior male line or on both sides of their family, for otherwise, as described below, they would have been forced to leave the original settlement.

Diagram Seven: *Tsimanovadrazana* by Bakarimanilahila
of Fanambana (Sept. 1975).

MARORENGY

Marorengy (*maro*: many; *rengy*: have heard of it). *Marorengy* has *ramogogo* on the right ear and a *vaky tendro* and a *latsakara ambany* on the left ear. It and other cattle ear marks with *ramogogo* on the right ear and no 'ear mark" on the left ear signify a segment of the Anjoaty ancestry associated with an area of land within Anjoaty country, but outside the originally settled area. The cattle cut with these cattle ear marks have been acquired by Anjoaty in association with such outlying areas. It appears that the greater the difference in the left ears of Anjoaty cattle ear marks, the greater the distance between the original settlement and the outlying one. Changes in the ordinary incisions on the right ear also affect the area of land signified by the cattle ear mark as a whole.

Diagram Eight: *Marorengy* by Bakarimanilahila
of Fanambana (Sept. 1975).

MANGALADRANGITRA

   Mangaladrangitra is an example of a cattle ear mark which takes its name from
one of its component "ear marks." It has *ramogogo* on the right ear and *mangaladrangitra* and *latsakara* on the lower side of the left ear. *Ramogogo* on the right
ear signifies that it belongs to the Anjoaty ancestry just as in the preceding examples.
Mangaladrangitra on the left ear signifies that the Maroserana played a role in the
acquisition of the zebu in question. The Anjoaty "ear mark" is cut on the right ear
to signify that the Anjoaty were the masters-of-the-land where the zebu were
originally acquired, whereas *mangaladrangitra* on the left ear signifies that the
Maroserana (specifically the Zafinivolafotsy) were outsiders on that land. As a
whole the cattle ear mark still signifies a segment of the Anjoaty ancestry (those
who are also descendants of the Volafotsy). As such it denotes an area of land within
Anjoaty country since an ancestry or a segment of an ancestry can only exist in
association with an area of land.

Diagram Nine: *Mangaladrangitra* by Bakarimanilahila
of Fanambana (Sept. 1975).

The Lateral Symbolism of Cattle Ear Marks

   Emil Birkeli wrote that the "ear mark" on the right ear of a
zebu represented the owner's paternal line of descent, while the
one on the left ear represented the owner's maternal line of descent.
He added that "ear marks" could be transferred from one ear to
the other to signify a change of ancestral affiliation:

> ...As we have already said, it is the mark on the right ear
> which is more important since it represents the right to
> paternal succession. There are exceptions however: if an
> individual descends from a father of modest origin and from
> a mother of good family or superior line, he is tempted to
> transport the mark from the left ear to the right ear to make
> himself henceforth part part of the maternal tribe. This act is
> rare however and the consent of the family head is necessary
> ...(Birkeli, *Marques*, 1926, 6).

This formulation derives from a view of cattle ear marks as products of "clans" or "tribes" and is consistent with what has been
called the optative nature of Malagasy descent groups. The idea

is that since a person can descend from several different "clans" as a result of clan exogamy, he or she can choose which clan to belong to, and can manipulate cattle ear marks accordingly.

However, cattle ear marks (as opposed to "ear marks") are products of descent groups which are also land groups. The "ear mark" on the right ear of a zebu signifies the ancestry which owns that animal by being master-of-the-land where it was acquired (not necessarily the paternal line), while the "ear mark" on the left ear signifies, in most cases, the particular land in question (not the maternal line). If a person acquires cattle in his or her father's land, then the father's cattle ear mark is cut on both ears of the zebu. If a person acquires cattle in his or her mother's country, then the mother's cattle ear mark is cut on both ears. In the special case of the origin of a cattle ear mark where a husband and wife act together to acquire the zebu, then the "ear mark" of the one who is master-of-the-land goes on the right ear, while the "ear mark" of that person's spouse goes on the left ear. In Birkeli's formula a person would have to change all the left ears on cattle inherited from the father and all the right ears on cattle inherited from the mother. Actually cattle ear marks inherited on cattle are *not* changed at all *except* with a change of *residence.* A change of residence *can* mean a change of ancestral affiliation as well as a modification in an inherited cattle ear mark. But it is misleading to call this optative. An ancestry or a family within an ancestry usually tries to keep as many of its members as possible to increase its power (and its means for keeping them is land). Nevertheless some of its members are forced out by disinheritance caused by rivalry within the family. Also new residences are often established after siblings divide the wealth of their parents. It is only in the latter cases (which no one chooses) that cattle ear marks are modified.

The Classes of Cattle Distinguished by Cattle Ear Marks

It has been mentioned that land is the primary means of acquiring cattle. Even inherited cattle are inherited from ancestors who got them by working the land. Moreover to inherit cattle in the first place a person must possess land to graze them on. While a fisherman, for instance, might acquire a zebu with the profits of his catch, unless he inteded to graze them underwater (in fact a common legend), he would have to possess land to support them or consume them right away.*

The Anjoaty of Vohemar have acquired cattle in several ways, but in each case the land of Vohemar is considered its ultimate source:

1. Several Anjoaty told me that the capture of sea-turtles and the sale of the shells was a primary way to acquire cattle in the past. Beampy, an Anjoaty of Manambato, said even that sea-turtles were the oxen of the Anjoaty (Fieldnotes, Feb. 1974). The Anjoaty method for capturing sea-turtles was to hunt them from the sand when they came ashore to lay their eggs. The sand was divided by the ancestry into delimited domains called *fahosa* which corresponded to similar divisions of land. A zebu acquired from the sale of a sea-turtle shell captured on a particular stretch of sand would be marked with the cattle ear mark associated with that *fahosa*.

2. Betsimiry, an Anjoaty of Manambato, told me that if he bought a calf with money he made by growing rice and then selling it for a profit, he would cut the cattle ear mark assiciated with his family ricefield on the newly acquired calf (Fieldnotes, Dec. 1974). The same is true for Anjoaty who have inherited access to more than one ricefield (like Jaojotombo of Vohemar). It is still the cattle ear mark associated with the ricefield used to acquire the zebu which is cut on that zebu's ears. (Fieldnotes, Feb. 1975).

3. Jaojotombo also told me that if he bought a calf with money he made by selling one of his steers, he would cut the cattle ear mark of the zebu he sold on the ears of the calf he bought. The land which was the source of the first zebu is still thought to be the source of the second (Fieldnotes Feb. 1975).

4. With changes brought on by modernization, some Anjoaty acquire cattle by working outside the traditional bounds of the ancestry. Belahy, an Anjoaty of Andravina, said that in this case a person could choose which of the cattle ear marks he or she had inherited to cut on the newly acquired calf. But in most cases a peson will choose the cattle ear mark associated with his or her home village and the land on which he or she intended to graze the zebu (Fieldnotes, Aug. 1975).

*This is exactly what happened to the Vezo fishermen of Vohemar in the 19th century according to Bernier (1834), see above.

If a person buys an unmarked calf he or she cuts the cattle ear mark associated with the source of the wealth used in the acquisition on that calf. If a person buys a cow which already has cattle ear marks, those marks are not changed, but that cow's offspring are cut with the cattle ear mark of the buyer and his land, not with the mother's cattle ear mark. Calves which are born into a family herd are simply cut with the cattle ear marks of their mothers which perpetuates the system. Therefore cattle with the same cattle ear mark in whatever herd they are found can be recognized as descendants of the same cow or group of cows, while a herd with cattle cut with more than one cattle ear mark have no common group of female ancestors. The *group* of cows were all acquired originally and maintained for the most part by one family working on area of land. They are thus property of the same kind, a category of social wealth corresponding to the division of land by a people of common descent.

Classes of People Distinguished by Cattle Ear Marks

Anjoaty trace their descent from male and female ancestors and transmit their wealth in land and cattle to male and female descendants. Since they practice both exogamy and endogamy, a cattle owner may possess many different cattle ear marks on the cattle in his or her herd, inherited from many different ancestors on both sides of the family. The greater the antiquity of the herd, the greater will be the number of different cattle ear marks in it since there will usually have been a larger number of ancestries which have contributed. On the other hand the existence of the same cattle ear mark in different herds is an indication that the owners are relatives. Still a person is identified with one of the cattle ear marks in particular by descent and residence. This cattle ear mark is usually inherited in the male line since descent links through males are considered stronger as links to the land. Thus residence is generally patrilocal and virilocal and people are most often buried in the cemetery of their father. As the proverb states: "Among cattle females rule, among people males rule."

Therefore one can expect to find a particular cattle ear mark on cattle in a particular place and that cattle ear mark and those cattle will most likely have been transmitted in the male line. If the herd contains other cattle ear marks, one can ask: how did these marks enter *(miditra)* the herd?* The required answer is that they entered through marriage between ancestries or between segments of the same ancestry and were brought by a spouse (usually a woman) moving into an affinal village. When women move to their husbands' village at marriage *(manaraka*: to follow), they leave their cattle in their natal village in the care of their brothers. But once they have children (heirs) in their husband's village their cattle are brought from their natal village to the natal village of their children.**

> For example, Bakarimanilahila lives in Fanambana, and is identified with the Anjoaty cattle ear mark called *araimatavy* (and-fat). Among the other cattle ear marks in his herd are *mantia*, associated with Manambato, and *mangaladrangitra*, associated with the Sahaka area of Manambato. *Mantia* entered his herd with his wife who, once she had given birth to heirs in his village, had her cattle brought from Manambato. *Mangaladrangitra* entered Famanbana with his father's mother's father's father's mother, an Anjoaty from the Sahaka area of Manambato named Minabe, who married an Anjoaty from Fanambana named Tsimanahaka around 1825 and had her cattle brought from the Sahaka to her children's village.

The reverse process where a man moves to his wife's village, acting like a woman *(jaloko)*, is not exactly the same since such a man probably won't have any cattle to bring with him. If he did he probably would have been able to stay in his natal village. This is what made Sinoa, a resident of Vohemar, say that the cattle ear marks of a woman could change place, but not the cattle ear marks of a man (Fieldnotes, March 1974).

As an ancestry descends over the generations, it loses some people and cattle through marriage with outside ancestries and also gains people and cattle in the same way. But it can gain only if it owns land; and the people it loses are mainly women since they have a weaker tie to the land. The cattle ear marks on the in-coming and outgoing cattle are not changed. Despite the fact

*Miditra (to enter) has definite sexual connotations in this context. Tsiahilika, an Anjoaty of Manambato, demonstrated by putting the index finger of his right hand through a circle made with the fingers of his left hand, thereby showing at the same time how males are associated with right and females with left.

**The circulation of women and cattle is cause for rivalry between her brothers and husband, and continues the next generation in the relations between her children and their mother's brothers.

that the cattle themselves move away, the cattle ear marks remain as a memorial to the ancestry and the land which first acquired them. Nevertheless, there are two ways in which cattle ear marks can be modified:

1. through a marriage between ancestries when the newly wed couple establish a separate residence within the ancestral domain of one of them and acquire cattle together;

2. and through the segmentation of an ancestry, when siblings divide the land and cattle of their parents, and some of them, usually women or junior men, are forced to move to an unsettled area within the ancestral domain.*

In both cases women are generally held responsible for the change, and in both cases it is the left ear which is usually more significantly modified. The two factors combined led Mahatoly of Andravina to say that women were responsible for the changes in the left ears of cattle ear marks (Fieldnotes, Oct. 1975). Birkeli envisioned a *"système boutonnier"* to explain such modifications, but it is not fully developed in his work and as a result there is as great a variety within the categories he creates (in some cases) as between the categories. The aim of the following history of Anjoaty cattle ear marks is to match the kind of changes that are made in cattle ear marks with the sorts of divisions which occur when an ancestry descends over the generations within a given territory.

The Creation of the First Anjoaty Cattle Ear Mark

There is a widespread Malagasy legend of the origin of cattle in which cattle are said to have come out of the sea. Anjoaty say that they emerged first in Antsinanana on the east coast, but returned to the ocean when they weren't treated with respect, and emerged again only in Bobaomby.** In the meantime, Anjoaty say nearly the same thing of themselves. They say that they came originally from Arabia to an island called Mijomby. When Mijomby sunk (another widespread legend), they were cast into the ocean. The survivors saved themselves in canoes (or in some versions, not directly concerned with the Anjoaty, on the backs of fish). They landed on the west coast of Madagascar.

*Exasperatingly, not all divisions of land result in new versions of cattle ear marks and not all newly composed versions get new names.

**Tsiahilika, Aug. 1975 and Bemanana, Sept. 1975.

Traditions differ as to their exact landing site; some say Toliamaeva (present day Tuléar), others name places on the northwestern coast. Nevertheless all agree that from their initial landing site they moved north along the coast to Bobaomby (and some put this in the context of the Maroserana invasions).*

In Bobaomby the Anjoaty consisted of a group of siblings, their families, and their dependants. One Anjoaty, Mahatoly of Andravina, told me that before they reached Bobaomby, they had no cattle and no cattle ear mark. "All they knew was fish." Fasanarivo, the eldest sibling, said: "Here there are cattle, so here I will have children." Since all they knew was fish, the Anjoaty made a cattle ear mark called *tsimanovadrazana* modeled on a fishtail (as shown in diagram ten).

TSIMANOVADRAZANA

Diagram Ten: *Tsimanovadrazana*, the first Anjoaty cattle ear mark.

...At the time the cattle climbed ashore, Fasanarivo wasn't yet in Bobaomby. There was no owner for those things. A long time after they gained the shore Fasanarivo arrived. He saw many cattle, perhaps there were one hundred, but coming from overseas, there was nothing they knew if not fish... "Here I will have children, for here there are cattle," he said. There were no cattle ear marks then, so they used a fishtail as a model. The triangular cut at the tip of the ear *(vaky tendro)* on the cattle ear mark *tsimanovadrazana* is modeled after a fishtail. Later they added features here and there; for instance the flab of ear left hanging at the base *(latsakara)*. You can't change *(tsy manova)* the cattle ear mark *tsimanovadrazana*, and that's what its name comes from... (Mahatoly, tape xiii, Oct. 1975).**

*Many Anjoaty say that at this epoch the Anjoaty were one people *(olo araiky)* with the Zafitsimaito, who subsequently migrated to the Matitana region of the southeastern coast. Zafitsimaito means "descendants-of-those-whose-common-ancestry-is-not-broken," and was said to be given in memorial to their common heritage. Bakarifeno of Ampanobe said that the Anjoaty and the Zafitsimaito possessed a common cattle ear mark called *manalobe* (but couldn't diagram it).

Fasanarivo sent his younger siblings to Vohemar and they claimed it by saying prayers at the mouths of all the important rivers and bays. Later they returned to Bobaomby, and when this generation of ancestors died, they were buried at sea. Their children returned to Vohemar to live. Some say that the first village they established was near the embouchure of the Manambato river (for instance Jaonatana, yellow notebook three). Sinoa of Vohemar was among those who said that before siplitting up to occupy all of Vohemar, they divided the cattle ear marks in Ambatoharanana, on the banks of the Manambato river (Fieldnotes, March 1974). Unfortunately, nobody could narrate this in detail. From this beginning, the Anjoaty eventually established themselves in Manambato and Andravina, Iharana, Fanambana, and Ampanobe. The cattle ear marks of these regions will be discussed separately and will then be related in the conclusion.

Manambato and Andravina

Fasanarivo's son, Ndranahalanana, settled in Manambato and Andravina. He continued to cut the cattle ear mark *tsimanovadrazana* which he had inherited from his father, so this cattle ear mark came to be associated with the main portion of land in

ANTAMPATANA

This cattle ear mark is identical to *tsimanovadrazana* except that it lacks a *vaky tendro* on the left ear. That it has *ramogogo* on the right ear means either that the Antampatana were one of the class of people who cut this ear mark or that their ear mark was changed through contact with the Anjoaty. That there is no *ramogogo* on the left ear (since there is no *vaky tendro*) shows that the territory it represented was considered to be a part of the territory represented by *tsimanovadrazana*, though I never heard it clearly delimited.

Diagram Eleven: The cattle ear mark *antampana*
which entered the Anjoaty ancestry through Ndranavaratra,
son of Sarahina, an Antampatana, by Jaona Jaofeno of Manambato.

**Mahatoly's version of events is self-serving since he is one of the Anjoaty who continues to cut *tsimanovadrazana*. He is implying that he descends in the male line from the senior Anjoaty ancestor. However his information is entirely consistent with other versions collected from a score of people as will be demonstrated in what follows.

Manambato and Andravina. Ndranahalanana was accompanied
by his son Ndrantiniky and his sister's son Ndriapiavonnona.
Once settled in Manambato he married Sarahina, the daughter
of the headman of the Antampatana, the people who occupied
Manambato before the arrival of the Anjoaty, and had Ndranavaratra. Sarahina's cattle ear mark, called *Antampatana* (as shown
in diagram eleven) entered the Anjoaty ancestry through Ndranavaratra, her son.

When Ndranahalanana died, Manambato and Andravina were
divided among his sons and his sister's son. His sons disputed
their share. Ndrantiniky, the elder, was pushed north of Andravina
since he was not the child of Sarahina and thus not a descendant
of the former *tompon-tany*. Ndranavaratra got the main bulk of
land: south of the bay of Andravina, north of Antranovato, and
west of the Andramalao river. Ndriapianonona the sister's son
got a small area of land near the mouth of the Manambato
river, generally considered to be a part of the land inherited by
Ndranavaratra. While Ndrantiniky and Ndranavaratra continued
to cut the cattle ear mark *tsimanovadrazana* which had belonged
to their father, Ndriapiavonona began cutting a variation of it
called *mantia* which became asociated with his small parcel of
land.[23]

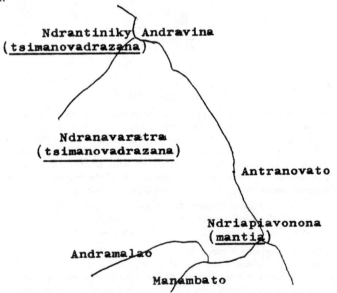

Map Three: The cattle ear marks of Manambato and Andravina.

MANTIA

Mantia has *ramogogo* on both ears, but no *latsakara ambany* on the left ear. This indicates that it is associated with a territory considered to be within the general domain of the territory associated with *tsimanovadrazana*.

Diagram Twelve: The cattle ear mark *mantia* which began with Ndiapiavonona by Jaona Jaofeno of Manambato.

To give some historical perspective on these events, Ndriapia-vonona's widow, Volamintariana, and two of his sons, Keliman-deha and Alimana, were seen and named by the Frenchmen Mayeur and Corby when they passed through Manambato in 1775.[24] Several generations later another cattle ear mark was introduced among the descendants of Ndriapiavonona. It is said to derive from a marriage between two of his descendants in Manambato (though I never learned the genealogy or the particular territory involved). The name of this cattle ear mark was *ramogogo aroe* (two *ramogogo*).* It was diagrammed slightly differently by two different men (as shown in diagram thirteen).

RAMOGOGO AROE   RAMOGOGO AROE
(by Aly of Manambato)   (by Jaozamany of Ampanobe)

Both versions have *ramogogo* on both ears. Aly's has no *latsakara*; Jaozamany's has a *latsakara ambony* on the left ear. It is difficult to determine whether the difference is due to error or whether the cattle ear mark is actually cut differently by different people. Both versions still indicate that *ramogogo aroe* is a variation from *mantia* and *tsimanovadrazana* and applies to a territory with the land signified by them.

Diagram Thirteen: *Ramogogo aroe* by Aly of Manambato and by Jaozamany of Ampanobe.

*Bakarimanilahila of Fanambana said that the first cattle ear mark in Manambato was called *tsineniko* (May '75), but Jaona Jaofeno of Manambato said that this was a synonym for *ramogogo aroe* (June '75).

Tsimanovadrazana (cut by the descendants of Ndranahalanana) and *Mantia* (cut by the descendants of Nrdiapiavanona) are the two dominant cattle ear marks in Manambato today. Since there has been marriage between the descendants of these two men, many Anjoaty possess cattle with both cattle ear marks in their herds. Yet they are still identified with one of them more closely by residence. If they live near the mouth of the Manambato river, they are identified as descendants of Ndiapiavonona and cut *mantia*; on newly acquired calves if they live elsewhere in Manambato or Andravina, they are identified as descendants of Ndranahalanana and cut *tsimanovadrazana* on newly acquired calves. Jaona Jaofeno, a descendant of both men, is more closely identified with *tsimanovadrazana* since he is a descendant of Ndranahalanana in the male line. Yet he told me that he had worked out a personal arrangement. When he grows rice in his inherited ricefield in Anramalao and sells it to buy zebu, he cuts the cattle ear mark *tsimanovadrazana*; but when he grows rice in the ricefield he broke south of the Manambato river, and sells it to buy zebu, he cuts *mantia* to balance things out (Fieldnotes, April 1975). Thus it is his place on the land which indicates his affiliation, but in fact, his place is determined by the manner in which he has descended from the ancestors.

Iharana

The names of the Anjoaty who settled in Iharana are known

ANTIHARANA   ANTIHARANA
(by Aly of Manamboto   (by Jaona Jaofeno
whose mother's family   of Manambato)
hails from Iharana)

Antiharana by Aly has a *vaky tendro*, a *lelam-pamaky ambany* and a *latsakara ambany* on the right ear, and a *kompa ambony*, a *tondro araiky ambany*, and a *latsakara ambany* on the left ear. *Antiharana* by Jaona Jaofeno has *ramogogo* on the right ear and *tondro araiky ambany* on the left ear. These differences conform to the complex ethnographical situation in Iharana, and without a more detailed genealogy, nothing can be said to explain them.

Diagram Fourteen: *Antiharana* by Aly of Manambato and Iharana and by Jaona Jaofeno of Manambato.

only in fragments. When they arrived in Iharana they came in contact with the Antiharana, the native people, and intermarried to the point where their common descendants are known both as Anjoaty and Antiharana.* They only cattle ear mark which has been transmitted by the Antiharana/Anjoaty in Iharana is called *antiharana* (and shown in diagram fourteen).

Ndramalony, a son of one of Fasanarivo's younger brothers, settled originally in Anorontany in Ampanobe. His son, Vonimbola, moved to Makira on the upper Fanambana. Bakarimanilahila of Fanambana said that Vonimbola's cattle ear mark was called *tsimahatoro*, but didn't diagram it.** Vonimbola had two sons, Ndrampisaora and Ratsima. When he died his sons divided the land of Fanambana and his cattle. Ratsimay, the junior, said of his share, "Ah, mine is fat," and began to cut the cattle ear mark *ariamatavy*. Ndrampisaora, the senior, said of his share, "And mine is sweet," and began to cut the cattle ear mark *koamamy* (and-sweet). The division of the cattle ear marks corresponded to a division of the land in Fanambana (as shown on map four).

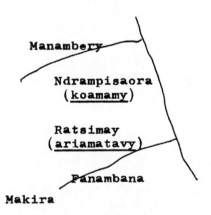

Manambery

Ndrampisaora
(koamamy)

Ratsimay
(ariamatavy)

Fanambana

Makira

Map Four: The division of land in Fanambana,

*When Corby entered Iharana in 1775, he met Raminty, whom he called a "chief from Sakalava country." This has been taken as an indication of Sakalava invasions said to have destroyed the early settlement in Iharana (P. Vérin, "Histoire Ancienne du nord-ouest de Madagascar," *Taloha*, 5, 1972). But Raminty was an Anjoaty, according to his descendants, so Corby's statement is really the first European account of the migration of the Anjoaty to Vohemar from the west coast.

** There is also a Tsimihety cattle ear mark called *tsimahatoro* (Molet, "Le Boeuf," 1953, p. 21).

Vonimbola

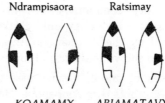

Ndrampisaora　　　　Ratsimay

KOAMAMY　　ARIAMATAVY

Koamamy has *ramogogo* on the right ear, and a *lelam-pamaky ambany* and a *latsakara ambany* on the left ear. *Ariamatavy* has *ramogogo* and *latsakara ambany* on the right ear, and *vaky tendro*, *lelam-pamaky ambany*, and *latsakara ambany* on the left ear. Both differ from *tsimanovadrazana* by not having *ramogogo* on the left ear. They differ from each other less significantly, by a *vaky tendro* on the left ear and a *latsakara ambany* on the right ear.

> **Diagram Fifteen:** *Koamamy* by Bakarimanilahila of Fanambana and Tsiahilika of Manambato and *Ariamatavy* by the same men.

Ndrampisaora's descendants continue to cut the cattle ear mark *koamamy;* some modifications have been introduced, but the name hasn't changed. His daughter's son, Ndranatoro, lived during the reign of Radama I, the Merina King. When Radama's armies conquered Vohemar in 1823, Ndranatoro moved from Fanambana to Vohemar and became the civilian commandant of that town.* His descendants cut a version of *koamamy* (as shown in diagram sixteen).

NDRANATORO'S *KOAMAMY*

The modification introduced by Ndranatoro was to cut an *afaka latsakara ambany* on the left ear in place of a simple *latsakara ambany*.

> **Diagram Sixteen:** Ndranatoro's *Koamamy* by Bakarimanilahila of Fanambana.

*This is common knowledge in Vohemar; see also James Hastie, "Journal," 1823-1824, original mss. in Government of Mauritius Archives; French text in *Bulletin de l'Académie Malgache*, vol. III (1904), 17-36; and the cited "Rapport" (1834) of Bernier.

Ndranatoro's family expanded throughout Iharana and into Manambato with the support of the Merina. For example his great-grandson, Osiny, founded the village of Andramalao avaratra in Manambato, Osiny's descendants still cut the cattle ear mark *koamamy*. But Osiny was also a descendant of the Anjoaty of Manambato and so also inherited the Anjoaty cattle ear mark *tsimanovadrazana*.* When asked to identify his cattle ear mark, Beampy of Andramalao avaratra, singled out *tsimano-vadrazana* (which had been inherited through females) and not *koamamy* (which had been inherited through males) since his family lived in Manambato.

Back in Fanambana Ratsimay's descendants continued to cut the cattle ear mark *ariamatavy*. His great-grandson, Osinikely, made a significant modification in that cattle ear mark without changing its name (as shown in diagram seventeen).

OSINIKELY'S *ARIAMATAVY*

Bakarimanilahila said that Osinikely had merely introduced a *famantarana* (a small nick used to distinguish his own cattle from those of his siblings). But the way Aly diagrammed it, it is completely different. Significantly it had no *vaky tendro* on the right ear and thus no *ramogogo*. I could not learn why such a significant modification was made.

Diagram Seventeen: Osinikely's *Ariamatavy* by Aly
of Manambato and Iharana.

Ampanobe

Ampanobe is the southernmost region of Vohemar inhabited by the Anjoaty. It was settled by descendants of Fonaomby, a sister of Fasanarivo. Fonaobmy's son, Lavakantsa, was the first person to be buried in the Anjoaty cemetery at the mouth of the Ampanobe river. His cattle ear mark was *marorengy* (as shown in diagram eighteen).

*Osiny's mother's mother's mother's father's father's father was Ndranahalanana.

MARORENGY

This version of *marorengy* has *ramogogo* on the right ear and *vaky tendro* and *afaka latsakara ambony* on the left ear.

Diagram Eighteen: *Marorengy* by Jaozamany of Ampanobe (Sept. 1975).

One of Lavakantsa's grandchildren, Ndranaharoana, was called "the chief of the banks of the Ampanobe river" by Mayeur in 1775,[25] He inherited the cattle ear mark *marorengy*. At the same time, he sent his sister, Mahoriaka, to settle the region of the Manambery river, and she introduced a version of *mororengy* called *bobalahy* (*boba:* many; *lahy:* males) in recognition of her new territory.

BOBALAHY
(by Jaozamany
of Ampanobe)

BOBALAHY
(by Jaozara
of Manambery)

Jaozamany's *bobalahy* is identical to Bakarimanilahila's version of Ndranatoro's *koamamy* (which may be due to a mistake). Jaozara's *bobalahy* id the second Anjoaty cattle ear mark without *vaky tendro* on the right ear.

Diagram Nineteen: *Bobalahy* by Jaozamamy and Jaozara.

Another woman from Ampanobe introduced the cattle ear mark called *manjo* (*manjo:*profit). Versions of this story differ: some say her name was Rahotsaka, that she married in Antsinanana and died there; one man said that one of the ears of *manjo* was Betsimisaraka (but this is not apparent from the diagram); some say that her daughter, Tompoemilaho, returned to Ampanobe with her cattle and her cattle ear mark; but others say that Tompoemilaho was a sister of Ndranaharoana.

MANJO

Manjo has *ramogogo* on the right ear and a *vaky tendro* and an *afaka latsakara ambony* on the left ear.

Diagram Twenty: *Manjo* by Jaozamany of Ampanobe.

Tompoemilaho's daughter, Norosariaka, married into Ndranatoro's family in Iharana and she began the cattle ear mark *tsimahateky* (as shown in diagram twenty-one).

TSIMAHATEKY   TSIMAHATEKY
(by Tsiahilika)   (by Bakarimanilahila)

Tsiahilika's *tsimahateky* has *ramogogo* and a *tombolomaly* on the right ear and a *vaky tendro* and a *latsakara ambany* on the left ear. The *tombolomaly* appears to come from a foreign ancestry. Bakarimanilahila's version has *ramogogo* on the right ear and a *vaky tendro* and an *afaka latsakara ambony* on the left ear. I do not have enough information to explain the differences between the versions.

Diagram Twenty-one: *Tsimahateky* by Tsiahilika and Bakarimanilahila.

MARORENGY

The *famantarana* is on the upper side of the left ear.

Diagram Twenty-two: *Marorengy* with a *famantarana* by Bakarimanilahila.

Finally, *marorengy* is the primary cattle ear mark in Ampanobe. Thus the people of Amboditsiandriana, twelfth generation descendants of Lavakantsa continue to cut it (but with a *famantarana* as shown in diagram twenty-two). The other cattle ear marks which come from Ampanobe derive from it and were created by women who were forced to settle new areas outside the originally inhabited area.

The History of the Cattle Ear Mark Mangaladrangitra

The cattle ear mark *mangaladrangitra* is shown in diagram twenty-three.

MANGALADRANGITRA

Mangaladrangitra has *ramogogo* on the right ear and *mangaladrangitra ambany* and *latsakara ambany* on the left ear.

Diagram Twenty-three: *Mangaladrangitra* by Bakarimanilahila.

There are three versions of the origin of this cattle ear mark which also explain its component incisions. Two concern the Antiharana/ Anjoaty (though they differ slightly in genealogical detail). The third concerns the Anjoaty of Manambato. All relate the same basic events: that *mangaladrangitra* came from the marriage of a Zafinifotsy prince with an Anjoaty woman in the Sahaka or Andravina area of Manambato.

Asanijoby, an Antiharana/Anjoaty, who lives in the Sahaka region of Manambato, said that the history concerned Manorobe-faneva, one of his Antiharana/Anjoaty ancestors:

> ...Andrianamisotry, a prince from western Madagascar, came here by boat looking for sea-turtles. He married Manorobefaneva and they had Ndranokona and Manetika. Once the children were born, Andrianamisorty prepared to return home to the west. He wanted to take his children with him, but the Anjoaty said, "We won't let our children go." Manorobefaneva would not let him take the children.
>
> "If that's the way it is, here are some silver pieces *(volafotsy)* to help raise the children. If you acquire cattle with them, cut the cattle ear mark *mirangitra*, because we are princes," said Andrianamisotry, who then departed.

But the Anjoaty thought it over. "What sould we do? If we cut the cattle ear mark *mirangitra*, the prerogative of the princes, they'll come and raid our cattle. So let's cut *mangaladrangitra* instead so they won't come." From this came the cattle ear mark *mangaladrangitra*...(Fieldnotes, Sept. 1975).

The second version of the *mangaladrangitra* history was written by Jaonatana in the early 1900's. It concerns a marriage between a Zafinifotsy named Andrianaka and an Anjoaty named Manoroantsa, and the birth of their daughter, Manorobefaneva:

> ...Manoroantsa was the mother of Manorobefaneva and Andrianaka was her father. Andrianaka asked for his daughter (to take away with him) but didn't get her. So he said, "If you won't give me the child, this is what you should do with the riches she gains by the work of her hands. If she acquires cattle, cut the cattle ear mark *mangaladrangitra.*" Manorobefaneva had Ndranokona and Manetika, so their descendants cut the cattle ear mark *mangaladrangitra* which came from Andrianaka, Maorobefaneva's father (Yellow notebook three).

Finally, Mahatoly of Andravina told me that the *mangladrangitra* history concerned an Anjoaty women named Masy, grand-daughter of Ndranahalanana (the first Anjoaty to settle in Manambato), and a Zafinifotsy prince named Fay:

> ...Fay was a child of the Zafinifotsy defeated in a war, a civil war, a fight for the flag. He came here from Ankarana and lived in Rantalava. His wife was named Masy. Together they waited over the sand in Rantafanasina. They captured sea-turtles, sold them, obtained money, and bought cattle. One of the cattle they acquired was a female with one calf. When the calf was a year old, Masy, the owner of the sand *(tompon-djia)*, cut her cattle ear mark, *tsimanovadrazana*, on the right ear of the calf. Fay's cattle ear mark, that which made him a prince, was cut on the left ear of the calf. But they disputed.

> "Mine is the master-of-the-land *(tompon-tany)*," said Masy. "Mine goes on the right."

> Fay disagreed at first, but in the end he consented. He said at first, "I'm a prince."

> "I know you're a prince," Masy replied, "but you are not

a master-of-the-land here. This is my land and my sand as
well, and that is how we acquired the cattle."

Fay agreed in the end and his cattle ear mark, *mangaladrangitra*, was cut on the left; the *tsimanovadrazana* of Masy, an
Anjoaty, was cut on the right...(tape xiii, Oct. 1975).

In all three versions the decision to put the Anjoaty cattle
ear mark on the right ear of the cattle and the Zafinifotsy ear
mark on the left ear is consistent with the fact that Anjoaty were
able to keep the children. Both derive from the fact that the Anjoaty were the masters-of-the-land.* It is interesting that the
versions of this tradition are linked to two separate genealogies.
Apparently the same cattle ear mark was created twice. The fact
that Birkeli recorded an identical cattle ear mark from western
Madagascar (as noted above) makes it appear that there was
frequent marriage between the Maroserana and other ancestries
such that *mangaladrangitra* was applied to a class of actions,
not just in isolated cases.

A Comparison of Anjoaty Cattle Ear Marks

The first Anjoaty cattle ear mark, *tsimanovadrazana*, is the
most complete Anjoaty cattle ear mark (containing *ramogogo*
on both ears and *latsakara* on both ears), and has been transmitted
unchanged (as its name implies) by the descendants of its founder
who have remained in the land of the founder. Modified versions
of *tsimanovadrazana* have been introduced by members of the
ancestry forced out of this region, and these people have been
mainly sisters and younger brothers. A comparison of *tsimanovadrazana* with derivative cattle ear marks (like *mantia, ariamatavy,*
and *marorengy*) shows two major ways in which Anjoaty cattle
ear marks have varied over time:

1. On the one hand they have lost incisions. Ordinary
incisions have been taken off altogether, and complex
incisions (like *ramogogo* an *mangaladrangitra*) have been
taken off in part. For example, *mantia* derives from *tsimanovadrazana* and differs from it by lacking a *latsakara* on the
left ear. The derivative cattle ear marks *koamamy* and
ariamatavy of Fanambana differ from it even more by lacking

---

*As noted above, normally a father controls his children. But when children are
born in their mother's country, she may act like a man, and keep them for herself.
In these cases, her brothers or her father are the power behind her.

a complete *ramogogo* on the left ear. The cattle ear marks from Ampanobe (notably *marorengy*) differ from it even further by not having any part of the *ramogogo* on the left ear.

2. On the other hand Anjoaty cattle ear marks have varied over time by gaining incisions through contact with other ancestries. The cattle ear mark *antiharana* has two ordinary incisions not found on any other Anjoaty cattle ear marks (*kompa* and *tondro araiky*), and it appears that they came from an Antiharana cattle ear mark adapted to the Anjoaty. Similarly, *tsimahateky* has the incision *tomolomaly*, not found on any other Anjoaty cattle ear mark. Finally, the most significant example of this is the cattle ear mark *mangala-drangitra* which includes part of an "ear mark" representing a foreign ancestry.

The general rule seems to be that the greater the distance between the founder of a cattle ear mark and the founders of its derivatives, expressed genealogically and in land, the greater the number of incisions taken off an ear and thus the greater the likelihood that foreign incisions will be added to it.

Conclusion

The Anjoaty cut *ramogogo* on the right ears of their cattle and thus belong to Birkeli's fishtail category. Birkeli explained the composition of this category by saying that the peoples in it became related through ethnic links (and there is some evidence for this in the relations of the Anjoaty, Antampatana and Antiharana). Given the significance of land, however, it is possible that peoples cut the same "ear mark" not because they have intermarried, but because they have shared the same land (or exploited the same ecological zone). It is thus possible that the people who cut fishtail marks are Antandrano or once were Antandrano.

Finally, while the Anjoaty are Antandrano and members of the fishtail category, they are unique by their common descent and their common land. This is expressed in cattle ear marks through the integration of *ramogogo* with other incisions on both ears of the zebu. Cutting a cattle ear mark of a zebu thus signifies a change from a descent group which is a member of a larger category of such descent groups, to a descent and land group or a *kind* of people. More fieldwork is necessary to discover how this process has occured in Madagascar as a whole.

NOTES

1. It is impossible to discuss the sources here or to consider the relations between the Anjoaty of northern Madagascar and those of the southeast (usually written Onjatsy). See A. Grandidier, *Ethnologie de Madagascar*, vol. I, Paris, 1908, pp. 121-127. This essay is based on fieldwork, 1974-1975, in Vohemar Madagascar supported by the NSF and NIMH, to which I am grateful.

2. J.V. Mellis, *Volamena et Volafotsy - Nord et Nord-Ouest de Madagascar*, Tananarive, 1938, 15-16.

3. N. Mayeur, "Voyage dans le nord de Madagascar," *Bulletin de l'Académie Malgache*, X(1912), 93-156 (with addenda), 114-131. The period of this voyage by the peripatetic N. Mayeur was November 1774 to January 1776.

4. P. Verin, "Histoire Ancienne du Nord-Ouest de Madagascar," *Taloha*, no. 5, 1972, University of Madagascar, Revue du Musée d'Art et d'Archéologie, pp. 133-150 and 165-174, being a summary of earlier literature.

5. Rev. H. Maudrell, "A Visit to the North-East Province of Madagascar," *Journal of the Royal Geographical Society*, XXXVII(1867), pp. 108-116.

6. F. Guinet, "Population du Nord," *Documents sur la Compagnie de Madagascar*, Paris, 1867, edited by Baron P. de Richemont.

7. A. Grandidier, *Ethnographie de Madagascar*, I(1908), Paris, 121.

8. Levy, "Le Nord-Est de Madagascar. La Province de Vohemar," *Revue de Madagascar*, XIII(March 1911), 687-699.

9. Verin, "Histoire," *Taloha*, 5, 1972, p. 87.

10. Ch. Bernier, Rapport sur une mission sur la Cote nord-est de Madagascar," 1834, mss., see R. Kent, *Early Kingdoms in Madagascar, 1500-1700*, 1970, New York, pp. 268 and 274 for a bibliographical context. The original mss. is in the French National Archives, Overseas Section, dockets 15³⁰/dossier 8B. following the new classification.

11. Levy. "Nord-Est Madagascar," 1911, 691.

12. A. Van Gennep, *Tabou et Totemisme à Madagascar*, Paris, 1902, pp. 190-191.

13. E. Birkeli, *Marques de Boeufs et Traditions de Race; Documents sur l'Ethongraphie de la côte occidentale de Madagascar*, Oslo, 1926, *Bulletin* no. 2 of the Oslo Ethongraphic Museum, pp. 12 and 17.

14. Birkeli, *Marques*, 1926, p. 20.

15. Birkeli, *Marques*, 1926, p. 20.

16. Birkeli, *Marques*, 1926, p. 55.

17. Birkeli, *Marques*, 1926, p. 30.

18. Birkeli, *Marques*, 1926, p. 55.

19. Birkeli, *Marques*, 1926, p. 54.

20. Birkeli, *Marques*, 1926, p. 55.

21. Birkeli, *Marques*, 1926, p. 5, and L. Molet, "Le Boeuf dans l'Ankaizinana," *Mémoires* (Institut Scientifique de Madagascar), Tome II, serie C, 1953.

22. Birkeli, *Marques*, 1926, P. 6.

23. Hosen Donto, *Interview*, Nov. 1975.

24. N. Mayeur, "Voyage," (1774-1776), *BAM*, 1926.

25. N. Mayeur, "Voyage," (1774-1776), *BAM*, 1912, p. 116.

Religion and State:
A Comparison of Antanosy
and Sakalava in the 1600's

R.K. KENT
University of California
Berkeley

Ils meritaient que je leur otasse tout, ainsi que faisaient les ZafeRamini, mais je me contentai de prendre seulement six boeufs." (Etienne de Flacourt, 1661)

"Ny nataon'ny sakalava azy dia Andriamisaraefadahy; io no maha sakalava ny sakalava." (Tsimanohitra Tombo and Mamoribé, 1965)

There is much ongoing discussion about the historical study of religion in traditional societies* and strong ties between religion and government have been and are widely noted in them. Nonetheless, Madagascar remains at best on the periphery of such international discussions while within it the older connections between religious symbols and political authority continue to be understudied by historians. The Great Island can undoubtedly add rich materials and offer valuable insights for this dual subject. It is clear, for example, that much of what has been written in some depth about traditional states in Africa derives from studies which rarely venture beyond the last century. Moreover, antecendent states tend to be explained away through intrusive state-builders whose own religions attain supremacy in the process, often because evidence is hard to come by and may no longer be obtainable in some cases. The Antanosy of southern Madagascar and the Sakalava of its western littoral provide two older settings which deserve and need to be compared.

*See, for example, T. Ranger and I. Kimambo (eds.), *The Historical Study of African Religion*, 1976.

Both have had intrusive elements associated with local states. In Antanosy they called themselves the Descendants of Raminia or *Zafindraminia*, after the ultimate ancestor and subject of a well-known local legend.[1] Among the Sakalava they were called the *Maroserana*, name which has received several interpretations.[2] Both, moreover, yield written sources situated close enough in time to throw light on the ways in which temporal authority and religious sanction came together. Two Jesuits, for example, spent a year just where the first Sakalava state of Menabé would see its birth. One of them, Father Luis Mariano, was a prolific writer and left behind a number of letters and reports written between 1613 and 1620.[3] The Antanosy land was not only visited by literate Europeans, including the ubiquitous Father Mariano, but was also the site of a French settlement, Forth-Dauphin, for over three decades (1643-1674), circumstance which produced an even greater number of sources written by visitors and residents alike. The most extensive as well as valuable contribution to come out of this period consists of two volumes by Etienne, de Flacourt, Fort-Dauphin's Governor between 1648-1655.[4] Lastly, both the Sakalava and the Antanosy are subjects of monographs in the making for some time,[5] work which should mitigate against unfamiliarity with wider contexts. Unlike the Zafindraminia in Antanosy, the Maroserana became in effect the family from which the Sakalava obtained their monarchs. As will be seen through the Zafindraminia failure and the Maroserana success, religion was pivotal in the acceptance of political authority but it may well be that the formula mentioned earlier is worthless as an explanation if what can be learned from Madagascar will encourage further comparisons elsewhere as well.

The Antanosy

The first visual impression of the Antanosy Zafindraminia must be attributed to Father Mariano in 1613. All of the "kings of various neighboring districts" who came to see the Portuguese visitors seemed less impressive than the ruler of the "Maticassi kingdom."* His party consisted of about 500 men armed with spears and axes, numerous relatives and progeny. Many appeared "almost" European as well as more refined in dress and ornaments than the crudely dressed soldiers and sailors who had gone ashore.

*A small area within Antanosy.

Mariano was shown a book "written in Arabic characters." The Maticassi ruler told him of trading relations with the Dutch and mentioned that there had once been in his land a small Portuguese fort, that these earlier Portuguese were absorbed into some local families through inter-marriage, and that his line of Descendants of Raminia went back seventeen generations on one side and fourteen on the other.[6] Some forty years later, Flacourt even came by a genealogy with 17 descendants of Raminia and calculated, at thirty-year generations, that Madagascar was attained some five centuries before his time (ca. 1150), but pointed out that the Zafindraminia settled in Antanosy much later, around 1500.[7] There is no firsthand description of the Zafindraminia in Antanosy during the 1500's. A brief Portuguese account could be interpreted in a way favorable to the Zafindraminia presence[8] but there are no reasons to doubt that they were in Antanosy at least since the time of Maticassi ruler's grandfather.[9]

Three years after Mariano's visit to Antanosy, two other European priests perceived the local society in terms of two "castes," one white the other dark. They felt that the local whites could "learn anything" but were completely amoral in the use of their intelligence. Both "castes," the priests held, were addicted to the same forms of sorcery as prevailed "among the Arabs."[10] The Portuguese were seeking a foothold in southeastern Madagascar at the time and the two priests escorted to Goa *Dian Ramach*, son of the Maticassi ruler who returned home as a Christian convert.[11] In the late 1630's as the new Maticassi king, Dian Ramach placed under his protection François Cauche who thus lived in Antanosy several years before his compatriots founded Fort-Dauphin. Cauche did not make sharp distinctions in terms of pigment, rank and power. The society did not consist only of *blancs* and *noirs* as there were many *olivatres*, too. As ruler, Dian Ramach alone wore red robes. "His *blancs*" (the Zafindraminia) and the *noirs* wore blue cottons generally with some of the more important *blancs* displaying a few red threads and some of the more important *noirs* wearing trousers. There were no distinctions in armaments as everyone carried a shield and a handful of throwing spears which varied only in the size of their heads. In one respect, the *blancs* seemed to have an advantage as it was an observable practice to have animals for consumption slaughtered only by a *blanc*.[12] According to Flacourt there were two parallel hierarchies in Antanosy for the *blancs* and the *noirs* or

Negres. The *blancs* had three estates, the *Rohandrian* (from *andriana* for Lord, Lords), the *Anacandrian* (*anak*-children of Lords), and the *Ondzatse*; the *noirs* had four, the *Voadziri*, *Lohavits*, *Ontsoa* and the *Ondeves.*[13]

Flacourt argued that the Rohandrian were the "race of princes" among whom the *Grands* (rulers) were selected but it is clear from his entire text that this term did not at all apply strictly to the Zafindraminia and it did not always indicate or imply an office or political function.[14] Indeed, the "children of Rohandrian" became increasingly "bastards' descendants," sired by the *Grands* and not, in fact, the immediate issue of Rohandrian. Since an Anacandrian could issue from a female of any "estate," *blanc* or *noir*, as long as the father was considered to be a Rohandrian, the Zafindraminia did not practice endogamy in Antanosy. The *Voadziri* and the *Lohavohits* were the analogous *noir* "estates," the former hereditary chiefs, richest and most powerful among the *noirs* (Antanosy), the latter their progeny. Among the *blancs*, the third estate consisted of "reddish-skinned" *Ondzatse* who were mainly fishermen and guardians of the *Grands'* tombs. The *Ontsoa*, third *noir* estate, were children of Lohavohits but whereas the Voadziri usually ruled over several villages and their sons over their own village, the Ontsoa could not hold an office and were, in contrast to the upper two estates, "poor." For this reason, the *Ontsoa* often attached themselves to a powerful Rohandrian. The fourth estate was composed of slaves or *Ondeves*. One could become an *Ondeve* through debt, purchase or capture in war but the Rohandrian and the Voadziri could not be enslaved.[15]

The Zafindraminia did not introduce or impose a hierarchy in Antanosy. As they came already *métissé* from elsewhere in Madagascar the Zafindraminia saw a clear Andriana-progeny analogy in the Voadziri-Lohavohits "estates." Lands under the Antanosy occupation did not have to be alienated since land was not scarce and the Zafindraminia established their own villages with facility. The old chiefs, sometimes remembered as *Antebobaka*, continued to rule over most of Antanosy and since a military conquest by the Zafindraminia was out of question, the Rohandrian needed to attain an economic or religious hold over the original inhabitants or find a combination of both through the manipulation of cultural symbols. A large number of followers could mean political power but real wealth was perceived in

terms of cattle. A *Grand* was often expected to feed large numbers
of people on festive occasions, an act resulting in the slaughter
of many head of cattle.[16] Acquisition of cattle in an agricultural
society went into the making of the local "cattle-barons." The
Zafindraminia are known to have stored away their harvests
until these could be traded for cattle at great advantage to themselves.[17] Still, the preferred method of acquiring already domes-
ticated cattle was a raid on someone else's pen allowing for
continuous redistribution of wealth among the upper estates.
Abbé Nacquart, who wrote a number of letters from Fort-Dauphin
to the head of the Lazarists, pronounced warfare in Antanosy
as nothing more than raids for livestock.[18] To Flacourt, many
local *Grands* "would hardly make war upon their neighbors"
because of an offense. The real cause of war involved the actual
"possession" of large numbers of *boeufs* and the capture of
slaves. The *Grands*, he wrote, even used to say "haughtily"
that anyone who owned many *boeufs* became thereby their
enemy.[19] Virtual monopoly over cattle and two other features,
one imported and the other local in origin, combined to give the
Zafindraminia preeminence in Antanosy.

In old Antanosy law inheritances went to kin of the deceased
in practice although the chiefs "owned" everything in theory.
There is no evidence that the Antanosy chiefs applied this theoretical
prerogative to accumulate personal wealth and where it was
exercised at all it must have been to *avoid* concentrations of
wealth in families and lineages through inheritance uncontrolled
by authority. Communal rather than individual wealth and election of chiefs provided the older society with mechanisms which
reduced political tension. The link between economic wealth and
political power was not allowed to be made in any lasting ways,
reason which suggests why larger states would not evolve out
of the internal situation. It was the right of all free Antanosy to
take part in electing their *Grands*. Whenever a *Grand* or *Roi*
passed away, "it was licit for the Voadziri, Lohavohits and Ontsoa
to place themselves under any *Grand*" of their choice. The
ritual which ratified this relationship between an incoming ruler
and his subjects was called *lafic-douve* which meant "mat given
to one's potential enemies" whose possible opposition was
diffused by acceptance of voluntary submission, of the "mat."
By Flacourt's own definition, *lafic-douve* was an engagement
for succession through a *Grand*'s gift committing him to the

protection of his wards in return for his right to inherit from them upon death.[20] The local custom of theoretical ownership was endowed by the Zafindraminia Rohandrian with new ritual, taken in part from a divination *(sikily)* formula as the term *douve* reveals.[21] And, as Nacquart observed, it was the common practice in his time for the *Grands* to "take everything" for themselves leaving nothing to the heirs and kin of the deceased.[22]

As founders of their proper villages in Antanasy, the Zafindraminia obtained *Grands* among the *Roanorian* a majority of whom held no political office but most of whom possessed wealth in cattle. The Zafindraminia ethos did not aim at the creation of a centralized state in which the newcomers would monopolize the political function and there is absolutely no evidence to suggest that the Zafindraminia were sophisticated state-builders. They did, however, believe in amassing wealth, especially in cattle, and wealth attracted followers from the *noir* estates as well, especially among the *Lohavohits* and *Ontsoa*. In time, there grew two paralled societies — the old and the new but the new one would gain ascendancy based on materialism, on "amoral intelligence," as the Jesuits observed in 1616. As *Grands*, the descendants of Raminia, readily copied the covenant between old chiefs and the people, adding the "mat" ritual. There was, just the same, a fundamental difference between the traditional chiefs and the Zafindraminia *Grands*. The former were regarded as "fathers" by their subjects, partly the reason why even later in time, in the 1600's, *Grands* could not hold office unless of age.[23] Being of the local people and taking a nonhereditary position in society the old chiefs assumed the role of parent which came with authority. But, the Zafindraminia — as newcomers to Antanosy — did not understand the web of real and psychological relationships which had formed within the covenant. By the time the French residents could observe the Antanosy society, the *Grands*, in Nacquart's indignant words, took "everything without leaving anything to the children of those who had spent entire lives in gathering a few possessions." Indeed, the very success of the new society produced intermarriages between the *Roandrian* males and *Voadziri* females while the old covenant became devoid of its meaning and the *Grands*, whether *blancs* or *noirs*, came to behave not as representatives of two societies but as men *above* both, possessors of the best lands and most of the cattle. As Nacquart perceived:[24]

"Each section has a *Grand* who is its acknowledged ruler
and who behaves like a *petit Roi*. The vassals of these
kinglets range from three to four thousand men. Their riches
consist of three to four thousand *boeufs* which they personally own and of the tribute paid by their subjects, namely
a fifth of the rice and the yam harvests. The title of King
would not be appropriate to them as they are not at all
absolute...The royalty cannot be inherited by the children
unless they are sufficiently advanced in age at the death of
their father. Under these kinglets are other *Grands*, just
about as powerful and rich as they are (themselves)."

And the wealth in cattle was undoubtedly also protected by the
imported feature, the prerogative to slaughter animals for consumption which was known elsewhere in the island as *sombili*.[25]

Again according to Nacquart, "wherever they have managed to
become masters the *blancs* have monopolized the right to cut the
throat of animals to be eaten." In areas, however, "where the
negres have remained masters, the *blancs* would not dare
slaughter their animals at all."[26] François Martin saw a different
dimension by noting "il y a un degré de science parmi eux pour
avoir la liberté de couper la gorge au bétail; ce degré dépend
d'être nés des premiers d'un village et de savoir une espèce de
prière qu'ils disent tout bas avant que d'égorger la bête."[27] Indeed,
if one looks closer at the principal contemporary accounts these
reveal that much of the actual killing and butchering of cattle
in Antanosy was *not* done by either the Rohandrian or the Voadziri but by priests or *ombiassa* who were the ubiquitous immo-
lators at important as well as ordinary occasions. The *ombiassa*
were "wondrously feared by the people" who regarded them as
"sorcerers," and they subdivided broadly into "writers" (*ompa-
norats*) and "diviners" (*ompitsiquili*). The "writers" were particularly respected and writing itself was perceived as a high form of
magic by the Antanosy. Even ink, washed off cabalistic scrolls,
was at times administered to the ill, perhaps as the ultimate
cure.[28] In the eyes of the local populations, the Zafindraminia
were intimately associated with the art of writing, form of *magic*
which had arrived with *them*. Even Flacourt believed that the
writers were Zafindraminia, in contrast to the diviners, throwers
of *siquili* (modern Malagasy *sikily/sikidy*, pronounced *sh'kidd*),
who were mostly "Negres" (pre-existing *tompontany*, owners-of-

the-land) with some *Anacandrian* or *métis* in this context. If
the writers were associated with medicine, as the books examined
by Flacourt confirm, they tended to serve generally the upper
estates in Antanosy. Flacourt, who in time came to be regarded
as a local potentate, was himself taught to read Arabico-Malagasy by an *ombiassa* named *Dian Radam* who later acted as an
unofficial go-between, acting on behalf of *Roandrian* hostile
to Fort-Dauphin in a rather high diplomatic capacity.[29] The
diviners, in contact with all the estates, applied their art not only
to determine the nature of illness and its most likely cure. Their
endeavors were also directed at individual hopes and fears,
accumulated tensions and problems of any type and at any level.
Some of the Antanosy were becoming dependent on the "oracle
of *siquili*" to an extreme, refusing to leave their huts until it could
be learned what "awaited" them outside. Some individuals in
Antanosy even refused to trade, plant, marry, construct a
residence or travel until the *siquili* became favorable.[30]

The *siquili* (*sikidy* today) is and was impersonal, becoming
personalized only during the divination itself. It is thrown,
"awakened," by the *ombiassa*-diviner as well as interpreted by
him. While the "awakening of the *sikidy*" usually involved a
formula that might be memorized by someone else, the *ombiassa*-
diviner could not be separated from the divination itself, at
least not in the Seventeenth century. If Antanosy land is taken
in its broadest possible geographic sense it contained 110 villages
of varying sizes around 1660.[31] Even if each village had at least
one *ompitsiquili* (or *ombiassa*-diviner) there were never enough
diviners on hand to meet the real or imagined needs of thousands
in Antanosy. The bulk of local inhabitants did, however, have
recourse to their personal amulets, the *auli* (*oly/ody* in modern
Malagasy, pronounced *oodd*) for prediction, explanation and
succor. Abbé Nacquart, who described the *auli* (or *oli* and *olis*,
plural, in his own text) as "idols," was convinced that both the
Grands and "their subjects" alike turned to the *auli* — an
"espèce de culte" which would be hard to "dislocate." The
"idols" were in effect made and sold by the *ombiassa* and:[32]

> "these little idols consist of a piece of wood or hollow root
> and are attached to a belt. Thereafter powder and oil are
> inserted and figures of small men are carved in the belief
> that they are alive as well as capable of providing whatever

might be desired...Everyone has them inside the homes and individuals take them along into the fields. They turn to (the idols) in times of need as we do to God. They will do nothing when uncertain without consulting them; and any thought that might occur to them is believed to have been suggested by their *Olis*."

In effect, the *auli* were seldom far away from their owners. Flacourt — whose description of the *auli* as small boxes embellished with glass beads and crocodile teeth reveals that he saw mainly those belonging to the wealthier Antanosy — also knew that the *auli* were placed on wooden staffs inside the residences of their owners. This is where the *auli* were addressed "as if they were endowed with reason." Their owners could talk to the *auli* "for two hours at a time, even fall into extatic trances while so doing," and they ascribed the content of their dreams to the "will of the *auli*."[33]

It was Abbé Nacquart's firm conviction that the Antanosy were "simple de leur nature" and having "neither laws nor religion" could easily be attracted to the "superstitions of Mohammedanism."[34] Although some of the features among the Zanfindraminia *Roandrian* point to probable Islamic antecedents — such as a form of fasting during Ramadan for example[35] — they were at best highly "diluted" Muslims, hardly capable of imposing a Muslim culture upon the Antanosy. If, as is quite probable, the Zafindraminia did introduce *sikidy* into southeastern Madagascar, its succesful diffusion within Antanosy (and elsewhere) was made possible precisely by the pre-existing cult of the *auli*, by the presence of religion which allowed for the *sikidy* to become one of the highest forms of sacerdotal consultation. Like the amulets which contained cabalistic writing, itself relatively novel in the area, or even the Christian agnus which a successor of Abbé Nacquart requested because the Antanosy would carry it "like their *Olis*," around the neck,[36] the *siquili* became incorporated into a cosmology concerned with assessment and prediction, prevention and cure. Nacquart himself described a healing process in which the interaction of the *siquili* and the *auli*, with the *ombiassa* as intermediaries, is clear:[37]

"First (the *ombiassa*) perform their abstractions and look busy (then) taking a board (into their hands) they spread sand on it and make a number of calculated points, what they call *squile*, and they repeat this often in order to assess the disease's nature. A part of the sand (thus used) is sold within a piece of wax which they place around the neck (of the ill) in order to obtain health."

An *auli* which produced the desired result, such as the end of illness, would continue to be worn long after the need had passed. In time, the fundamental *tompontany* belief that disease was either supernatural or unnatural, willed by displeased ancestors or living personal enemies, led 'to ever wider use of the *siquili*, not only as detector of the nature and source of illness but also as counter-measure and weapon of the will. The last two in particular strengthened the association of the *siquili* as the higher sacerdotal adviser and the *auli* as its faithful agent, the *ombiassa* both prescribing and manufacturing appropriate amulets for healing or prevention, even for someone else's death. The *auli* roles are best depicted not for the commoners in Antanosy but — as could be expected — for the *Roandrian*, around the mid-1600's. A list of some thirty *auli* belonging to the *Roandrian* reveals their strong desire for control, power and absolute protection: control over natural pests, like the locust, and natural phenomena like rain, wind, thunder and lightning; control over cattle and cattle-theft; control over women; control over subjects who must serve the *Roandrian*; power to punish instantly those who speak ill of the *Roandrian* in public or in private; power to cast spells on anyone; power to turn invisible at will; power to deprive an enemy of will to resist; power to crush enemies; protection against all attempts to put spells on the *Roandrian*; protection against ulcers and against venereal disease.[38]

Flacourt also notes that not all of the *Grands* believed in the *auli*. The matter is however one of mere form, not of real substance since the *Roandrian* and *Grands* who had not "converted" to the *aauli* were just as attached to the "Muslim" talismans, the *hiridzi*, manufactured by the *ombiassa*-scribes, with purposes and functions identical to those of the *auli*, the only difference being in the interior contents as the *hiridzi* were encasing Quranic verses as general protectors or astrological incantations geared to specific tasks.[39] Carpeau du Saussay, who composed his account of the southeastern Madagascar in 1663 and who spent some four months exclusively devoted to an attempt to understand the

Oly, "ce Dieu," readily perceived the point. The *Grands* placed the *Oly* box into another, made of gold or silver and carried around the neck, suspended on a rather slack chain. But, when the *Grands* resorted to the "other" style of carrying boxes around their necks, the "*boëtes* were replete with "caracteres magiques, & d'espece de Talismans." The "Commissaire Provincial de l'Artillerie de France" left no doubt that he considered the boxes filled with a variety of "drogues" and those containing writing to be *Oly* just the same.[40]

The two-way flow of the *tompontany auli* and the Zafindraminia *hiridzi* reveals with slight chance of error that the parallel societies were not simply in a state of interpenetration but an ascending one at that. An increasing involvement of the *Roandrian* with the *auli* cult was a process of both manipulative and sincere adaptation which brought them closer to the Antanosy cosmology. Conversely, the Antanosy ould readily assign both religious and magical value to the *hiridzi* and even the ink in which the contents were written and adopt them as another form of *auli*, the pivotal element of their religion. The Zafindraminia did not bring with them a coherent idea of state or a discernible political theory but they were — just the same — moving in the direction which would centralize political and not mainly economic power in the hands of the *Roandrian* who were active rulers at the same time, having attained preeminence through the cultivation of acquisitive impulse and, as *ombiassa*, through association with ritual, immolation, circumcision, writing, divination, medicine, and magic — both white and black. This preeminence was even to be sanctioned by a myth of origins in which the six estates in Antanosy had issued forth from six women that God had fashioned out of Adam's brain, neck, shoulders, thigh, legs calf, the seventh female deriving from his heel as mother of slaves. The upper estates were all above the waistline while the *Roandrian* alone were "of" Adam's brain.[41]

Despite the myth that everyone in Antanosy had a common ancestor in *Radama* (Adam) the ancestral trees of the original settlers (*tompontany*) and of the Zafindraminia could not merge in the presence of parallel societies. The specific *auli*, espoused by some of the most powerful *Roandrian*, could not become the national "idols" of all Antanosy. As the *Roandrian* had adapted the inheritance covenant to their acquisitive drive so they came to perceive the *auli* not as benevolent helpers of men and women coping with daily life but as coercive magico-political tools having a dual purpose: to gain control through fear and to insulate this control from challenges to it, again through the agency of fear. The *Roandrian* will-to-power, as their *auli* attest, was intense and, at least under Dian Ramach, as a response to the French fort and its local impact, the Antanosy in general began to move toward centralization. But, lack of unity and discipline among the *Roandrian* and their inability to seek support by means other than coercion would have made it impossible to have a single political authority in Antanosy even if the French fort had not prevented its establishment.

The Sakalava

"One searches in vain," noted an observer in 1895, for "those Roandriana, the lordly families of yore...they have disappeared" from Antanosy land.[42] No Zafindraminia *Grand* is recalled in this area by tradition and the last of Raminia's known Descendants left Antanosy back in the 1840's.[43] The Maroserana, oldest dynastic family in Madagascar, are, in contrast, still around among the Sakalava. If they no longer rule the memory of Maroserana kings is preserved among the Sakalava through the *dady* cult, an enduring feature of local society. In general, the term *dady* stands for "ancestors" but it is used among the Sakalava only for the relics of departed male monarchs, great men of the past, the *Ampagnoto-bé*. There are ten *dady* in Menabe, area which saw the birth of the first Maroserana-Sakalava kingdom, and four main *dady* in Iboina, second of the two states located along the coast of northwestern Madagscar. Succesive monarchs could not mount the throne and rule without being in possession of the *dady*; they were housed in the inner court of the royal village; and they were taken out every two years for the ceremony of *Fitampoha*, ritual bath of the relics.[44] The relics, fashioned shortly after a royal death, contained:[45]

> "une touffe de cheveux au-dessus du front, les deux canines, l'ongle du petit doigt de la main droite, un fragment du frontal et un éclat de l'occipital...Chaque 'dady' renferme ses dépouilles royales dans deux dents de crocodile, jumelées, des dents en argent...remplacent les dents vétustes, décomposées par l'âge; ces dents sont encastrées, avec plusieurs

tubes de bois fermés par une rondelle de calebasse, dans un bandeau, dans une armature d'argent, décoré de figures géométriques au repoussé; les tubes de bois contiennent des ingrédients végétaux mélangés de cire, de graisse de boeuf et de miel; ils furent préparés par des 'omasy'" (*ombiassa*).

Although ceremonies of the royal ritual Bath took place also in two other societies within the island they involved *living* rulers and they came to end with the respective monarchies. The cult of the *dady* continues. Despite the fact that most Malagasy respect their ancestors in a variety of religious ways, the cult of the *dady* is unique in Madagascar. It literally defines the Sakalava. The central feature of this cult is the incorporation of defunct monarchs into one's family at the exclusion of the more immediate familial ancestors. It is hence no accident that the Maroserana *Ampagnito-be* are at the same time the *dady* of all Sakalava.

It has been an established feature among the Sakalava that only their nobility could maintain ancestral trees and that their oral traditions recorded, in effect, only the deeds of the "upper estates," to use Flacourt's terms. Guillain was struck in the early 1840's by the widespread recall of ancestral names among the Sakalava, who invoked them "in all (the) important activities of their social life," and by the pride with which events relating to ancestors were told.[46] His text leaves no doubt that the ancestors in question were mainly rulers and nobility. Some decades after Guillain, Captain Rey was even more explicit. The common people in Sakalava land had completely accepted the idea that they had no *razana* (family) traditions since they did not "need" them. Ancestral trees and traditions of the past were confined to the *Mpanito-be* and *Mpanito-taloha* (living and departed kings and princes), to the *longon'mpanilo* ("lateral friends," from *anila* or side, aside), and to the *vohitsy-mananila* (commoners elevated to nobility laterally).[47] In our own day, an educated Sakalava, has made the point that it is difficult to separate the exercise of power from religious functions involving the great Sakalava chiefs, the *Mpanjaka-be*, "Sovereigns and Pontiffs" at the same time. As the supreme guardian of royal relics and head of the ritual, the *Mpanjaka-be* remains human but has a sacred quality; posthumously he becomes the object of the cult himself. When the colonial authorities abolished royal government among the

Sakalava the act itself did not alter the mass-veneration of the royal ancestors; the possession of relics remains more important than even the principle of heredity; and the relics symbolize to this day both the cult of the *dady* and the origin of unity among the *Zafimbolamena*, ruling branch of the Maroserana.[48]

As a long-time student of the Sakalava observed not very long ago, ancestral spirits in the act of possession *(tromba)*, especially the benevolent ones *(tromba tsara)*, turn out to be those of the earliest Maroserana.[49] Custom dictates that departed monarchs may be recalled only through their *fitahina* or posthumous names and the most common of such names are those of *Andriamisara* and *Andriamandazoala* in Menabé, with *Andriamandisoarivo* being added in Iboina, which he had founded. If there is a single name for the four main *dady* of Iboina it must be *Andriamisara efa dahy..*[50] There is also the specifically royal *tromba* through which designated mediums (generally called *vaha* or *famahavaha*) assume the personality of a previous king at the site of the royal tomb and then "speak to the people," usually to urge them not to adopt any new ways. After such a speech, the *vaha* would enter the inner and sacred chamber of the royal enclave *(Zombabé)* to receive the sacred lance which princes of the Maroserana line had dipped in water; and he would sprinkle anyone approaching with it to dispense the "benediction of Andriamisara" upon all of his descendents.[51] How and when did a family of outsiders manage to become venerated like gods and personal ancestors after death, to become the powerful guardians of tradition even from the tomb? They founded Menabé as conquerors, as "spearheads," mark which they placed on the ears of their cattle.[52] Did they in fact impose a religion defining their own family as one of the populations under their control, affirming that venerable dictum of *cujus regio ejus religio?*

If one consults the internal source of Sakalava past, namely their own oral traditions, a sacerdotal person is connected almost invariably with the founding of Menabé as kingdom under the *Volamena* (Zafimbolamena) or golden branch of the Maroserana family. Because the Maroserana became a dynasty first among the Mahafaly populations in Madagascar's deep southwest the Sakalava traditions have come to reflect a certain amount of confusion as to where in the Maroserana family tree the Volamena should properly begin. It is generally agreed in the traditions that Menabé's conquest took place under *Andriandahifotsy* (d. ca. 1685) who is thus its founder but it is still an open question as to whether the Volamena branch of the Maroserana began with his father, uncle or grandfather. The father-and-uncle traditions often give both as *Andriamisara* while the grandfather is given as *Andriamandazoala*. There is, however, no disagreement in traditions relating both the advent of Volamena and birth of Menabé that a *moasy* (Sakalava equivalent of *ombiassa*), especially the diviner variety, occupied a central place in both events. In the northwest, a long distance from the southern reaches of Menabé, there is a composite version which accounts for the Maroserana success in creating their first Sakalava kingdom and which seeks to explain how the royal relics came into being. In it, a *moasy* named either *Ndramboay* or *Tahezamboay* (noble or violent crocodile) advises through divination that Andriamandazoala must offer in sacrifice his favorite spouse if Menabé is to be his. The spouse herself exonerates Andriamandazoala from an unpleasant decision favoring the *moasy*'s advice. In return, her progeny acquire lasting primacy over children of all the other Maroserana female spouses. It is she who fashions the first Volamena royal relics with a lock of her own hair, a nail and one of her canines; and following her sacrifice, the *moasy* dips a spearhead into her blood, recasts the iron, mounts it on a royal staff and proclims Andriamandazoala as king of Menabé.[53] In contrast, traditions prevalent between rivers Tsiribihina and Onilahy, tend to remain silent on matters of human sacrifice, on the royal relics, and even to downplay the role of *moasy* in favor of those who ruled. They insist nonetheless that Andiamisara was the first Maroserana in contact with the Sakalava and Guillain was able to learn that the very name "Sakalava" was given to those who willingly placed themselves under Andriamisara's authority[54] which Guillain did not difine as either secular or religious. Still, the unembellished *moasy* does often appear in one composite tradition from Menabé as the originator of the idea to use a red bull in a ruse directed at opponents of the Maroserana, ruse which was successful, which made the red bull a sacred animal and the red color itself a part of the kingdom's name.

If such symbolic traditions are not apt to command attention as good history their links to the past should not be dismissed either. The female spouse represents a local kingship base for the Maroserana. She is the fundamental link of local populations to their new monarchs. Through her, voices of the past suggest that the royal relics' origin should be sought locally and not among outsiders; and the ubiquitous *moasy*, especially the *mpiskidy* or diviner, has in fact been a fixture at the court of Sakalava rulers. If his advice worked, the ruler would get most of the credit; if it failed, the *moasy* would earn most of the blame and a "mistaken" priest could be put to death by a disappointed Maroserana ruler.

There is, however, in the single instance of Andriamisara, a priest-king problem which yields both symbolic and historical traditions and which leads into the advent of *royal* relics. Henri Rusillon was among the first to discuss the "Andriamisara problem." "On veut," he wrote, "que (le) père (d'Adriandahifotsy) soit Andriamisara. Les uns en font un guerrier farouche, les autres un...moasy sans pouvoir autre que celui de ses remèdes ou de ses charmes...on se trouve devant un problème qu'il n'est pas possible d'éclairer complement."[55] On linguistic grounds, Rusillon also held that Andriamisara was a noble *(andriana)* noted for his constant efforts to purchase *(misara)* a variety of magico-religious objects, the *ody;* more recently, it has been proposed that the root-word in this name is *Isara* or Arabic for "divination," that whole clans are extant in Madagascar claiming the name of *misara;* that *Andriamisara* crops up in divination formulae in many parts of the Island; and that we are hence dealing with the figure of a noble who became a diviner or a diviner who was elevated to nobility at the highest possible point, as the "father" or "uncle" of the conqueror of Menabe.[56] Indeed, it is difficult to find anything about Andriamisara as a *ruler* in the Sakalava traditions, while it is common to find him associated with religion, magic and service to the Maroserana. There is also an important text collected from attendants of an *Mpanjaka-bé* in Iboina, attendants who had no stake in shielding the past. They were Makua and not Sakalava and, moreover, they resided among the Iboina Sakalava who generally believed and still do that Andriamisara was "chef de la famille royale sakalava qui regna dans le Menabe."[57] According to the Makua text:[58]

> The dady go back to Andriamandresi and Andriandahifotsy, who had subjected several villages in Menabe, extended and augmented their father's kingdom. They had a moasy of great renown. At the death of Andriandahifotsy, king of the warriors and the moasy's master, the moasy cut his hair

and his nails and pulled his teeth out, placing them together
with his own ody (amulets). Then he prepared a wooden
box, ornamented with pearls, and placed the remains of the
deceased monarch into it. The box came to be respected
as much as the king when still alive. As the conquests went
on, Andriamisara took the box along saying "the king's
body is in here and those who do not obey me... take
away the ancestral force from the box." The people submitted
to the Zafinimena kingdom. No one could handle the dady
as well as the moasy, Ndramboay who —after his (own)
death— became Andriamisara. When he died and in accordance with the will of Andriandahifotsy, his own hair,
nails, and teeth were placed in the box. He was thus greatly
honored and considered as the king's son although this he
was not, no more than being the king's father. Andriandahifotsy's son, Andriamandisoarivo, when sent by his older
brother to conquer the north, would not leave without the
wooden box. This is how the royal ancestors became the
Zanahary (Gods).

This is by far the most lucid resolution of the Andriamisara
problem and a key to how the *dady* were put to use.

Andriandahifotsy died around 1685 and his conquests and fame
are attested as far back as the 1650's. It is when one turns to the
first half of the 1600's, to an important society within future
Menabé, one for which records are available, that the real
origin of the *dady* cult comes to the fore, with all of its fundamental and associated features. It emerges from the letters and
reports of Father Mariano that the most important place in the
area of future Menabé or, for that matter, between Boina Bay in
the north and Onilahy River in the south, was *Sadia* located in
the Manambolo delta. During his first visit in 1613 it had some
10,000 inhabitants and around a thousand dwellings. Sadia's
people were agriculturalists, millet was the main crop, and some
cattle-keeping was present. The local ruler, *Capitapa*, was well-
advanced in years, he befriended Mariano and offered his son and
heir-apparent *Loquexa* as a guide to further coastal exploration.[59]
A treaty was concluded with the Portuguese and Capitapa
permitted a future posting of Jesuit priests at Sadia.[60] Mariano
returned to Sadia in June 1616 with his companion António de
Azevedo. They remained until June 1617. Although Father de

Azevedo did pen some pages of reports at Sadia, Mariano is the principal writer. His religious bias is clear but his descriptions retain undisputable value. In disapproving of polygyny and of levirate, for example, he described local marriage and family; and in being repulsed by "witchcraft" Mariano depicted some of the most salient features of local religion.

The Jesuits noticed fairly soon that there were no priests in Sadia for otherwise they would assist at such events as circumcision and sacrifice to a diety. Still, the inhabitants of Sadia undertook virtually nothing of any importance without the aid of divination which many practiced on sand. There was in Sadia, however, a high diviner, called *Maganga*, who had the "attributes" of a *Cacis* (priest). He was a close relative of the ruler holding a public office and at the same time much sought after by other important men of the land. In the town of Sadia, this dual function was exercised by a brother of Capitapa, uncle of the heir-apparent, Loquexa. In other sections of the state it was exercised by the most respected members of nobility. Although the *Maganga* was frequently in error, as perceived by the Jesuits, he was the object of such blind faith that his slightest whims were responded to without question.[61]

The absence of local priests was indeed in sharp contrast with the many divinities. Local dieties were infinite in number because anyone who passed away in adulthood would become an *Afo* or ancestral spirit. The very aged and heads of families were venerated in particular after death but the greatest honors were reserved for the spirits of departed nobles and princes of royal blood. Any males of royal blood who passed away in very old age would be honored posthumuously "by the entire population, like national dieties." The *Afo*, continued Mariano, were objects of a cult similar to the one rendered by Christians to their Saints yet obviously "in error." The Sadians knew nothing of Hell and Damnation and they regarded the *Afo* as benevolent, begging them for help and honoring them "incessantly." They could not even spot the Devil who was nonetheless present, taking the name of an *Afo* and possessing someone to preach to an assembled crowd "about wars past or yet to come, to incite those listening into some enterprise." The Devil wasted no time as only a day or two after someone's death he would come to speak in the deceased person's name, "assuming its voice." It was "strange and lamentable" for the Jesuits to see a people in communion with the Devil "as if they were speaking with their fathers, brothers or friends."[62]

Sadian gods and *Afo* were represented by "wooden images," "mis-shapen and ugly," yet decorated with glass beads and "other crude jewelry," and carried crosswise while attached to some "sort of scarf." In wartime or when a dangerous journey had to be undertaken, the "representations" would be anointed with lard. There was a "general custom" for commoners and nobility alike, which required the eldest sons to cut the beards and nails of their departed fathers, usually on the day of death. But, whereas the commoners would also add a piece of the deceased's loincloth to "these relics" and sew them up into some cotton, the nobility placed "these objects into an evil little reliquary attached to a belt," usually brought out during festivities and always carried in times of war.[63] In many parts of his text, Mariano repeats with consistency that the specific customs described for Sadia were in fact widespread along the western littoral of Madagascar in areas which include the central and northern Menabé as well as southern Iboina.

It is clear that such innovations as may have arrived into Menabé with the Maroserana did not include a "new" or "superior" religion. As in Sadia, commoners and nobility venerated their departed males over much of Sakalava land long before Mehabé and Iboina were created. The inclusion of conqueror-kings like Andriandahifotsy or Andriamandisoarivo into a wide-spread and tailor-made ancestral cult could not have been an act hedged with great difficulties. On the contrary, it must have been *impossible* to do otherwise and retain the fruits of conquest. If the initial inclusion was a calculated effort, suggested or made easier by diviners and elders, one of whom entered the Maroserana family tree as a result, in time the royal ancestors could not be "controlled." They became the "national dieties" (an apt expression by a Jesuit priest) and the Sakalava government could not function until royal successors attained legitimacy through the formal pos-session of the *dady*. In contrast to the Zafindraminia, who settled among the relatively homogenous and culturally-resistant Antanosy, the Maroserana faced some very diverse populations, dispersed over a vast area. The diverse gropings, clustered for the most part along river-mouths of the western littoral, shared the same religion and spoke a language barely penetrated by Malagasy loan-words. In the Sakalava, the Maroserana had the formidable warriors needed to induce a host of self-governing clusters into becoming "Sakalava" themselves. In the widespread ancestral cult the Maroserana found an avenue for the acceptance of their dynasty by isolated and self-sustaining groupings. Neither the Zafindraminia nor the Maroserana can be perceived as particularly astute in the domain of religion; the former could not accomodate to the pre-existing cult of the *auli* and the Moraserana came into a highly developed ancestral cult. In neither case can religious innovation be remotely perceived but while the Zafindraminia copied the Antanosy "estates" the Maroserana brought with them their own political ideas and did not subscribe to the acquisitive impulse of Raminia's Descendants. There is a great deal of oral and written evidence to support such a conclusion but that is another subject.

NOTES

1. See G. Ferrand, "La Légende de Raminia," *Journal Asiatique*, 9th serie, XIX/2(1902), 185-230.

2. *Cf.* Ch. Guillain, *Documents sur 1'histoire, la géographie et le commerce de la partie occidentale de Madagascar*, 1845, 11, note 1; J.V. Mellis, *Volamena et Volafotsy -Nord et Nord- Ouest de Madagascar*, 1938, 12; R.K. Kent, "Madagascar and Africa: The Sakalava, Maroserana, Dady and Tromba before 1700," *Journal of African History*, IX/4(1968), 538.

3. Six *Letters*, dated July 1616; 9-17-1616; 10-22-1616; 8-20-1617; 8-24-1619; 9-9-1630; a seventh letter-report, *"Relação da Jornada e Descobrimento da Ilha de S. Lourenco,"* was prepared by Mariano in 1613-1614. One of the letters may have been written by his companion António de Azevedo.

4. *Histoire de la Grande Isle Madagascar*, 1658 and 1661 editions; *Relation de ce qui s'est passé en 1'Isle Madagascar depuis 1'année 1642 iusques en 1660*, 1661. On the author himself see A. Malotet, *Etienne de Flacourt ou les origines de la colonisation française à Madagscar, 1648-1661*, 1898.

5. R.K. Kent, *Western Madagascar under the Sakalava, 1650-1896*, 1980; *Southern Malagasy and the French, 1638-1675*, ca. 1981/2.

6. Mariano, *Relacao*, 1613-14, French translation, in *Collection des Ouvrages Anciens Concernant Madagascar* (henceforth cited as *COACM*), II, 1904, 48-51.

7. *Histoire*, 1661, 5 (for modern text see *COACM*, VIII, 1913, 13, 25 and 86-7).

8. Visit of Diogo Lopes de Sequeira, *COACM*, I, 1903, 49.

9. One of the most aged men encountered in Antanosy had vivid recollections, supported by good detail, of events going back to his youth, while the Maticassi ruler virtually stated that his father's and grand-father's times were alone still in his memory.

10. Father Manoel de Almeida, "Report," 5-25-1616, *COACM*, II, 1904, 139.

11. Dian Ramach was taken to Goa in May 1614 and returned home in April 1616. He returned as a Christian convert with the name of Andreas de Azevedo. He eventually repudiated the new faith and turned against the Europeans very much like his African contemporary, prince Yusuf bin Hasan, sent to Goa from Mombasa re-named Dom Jeronimo Chingulia, and converted by Augustinian friars. It is interesting to note that after Yusuf's rebellion against the Portuguese he had fled temporarily to northwestern Madagascar and remained hidden among the "East African Arabs" of Boina Bay. *Cf.* Justus Strandes, *The Portuguese Period in East Africa*, (1899), 1971 (English transl.), 171-179; and Flacourt, *Histoire*, 1661/1913, *COACM*, VIII, 60-61.

12. François Cauche, *Relations veritables et curieuses de 1'Ile de Madagascar..*, 1651, *COACM*, VII, 1910, 131-132.

13. *Histoire*, 1661, 47.

14. For example, Flacourt reported factually that the "village of Amboule" was *ruled* by a member of the "*Noir* estates" who was at the same time the head of all the *Grands* in "this area."

15. *Histoire*, 1661, 47-48.

16. Also during funerals all those attending were fed beef, see Flacourt, *Histoire*, 1661, 101, and *passim*.

17. Flacourt, *Histoire*, 1661, 87.

18. Nacquart, *Letter*, 5-2-1650, *Mémoires de la Congregation de Missions (a Madagascar)*, IX, book 4, 1867.

19. *Histoire*, 1661, 95-96.

20. *Histoire*, 1661, 48.

21. See J. Richardson, *A New Malagasy-English Dictionary*, 1885, 128. Noting that the term "is used chiefly in the Sikidy divination" and that it means "enemy," Richardson gave it the Arabic etymon, *aduva*, "enemy."

22. Nacquart, *Letter*, 5-2-1650, 1867, 69.

23. Nacquart, *Letter*, 5-2-1650, 1867, 60.

24. Nacquart, *Letter*, 5p2-1650, 1867, 60.

25. The term *sombili* has been used among the Antambahoaka of eastern Madagascar; see also G. Ferrand, *Les Musulmans à Madagascar et aux Iles Comores*, II, 1893, 32.

26. Nacquart, *Letter*, 5-2-1650, 1867, 69.

27. *Mémoire concernant 1'ile de Madagascar*, 165-1668, *COACM*, IX, 1920, 608-9.

28. *Histoire*, 1661, 189.

29. *Relation*, 1661, 293.

30. *Histoire*, 1661, 25 and 175.

31. See "Carte Carcanossi," *Relation*, 1661, 203bis and *COACM*, VIII, 1913, 24bis. By "villages" one means village-concentrations on about 110 sites in Antanosy.

32. Nacquart, *Letter*, 5-2-1650, 1867, 67.

33. *Histoire*, 1661, 191-2.

34. Nacquart, *Letter*, 5-2-1650, 1867, 61.

35. *Histoire*, 1661, 67-70.

36. Abbé Bourdaise, "Evénements Divers," (ca. May 1655?), *MCM*, 1867, 232.

37. Nacquart, *Letter*, 5-2-1650, 1867, 66.

38. *Histoire*, 1661, 192-3.

39. *Histoire*, 1661, 16, 171 and 192.

40. Carpeau du Saussay, *Voyage à Madagascar*, 1722 (written in 1663), 258-260.

41. *Histoire*, 1661, "Avant-Propos."

42. Louis Catat, *Voyage à Madagascar, 1889-1890*, 1895, p. 379.

43. On the so-called "Antanosy émigrés," see A. Grandidier, *Ethnographie de Madagascar*, IV/1, 1908, 211-12.

44. For a description of *Fitampoha* see J. Valette and S. Rharijaona, "Les grandes fetes rituelles des Sakalava de Menabé," *Bulletin de Madagascar*, IX, no. 155 (1959), 218-313.

45. Ch. Poirier, "Notes d'Ethnographie et d'Histoire malgaches," *Mémoires de l'Académie Malgache*, XXVIII, 1939, 13-15.

46. Guillain, *Documents*, 1845, 9-10.

47. H. Rey, "Le Folk-Lore Menabé," *Bulletin de l'Académie Malgache*, XII/2 (1913), 1930 reprint, 70-71.

48. Ch. Betoto, "Histoire de la Royaute Sakalava," typescript, 1950, 30-32.

49. A. Dandouau, "Le Trumba - Razana ou Angabé," in Kent, *Early Kingdoms in Madagascar, 1500-1700*, 1970, Appendix, 324-332.

50. H. Rusillon, *Un Culte Dynastique avec Evocation des Morts chez les Sakalaves de Madagascar. Le "Tromba,"* 1912, 180.

51. H. Rusillon, *Culte Dynastique*, 1912, 70-71.

52. E. Birkeli, *Marques de Boeufs et Traditions de Race. Documents sur l'Ethnographie de la Côte Occidentale de Madagascar*, Oslo Etnografiske Museum, *Bulletin*, 2, 1926, 30-41. *Cf.* R. Drury, *Madagascar...Journal*, 1729, ed. of 1890, 271, where the Moroserana cattle-marking is named for the first time with certainty by an external source.

53. Betoto, "Royaute Sakalava," 1950, 3-5.

54. Guillain, *Documents*, 1845, 9.

55. H. Rusillon, "Notes d'Histoire Sakalava," *Bulletin de l'Académie Malgache*, new serie, VI(1922-1923), 1924, p. 3 (offprint).

56. Rusillon, *Culte Dynastique*, 1912, 180; Kent, *Early Kingdoms*, 1970, 134-135.

57. Sgt. Firinga, "La Dynastie des Maroserana," *Revue de Madagascar*, III/9 (September 1901), 661, quoting Ch. Benevent.

58. Anonymous mss. Document 2238/2, Archives of the Académie Malgache, *Niandohan'ny Fivavahan'ny Sakalava* (Origins of Sakalava Religion), 1-7, sat on paper ca. 1908.

59. Mariano, "Relation," 1613-14, *COACM*, II, 1904, 20-21.

60. Paulo Rodrigues Da Costa, *Diario*, 1613-14, in H. Leitao (ed.) *Os Dois Descobrimentos da Ilha de São Lourenço*, 1970, 120.

61. Mariano, *Letter*, 10-22-1616, *COACM*, II, 1904, 230, 254 (small print).

62. Mariano, *Letter*, 10-22-1616, *COACM*, II, 1904, 228, 253 (small print).

63. Mariano, *Letter*, 10-22-1616, *COACM*, II, 1904, 229, 253 (small print).

Royal Authority
and the Protector System
in Nineteenth-Century Imerina*

G.M. BERG
Sweet Briar College

A king of ancient times observing the influence obtained by masters of families, in consequence of their acting as their own priests and consecrating their own household gods, adopted the plan of consecrating an idol for the people, calling them his family and children.[1]

Their idols are numerous and of different degrees of honour and renown, the most renowned in this part of the Island, are those which belong to the sovereign, these are (as far as we can ascertain) about twelve in number. The government appoints the guardians of these idols and the office is usually hereditary. These are exempt from all other services and as the service to the government, at present, is a great burden to the people, it is no small privilege to be thus exempted.[2]

A history of the Merina national pantheon sheds light on the means by which kings preserved their authority and the populace maintained their kings. By including local deities in a national pantheon and incorporating them in a royal cult, kings of early

*Research for this essay was supported by grants from the Regents of the University of California and the Mabelle McLeod Lewis Memorial Fund. I am indebted to Marie Krekling Johannessen and Per Rekdal of the Ethnographic Museum, Oslo; Nicole Boulfroy and Elie Vernier of the Musée de l'Homme, Paris; J. Picton of the Ethnographic Section of the British Museum, London, for assistance in examining various collections of Malagasy protectors. I wish to thank Raymond K. Kent, Maurice Bloch, Elizabeth Colson, and Margaret Mooney for comments on earlier drafts, though I alone am responsible for what appears here.

Imerina directed regional loyalty towards the sovereign. In the early nineteenth century, however, Radama I entrusted the task of national unification to the army rather than the pantheon. But, though the army gained territory, it could not contain the social turmoil which spread in the wake of literacy and of Christianity. When a Christian queen abolished the pantheon in 1869, many councilors warned that her throne's authority would suffer since it rested upon popular belief in the pantheon. They were right. The crown lost a major claim to popular loyalty, and the disunity which followed could be allayed neither by the army nor by competent administrators.

The Ody-Sampy Complex

In the first half of the neneteenth century, personal protectors, *ody*, were popular among Merina at all levels of society. The personal protector usully consisted of wood chips, either strung together, or placed in an ox-horn container with various organic substances and worn around the neck or suspended from a belt around the waist. Such a protector guarded its owner from injuries in war, its owner's house from fire, its owner's fields from hail and locusts. It could find lost cattle or a desirable wife. In short, the personal protector, *ody*, insured an individual's well-being.[3] In addition, there were group protectors, *sampy*, which had a more pervasive power than the individual protector. The *sampy* could protect an entire village or household from misfortune, and each group had at least one. In form, the *sampy* was identical to the *ody*, and this similarity has led many observers to use the two terms interchangeably thus obscuring an essential difference in function. The principle difference in personal and group protectors lay in the more pervasive and transferrable power ascribed to the group protector *(sampy)*. The personal *ody* had no power except through consecration by the group *sampy*.[4] Protective power was transferred from the group to an individual when an individual made gifts to the group in return for pieces of wood which were consecrated by the group protector.[5] Thus group protectors, *sampy*, created personal protectors, *ody*.

If the owner of an *ody* became wealthy and successful, admirers could buy offshoots of his protector in which case the successful *ody* became group protector, *sampy*. In this way the transformation of an *ody* into a *sampy* mirrored the change in status of the

protector's owner and tied inferiors to superiors. The connection
between the group *sampy* and the personal *ody* is so strong that
Merina expressed it in kinship terms. The group protector was
known as the "mother protector," *reni-sampy*, which would give
birth to a "child-protector," *zana-sampy*.[6] We will refer to derivative
personal protectors *(ody)* as talismen, and to generative group
protectors *(sampy)* as palladia. As we have seen, the distinction
lay in the protector's extent of power which may change over time.

The supreme rank of palladia *(sampy)* were those which belonged
to the King and were operated in his behalf by hereditary priests.
Just as palladia could consecrate talismen *(ody)*, the royal palladium
could bestow effective protection upon either a group or an
individual. Thus the priest of Kelimalaza, the foremost royal
palladium, exchanged bits of wood from the palladium for oxen
or sheep.[7] This exchange was often attended by great ceremony
which emphasized the distinction in status between ruler and
ruled as well as their mutual dependence. It is precisely this
relationship between royalty and lower status groups, expressed
in a national system of palladia which allowed otherwise independent groups to unite in support of royalty.[8] When it backed
a successful pretender to the throne, a group entered into alliance
with royalty and the group palladium entered the royal pantheon.
Thus, when Adrianampoinimerina secured the support of the
Ambohimanambola, its palladium, Kelimalaza, became a part of
the royal pantheon. As sovereign, Andrianampoinimerina then
placed Kelimalaza at the tomb sites of his ever-expanding ancestral
lands *(tanin-drazana)* wich included Ambohimanga, Tananarive,
and Amparafaravato as well as Ambohimanambola. The people
of Ambohimanambola rose in status. For their support of
Andrianampoinimerina, they retained legal autonomy and performed crucial functions in royal ritual. Their relationship with
royalty was expressed through their palladium's membership
in the royal pantheon. In this way the royal pantheon assimilated
many group palladia while preserving the palladia's regional
association. The royal pantheon of group palladia represented
mutual dependence between sovereigns and groups. It also was
a symbol of national unity which bound the sovereign to law.

Though each ruler owed special consideration to the one or two
groups which brought him to power, the royal pantheon contained
all group palladia ever associated with royalty in the past and

could be invoked by the sovereign to broaden his claim to group loyalties. While the palladium Rabehaza represented the Zanakambony of Betsizaraina and was instrumental in Adriantsimitoviaminandriana's accession to power in the late seventeenth century, it was neverthless, revered in the nineteenth century and was included in most lists of royal palladia. The royal pantheon preserved its past status and lent legitimacy to nineteenth-century monarchs. Ranavalona I, though using palladia such as Rabehaza, usually called upon Kelimalaza, Fantaka, Mahavaly, and Manjakatsiroa to unite her kingdom. The first three had nearly universal appeal owing to their antiquity while the last, Manjakatsiroa, was closely, if not exclusively, associated with Andrianampoinimerina through whom Ranavalona I claimed rights to the throne. Shifting political conditions and the desire to appeal to different groups at different times determined the names of royal palladia invoked on any given occasions. Appeals to unity of course would include as many names as possible. Discrepancies in lists of royal palladia collected in the nineteenth century indicate that the royal pantheon aptly responded to momentary political exigencies.[9]

The incorporation of deme palladia into the royal pantheon drew disparate groups gogether and expressed group solidarity through ritual. The royal pantheon transcended local loyalties. It codified the cooperative relationships between groups required for large-scale irrigation projects and also provided an means of royal control. Loyalty ran from the individual *ody* owner to its "mother," a group *sampy* and in turn to the royal *sampy* of the pantheon. The system promoted social coherence by tying individuals to ever larger groups.

Many authors have confused *ody* (personal protector, "talisman") and *sampy* (group protector, "palladium") in a way which obscured their function. Abinal, Renel, Edmonds, and Otto Dahl derive *sampy* from *asampy* which means "astride" or "suspended." This derivation would refer to the form of the amulet rather than its function.[10] There is some support for this from *Tantaran'ny Andriana eto Madagasicara* which uses the word "asampy" in describing how amulets are worn.[11] An interpretation which is based on form, however, neglects the significance of *sampy* and is, moreover, inconsistent with common usage. If the term means suspended, why would it be applied universally to *sampy* of the royal pantheon which are always attached to a staff rather than suspended?[12] Moreover, while all royal or deme protectors usually appear in traditional literature as *sampy*, personal amulets, which are always suspended, are never called *sampy*. Clearly then the term does not refer to the amulet's form. In light of the preceding discussion of *sampy*, the term may instead be seen as a description of function since the word derives from the Malagasy *samy*, "together," "united." A group protector then, which represents group solidarity would reflect this function in its name. Birkeli has observed that West Coast groups which have migrated from the interior long ago, designate clan names with the prefix, *sami*, *sampi* or *sambi*. He notes resemblance to the Malagasy *samy*, but also to the Arabic *jami*, "united," and East African *jama*, "family," or Kongo *nzambi*, "clan."[13]

Birkeli's association of *sampi* with group leads to a re-evalution of the term *sampy* in the context of function. *Sampy* aptly describes the protector's purpose as the focus of group loyalty whether the center of that focus be the sovereign or the deme elder. That it also coincides in part with a description of the amulet's form increases the likelihood of widespread adoption of the term when describing the item to Europeans.

Palladia and the Royal Cult

In the nineteenth century, the *ody-sampy* complex tied individuals to larger groups, and at the highest level of social organization, the royal pantheon united demes. Loyalty flowed towards the sovereign. Though Radama I doubted the efficacy of the royal pantheon, the system remained in force. Bojer and Hilsenberg in 1822 mention a "national divinity" but Duhautcilly in 1825 was the first to describe it in terms of a royal cult:[14]

> ...ils ont pour le roi et la nation le préservatif général auquel ils rendent une espèce de culte. Ce préservatif se compose de quelques racines d'un certain arbre et de chaînes d'argent le tout enveloppé dans du drap rouge et continuellement gardé dans l'enceinte du palais du Roi par le prêtre habillé en soie couleur puce; c'est pour les Hovas une espèce de Divinité; autrefois ce préservatif suivait toujours le roi à la guerre. Rhadama le fit encore porter à sa suite dans la fameuse guerre de 1820; mais depuis qu'il a une armée per-

menante, regulière et disciplinée il dise que c'est le meilleur presérvatif....

The system of unity emerged from historical circumstances. Before assuming a position in the pantheon as a royal palladium and acquiring special power to protect the nation, protectors were ordinary group palladia, or even personal talismens with powers limited to a small territory, in the case of group palladia, or to specific problems of an individual such as finding a wife, in the case of personal talismens. The *Tantaran'ny Andriana* notes that in ancient times all palladia were equally powerful until chosen by a sovereign for national duties.[15] Elevation to national status depended on the political circumstances which brought a group into alliance with royalty. Understanding a group palladium's involvement in the royal pantheon provides a view of the character of Imerina's national cohesiveness and of the process which created royalty.

It is extremely difficult to study royal palladia of the distant past due to the highly mythic nature of traditions concerning the origins of religious institutions, though several general observations can be made. First, from the time of Ralambo onwards, royal palladia won territories for the monarch and assured national prosperity by making known the proper time for planting rice.[16] Second, royal palladia enhanced a monarch's status in Merina society. Andriamifidy's traditions report, for example, that the red coral bead *(voahangy)*, a principal component of protectors and a symbol of leadership, was used initially by Ralambo to distinguish royalty from the populace.[17] Later the palladia acted completely at the behest of the sovereign so that when Matsatso disobeyed Andriamasinavalona, it was excluded from the royal pantheon and its group reduced in status.[18] In the remote past then, group palladia included in the pantheon represented political relationships and relative status between monarch and group.

A more complete picture emerges for the nineteenth century. As in the earlier period the royal pantheon promoted national unity by fixing group loyalty on the king. The Vig manuscript thus reports that Kelimalaza, in addition to having the power to increase fertility, protect rice, and heal disease, made kings kind to their subjects and made subjects loyal to their kings.[19] All sources emphasize the royal palladium's ability to expand the kingdom and preserve order. Specifically, a royal palladium would protect the king's army and safeguard the people from attacks by bandits. The emphasis on preserving order and efficient administration was a reaction to the social turmoil of the mid-nineteenth century when most of the traditional Malagasy sources were collected.[20]

In the 1830's when Merina saw missionaries and Christianity as the principal cause of unrest, they attributed to the royal palladium, Mahavaly, the power to "smell out" Europeans and their converts. Ranavalona observed that her kingdom's viability depended on loyalty to the ways of Malagasy, not European, ancestors and so she insisted that her subjects call for aid upon Kelimalaza, not Jesus.[21] As the crisis of order grew, the royal pantheon and the guardians of its palladia assumed a paramount position in traditionalist attempts to reduce social discord.

Palladium Rituals and Sacred Kingship

Both group and national ritual using palladia had similar objectives. In the nineteenth century palladia served as symbols of unity in rituals which sought to preserve traditional social order in the face of unprecedented foreign influences. Most of the oral literature collected during the period of upheaval in the mid-nineteenth century abounds with lengthy descriptions of palladia ritual as well as exhortations to continue in the ancestors' ways.

Kelimalaza was the palladium of the Ambohimanambola as well as the principal component of the royal pantheon. The Vig manuscript provides an excellent description of a palladium ritual in the tumultuous times of Ranavalona I when Andriantsavo headed the Ambohimanambola.[22]

> Then Andriantsavo returned carrying water in a white horn (*tandrompotsy*) in which was the ginger of God; with his hand he sprinkled the people present and said "May you be blessed by the water of this white horn with which I sprinkled you, for this is not ordinary water but the water of the divine Kelimalaza, so you will be blessed by Kelimalaza." And when the water was sprayed upon the people, he returned to Kelimalaza and dressed him in a *lambamena* arranging it so the ends hung around his shoulders just the way people usually wear it; and then Kelimalaza was taken outside and

shown to the people. Then he was carried on a long staff and two people preceded him.

A central element in palladium ritual is the sprinkling of water upon those of lower status, and this element assumes paramount importance in rituals of the royal pantheon in times of crisis. Each palladium possessed a "white horn" *(tandrompotsy)* filled with sacred water. In order to assuage widespread public discontent in 1854, Ranavalona I had a zebu killed in honor of Kelimalaza. The ceremony, however, was preceded by a gathering of all "courtesans" at the hut of yet another royal talisman where the sovereign had the crowd sprinkled with water in order to purge them of sorcery.[23] Sibree described a similar ceremony performed by Queen Rashoherina in 1864. The royal rite paralleled deme rites:[24]

> Holding in her hand the horn (N.B. *tandrompotsy)* filled with warm water, and attended by the high officers, the Queen passed through the people, sprinkling them on either hand, and then the soldiers and officers of the guard in the veranda.

Kelimalaza's white horn of sacred water, often mixed with ginger *(sakamalao)*, protected the sovereign and his subjects from sorcery, banditry, and the ravages of war. The "white horn" resided alongside the palladium itself in the sacred northeast corner of its guardian's hut and was brought out for use in various rites including blessings on the birth of a royal child and on the sovereign himself during the national bath festival *(Fandroana).*[25]

Palladium rites combined with water sprinkling mark a relatively recent phase in the evolution of the royal pantheon as an instrument to connect social unity with the well-being of the sovereign. Though water sprinkling and palladium rites emerged in the remote past, they existed as separate rituals. Traditional sources observe that only in the times of Andrianampoinimerina and later did the two ritual systems combine. The merging of these rites is best explained by the extraordinary symbolic efficacy of water in Merina ritual and the support it might add to royal dominance in political alliances with groups expressed in the royal pantheon system. Renel has long since observed the pervasive role of water in a variety of Merina rites.[26] Bloch's recent study of circumcision suggests that the water sprayed on a child's head by an elder represents the "continuity of the generations" making the child a part of the group's "stream of life" which leads from dead ancestors through elders to the young. Sprinkled water then is a transmission line of group membership.[27] By incorporating a similar rite into the royal pantheon ritual, the sovereign interceded symbolically in the "stream of life" between ancestors and the living. Thus, it was through him that groups obtained and conserved membership in a wider social grouping ordained by the hoariest of ancestors. In this way the kings transformed political alliances into relationships approximating kinship *(fihavanana).*[28]

The evolution then, of a royal cult began with a pantheon representing political arrangements between groups and sovereigns. Such an alliance was expressed in ritual by the inclusion of a group palladium into the royal pantheon. Oral literature examined above repeatedly reports this form of ritual for the earliest sovereigns from Ralambo and Andrianjaka to Andriamasinavalona. For the same period water sprinkling played an important role in royal ritual though it was in no way connected to the royal pantheon. Subsequently, however, the purely political and consentual nature of pantheon ritual gave way to rites that expressed a superior-inferior relationship between group and sovereign when water sprinkling and pantheon ritual combined, placing the king directly in line between ancestors and demes. This transformation of ritual combining water sprinkling with pantheon ritual appears in oral literature during the reign of Andrianampoinimerina in the late eighteenth century and it reflected the increased sacrilization of kingship, a development which coincided with the growing secular power provided by a professional standing army. While the pantheon ritual system had previously promoted unity between groups and sovereigns based on consentual political arrangements, its coordination with the water-sprinkling ceremony tied national unity to the elevation of sacred kingship.

Hasina Ceremony and the Royal Pantheon

The presentation of *hasina,* as well, was grafted onto royal pantheon ritual and the combined ceremonies defined a group's status relative to other groups and to royalty itself. Whereas pantheon ritual in the remote past represented a contract of mutual dependence between group and sovereign, the *hasina* ceremony, just as water sprinkling, changed the ritual into an expression of relations between superior and inferior.

Maurice Bloch suggests two meanings for the word *hasina*. The first, *hasina* mark I, is the possession of "innate religous superiority," or as Richardson put it in 1888, "an intrinsic or supernatural virtue which renders a thing good and efficacious." The second, *hasina* mark II, is the homage rendered by inferiors to superiors. In practice, *hasina* mark II is offered in the form of gifts such as an uncut silver coin *(vola tsy vaky)* or parts of prized cattle. In the *hasina* ceremony, *hasina* mark II is given by inferiors to superiors in exchange for *hasina* mark I in the form of blessings of fertility and efficacy. The transaction often takes place between groups of unequal status and the oppsing flows, *hasina* mark II upwards and *hasina* mark I downwards, form a hierarchy in which all groups are ranked in order of status with royalty at the apex.[29]

While offerings to superiors, and royalty in particular, represent an institution dating to the distant and forgotten past, *hasina* rites merged with rituals of the royal pantheon only from the reign of · Andrianampoinimerina onwards. Traditional literature notes that from the very inception of the palladium system, a palladum's guardians required gifts (*hasina* mark II) in exchange for the palladium's protection (*hasina* mark I).[30]

Before the creation of a royal pantheon, or in later years, if a group palladium was not a member of the royal pantheon, the *hasina* transaction occurred between the group's palladium guardians (the superiors) and inferior groups or individuals. As group palladia were included in the royal pantheon, however, an additional transaction arose in which *hasina* mark II offerings went first to the king at the apex of the hierarchy and then to the group's palladium's guardians. Just as the king interposed between dead ancestors and the living through his manipulation of the water-sprinkling ceremony, Andrianampoinimerina placed himself between group palladium guardians dispensing *hasina* mark I and supplicants offering *hasina* mark II. The Vig manuscript observes that the populace presented *hasina* mark II in the form of the unbroken coin (*vola tsy vaky*) to Andrianampoinimerina during the royal bath festival (*Fandroana*) as well as cattle (*volavita, omby malaza*) on yet other occasions in exchange for his blessings of *hasina* mark I. But on such occasions Andrianampoinimerina himself, though at the apex of the status hierarchy, turned over such gifts of *hasina* mark II in an offering to the guardians

of his wife's deme palladium, Imanjakatsiroa, also a member of
the royal pantheon. In return, the king received blessings (*hasina*
mark I) which could then be passed on to the population at
large. In effect, the guardians of Imanjakatsiroa received their due
offerings of *hasina* mark II, but only through the auspices of the
king.[31] Thus the *hasina* hierarchy combined with royal pantheon
ritual to bolster the purely sacred nature of the king's authority.

By the third decade of the nineteenth century, the new Queen,
Ranavalona I, attempted to counteract European influence not
only by expelling missionaries and persecuting converts, but also
by re-establishing rituals of a royal cult which had been created
in the late eighteenth century by Andrianampoinimerina which
had lapsed subsequently during the pro-European reign of Radama
I in the 1820's. During the "nativist" reaction presided over by
Ranavalona I the guardians of Kelimalaza again rose to prominence
and emphasized repeatedly that the Queen's authority rested on the
sovereign's dominant role in *hasina* and pantheon ceremony,
insisting that as in the times long past, the sovereign should
offer the unbroken silver coin and ginger to Kelimalaza in order
to strenghten the kingdom.[32] The impending threat of social
disintegration after the death of Radama I and the rise of traditional
zeal in the late 1820's assured that Ranavalona I's investiture ceremony in June 1829 would consist of an almost baroque amalgam
of ritual intended to emphasize the sacred character of her reign.
Attention centered upon the royal pantheon. At the tomb of
Andriamasinavalona, Ranavalona offered *hasina* in the form of
scarlet flags to the guardians of Fantaka and Imanjakatsiroa
saying "my ancestors have given you to me, therefore support
me."The royal palladia were brought out and displayed to the
population. They were fastened to a long staff with other symbols
of royal authority including scarlet cloth, a coral stone (*arana*),
a green diamond-shaped stone (*andriantsiriry*), a six-link silver
chain. After the royal presentation of *hasina* mark II to the
palladia, in return for *hasina* mark I assuring her royal power,
each group presented *hasina* mark II to the sovereign in exchange
for *hasina* mark I blessings.[33]

The preceding discussion shows a gradual merging of ritual
elements into a royal cult. In the remote past, water sprinkling,
hasina ceremony, and the palladium system expressed group
corporateness and relative status. As the power of royalty

grew, sovereigns appropriated an increasingly dominant role in these rituals and combined them into a royal cult which sanctioned political rule over groups by emphasizing innate sacredness of kingship. Wereas, in the days of Ralambo, membership in the pantheon represented a relatively consentual relationship, such membership by the time of Andrianampoinimerina reflected an unequal relationship, religious superiority clearly belonging to the sovereign who alone could transmit well-being from ancient ancestors to his subjects. The emphasis upon royal sacredness lapsed under Radama I, who depended more on a European-trained army to exert his authority, but in the chaos which followed his reign, the sacred aspects of kingship again became significant in Ranavalona I's attempts to hold the monarchy together.

Political Equality and Ritual Inferiority

On the group level, palladia represented group unity so that several towns composing a group's ancestral lands (*tanin'drazana*) would possess a common palladium. Though no group was exclusively charged with priestly duties it generally fell to elders to manage palladium ritual. The palladium, Rabehaza, united six villages, and responsibility for its maintenance rotated among the elders of each village.

More often a single family was charged with sacerdotal duties. Thus, though the Ramahavaly palladium had a following which crossed group divisions, its guardians were chosen from descendants of Riamangidy. Similarly the guardians of Tsimahalahy belonged to the same family.[34]

The most well-known group palladium, Kelimalaza, was the principal component of the royal pantheon as well and represented the deme of Ambohimanambola, who trace their ancestry to Ravololonandriana, allegedly the daughter of Ralambo and the sister of Andriantompokoindrindra.[35] The Ambohimanambola represented by their palladium guardians have played a significant role in royal politics and received a special place in the status hierarchy of demes represented in political rights as well as ritual duties. At the height of the "nativist" reaction under Ranavalona I, Ambohimanambola received from 200 to 300 bullocks a year from the Queen as well as sheep, fowl, and hard currency.

Financial support was only a part of their due. The Ambohimanambola were almost an autonomous group with few legal
responsibilities to the sovereign other than bestowing Kelimalaza's blessings upon the king. They had the right to judge and
condemn criminals without interference from the sovereign
("*ketsa mahafehy tena*") and could not be prosecuted for crimes
committed ("*tsy maty manota*"). In addition Ambohimanambola
were exempt from corvée labor and army servive ("*tsy atao
miaramila*") as well as various state taxes (*isampangady, landin'ny
manjaka, variraiventy*) and the *vodivona* offering to the king
which they were entitled to receive from other groups. They were
considered by the king as kin ("*havako, hoy ny Mpanjaka*"), as
the "one third of Imerina" (*fahatelon'Imerina*) and finally as
nobles who are sufficient unto themselves (*Andriana mahavita
tena*). These rights were granted before Andrianampoinimerina
and were subsequently re-enforced. Ranavalona I exempted the
Ambohimanambola from mission school attendance.[36]

Political autonomy for groups, it seems, was not reflected in
pantheon ritual. The picture which emerges from a description
of Ambohimanambola political rights presents a striking contrast
between their inferior status manifested in royal pantheon ritual
and their actual power in the political sphere. While their palladium, Kelimalaza, operated in ritual at the behest of the sovereign
in a *hasina* transaction which emphasized subservience to royalty,
in legal practice Ambohimanambola assumed a more equal status.
This discrepancy derived from historical movements discussed
above. Ambohimanambola's juridical independence carried over
from the remote past when inclusion in the royal pantheon
represented a consentual relationship. Their ritual inferiority
resulted from comparatively recent attempts by sovereigns since
Andrianampoinimerina to emphasize royal sacredness through
pantheon ritual. Nevertheless the ritual itself recognized to some
extent the real political power of Ambohimanambola in rites in
which the king presented *hasina* to them. But insofar as the entire
ceremony came to center upon the king and was led by him,
royal legitimacy depended more and more on rites, such as water
sprinkling and *hasina* which emphasized the innate religious
superiority of the king. Dependence on this religious sanction
held monarchy together despite the actual equality of political
power of so-called "subservient" demes. When traditional
sacredness itself was questioned by Christianity and eventually

eclipsed by it after 1868, the last prop of monarchy fell and disunity followed.

Priestcraft and the Tarnished Crown: The Pantheon's Decline

The decline in the belief of traditional sanctions is best illustrated in the uncertain fate of palladia guardians throughout the nineteenth century.

With the establishment of the London Missionary Society's station in Tananarive in 1818 and Radama's encouragement of mission schools in the following decade, Christianity first presented an alternative to traditional belief. Though Radama I continued the rituals ordained by ancestors, he placed as much faith in European technology, in the form of a modern army, to maintain his authority. The apparent success of European influence led to widespread anxiety among the traditional religious elite, and when Radama I died in July 1828 they rose in support of a monarch who would stem the Christian advance. Ranavalona I came to power.

> Now the idol Kelimalaza and the divination sikidy are entered into Court, which Radama has chased away for some years past, and they now direct and govern all things as they did twenty years ago. Every superstition is renewed....[37]

Radama I had paid the salaries of mission school teachers and the payment could have been construed by palladium guardians as a misdirected form of *hasina* offering. Moreover, he required that each deme send a number of students to mission schools. In 1829, however, Ranavalona abolished teachers' stipends and exempted Ambohimanambola, the deme represented by the Kelimalaza palladium from mandatory school attendance.[38] Traditionally, various taboos (*fady*) associated with Kelimalaza emphasized the sacredness of the palladium, and the principal interdiction was against pigs. By established custom no pigs were allowed east of the Ombifotsy River or within about 30 miles of the capital.[39] By late 1822, however, Radama I had allowed the interdiction (*fady*) against pigs to lapse to the point where only Ambohimanambola and Ambohimanga, the two principal sites of Kelimalaza, maintained the traditional interdiction. But when Ranavalona I came to the throne, she consented to the demands of palladium guardians and proclaimed in 1830 that pigs would be excluded from all Imerina "according to the custom prevailing in the days of Radama's father," Andrianampoinimerina.[40]

In the early 1830's a court struggle ensued between Christian and palladium partisans. Palladium guardians from various groups represented in the royal pantheon brought their grievances to Rainiharo who implored the Queen to recognize that it was through the pantheon system alone that sovereigns could rule effectively. He was opposed at court by Andriamihaja who argued that European learning and techniques would assure the throne's authority.[41] Traditional forces won the day and from the mid-1830s to Ranavalona's fall from power after 1857 Christianity in all of its forms was purged and ancient ritual, particularly the rites of the royal pantheon were restored as described earlier.[42]

The traditional restoration under Ranavalona I was, however, by no means a complete triumph for belief in the palladium system and an utter defeat of the Christian ideal despite the exaggerated accounts of European missionaries. The two ideals co-existed, the palladia backed by guardians and royal policy and Christianity by large numbers of displaced converts who worshipped secretly. But the years of Ranavalona I's reign marked the last phase of the pantheon's efficacy. When Radama II replaced Ranavalona, Christianity emerged stronger than ever and led to a period of acute uncertainty for palladium guardians who tried in vain to persuade the young monarch to forbid Christianity.[43] A "possession epidemic" led by disenchanted palladium guardians swept Imerina three months before the dethronement of Radama II and warned of imminent destruction lest the ancestors' ways were strictly adhered to.[44] Rasoherina assumed power in 1863 and the palladium system seemed headed for destruction as the new queen espoused increasingly pro-Christian ideas. As Ranavalona II, she no longer called on the royal pantheon as a sanction of her reign. When she was officially crowned in 1868, references to palladia were absent, and during the national bath ritual (*Fandroana*) of 1869 all palladium rites previously associated with the bath had been eliminated. In February 1869 Ranavalona II was baptized.[45]

At the same time as palladium ritual disappeared from the royal court, palladium guardians lost their special political rights. The

Ambohimanambola, the deme of Kelimalaza, were deprived of autonomous jurisdiction (*tsy maty manota*) and forced now to contribute as all other demes to military and other government service. All outward signs of their special status, including the right to be greeted as nobles and to carry red umbrellas, were abolished.[46] To be sure, palladium guardians continued to press their cause at the Court, but with no avail. On September 8, 1869, Ranavalona II had Kelimalaza burned and on the following day, Ramahavaly, Manjakatsiroa, Fantaka, Rabehaza, and Ranoro were destroyed.[47] The burnings were supervised by a crack division of the royal army which now served as the principal source of the sovereign's authority, a development which Radama I foresaw 45 years earlier when he recognized the potential power of European military techniques.

In the years that followed, Christianity became the dominant faith, even among the Ambohimanambola, whose first pastor, Rakotomainty, was a former guardian of the palladium, Kelimalaza.[48] In the political sphere a new system based on European legal and administrative practices arose under the stewardship of Prime Minister Rainilaiarivony.[49] Most Merina, however, continued to believe in the *ody-sampy* complex and expressed their dissatisfaction with official neglect of ancient custom in a number of "possession epidemics," the most famous of which, led by the palladium guardians of Ravololona, occurred as late as 1895 just as French occupation of Madagascar seemed imminent.[50]

The evolution of the *ody-sampy* complex in Imerina comprises four phases. In the first, occurring in the remote past when demes existed autonomously, *ody* protected individuals and palladia (*sampy*) provided for the general well-being of each group. The second phase coincided with the rise of lowland riziculture and large-scale irrigation which required cooperation between groups and promoted a central authority under the first kings from Andriamanelo to Andriatsitakatrandriana. The royal pantheon emerged as a structure of consensus between group and sovereign expressed in ritual by the inclusion of a group's palladium in the royal pantheon. Increased sacrilization of the royal pantheon marks the third phase which took place towards the end of the eighteenth century under Andrianampoinimerina. Though demes retained a great deal of legal autonomy, pantheon ritual stressed inequality between king and deme by emphasizing the innate religious superiority of royalty. In the final phase, Christianity replaced belief in the pantheon as a sanction of royal authority, and European administrative techniques superceded royal ritual.

NOTES

1 An "elder" to D. Jones in William Ellis, *History of Madagascar* (London, 1838), I, P. 397.

2. D. Johns to W. Ellis (30 May 1833), London Missionary Society, Letters received (LMS-LR), IV/4/B.

3. The first mention of a war charm in Imerina occurs in 1787 in La Salle's description of a bandolier of ox horns filled with a substance which rendered soldiers invulnerable to bullets. See Responses de M. La Salle, 1816, British Museum, Add. Ms. 18135, fol. 219. At a *hova* war camp near Tamatave in 1830, Jourdain saw two small wooden "idols" which soldiers would polish with honey. Soldiers also carried crocodile teeth to insure victory. See Jourdain's, Notice sur les Ovas (18 juill. 1830), Archives nationales — Section Outre-mer, Madagascar (AN-OM), 16/31, pp. 35-36. Charles Renel, "Les Amulettes malgache. Ody et Sampy," *BAM*, n.s. II, (1915), 281 pp., and Lars Vig, *Charmes. Spécimens de magie malgache* (1908), Musée d'Ethnographie de 1'Universite d'Oslo, *Bull.* No. 13 (1969), are the most comprehensive studies of Merina protectors. Renel's study includes a catalogue of hundreds of *ody* with one line descriptions as well as many of the oral traditions surrounding them which he collected from "indigènes instruits" over the eleven years he spent around Tananarive. It is the most exhaustive work on religious amulets and although it remains a landmark in painstaking descriptive ethnography, there is little understanding of the *ody* system's place in society nor any synthesis of contradictory historical data. Vig's *Charmes*, translated from Norwegian by Otto Christian Dahl, draws on information from an earlier period. Lars Vig (1845-1913) was a Norwegian missionary who arrived in Madagascar in 1875 and took up residence among the northern Betsileo and southern Merina near Antsirabe where he stayed until 1889. After a four-year leave, he returned in 1893 and remained until 1902. *Charmes* is a catalogue of *ody* sent to Norway in 1893. It was written in 1896 from notes and amended in 1908. *Charmes* gives the most detailed descriptions of *ody* made by someone with an intimate knowledge of the language and people. It also concerns an area considerably to the south of Renel's area of study and so provides a good control.

4. *Tantaran'ny Andriana eto Madagascar,* henceforth TA (Tananarive, 1908), p. 56; Johns and Freeman to Ellis (29 May 1833), LMS-LR, IV/4/B; Freeman and Johns, *Narrative of the Persecution of Christians* (London, 1840), p. 53; Ellis, *History...* (1838), I, pp. 395-96. Andrianaivoravelona, a Malagasy pastor, observed in 1885 that every clan had its own "idol" just as the government did. He calls it a system of totem. See H. Clark, *Antananarivo Annual* (henceforth *AA*), No. 9 (1885), pp. 79-81.Mondain notes that each village has its own "idols."

See Mondain, "Quelques idees...," *BAM*, I (1903), p. 31. For the local power of a group protector see M. J. Jeffreys' description of Rahodibato in "Extrait d'une relation ecrite sur un sejour accompli a Madagascar entre les annees 1822 et 1825," *BAM*, n.s. I (1914), pp. 142-44.

5. Johns to Ellis (30 May 1833), LMS-LR, IV/4/B, reported that pieces of an "idol" that belonged to four "clans" were sold to departing soldiers for two oxen, two sheep, and two fowl.

6. TA, p. 56; L. Vig, "Les usages religieux...," *Bull. du Comite Auxiliare de Paris. Miss. Luth. Mada.*, NO. 21 (1903), pp. 218-19, which is an extract from "Symbolikken i den Madagassiske Gudsdyrkelse og det folkelige Samfundsliv.," *Nordisk Missions-Tidsskrift*, n.s., V (1903), pp. 227-35.

7. Lars Dahle, *Madagascar og dets Beboere* (Christiania, 1877), II, pp. 133-34. I am indebted to Mr. Kjetil Anao for a translation from the Norwegian.

8. Mondain observed that often a village *sampy* is unknown to neighboring villages. See Mondain, "Quelques idées," p. 31.

9. Lars Vig, coll., Manuscript Notebooks, Boky I (c. 1875) in J.-P. Domenichini, ed. and trans., *Histoire des palladia d'Imerina* (Tananarive, 1971), pars. 82-96; Merina Mnuscripts (Manuscripts des Ombiasy), I (1864-1870), Boky 7 in *Sombintantaran'i Madagaskara nosoratan'ny Ombiasin-dRanavalona I* (Ambozontany, 1970), pp. 57-59; TA, pp. 550, 441; *Firaketana ny Fiteny sy ny Zavatra malagasy*, No. 186 (1957), pp. 62-63; David Jones, Journal, 1823, London Missionary Society — Journals (LMS-J), I/7, pp. 49-51; Raombana, Histoires I (1853-54), typescript edition of Simon Ayache, p. 60; Sibree to Mullins (21 Nov. 1870), LMS-LR, IX/2/C; Ranavalona I, *Proclamation* (9 March 1835); Renel, "Amulettes," pp. 146-49; Ellis, *History*, I, pp. 395-96, 402, II, 353; Dahle, *Madagaskar*, II, pp. 130-31.

Imanjakatsiroa is more properly associated with Andrianampoinimerina's wife, Rambolamasoandro, from whom descended Ranavalona's principal rival for the throne. See Vig, Manuscript Notebooks, Boky III, pars. 3-7, and Alain Delivre, *L'histoire des rois d'Imerina* (Paris, 1974), pp. 237-42. It is an indication of the extent of political expedience involved that Ranavalona would call upon Imanjakatsiroa once on the throne, and, by so doing, ask for the loyalty of the factions which backed her rival.

While specific appeals to the royal palladia name only a few *sampy*, lists supplied to Europeans by Malagasy informants tend to be much longer, including between twelve and fifteen names, because length suggested antiquity and awesomeness. Henige has recently described a similar situation for Maori king lists in his *Chronology...* (1974), pp. 97-103.

10. Abinal, *Vingt Ans à Madagascar* (Paris, 1885), pp. 264-65 and Renel "Amulettes...," p. 213, n. 1, claim that *sampy* means "califourchon." Edmonds, AA (1896), p. 421, n. 3 concurs. Dahl's comments on Vig's *Charmes...* (p. 167, n. 74) says that *sampy* was originally something which hangs astride like the legs of a rider.

11. *TA*, p. 130.

12. Bojer and Hilsenberg (1822-1823) in *Bulletin de Madagascar*, XV (1965), pp. 313-14.

13. Birkeli, *Memoires de l'Académie malgache* (1936), pp. 44, 59. J.Ruud, in *Taboo. A Study of Malagasy Customs and Beliefs* (Oslo, 1960), p. 188, notes that *sampy* is the common property of a family. Vig, *Charmes...*, pp. 158-59, and Otto Dahl's introduction to Vig, p. 13. The equivalent of *ody* in Betsileo

is *aody*, and in Sakalava, *aoly*. The possibility of applying either *ody* or *sampy* to royal palladia led many Europeans to observe that there was little difference between the two. See Vig (30 December 1887) in *Norsk Missionstidende*, No. 43 (1888), p. 256, and Renel, "Amulettes...," pp. 79, 265, 146-49.

14. Duhautcilly, MS., 1825, AN-OM, 11/25, fol. 11. He calls the divinity "Quely-malasa" (Kelimalaza) Bojer and Hilsenberg in 1822-1823 refer to "ramahawalu" (Ramahavaly) as an *ody* consisting of a sack of roots wrapped in red cloth with a silver chain attached. See their account in *Bulletin de Madagascar* (BM), XV (1965), pp. 313-14.

15. *TA*, p. 177; Renel, "Amulettes...," pp. 215-16; L. Dahle, *Madagascar...* (1877), II, pp. 138-39. Andrainaivoravelona reported that before the advent of "royal idols" there were only personal amulets. See Clark, *AA*, No. 9 (1885), p. 81.

16. *TA* (1953), p. 330; Renel, "Amulettes...," p. 52; *Firaketana*, No. 186 (January 1957), pp. 66-67.

17. Andriamifidy, "Andriana," *Mpanolo Tsaina*, V (1908), pp. 45-46: "voahangy sampan-dRalambo."

18. *TA*, p. 178.

19. Vig, Manuscript Notebooks (1857?), ed. Domenichini, pp. 14, 16: "Ho tian'Andriana, ho-tiam-bahoaka."

20. A typical statement of royal *sampy* powers occurs in the Merina Manuscripts, Boky 7 (1865), in *Sombin-tantaran'i Madagaskara*, pp. 57-58. For Kelimalaza: *"nentiny namory ny fanjakany (ny Andriana), nataony hampahery azy raha miady izy; ary haharesy ny fahavalo miady aminy... ary ho entiny mitana ny fanjakana efa azony."* (Rakelimalaza allowed the sovereign to bring his government together; it made him (the king) strong in battle and conquered the bandits in his kingdom and consolidated his rule over lands already his own.") See also Jones, et al., (1 April-26 September 1823), LMS-J, I/7, pp. 51-52; Hohns to Freeman, (14 November 1829), LMS-LR, III/4/B; Griffiths and Baker to Clayton (2 December 1831), LMS-LR, IV/1/C.

21. Ellis, *History...* (1838), II, pp. 418-21; Ranavalona, *Proclamation* (20 February 1835).

22. Vig, Manuscript Notebooks (c. 1875), ed. Domenichini, p. 72, pars. 163-64.

23. Raombana, Letter (8 January 1854) in *BAM*, XIII, (1930), p. 19.

24. J. Sibree, "The Fandroana...," *AA* (1900), p. 493.

25. Griffiths, Journal (18 January-19 July) entry of 19 June, LMS-J, I/4 for earliest description of the white horn and sprinkling; Griffiths and Baker to Clayton (2 December 1831), LMS-LR, IV/1/C and Ellis, *History...* (1838), ii, pp. 464-65 for military success; TA, p. 307; Callet, Letter (8 September 1875), *Ann. St. Enfance*, XXVIII (1877) pp. 180-81; and Lars Vig, *Charmes...*, p. 159, for white horn and water sprinkling in various benedictions. The method of consulting Kelimalaza described in *TA*, p.175, similarly emphasizes the role of the white horn filled with water which is sprinkled upon the people. See also, A. Grandidier, Carnets de Voyage, MS. Cahier 25 (1848-1856), Musée de l'Homme, pp. 1827-32.

26. Renel, "Ancetres...," BAM, pp. 113-17.

27. Maurice Bloch, Personal Communication, February 1975.

28. Kinship terms may donate positive moral value rather than genealogical relationships. Thus a political ally may be considered kin. See M. Bloch, "The Moral and Tactical Meaning of Kinship Terms," *Man*, VI/1, (1971), pp. 79-87.

29. Maurice Bloch, "The disconnection between rank and power..." in Rowlands and Friedman, eds., *The Evolution of Social Systems*, Duckworth, forthcoming.

30. *Firaketana*, No 186 (1857), pp. 71-72; Vig, Manuscript Notebooks, Boky I, en passim; TA, p. 175; Merina Manuscripts, Boky 7 (1865), p. 137, in *Sombintantara*, p. 57; K. Jeffreys, *The Widowed Missionary's Journal* (Southampton, 1827), p. 147; Freeman and Johns, *Narrative...*, p. 64. Even where *sampy* were not involved as in the case of holy stones *(vatomasina)*, some sort of offering *(sorona* or *faditra)* must be made to receive well-being.

31. Vig, Manuscript Notebooks, ed. Domenichini, p. 188, par. 18: "dia miantso sy nanasina azy (Andrianampoinimerina)"; an p. 214, par. 59: "Manalotra ny hasina ho anao aho (Andrianampoinimerina). See also ibid., p. 212. Rambolamasoandro, Andrianampoinimerina's wife at Ambohimanga, was the principal guardian of Imanjakatsiroa and is reputed to have come from Ambarasoa, a Sakalava town (ibid., p. 188, par. 16).

32. Merina Manuscripts, Boky 7 (1865), ed., Ambozontany (1970), p. 57: "...dia manasina vola tsy vaky sy sakamalao and'Rakelimalaza izy (andriana)."

Sampy guardians threatened by the new European religion saw Ranavalona's reign as an opportunity to regain their exalted status. Their zeal is openly expressed in the Merina Manuscripts which Grandidier elicited from them in the mid-1860's when it was becoming increasingly clear that their cause was lost.

33. Colonial Office Memorandum (March 1830), LMS-LR, II/3/B; Ellis, *History..*, ii, *pp.* 422-424-25.

34. Renel, "Amulettes...," p. 152; Rainivelo, *AA* (1875), p. 112; Ellis, op. cit., I, p. 401; Freeman and Johns, *Narrative*, pp. 54-55. Terms such as "family," and "elders" are admittedly vague but the sources do not allow more precision.

35. Vig, Manuscript Notebooks, Boky I, ed. Domenichini, p. 80, par. 186. Rasamimanana's relation of traditions concerning Andriatompokoindrindra makes no mention of Ravolonandriana.

36. Vig, Manuscript Notebooks, Boky I, ed. Domenichini, pars. 61-64; *Firaketana*, No. 26 (1939), p. 354 and No. 186 (1957). pp. 73-74; Gautier, "Ambohimanga," *Notes, Reconnaissances, Explorations*, I/1 (1897), p. 106; Dahle, *Madagaskar*, II, pp. 131-32; Johns to Ellis (30 May 1833), LMS-LR, IV/4/B; Cousins to Mullins (24 September 1869), LMS-LR, VIII/6/C; Grifiths and Jones, Report (December 1829), LMS-LR, II/2/C.

37. Jones to Arundel (10 October 1828), LMS-LR, II/4/D.

38. Griffiths and Jones, Report (December 1829), LMS-LR, II/2/C.

39. *TA*, p. 185; *Firaketana*, No. 186 (1957), pp. 69-70; A. Van Gennep, *Tabou et totémisme a Madagascar* (Paris, 1904), pp. 122-23; Griffiths, Journal (18 January 19 July 1822), LMS-J, I/4, entry of 26 May; Griffiths, Jones, et al., From Tananarive to the West (1 August 1822-10 April 1823), LMS-J, I/5a.

40. Jeffreys, Journal (15 January-19May 1823), LMS-J, I/6, entry of 21 February; Jones, et al., Tour... (1 April-26 September 1823), LMS-J, I/7, pp. 17, 49-51. Freeman to Orme (17 May 1830), Port Louis, LMS-LR, III/3/B.

41. Griffiths and Baker to Clayton (2 December 1831), LMS-LR, IV/1/C; Freeman and Johns, *Narrative...* (1840), p. 88.

42. John to Ellis (26 September 1835), LMS-LR, V/2/C; Baker to Ellis (9 November 1835), LMS-LR, V/2/C; Johns to Ellis (21 July 1837), LMS-LR, V/2/A; Jones to Ellis (20 July 1840), LMS-LR, V/3/C; Merina Manuscripts, Musée de l'Homme, Vol. III, cahier IIa; Rainandriamampandry, Tantarany, 2.e rec., Livre III, Archives de la Republique malgache, SS 12. The Missionary literature

on the return to traditional forms presents the movement as a triumph of darkness. The best examples are: Freeman and Johns, *Narrative of the Persecutions...,* en passim; Ellis, *History...,* II, Chapt. 18; Andriamifidy, *Ny Tany Maizina* (Tananarive, 1889); Gautier, "Ambohimanga," *Notes, Reconnaissances, Explorations,* I/1 (1897), p. 105; Pr. Rabary, *Ny Daty Malaza,* II, (Tananarive, 1930); Pr. Rajoelisolo, *Tantaran'ny Martiora malagasy farany* (Tananarive, 1957). A recent scholarly corrective to the traditional missionary view of Ranavalona's reign was presented by S. Ayache in *BM* (1963).

43. A. Davidson (4 May 1863), LMS-LR, VI/3/D. For political developments at the court between 1856 and 1863 see G. S. Chapus and G. Mondain, *Rainilaiarivony. Un homme d'etat malgache* (Tananarive, 1953); A. Boudou, ed., *Le Complot de 1857* (Tananarive, 1943); and R. Delvel, *Radama II* (Paris, 1974).

Caldwell reports that during Radama II's coronation, the "King paid no attention" to the guardians "neither did he affront them" though they pressed up "so close to the platform that they invaded the place of, and got mixed up with, the band of Les Enfants de la Ressource, directed by the Jesuit Missionaries...." See S. P. Oliver, *Madagascar and the Malagasy* (London, 1862), p. 87.

44. Ellis to Tidman (16 May 1863), LMS-LR, VII.

45. Ranavalona II, Address to the People (July 1868), LMS-LR, VIII/4/B; Andriambelo to Cameron (3 May 1869), LMS-LR, VIII/6/A.

46. Cousins to Mullins (24 September 1869), LMS-LR, VIII/6/C.

47. Ibid.; Vig, Manuscript Notebooks, Boky VIII, Norsk Misjonsskolen, Stavanger, for the burning of Ranoro and the Domenichini ed., pp. 82, 84, for Kelimalaza; TA, pp. 234-36; *Firaketana,* No. 186 (1957), pp. 75-78; Rabary, *Ny Daty Malaza,* II (1930), pp. 124-29; Rainivelo, AA (1875), 2nd ed., pp. 107-10; Ranavalona II, "Proclamation," in BAM, XXII (1939), p. xxii; G. S. Chapus, "La fin des idoles," BM (1953), pp. 82-86.

48. Vig, Manuscript Notebooks, Domenichini ed., pp. 86-90.

49. See Chapus, *Rainilaiarivony....* A collection of documents representative of his administrative innovations may be found in G. Julien, *Institutions politiques et sociales de Madagascar,* 2 vols., (Paris, 1908).

50. For continued belief in *sampy* see Cameron to Mullins (20 February 1873), LMS-LR, X/4/C and Woodward to Bullock (20 October 1878), SPG-LR, D.48. For the possession epidemic of 1863, see Ellis to Tidman (16 May 1863), LMS-LR, VI/3; of 1877, see Wills to Mullins (25 April 1877), LMS-LR, XIV/2/C: of 1887, see L. Vig (30 December 1887), *Norsk Missionstitende,* No. 43 (1888), pp. 276-77; and for 1895-1996, see Rev. M. Rasamuel, *Ny Menelamba tao andrefan'Ankaratra,* 6 fasc., (1948-1952). I am currently preparing a study on the relationship between the continued belief in the protector system and the rise of popular protest movements in late nineteenth-century Imerina.

Oral Tradition
and Historical Consciousness:
the Case of Imerina

A. DELIVRÉ*
Tours

The postulate "no writing, no history worthy of the name,"
accepted only yesterday without discussion, begot an enormous
misunderstanding at the very beginnings of the ethnographic
science and one that had hardly been dispelled at the end of the
Nineteenth century. In juxtaposing the two civilizations —that
of the West to the collectively "primitive" one— the early ethnographers were not remiss in efforts to compile recollections of
the past extant among the peoples they came to study.[1] But, the
results were meager when placed next to the harvest of observations one could make about the daily life, unexpected customs
or the strange and still vital myths; and, generally, the past
seemed either unimportant or else marginal at best. Given that
the historical evolution of such peoples was a slow one and that
their respective cultures had an unchanging quality in modes of
life, in thought and customs, it was quite permissible to assign
their histories to the category of minor phenomena and even to
deny them any historical value at all. Only in entering into contact
with us, at last, did they undergo in turn the extraordinary and
wondrous transformations of our modern world.

This way of approaching the history of peoples without writing
is now obviously out of date and many works have been able
to show that the historical evolution of illiterate peoples —even
if memorized in rudimentary fashion with all the attendant
lacunae— is as important to them in the last analysis as our

*Translated from French by R. Kent.

own is to us,* guarding the relative proportions. Is there a man who cannot remember his father? The merit of our professional predecessors resides precisely in the fact that they collected enough of the historical data among the peoples with whom they were in contact to allow us to turn fruitfully to the problem of their evolution anterior to such contact. We thus believe that the real question to pose is the following one: given that the past lives in the consciousness of man within traditional cultures could it not be held that, for him, the present has no significance except in relation to the past which had engendered him, and even that he perceives his own being as intertwined with this past? As this alone gives, in fact, this man a sense of value and hence a sense of his own history? We would like to pose in this essay the question in respect to the ancient Merina whose ethnography and history seem to be so intimately linked with their Nineteenth-century descendants that it would be in vain to study one without the other.

In pursuing the question and in seeking as good an approximation of the "time consciousness" as possible among the ancient Merina our method will be to match the traditional source types with the principal phases of the ancient Merina history from the most remote point in time. This will not be undertaken to discover an explanation of one or more historical events as such (as such an endeavor would have to integrate other data already known or yet to be learned through sources other than oral tradition, archaeology among others), but only to apply to the fundamental sequences of this tradition the manner in which the ancient Merina reported themselves the historical events, properly speaking, and the cultural innovations implemented by a few of their great monarchs.

In so doing, we continue to be aware of dangers inherent in this approach —the most important of which would be to come to believe that events relating to a given reign in a tradition are objectively attributed by it at the same time. This would entail not knowing a fundamental risk of oral tradition (which, in addition, is not buttressed by calendar-time computations), namely the risk of anachronism. As is widely appreciated, anachronisms derive as much from the backward projection of recent political

*The most important single work in this category is Jan Vansina's *De la Tradition Orale. Essai de Methode Historique*, Tervuren, 1961, translated into several languages. (Ed.)

events as from the use of the past to validate one or more projects in the making. It also derives from deformations which are, properly, semantic in nature but with such and such an allegation nonetheless preserved in its original form. Equally, one must be on guard to discern, in the endeavor we are developing, items which come forth from the texts of actual historical traditions from those which only possess an exterior link with them, either because of an already attained publication, even an old one, or because they were spontaneously passed on by informants not always up on the facts of the matter and may not even have been sure of the matchings in the course of inquiries made in the Nineteenth century.

Outline of the Traditional Sources and their Historical Contents

In order to grasp the possibilities which the Merina tradition can offer it is important to recall briefly the main stages of Merina history as we have come to know it. The published documentation can be reduced to a single monument of ethnography and history known as the *Tantaran'ny Andriana* (History of Kings), published between 1873 and 1881, and remarkably confirmed through the original manuscripts which were prepared for the most part toward the middle of the Nineteenth century.[2] Actually, the *Tantara* (as they are commonly referred to) are a collection of purely royal traditions, transcribed during the Nineteenth century's second quarter, and of group traditions compiled by the Nineteenth-century researchers (often by chance and through changes of residence), body of texts to which must be added a host of monographs and articles since the start of our own century,[3] to round off the available materials.

What is the content of this corpus? It is, certainly, very disparate in its form but, in the end, quite homogeneous in its perspectives.

The *royal traditions* are essentially genealogical,[4] and they adhere to the chronological thread as given through the succession of royal ancestors on the throne of Imerina (or to Imerina's principalities when the kingdom was not a unified one). These texts, as we have them, retain few of the facts. In the beginning, there were mainly some difficulties and struggles with the Vazimba, inhabitants of the central highlands of Madagascar encountered by the Merina ancestors upon their arrival. Along with this memory, there are recollections of the foundation of the Merina "kingdom" or, more accurately, of the *fanjakana** which implies a political order based on the undisturbed succession of kings. We are here roughly at the end of the 1400's. Without any loss of time, the early monarchs settle the Vazimba problem and they are Andriamanelo, then Ralambo and Andrianjaka. Still, internal dissent makes the just-constituted kingdom rather fragile; as the brothers of kings are in power struggles, until Andriamasinavalona, first monarch to succeed his brother, Razakatsitaka-trandriana.

Although still under the rules of succession to the throne, the Merina Kingdom is temporarily subdivided by Andriamasinavalona; decidedly, however, antagonisms are rampant, Imerina remains split into the four "kingdoms," and later into three, as the dynasty of Ambohimanga princes gained the upper hand within some three generations. This is also a period of destructions without end in sight, of famines, of the incursions by the Sakalava, then at the high point of their power. Finally, a prince of Ambohimanga, Ramboasalama, dethroned an uncle at Ambohimanga, unified Imerina once more, and, as much through cunning as by force, succeeded in extending the kingdom of Imerina beyond its traditional boundaries. It was also he who supplied slaves to the French who knew this ruler as Dianampouine. Indeed, Andrianampoinimerina would continue the work of conquest until his death in 1810. At this point, Imerina is powerful enough to allow his son Radama I to create an army with English help and to conquer stll òther territories until he became master of the major part of Madagascar as a whole.

The *traditions of nobility* are of interest basically because they confirm the different phases of organization recounted by royal traditions under three sovereigns, who thus extricate themselves from the Andriana line of descent through their political role, namely Ralambo, Andriamasinavalona and Andrianampoinimerina. For the remainder, they oppose one another on the matter of precedence, especially those which are related to kings in the greatest antiquity —factor which accounts for the interest they have for a reconstruction of the most remote history, one that they make more solid through indirect clarifications even where

*In common usage, *fanjakana* means "government." (Ed.)

they remain divergent. As for the *traditions of free men* (commoners) or those who found themselves at the lower end of the
social hierarchy, they obtain their own glory rather from the
roles played directly by their ancestors and not through some
lineage. They join nonetheless with the other traditions in that
an accordance exists on one point: the role of Andrianampoinimerina after the reunification of the Merina Kingdom and the
highly advanced social organization this monarch was able to
endow his people with. The traditions of commoners have a
capital importance for the study of recent history (throughout
the 1800's).

To be even clearer in respect to this outline of Merina traditions[5]
it should be recalled that the various Merina sub-groups lived
in well-defined locations, remaining —except in recent times—
in their own villages, nobles as well as commoners. This geographical dispersal is not without value for the preservation of traditions; and it also brings to bear some rather strong confir-
mations for the relatively remote events by allowing us to cross-
check, since not all of the sub-groups had the same role in the
course of local history. Their geographical context often confirms
what their traditions say, traditions memorized in their own
areas in the period before the advent of English influence, that
is to say before the reign of Radama I.

One could conclude that oral texts of kings are the skeletal
frames of Merina historical tradition to which they give historical
depth through the skewing of temporal schema that serves as
reference for the individual traditions, noble and otherwise. In
the absence of such temporal coordinates as the cross-reference,
this depth is an indispensible feature; and the role of individual
traditions is to give consistency to the royal ones, which they
enrich from every angle. It should not be lost sight of that the
Merina tradition is no vehicle for a direct transmission of custom,
transcribed only in the wake of European inquiries or else for
instruction —it would seem— given at the royal palace in Antananarivo. Customs were in full force in the Nineteenth century,
at least until the massive conversions to Protestantism in 1869,
and there was no need to set them down on paper.

The Merina tradition is, still, a vehicle for data *about* customs
but mainly through the slant of innovations attributed to some
monarchs in connection with a historical unfolding of holidays

that have as much religious as political significance —an important subject that requires no stressing and one to which we will
return in some detail. We can now turn to the events as they
spring from the main sources on hand by way of a *tableau* that
recapitulates the innovations, without neglecting to note that it is
developed by commencing with the textual analyses; in turn,
chronological connections can be made between an innovation
in custom (or the practice thereof) and the corresponding reign.
This should serve, in consequence, to bring into relief what the
Merina themselves thought in the Nineteenth century about the
history of their customs. In logical sequence, we have modified
the schema of the *Tantara* about these connections;[6] and, from
now on, attention will be focused on the early times of the
Merina monarchy, more precisely on the period from the origins
until King Andrianjaka.

Advent of a Tradition

When one looks closely at the earliest traditional texts it is
difficult to avoid making a rather startling find: there is no
memory antedating, in so far as the extant royal traditions are
concerned, the installation of the Merina on the high plateaux
of central Madagascar (an event that took place in the Fifteenth
century). A lone tradition relates a sojourn of royal ancestors
in north-eastern Madagascar which has been placed quite roughly
in the Thirteenth century.[7] It is certainly remarkable that memory
alone, still going strong during the Nineteenth century research,
could reach that far back in time. Yet, is it not peculiar that
details relating to the distant events by way of an allusion cannot
be found even transmuted into myths from which some reference
could be deduced? Such myths as are present in the different
pages of the *Tantara*[8] either allude to personages considered by
tradition as contemporaries of the Vazimba or else to the Vazimba
themselves, a people of strange beings; people, unfamiliar with
rice, whose males marry females descending from the heavens
as legend (*tantara angano*) would have it; people who, from
the point of view which interests us the most, knew no political
and social organization. "*Fa tsy mbola nisy ny manoa,*" states
the tradition quite simply, because "it was not known yet what
submission means" and, correspondingly, what the political order
itself was.

TABLEAU - EARLY TIMES OF MERINA MONARCHY

DATES	PERIODS - REIGNS	EVENTS	CUSTOMS AND INNOVATIONS
XIVth?	Vazimba Period	?	Astrology (*fanandroana*); Commencements (*santatra*); Divination (*sikidy*); Protector Talismans (*sampy*).
XVth?	Andriandranolava	Co-existence with the Vazimba	Institution of "royal discourse" - the *Kabary*.
	Rafohy	?	First rules for succession to throne.
Start of XVIth	Andriamanelo	First wars against the Vazimba	Institution of circumcision (*famorana*); Iron-smelting and smithing techniques.
	Ralambo	Combats	First use of talisman (*sampy*) by the king (*sampy* Kelimalaza) for military ends; Institution of the Royal Bath (*Fandroana*).
			Social Organization: Nobility
End of XVIth	Andrianjaka	Last fights with the Vazimba Installation at Antananarivo	Advent of firearms; Royal Funerary customs; First Royal Tombs at Antananarivo
	Andriantsitaka-trandriana		Rice cultivation; Weaving.
End of XVIIth Start of XVIIIth	Andriamasinavalona	Sub-division of Imerina	Further organization of society, especially: marriage within the royal family; slaves (*ankizy*); respect due to a sovereign.
		Internecine struggles	
(1783? - 1810?)	Andrianampoini-merina	Reunification of Imerina	Reorganization, conquest of territory and of society.
		External conquests	

On the other hand, the first royal ancestors related with precision by tradition to the subsequent rulers are known (in a summary fashion) through the genealogical lists spanning some ten generations or so; then, without transition, starting with the Queen Rafohy and her son Andraimanelo, these sovereigns are known mainly through their acts and the institutions attributed to them, as if the sole reason why the traditions themselves came to light was to commemorate the state —even a rudimentary one— or, more accurately, a charter forming the basis of a social order. This is why details about the struggles with the Vazimba are omitted. As for the connections that should have developed between these antecedent inhabitants and the newly-arriving Andriana no details are supplied by tradition, if not allusions which suggest an alliance, even a tacit one, with masters-of-the-soil (*tompontany* or original inhabitants).[9] For the ancient kings, there is only the laconic mention of a manuscript: "Very* tantara;" "their high deeds are not known." Still, with the earliest traditions, those which are most venerable through their antiquity, it is possible to discern a clear expression of the need for political order. To illustrate the point, two following texts have been selected, one concerning the link established betwen the king and the people, the other regulating succession to the throne. According to the first text:[10] "It was under Andriandranolava that appeared first domination and vassalage (*fanjakana ifanoavana*); one rules, the other obeys. Andriamoraony, the elder, submitted. It was then that the *kabary*** appeared. The Vazimba asked "but, then, what is *kabary*?" For the Merina, familiar with the royal *kabary*,[11] the sense of the question was clear: the *kabary* constituted essentially a dialogue between king and people; the former would not make an important decision without first exposing the underlying reasons to the latter, following the traditional formulas in which the royal ancestors played a fundamental role, aiding the projected innovations with their high authority. In more recent times, European observers were able to be present at ceremonies of this type, which sometimes lasted several days. "We are the master but we do not command," states, again, the paragraph of *Tantara* devoted to Andriandranolava and, through him, to

---

Very = "lost." (Ed.)

**See also the essays on folklore and on Rainilaiarivony below for explanation of *kabary*. (Ed.)

the sovereign relationship between the people and their king. In contrast, a Vazimba, no less-known among all the Merina and called Baroa, who exploited the people and under whose dominion disorder was the rule along with lies between the humble and the mighty, gave birth to a familiar expression —"domination by Baroa: the people cannot grow; it disperses."[12] The other selected text is in closer proximity to the accounts generally encountered in the old royal traditions:[13]

> "The rule of Rafohy, spouse of Ramanahimanjaka at Alosara: she gave birth to Andriamanelo and Andriamananitany; and Rafohy made her wishes known. Here they are: to you, Andriamanelo, all of the days, as you are the older (brother); but, it is in the end Andriamananitany who will rule. In his turn, Andriamananitany sired Andriamboninolona. And when Andriamanelo made his wishes known, this is what they were: it is you who are my older (brother), Ralambo, and thus I will make you rule. When Andrianamboninolona gave birth to Ratsitoinamanjaka she became wife to Ralambo when the interdiction was lifted, so that she could, at last, be sovereign (*ho tompon'ny farany*). And Andriamananitany submitted."

This text certainly shows the progress made in relation to the earlier one, attained in just a few generations.

It was the practice before Rafohy that descendants of one king submit to the authority of his successor; but, it was not known on what grounds. Henceforth, the matter became clear: it is by the will of kings that one is chosen to succeed. Another text puts the imagery this way: Andraimanelo will rule on Thursdays and Andriamananitany on Fraidays; not in their own persons proper but through descendants. From this derives the expression found ultimately in Merina history, "*manjaka zanaka*," to "rule through one's progeny." Right along with the "*fanjakana ifanoavana*" (domination and vassalage), extant before Rafohy, the Merina instituted what is called "*fanjakana arindra*,"* commented in the *Tantara* explicitly and relative to the problem of succession in a way meant to be without ambiguity.[14] It is known that Merina history since the time of the rule of succession reflects, in large part, the bitter struggles for the throne and family rivalries; but, whatever were the ups and downs of Rafohy's

*Government by equilibrium. (Ed.)

famous wish, it served constantly as a point of reference. an order was born, not at all in the even matchings of dominion and vassalage with available force, but of dominion and vassalage *based on the past.*

It seems profoundly significant that the birth of royal traditions had not been induced as a high event of external provenance, allowing thus the ancient Merina to become aware of unity in the face of an external opposition. In spite of the Vazimba presence it was not the struggle of Andriamanelo, with his iron-tipped spears against them, that served as point of departure for the exploits of the Andriana,[15] but the concept of a social and political order, concise but basic.

This embryonic structure would soon enrich itself, this time in a different way, namely through the integration of alien groups. The typical as well as earliest example was that of the Antehiroka, descendants of the Vazimba rulers who had helped Andrianjaka, the nephew of Andriamanelo, to take Antananarivo.[16] This is, apparently, the second major aspect, concerned not this time with the royal traditions' birth but rather with the advent of individual ones; in effect, the Antehiroka would always derive their glory from their association with the Andriana, especially glaring during the circumcision ceremonies. With this association there came into being in Imerina a principle of political structure that was not rooted in kinship but was founded on collaboration. This is a feature that returns very much amplified in the last few reigns before the coming of the Europeans in Madagascar and until the reign of Radama I himself, this time beyond the traditional boundaries of Imerina. What is to be noted here is that, concurrently with the royal traditions, there came in Imerina this type of very original accounts that are the traditions of groups, once antagonistic but always locating themselves in relation to the history of kings proper, to which they are both complementary and indispensible. The main function of these traditions was to link the groups from which they sprung to such and such a sovereign —source of historical "privileges" (*tantarany*) which form, at the same time, a memory of the high deeds historical in nature and the foundation of actual social relations as expressed in the daily life.[17]

Rather rapidly since the time of Andrianjaka, these individual or particular traditions overtake those which are royal or of nobility in the strict sense (that is to say, linked to royalty by blood); the traditions of nobility do not escape this process and even combine within themselves both elements at times, one original and based on kin ties, the other accessory but augmenting in the course of time and resting on the acts of a group or its representative.[18] Because of this phenomenon it is possible to hold with sufficient probability that whenever there is a cross-reference between one of these traditions and a royal one on a point concerning custom historical objectivity will be present in both. This is why, even in events that are rather remote in time, the Merina tradition seems to be (notwithstanding certain precautions in interpretation) fairly sure. The Antehiroka are a case in point. Their role in the circumcision of the royal children and the importance this custom took on during Andriamanelo's time, are not events artificially put together. They confirm, with considerable clarity, the association of the Antehiroka to the "*mpanasina Andriana*," to the power (*hasina*) of the nascent dynasty and, so to say, to its destiny as well.

In short, it should not be assumed that the poverty of the early traditions renders them unimportant. On the one side, there comes into focus a succinct but basic political organization, along with initial solutions to the problem of succession; on the other side, there is a barely discernible yet rich in promise *power of integration* rather uncommon for the first kings and tending to associate the enemies of yesterday and integrate them culturally as well. These two perspectives seem to be of capital importance for an in-depth understanding of later events as across these, from their multiplicity and variety, one can always find anew the orientation initially given to the Merina historical tradition, continuously simple in its principle and virtually self-contained and complete since its birth.

These findings serve to release, in the mind of the most faithful guardians of ancestral traditions, that which seemed sufficiently important to be worthy of memorization; and one could infer that the other events were not regarded as such and were hence spontaneously eliminated from the corpus while it was being formed. In fact, this conclusion should allow us to pinpoint at which time of the Merina past did the traditions start to acquire their importance. This would be, most precisely, at the moment when in Imerina the existence and continuity of the kingdom become the object of sufficient consciousness so that from the mass of details, known and relating to the just mentioned first sovereigns, facts are derived concerning the *fanjakana* according to its perspectives. This consciousness of the *fanjakana*, we believe, is very old. We will attempt to date it with some documentary elements that have not been dealt with until now: those of the customs and the manner in which, according to the tradition, they were to appear in the political life of Imerina.

History as Explanation of Culture

In truth, the events already related by the early Merina tradition have brought us into the field of "cultural" history if one understands concisely this expression to include the rough shape of socio-political organization already mentioned; what needs to be done here is to throw into relief this highly original aspect we have described of the Merina historical traditions which not only give us the events but which also recall the cultural innovations introduced during each of the early reigns. And, these are so important that they are sufficient to explain the whole of Merina culture such as it existed at the apogee of the Merina monarchy at the start of the Nineteenth century.

With slight fear of contradiction, it can be seen that the tradition has retained from the earliest times the asrological customs which are also linked with the proverbial wisdom of some great Vazimba personages.[19] Here, the question concerns an entire panoply of usages resulting from an Arab influence which comes out of the technical vocabulary for the usages themselves. Although tradition does not assign them directly to the Vazimba period, the usages were a part of it. Let us note that these are customs that have survived all historical changes which were politico-religious in nature within Imerina's countryside and that they are endowed with a retentivity that attests their depth. The same goes for the practice of divination (*sikidy*), described at length in the reign of Andriamanelo,[20] but the description itself establishes an even more ancient origin as can be easily deduced from the text; or for the game of *fanorona'** ascribed to the ensuing reign of Ralambo but explicitly linked to the Vazimba epoch.[21]

*Passionate game, played on a board; one of the earliest royal family members is said to have been excluded from succession to the throne because of his "addiction" to the game of *fanorona*. (Ed.)

The cultural repository here is the daily life; but, with Ralambo's reign, there begins a series of impressive innovations: techniques of iron-smelting and smithing are linked with the reign of Andriamanelo, who knew how to defeat the Vazimba thanks to his iron-tipped spears.[22] The circumcision ceremony was also instituted by the same king, associating, as was seen, the Antehiroka with his rejoicing.[23] Since Andriamanelo's son, Ralambo, dates the most important ceremony, without a doubt, of all the religious and political life of Imerina, that of the Royal Bath (*Fandroana*). The *Tantara* are rather discrete about the origin of this feature[24] but another and equally venerable source, the *Merina Manuscripts* put together by Queen Ranavalona's priest (*ombiasa*),* allows for a reconstruction of its main phases and gives it historical depth. Actually, the bath taken in public by a ruler predates the institution of ceremonies that emerged in Ralambo's time. This king was attached to the observance of his Zodiac sign of *Alahamady*, first of the twelve astrological signs.** By sacrificing a zebu and following this act with ritual mastication of the animal's hump,[25] Ralambo endowed the event with a great deal of solemnity; and it took about three generations for the *Fandroana* to develop in all of its splendor, retained well into the Nineteenth century as a magnificent national event enshrined in the contemporary *Tantara* descriptions. It was Andrianjaka, the son of Ralambo, who added to it another ceremonial component involving the tomb of his father and there is no doubt that invocations made at the royal tombs to mark the end of the *Fandroana* holidays date from his time. There are also texts other than the *Merina Manuscripts* of the *ombiasa* who served Ranavalona I (1828-1861) which furnish their own details about the evolution of *Fandroana*; and they allude to funerary customs which are explicitly placed in Andrianjaka's reign; and, if these customs did not quite owe their advent to the respect Andrianjaka had for his father —considered as the founder of the Merina monarchy— one can easily attribute their enhanced splendor to this respect.

Henceforth the Merina society, reorganized by Ralambo and made accustomed to discipline first under this king's father and

*The Merina (or Hova) Manuscripts were prepared between 1864 - 1866; a listing of their contents will be found in G. Grandidier, *Bibliographie de Madagascar*, I/2, Paris, 1906, pp. 730-733. (Ed.)

**Alahamady*, first month of the Malagasy year is also the month in which *Fandroana* took place before the fall of the Merina monarchy. (Ed.)

later his son (first to be at Antananarivo), could prosper in peace. The ensuing reigns no longer allude to the advent of new political customs as if the ones that had been instituted were enough to give the society all of its coherence. Traditions now become devoted to the cultivation of ricefields instead, without failing to do their part in respect to contemporary political problems, always and still those of difficult successions.[26] At the time of internecine but relatively short-lasting struggles which allowed Andriamasinavalona to assume power to which he had a legitimate claim, the Merina society was already the one that would be known at the start of the 1800's in so far as its political structure is concerned. No doubt, the reign of Andriamasinavalona would modify the hierarchy of noble families in profound ways;[27] the reign of Andrianampoinimerina would unsettle the territorial, economic and political organization even more; but all of this does not alter the fact that long before these great kings the bases of the social, political and religious order were solidly anchored in the mores of the inhabitants of Imerina.

What can one conclude in respect to this series of innovations given here in rapid outline form? In essence, there are, as we see it, three main facts.

First, there is the extremely powerful cultural substratum which survived not only the possible memory loss of events anterior to the foundation of the Merina monarchy but also everything that would come to affect the political stability of the fledgling kingdom (and even, in good measure, the vicissitudes of Merina traditional thought in the Nineteenth century). This is the core reason why the Merina society can be called *traditional*. All of the customs antedating the consciousness of political destiny and going back to the Vazimba epoch, belong to the daily life; and because of this fact they remained relatively independent of changes unsettling to the society at other levels. As noted earlier, some of the customs described in the first reigns, where they comingle with what can properly be called historical traditions, had only the most tenuous ties with these reigns; and, we could conclude that, still, the expediencies of composition taken by the compilers were continuously justified by the fact that these customs were in a way linked, in the traditional mentality, to the same reigns and not without reason at that: there have always been changes, even minor ones, justifying a chronological link of a custom with one of the first reigns, as in the case of circumcision, clearly a feature that antedates Andriamanelo but one linked to this king through a modification of the ritual; or, yet, for the funerary customs, tied to Andrianjaka by the ceremonial pomp at the tomb of his father.[28] In sum, the essential customs had been around long before and, what is remarkable, the Merina historical tradition, when correctly interpreted, allows us to discern this fundamental aspect without covering the tracks.

A second conclusion, no less important to the correct understanding of certain traditions, imposes itself: alongside the cultural substratum evoked in the preceding paragraph, the Merina state in formation elaborated another series of new usages, all functionally related to events as must be the case for the group of customs regarded much later by one of the most sensitive observers of Nineteenth century Imerina, Father Callet, author of the *Tantara*, as without peer in importance: circumcision, Royal Bath, and royal mourning.[29] Is it not curious that the first of the customs is assigned to Andriamanelo, the second to Ralambo and the third to Andrianjaka? If one adds the elevation of the regional *sampy* Kelimalaza to the status of royal protector (*sampy masin'Andriana*),[30] it follows that the basic underpinnings of the Merina state were established within the three generations, a rather remarkable feat.

Lastly, the following finding seems to be the most astonishing one: the new adjuncts worked out by the three sovereigns were not done in the abstract, independently of the cultural substratum. On the contrary, they were able to extract spontaneously the essential elements —the integration of man in time and space— to buttress ceremonies which were at the same time religious and political, attesting a social structure in the process of its own elaboration. To take only a single yet most significant example, it is the Royal Bath which became the quintessential pageant of the new monarchy. It is evident from all the relevant sources that the *Fandroana* rests on a pre-existing astrological system and does not attain its full sense without the most powerful sign, that of *Alahamady*, sign of Ralambo, sacred (*masina*) and powerful, sign preferred by the monarchs.[31] One can only come to grasp the Merina historical tradition by keeping constantly in mind the conjugation of cosmic features, which are properly traditional, permanent, repetitive, and socio-political transformations which are historical in nature and which provoked, we believe, the advent of this tradition. A unification of perspectives attained spontaneously from the earliest times of the Merina monarchy does not preclude that a monarch like Andrianampoinimerina could and did use and even provoke a similar process, with his well-known political genius. Yet, he did nothing more than pattern himself after the founders of the Merina monarchy who knew how to preserve this distant legacy, one integrated into the new solemnities.

It is not within the frame of the current essay to develop at the same time this legacy and show how it was integrated into the ascendant moments of the traditional politico-religious life; we have attempted, elsewhere, a synthetic presentation of the temporal concepts among the ancient Merina,[32] expressing the ambivalence and the mystery of the present torn between the possibilities of destruction and of progress. This tension is also evident in the structure of the *Fandroana* and, in this sense, the Royal Bath is properly a traditional element. But, it is also a testimonial of the past and, equally, a political symbol of virtually endless progress; and in this new sense (given by Ralambo according to tradition) it expresses the existence of a *historical consciousness*, rudimentary and limited to be sure, but clear for all to understand. It is a consciousness just as evident in the humble invocations made during the traditional sacrifices to the royal ancestors on which the *Tantara* give so many concrete examples and which emerge —according to the same text— in the time of Ralambo.[33]

Tradition and Objectivity

History had thus given the ancient Merina, at the same time, the genesis of *fanjanaka*, thanks to the memorization of events which became common recollections, political in nature, and the secret of the *fanjakana*'s preservation, with the panoply of customs relating to the royal person. The first aspect was brought out during the analysis of the tradition's advent; the second came out during the recall of cultural innovations as well as from the sense in which these should be appreciated. To put it another way, the first concerns events and the second culture. To disassociate them would be to know them badly, so much are the two linked in Merina tradition, which becomes original thereby.

To go a step further and attempt to resolve a delicate problem but one which serves as counter-proof, a necessary one, to the analyses so briefly outlined above: why and when did events start to be retained not through a family or clan perspective any longer but in accordance with a fundamentally new perspective, a properly political one? Since the selection (which seems established beyond dispute) of the themes retained in the royal traditions must of necessity have a point of departure; it was at a certain point in time that the threshold was crossed and not at any other.

In what concerns the problem of objectivity of ancient Merina historical recollections it is necessary to recall two extremely important facts: the fundamental event is external in nature but, it should be noted here, it is external only in the sense that it does not concern the letter of historical texts but the manner in which these are memorized by the geographically-dispersed groupings. It is certain that the different groups or different families allied to the king's own preserved in something of an airtight chamber their own recollections (especially in the epoch of the Royal Bath), precisely because these recollections amount to nothing less than *privileges*. The *Tantara* are —if one considers them from the Merina point of view and not the western one— at the same time an event of the past and a justification of social situations inherited from history and, indeed, for the most fame-laden of families, of their roles in the great royal ceremonies.[34] Two consequences emerge from this: individual traditions are not always in accord among themselves when it comes to this justification, aspect that predated the arrival of Europeans on the historical stage of Imerina. One should not lose sight of the fact that Andrianampoinimerina did query some of the families on the origin of their privileges[35] and had to decide between the versions; and, Radama I did the same at the beginning of the Nineteenth century. Yet, these same traditions are in accord on the basic historical schema to which, they make spontaneous references. There is, in this, undoubtedly, the best condition for a genuine preservation of common memories that royal traditions have become, traditions which in the Nineteenth century were not even considered as *tantara* (history, histories) but as *tetirana* (genealogy, genealogies), more or less enriched with details of events within the different reigns but serving as canvass, as noted earlier in the text.

The second fact to be noted concerns the cultural events of Imerina, this time: they tally perfectly with *internal* indications which are interspersed in the historical texts. This point has been made explicit in so far as it concerns the correspondence between cultural indications of the three early great kings of Imerina and the necessity for a political order which they had the role to confirm. One could also recall, without persisting on the point, that similar phenomena would come about later, for example in the evolution of the royal *sampy* in perfect correspondence with the political problems of the moment.[36] Already, Kelimalaza, as royal *sampy*, was elevated to a military function by Ralambo; the other *sampy*, whose cosmic and curative roles are both ancient and original, were given political roles under Andriamasinavalona, all the way to the creation of the supreme *sampy*, the unique symbol of unity of power under the rule of Andrianampoinimerina, *sampy* called *Manjakatsiroa*, literally "two cannot rule."

The historical tradition of the Merina was certainly an *oral* tradition but it was inscribed (one would almost be tempted to say *written*) in the political life of the Merina, too deeply, through the great ceremonies and the regional memories, to be false. This makes it possible to bring back, in a valid way, the question posed earlier on: when did the unembellished Merina tradition start? And, since the historical traditions will evidently not give us the answer themselves, the question merits to be transformed into a different one that will allow for the probability of reasoning the answer out: what is the determining reason for the advent of Merina historical tradition?

To seek the answer one must go around the period in which the memorization of particular aspects of the past and their alliance with the "traditional" cultural substratum (going back to the Vazimba period and anterior to those political events that make up the success of the early Merina monarchy) came to light. This phenomenon can only be an ancient one since royal traditions give notice of the basic political innovations of Rafohy and Rangita* (regarding succession) and are cross-referenced (what

*Sometimes given as daughter or sister of Rafohy in traditions. (Ed.)

is of major importance) by traditions of nobility, srongly opposed to the theses of succession stated in these royal counterparts in respect to individuals designated to succeed but not to the process of *designation itself*.[37] The representatives of the ancient royal family would never tire of insisting and on thus confirming this point in respect to the three first historical sovereigns who saw the separation of this family from the throne.

The advent of royal historical traditions could not, besides, have taken place until the moment at which the *fanjakana* was already perceived with its essential component-parts; and this is something that could not have occurred before Ralambo organized the noble strata of Merina society and before he gave pomp to the monarchy itself by instituting the Royal Bath. We are thus willing to date the advent of royal traditions to the reign of Andrianjaka, sovereign hardly less important than Andriamanelo and Ralambo, one who made Antananarivo the seat of his kingdom. It was Andrianjaka, as was related, who first saw the need for rendering homage to Ralambo on the tomb of this king itself, during the *Fandroana* ceremony. No doubt, tradition does recall that it was Ralambo who evoked the ancestors but, with Andrianjaka, we are dealing with an institution that would survive as long as the Royal Bath would be observed in Imerina. While being aware of the contextual differences, one can point out that what happened for Ralambo was a phenomenon analogous to the one to which Andrianampoinimerina would give birth; in a like manner, Radama I, too, would go to meditate at the tomb of his father.[38] It was necessary that memories concerning Rafohy, Andriamanelo and Ralambo were sufficiently robust to have been conserved along with the sites of their respective residences; besides, it was also necessary for the *fanjakana* to be quite explicit so that the selection of themes to be retained was done as a function of one successor only and no other, in accordance with a formulated and frozen ritual (the same one which made it possible to find the distinction between the royal and individual traditions). This observation confirms that royal traditions were selective from their start. They did not aim at explaining the past or even the present as a function of the past (from this angle, individual traditions are for closer to history as it is perceived by westerners); their role was a subtler one, namely to sustain the present. What constitutes a feature undoubtedly very rare in a society called "traditional," royal traditions arrived not at a pure and simple repetition of what the ancestors so honored had done but at a progress they wanted consciously to be rooted in the thought of ancestors to such a degree that monarchs could always justify a new project by the fact that it had been conceived by the preceding royal person.

One must also nuance this conclusion. In the formal sense, it is accurate to say that time had indeed acted upon the oldest of royal traditions and that it made their presentation frozen in a way —this is where the stereotypes stem from, ones that are constantly found for all of the early sovereigns, with the names of their residences, spouses and children. But, in respect to the base and texture of the ancient historical texts they are not the product of a backward projection of new political situations. Paradoxically, they seem more unerring than many of the more recent rather poetic and over-elaborated accounts.

Our sketch of the most remote Merina past, outlined rather quickly, merits to be amplified but, across the humble accounts of the Merina royal origins —sometimes reduced to just a few lines, already transcribed in full in the Nineteenth century and piously at that by the faithful guardians of tradition— let us know how to discern, as they did intuitively, the secret of their becoming.

NOTES

1. One could recall here for Madagascar, among others, the contributions of Charles Guillain, Vincent Noël, Father François Callet —all in the Nineteenth century— or of Etienne de Flacourt in the mid-1600's; for other areas one could mention, among the many, Maurice Delafosse for Africa or Todd for India.

2. There have been several publications of the *Tantara*: first from 1873 to 1881 by Father Callet (last volume published by Malzac in 1902); then a reference edition, the most widespread, published in 1908 by the Académie Malgache; finally, a French translation in four volumes by Chapus and Ratsimba (1953 - 1958).

3. The publication of monographs was almost entirely due to the initiative of the Merina in Tananarive since the start of our century. We have also received other manuscripts. Two important sources (since they are embarrassing to the whole of the ancient Merina thought) are the manuscripts of Rainandri-

amampandry, prepared independently of the *Tantara*, between 1875-1880, as well as the manuscripts collected by Alfred Grandidier (see Alain Delivré, *L'Histoire des Rois d'Imerina — Interpretation d'une tradition orale*, Paris, 1974, pp. 423-24) known as the *Merina Manuscripts*. (See same for the different *Tantara* editions, pp. 424-426. Ed.)

4. The *royal traditions* were put together by some individuals whom Queen Ranavalona I had engaged to put down on paper the events concerning the ancestors. One of the individuals, Rabetrano was regarded as having given an exact schema of the past. We have been able to determine that this manuscript, prepared in 1844, had served as canon law and that it was copied several times before the research undertaken by Rainandriamampandry. Some of the same texts are also found in the *Tantara* but in dispersed form, and the same holds for the *First Collection* of Rainandriamampandry (the one from 1875-1880).

5. We have established the distinction between *royal traditions* and *individual traditions* through the existence of manuscripts and through a philological analysis of the parallel texts already published in the *Tantara* (of Callet). Examples of individual traditions in the *Tantara*: p. 555 (Andrianentoarivo); pp. 149-153 (Andrianteloray); p. 308ss (Antehiroka); pp. 614, 621-623 (Tantsaha), etc.

6. Delivré, *Interpretation*, 1974, pp. 30-31 (schema of the *Tantara*, pp. 7-374).

7. A Zafimamy tradition published by E. Ramilison, *Ny loharanon'ny Andriana manjaka teto Imerina*, Tananarive, 1951-1952.

8. *Tantara*, p. 11, note 1; p. 15, note 1; page 18, note 1.

9. For the Vazimba see the following *Tantara* references: pp. 7-8, 12-14, 17-19, 141-150; and by allusions to, *Tantara* p. 837, note 1, pp. 944, 994-996.

10. *Tantara*, p. 14 §2.

11. For the *Kabary* of the 19th century, see those which have been published by W.E. Cousins under the title of *Malagasy Kabary*, Antananarivo, 1873.

12. *Tantara*, p. 14 §3.

13. (From a manuscript), *Tantara*, p. 9 §3.

14. *Tantara*, p. 14 §4.

15. *Tantara*, p. 67 §2; First Collection of Rainandriamampandry, folio 54v.

16. *Antehiroka* or *Zanadahy*, *Tantara*, pp. 8, 18, 254-255, 306-310, 543-548, etc. There is a text which is not favorable to this group, *Tantara*, p. 496.

17. Analysis of the term *tantara*, Delivré, *Interpretation*, 1974, pp. 163-164.

18. This is the case of most of the traditions of nobility, famous by virtue of their ascendancy but also for having played an important role in the more recent history, for example the Andriampolofatsy, *Tantara*, pp. 151-152.

19. There are numerous essays on Malagasy astrology, among them, R.P. Abinal, "L'Astrologie Malgache," *Les Missions Catholiques*, Lyon, September 1879 and October 1879, pp. 432-434, 445-448, 458-459, 481-484, 492-494 and 505-507; A. and G. Grandidier, *Ethnologie de Madagascar*, IV/3, Paris, 1917, pp. 445-457.

20. *Tantara*, pp. 90-137.

21. *Tantara*, p. 143.

22. *Tantara*, p. 67.

23. *Tantara*, pp. 73-82.

24. The description of this ceremony in the *Tantara* is that of its observance in the 19th century, see pp. 157-168 as well as 163-170.

25. The *Merina Manuscripts,* collected by A. Grandidier give an extremely valuable schema for the evolution of this particular ceremony (Mss. housed at the Académie Malgache, in form of copy, pp. 123-129). See also the *Fomba Malagasy* in *Tantara,* pp. 450-455.

26. The reigns of Andriantsitakatrandriana and of Andriantsimitoviaminandriandriandehibe, *Tantara,* pp. 284-287.

27. *Tantara,* pp. 303-310.

28. *Tantara,* pp. 238-273.

29. *Letter,* i the Archives of the Company of Jesus at Toulouse, dated August 1870.

30. *Tantara,* p. 773; this is a prologue to a long study of the *sampy,* both royal and regional (*Tantara,* pp. 173-235), which were publicly destroyed in the mass-conversion of 1869, acts which were unsettling to many.

31. *Tantara,* p. 157.

32. Delivre, *Interpretation,* 1974, p. 158.

33. *Tantara,* p. 148; see also p. 13.

34. A typical example concerning circumcision, *Tantara,* p. 49, which cite the Zanakandriamitondra (from the Ankarata area), the Zankadriampenitra (at Alosara), the Antehiroka, the Zafinandriamilaza, the Zanakandrianato, the Zanamarofotsy (west of Ambohimanga), etc.

35. *Tantara,* p. 705, and pp. 1211-1214. The second passage is a follow-up of the accounts transcribed at the time of Father Callet and completed through his own investigations.

36. Delivre, *Interpretation,* 1974, 192-198.

37. This is essentially a tradition of Zanakandriantompokoindrindra, published by J. Rasamimanana and L. Razafindrazaka, *Contribution à l'histoire des Malgaches,* Tananarive, 1909 (re-edition, 1957).

38. As observed by Europeans; from his arrival at the sacred sites relating to the advent of his father, Radama I mounted the sacred stone on which Andrianampoinimerina had stood at Ambohimanga, *Tantara,* p. 159.

EDITOR'S NOTE

As the present volume went into negative-photography layout its editor received an interesting paper from Professor Paul Ottino entitled "L'Ancienne Succession Dynastique Malgache: l'exemple Merina." Written in July 1979 and dealing with the subject to which Alain Delivré has given such a close and fruit-bearing attention, the paper is at once a continuation and a departure, an elaboration from a different perspective. As it was not possible to translate and include here the entire fifty-seven page paper upon its late arrival from Reunion, Professor Ottino has kindly consented to allow an editorial outline of its main points concerning only ancient Imerina in a note appended at the end of Alain Delivré's contribution above. A brief summary which follows cannot do justice to the original text since it excludes all of the paper's comparative aspects inside and outside Madagascar while over-simplifying the intricacy and sophistication of Professor Ottino's framework, which includes a number of important visual schema that are left out. Since there are many implications in the important work of Alain Delivré which deserve to be pursued by historians and anthropologists concerned with Madagascar and other parts of the world, even a summary cannot fail to contribute to the larger task at hand.

Looking at succession in a method similar to the process-model, not as one or more monarchical events in ancient Imerina, and adhering deliberately to the *letter* of various *Tantara* in print without concern for any ascending or descending ana-chronisms found in the Merina oral tradition, the paper focuses on the "interplay of concepts and political principles throughout...the Vazimba times and at the start of the Merina period." Identifying local sacerdotal persons (*ombiasy/omasy*, lit. "holy men") as theorists who translate the "theological and religious ideas" of their culture into "applied policies," Professor Ottino wants to know how the concept of "segmentary" state (in its original Durkheimian sense) was abandoned in Imerina in favor of a new state rooted in the idea of "center" and "periphery" and marking a transition from "loose" structure affected first by celestial-descent ruler and later by magician-king to the highly stratified heights of "hydraulic state" at its apex around 1800. The norm of single-ruler, of sovereignty, attained its status as the "sole alternative to death." It started out as vehicle for submission (*fanoavana*) to a single master (*tompo*) with celestial kinship ties which were immediate. As such ties grew visibly more and more distant, without any new arrivals, it became necessary to invent intermediaries between celestial and human descent, between men and women who had long ago fallen from the Heavens on mountain peaks of Imerina and their less elevated earthly counterparts. This role was filled by the *andriana* ("lords," "nobles," "princes"), humans with divine attributes, possessing the mysterious power of *hasina* which confers divine right to rule over men. "Celestialism," to coin a term, continued through female descendants. As Delivré has shown, while political power was "normally" exercised by males it could only be transmitted through royal females, principal spouses (*vady-be*) and sisters of the reigning monarchs who carried the royal *line* if not the power itself. The twin concepts of sovereignty and "vassalage" (term which does not quite duplicate the Merina meaning), long in the making during the "Vazimba times," manifested yet another type of duality but did not provide for a way of determining just who must submit (*mpanoa*) and who should rule. It is from this "no-man's land" within the structure of sovereignty and submission (*fanjakana ifanoavana*) that there developed an elaboration aiming at equilibrium through *pre-arranged succession* to royal government (*fanjakana arindra*) based on uterine affiliation and endogamy within the "royal order." Monarchs in Imerina, by way of "double-designation," came to 'have two generational successors, the eldest and youngest sons. The eldest or first-designated inherited the reign but could not pass on the royal line to his own progeny along with royal power, both flowing downward temporarily through the youngest or second-designated only. The norm that there can be only one head of state at any time formed a bridge between *fanjakana ifanoavana* and *fanjakana arindra*, two major aspects of Merina political theory. As long as the first-designated successor actually rules the second-designated one must submit to the reigning monarch's authority but since such *fanoavana* would have to expire sooner or later there is little doubt that a monarch who ultimately could designate *his* two sons as generational successors would have greater power as well. If pre-arranged succession to royal government became an elaboration attributable to the early Merina epoch or to the transitional Vazimba-Merina period under Rafohy and Rangita, Ottino makes the most important point that the principle of ultimate submission of the older to the younger successor goes itself to the very "dawn of the Vazimba dynasty," at least six generations *before* the Vazimba ruler Andriandranolava with whom it is supposed to have started and who has been tentatively placed in the Fifteenth century. Even the name *Andriandranolava* (Lord-of-water-in-constant-flow) conveys the idea of continuity. Thus, from an anthropological perspective and through textual analysis, Ottino lends additional support to the "revisionist" and fundamental claim of not only Delivré but several students of Madagascar before him as well that the Vazimba *tompontany* (masters-of-soil, original inhabitants), so far from being simple enemies and inferior subjects affected Imerina's kinship, religion and government in some lasting and decisive ways.

Obviously, rules of succession, whether understood as ancestral testament (*hafatra*) or observed and enforced to keep a particular royal lineage in the "center" and not on the "periphery," are subject to violations, by chance or by design. What happens, for example, to the whole system when the second-designated successor dies naturally or through an act of violence before mounting the throne, before having the right to designate his two generational successors? Here, Merina political theory provides for just such an eventuality through the concept of accesion to royal authority "in the last instance" (*amin'ny farany*) whereby descendants of the defunct second-designated successor "allow" *him* to come to rule through *them*. It is quite clear that this reverse-proxy situation is connected with legitimacy itself and that it can be used as a political tool by the first-designated successor seeking to pass on royal power to one of his sons via marriage with an "appropriate" royal female. This is, indeed, what did happen, with the very first *Merina* monarch, Andriamanelo, the first-designated successor. He "restored all rights" to his assassinated (second-designated) brother's son and his *uterine nephew*, had the young royal marry Andriamanelo's own sister (the orphan's paternal aunt), and married off the royal female issuing from this union to his own son Ralambo. It will not be lost on those familiar with Merina society and history that the descendents of Ralambo (Zafindralambo) had been uppermost in the seven *andriana* noble classes which Ralambo himself began to create in relation to their *proximity* to the "center." As Delivré notes, the *"uterine nephew* of the king came to be considered as his *closest relative*," (ed. italics). In fact, Ottino sees much of the subsequent dynamic in Merina history as a consequence of "new lineages detaching (themselves) from the central uterine one" and of continuous attempts to be as close to the "center" as possible, attempts countered by the strategies of strong monarchs who sought to keep their numbers down and most of them as far from the "center" and into the "periphery" as could be enforced. Lastly, Ottino makes a very useful and timely double contribution to the understanding of ancient Imerina. In one, he shows that the shift from generational successors (eldest/ youngest) to co-successors (son/uterine nephew) added a third "player" in the historical drama of succession but did not change the "pivotal" nature of uterine or matrilineal succession. Going beyond Andriamanelo and Ralambo into the period of Andriantompokoindrindra (first-designated) and Andrianjaka (second-designated), Ottino sketches out the mechanics of matrilineality involving the female-spouse-giving lineage and the female-spouse-taking lineages, the (central) uterine lineage being itself *sacred* as giver of female spouses with unquestioned celestial origin, the *vady santatra*, who dispense the sacral quality of *hasina* without which one cannot hope to rule. In this most telling example of an "inherited" charisma it is the conjugation of the three "players" (the first-born, last-born and uterine nephew) and their lineal satellites that reveals the continuing vitality of Merina royal order and, ultimately, its very real *capability* to implement far-reaching changes. In the other contribution, Ottino offers a reassessment of King Andriamasinavalona, monarch maligned and castigated by many as having been "destructive" for Imerina because he sub-divided (*zara taiza*) a single kingdom into four, each one under his own son, in what appears as a radical departure to the critics. Actually, argues Ottino, this king did nothing to alter the principle of succession; his act aimed first at expansion through administrative use of progeny and secondly at unification of Imerina he had inherited. He was seeking a compromise "between the old norm of 'loose' structure" and the mounting "exigencies of unified state" not by breaking with the precedent but by being guided quite clearly by it. Thus, his *four* sons were the simultaneous *single* and first-designated successor attesting to an expansionism and *all* would in turn have to be succeeded by the son of Andriamasinavalona's sister, Andrianamboinimena, prince of Alosara, the ancestral home of the first Merina monarch. Once again, it is the anthropological perspective that comes to assist historical reconstruction; and, if Alain Delivré has shown us how the Merina reified the cultural position of history in their society, it seems to this editor to be the merit of Paul Ottino to highlight a coherent political theory as one of its dynamic components.

The Folklore Component
in Malagasy History

L. HARING
Brooklyn College
City University of New York

All folkloristics is a historical study insofar as it examines
facts, movements, or attitudes that have existed in some place at
some time. The origins of folklore, a historical question, absorbed
the attention of Victorian folklorists; that their successors no
longer care much about it is a fact of their history. India originated
a story in which a clever peasant girl attracted a king's attention
with impertinent remarks that turned out to be pertinent; she later
wins him as her husband. How and why this story subsequently
appeared in Madagascar is a kind of historical reconstruction
that was the principal objective of the so-called historic-geographic
school of folklorists.[1] Even a morphological classification of
Malagasy tales based on African models would make a historical
statement about the possible past relations between Malagasy
and Arfricans. Historians now recognize the value of oral traditional
history in enlightening them about the African past, and folklorists
recognize that proverbs and riddles have almost no meaning outside
a specific setting that must be learnt from ethnography, which
begins to aspire to the condition of history.[2] Not only to oral
traditional history, however, must historians of Madagascar look
if they hope to tell the full story of the Great Island. Many other
forms of folklore offer much to the historian. Seeing national
character through proverbs or a value system through traditional
oratory, finding the Malagasy hero, if he exists, even watching
the cultural expressions of the enduring Malagasy hostility to
outsiders are all folkloric topics with historical dimensions. The
study of Malagasy folklore, while inevitably entailing its own
historical problems, offers as much to the writing of history as
it receives from the reading of history.

From the beginning, observation of Malagasy folklore has been carried out by the writers of Malagasy history. Again and again the principal works of Malagasy historiography, such as the monumental ethnographies of Alfred and Guillaume Gnandidier and the Arabico-Malagasy manuscripts edited by Gustave Julien, are of equal use to both historian and folklorist.[3] Indispensable to both are the three volumes of royal history, the *Tantara ny Andriana eto Madagascar*, compiled from dictation and manuscripts of the mid-nineteenth century.[4] Father Callet combined the Victorian folklorist's passion for capturing old and fading facts with the historian's insistence upon comparing and evaluating his informants' accounts. Recent evaluation of Callet's work in the light of present-day standards of historical writing[5] has not diminished his stature as a recorder of folklore: no continental African country can show such a compendium of traditional narrative, custom, and belief captured so early in the period of European contact. A full catalogue of Callet's folklore has yet to be made, but the reader quickly sees the folktales and legends in his work along with many details of folk religion and custom, framed in a general account of the past as his informants believed it really happened. While the *Tantara* were told as true, those contents that correspond to other stories told elsewhere can be identified through the collections and indexes of the comparative folklorist.

An obvious example of Merina folklore reported by Callet is the giant Rapeto, possessor of humpless cattle, able to encompass prodigious distances in a single step, a *vazimba* (aborigine) who fathered two daughters on his wife Rasoalao as well as some other children.[6] In all his features and deeds we recognize the giant of international legend, especially in his most famous exploit, when, out of pique at Rasoalao because she would not let him borrow her cattle to trample the fields, he blocked off her rice-fields and created the present Lake Itasy. Folktale motifs for Rapeto include F 531.6.8, Mutual relations of giants, F 531.3, Gargantuan feats, and A901, Topographical features caused by experiences of primitive hero.[7] Rapeto represents the gargantuan component of the nineteenth-century image of the *vazimba*, the anterior population of Madagascar, who are elsewhere described as diminutive. So also Rapeto's east coast cognate Darafify personifies a group said to be anterior to the present inhabitants. Darafify, they say, was a powerful chief of the east coast, born

of parents from beyond the seas (F531.6.1, Origin of giants).
His great stature caused his head to reach the sky (F531.2.5);
thus he became bald. The debris of his giant cooking tripod can
still be seen at Ambosidiny, where he lived (F 533.4, Gigantic
possessions of giants). The ricefields he gave his two wives are
now two large swampy lakes. A stone he cast aside when he
changed his mind about erecting it as a memorial lies in the river
near Vatomandry (F531.3.2, Giant Throws a great rock). His
predictions about the future destiny of places have all come true
(D1812, Magic power of prophecy). At his death the splash of
his legs, arms, and head into the ocean caused the first tidal wave
(F531.6.12, Disappearance or death of giants).[8]

Both giants perform gargantuan feats. The behavior of both
sets important precedents or predicts present reality — a wife
is directed to let her husband make free use of her property,
the erecting of memorial stones is shown to be a practice of great
antiquity. An enlarged visual scale to enhance such precedents
and predictions has been imagined many times: tales of giants
and their deeds are found in Togo and Sweden with no connection
to Madagascar. Rapeto and Darafify should make a historian
wonder about the validity of Malagasy accounts of anterior races.
Vazimba that are now gargantuan, now diminutive, strike a
folklorist as being the construct of nineteenth-century Merina who
needed a contrasting race against whom to define their self-image.
The nature, characteristics, and meaning of the *Vazimba* should
be rigorously examined from the point of view of comparative
folklore..Perhaps they never really existed.[9]

Writers on Madagascar have given more than their share of
attention to some of the island's groups. Tales, proverbs, songs,
folk religion and oratory of the Merina have been so extensively
collected that the group seems to have persuaded scholars of
their primacy, as they did the British and French authorities from
1820 on. *Malagasy Proverbs* (1871), by Cousins and Parrett, a
landmark of folklore studies, collected several thousand Merina
proverbs. Dahle's 1877 collection of tales and songs and Houder's
1884 proverb collection are continuously in print and are offered
by literate Merina as the embodiment of what folklore means.[10]
The twin trickster tales unique to Madagascar appeared in Dahle's
collection and elsewhere.[11] Jean Paulhan's publication of Merina
traditional poetry put these extraordinary pieces before the French-

reading public in 1913 and again in 1938, though perhaps obscuring their manner of performance as courtship rituals. Fortunately, not all those who were interested in tradition found themselves confined to Imerina. Especially in the realm of folktales, certain other groups are better represented. Gabriel Ferrand, who resided on both east and west coasts, anthologized Sakalava and Betsimisaraka tales in his *Contes populaires malgaches.*[12] Soon after, Charles Renel, director of schools for the colonial government, produced his island-wide *Contes malgaches* in two volumes, the third issued after his death.[13] The 1920's brought two great monuments of Malagasy folktale studies, André Dandouau's and Emile Birkeli's collections of Sakalava tales, which tipped the balance in favor of western and northwestern peoples.[14] Exceeding their already high standards of linguistic fidelity, and providing in addition extensive background information, Jacques Faublée's *Récits Bara* placed before us the tale repertoire of one of the less influential, less numerous Malagasy groups.[15] While the Bara, Betsimisaraka, Sakalava and Merina are over-represented in these and other tale collections, there are few or no tales from the Antanosy, Antaisaka, or Antaimoro.

It would be absorbing and productive for comparative folklore to compare the tale repertoires of these Malagasy groups seeking analogies to dialectal variation in language, and to discover the affinities of Malagasy tales with counterparts in Africa and Indonesia, so far as the existing collections with their sampling deficiencies will allow. But there is a limit to what such comparative study can reveal. Because the centuries since major settlement in Madagascar by non-Europeans have allowed ample time for the development of specifically Malagasy styles in storytelling, as in wood sculpture or music, the folklorist will not be offering the historian any new keys to the vexed and battered problems around the peopling of the island. Much additional research in the field is needed, especially on the paralinguistic aspects of Malagasy storytelling events, to facilitate comparison with folkloric communication in Africa and Indonesia.[16]

All genres of Malagasy folklore, like other forms of art and communication, have their own history. The specialization of singing and dancing has professionalized the minstrel into the commercial *mpilalao* of Tananarive in the 1970's. As in many countries of Africa, the tradition of singing topical songs has been adapted to mocking the European, who also gets cast as the butt in post-contact versions of jocular tales that exited long ago.[17] In Imerina, place-names like Betsimitatatra, "the big undrained (place)," have preserved the memory of the building of the dikes by Andrianjaka around 1600.[18] The tradition of ceremonial speechmaking (*Kabary*, meaning both the activity and its occasion), itself a distinct folklore genre approaching a form of theater, has included such minor genres as proverbs and parables.[19] A foreign observer could remark in the eighteenth century, "Nothing is more solemn than the grand *kabar*(y) of the Malagasy; therein language is in all its   glory. The European who is present at these gatherings is captivated by the harmony of these sounds, the movements and grace of the orator."[20] In 1949 a poet could still see orators speaking for hours in a marriage proposal ceremony, "now in *hain-teny* (a traditional poetic form), now in proverbs, using for each figure a parallelism extending to twenty or thirty images, symbols, or comparisons. These in Imerina are the most sought-after *kabary* speakers."[21] The fondness for public verbal eloquence links Madagascar with the continent of Africa, where the man who knows and can manipulate words has often been accorded respect analogous to, maybe deriving from, the awe of the shaman's knowledge of secret words. From ceremonial oratory it is a short step to political oratory. Unlucky indeed would be the public man who could not oblige the crowd with a speech performance when the occasion called for it. Speeches attributed to historical figures in the *Tantara* are lengthy and numerous. The large amount of speechmaking recorded in Merina history, while attesting to the high place of this art in community life, suggests that it has been a component of successful leadership.

The prominence of *kabary* in the *Tantara* contrasts with the small amount of direct discourse in the recorded oral histories of African countries. Gideon S. Were's *Western Kenya Historical Texts*, "the actual fieldwork information as given by my informants" on which he based his history, contain almost no direct quotation.[22] Extensive quotation does, however, appear in all malagasy storytelling. Malagasy animal tales are as notable as the *Tantara* for the amount of dialogue assigned to the characters. It is therefore a trait of Malagasy narrative style to use dialogue as a means of narration and characterization, whether the accounts are presented as true or fictional. The *kabary* attributed to the greatest of Merina kings, Andrianampoinimerina, often have an authoritarian tone, since they contain laws and prescriptions and serve at the same time to enhance his traditional portrait.[23] Properly these orations should be read as an especially forceful frame for the code of laws, a frame that purports to explain how the laws came to be, a secular myth in which a culture hero establishes law and order (Motif A530). How much validity, then, have these recorded speeches as historical evidence? Is their style expressive of the individuality of Andrianampoinimerina or of a tradition which he is made to personify by their attribution to him? Would oral traditional history attribute so many speeches to a less eminent leader? It has not done so. Are the speeches the evidence for his eminence, as they purport to be, or its cause, by showing him to us scenically instead of through indirect discourse?

Whatever answers historians may find for these questions, speechmaking ability was probably a measure for the prospects of a new political leader in Madagascar. About 1750, Ratsimilaho, the founder of the Betsimisaraka federation, illustrated the power of the knowledge of words when he persuaded the chiefs to follow him in liberating the "nation" from the tyranny of Ramangano. According to one account, Ratsimilaho's modesty, prudence, and ambition as evidenced in his *kabary* were sufficient to decide the chiefs to support him.[24] While the speechmaking function is still the obligation of the eldest male in a family or any male in a position of responsibility, an ability to sway the people with speeches must have characterized the man who sought power.

At the same time that he excelled his people in speechmaking ability, the Malagasy orator had to learn to disclaim his excellence. Fulfilling his leadership obligations publicly and audibly, he yet had to deny that he was separate from his group.

> We are met here, and if I begin to speak before you, please excuse me for it. I am not a father but a son, not an old man but a young man, not a senior but a junior. I must "carry the spade on my shoulder and the basket under my arm,"... To speak before such persons is like talking of cooked rice before the rice is ripe... Before speaking , I excuse myself seven times and bow seven times.

The self-effacement enforced by traditional *kabary* style has been remarked on more than once by gifted Malagasy men of words;[25]

Is it a component of successful leadership in Madagascar? Has the Malagasy man of power concealed his inevitable separation from the group?

Both proverbs and folktales have been utilized to enlighten obscure recesses of Malagasy history. One very explicit though eccentric historical thesis employs proverbs as its principal evidence. According to J.-B. Razafintsalama, the earliest Malagasy, despite their variety of physical types, were unified by being fervent Buddhists. In his reconstruction, the early Malagasy must have lived together in one place for a substantial period before settling in Madagascar. Near the end of the twelfth century, with the expansion of the "Aryano-Buddhist" religion into Java and Sumatra, they moved to Madagascar with their Buddhist monk leaders. Although their descendants inexplicably forgot any shred of their debarkation and passage inland, the later political hegemony of the Merina should actually be traced to Buddhist influences. "We know today from certain knowledge that the Malagasy, at the beginning of their history, had as their guide a college of religious men or various denominations, Buddhist monks, Shakti Tantrists both Shivaite and Vishnavite."[26] Prime evidence is the heavy debt of Malagasy to the Sanskrit language and others derived from it.

Along with language, Razafintsalama's further evidence for the Buddhist origin of Malagasy people and philosophy was the doctrine he created by arranging and commenting on their proverbs. By reorganizing the Cousins and Parrett collection, Razafintsalama revealed what he identified as a basic Buddhistic doctrine harmonized with Tantric monotheism. Large categories arranged the proverbs by subject. Observe his method of illustrating the second of the Four Noble Truths of Buddhism, "the cause of suffering is rooted in desire." According to Razafintsalama, many Malagasy proverbs urge the idea that man is driven by a thirst for pleasure that can never be satisfied. Sometimes he drowns himself in pleasure: the miser of some proverbs is the type of a man wholly driven by desire. Other proverbs demonstrate the difficulty of overcoming desire, the error of desire here on earth, the rejection of desire at some more enlightened times in life, and the role of reason in establishing standards for success and failure. Other proverbs are classified so as to support the doctrinal interpretation, in such classes as the vices, the passions, misconduct, anger deception, jealousy, suspicion, distrust, laziness, lying, hypocrisy, betrayal, vanity, pride, contempt, hatred.

In his conclusions, Razafintsalama systematized the doctrine that arises, plausibly enough if we grant his scheme, from the arrangement of the proverbs — "a rigid determinism of immanent causation which imposes a pre-established order upon all events."[27] What this author was really studying was the national character of his people: the statements that resulted from arranging and interpreting the proverbs as outgrowths of ancient Buddhist doctrine are statements about the essential nature of the Malagasy mind. His thesis, however, proclaimed itself historical. Since the time of Radama I, Madagascar had been undergoing a regressive maladaptation to European civilization; in the same period, Buddhistic humanitarian conceptions re-emerged which should now unify all the diverse groups in the nation. Proverbs were a product of authentically Malagasy culture, surviving half-understood into the twentieth century.

Neither Razafintsalama's interpretation of history nor his handling of proverbs has much merit. That the proverbs which Cousins and Parrett happened to be able to collect amongst Merina in the 1860's lend themselves to an arrangement by topics proves nothing about the time when any of them originated. Rather, Malagasy proverbs represent an unsystematic and *ad hoc* process of invention and repetition, fostered by the traditionally high value of verbal eloquence. Their only reality derives from their occurrence in speech, as Alfred Grandidier seems to have recognized: "In their conversations, at every instant they quote proverbs which very well express, in lapidary style, their feelings and thoughts, and they amuse themselves by making ingenious comparisons...."[28] The possibility of harmonizing all the sentences found in a collection of 1,477 is now more commendable an analytic procedure than the missionary Cousins's own demonstration through proverbs that the Malagasy were skeptical about their own belief system.[29] It would be equally easy and futile to reclassify proverbs to show their contradictions. Yet the folklorist can afford to feel for Razafintsalama as he struggles with the labor of proverb classification. Seeking to reveal a latent order, unaware that he was imposing one, he saw Merina proverbs as an expression of pan-Malagasy character and therefore a basis for asserting the value of Malagasy culture against the colonial power. His attempt to show the historical content of Malagasy proverbs must be credited as one of the few attempts to examine any Malagasy folklore against the background of the island's unique history, but his tendentious reasoning is a fatal demerit.

A more successful effort to reveal history through folklore was made by J.C. Hébert, who analyzed a Malagasy coastal legend and its historical cognates.[30] Through this investigation Hebert showed a tiny but distinct connection between Madagascar and Polynesia. In the Malagasy tale, during a famine in the Seychelles, two children, Lema and Nio, die and are buried by their father. A tree grows near Nio's tomb; the father says, "Its fruits are the fruits of Nio (*voanio*, coconut palm)." A Tahitian tale narrates the origin of the bread tree and coconut palm from the head and body of a buried eel. In both stories a tree is born from a real or symbolic head buried in the ground; the coconut palm and bread tree appear in both; the Indonesian name for bread tree, *rima*, appears as a character name in the Malagasy tale (Lema): and the Indonesian *nijugh* (*niu*) has its analogue in the word *voanio*, fruit, which in Flacourt's mid-seventeenth century may also have meant the fruit-bearing tree. Hébert concluded that the Malagasy and Tahitians are cognate groups (as confirmed by other evidence), which separated long ago in an area where both originated and where the coconut and bread tree flourish, namely Indo-Oceania. Customs and beliefs of more recent time in Madagascar are connected to this tale, such as a widespread recognition of the coconut as a head symbol, a taboo against young persons' putting coconut plants in the ground, and the banana as a life-token. Hébert's conclusion assumes other evidence that Madagascar was settled by people from Indonesia, a point not under debate. The resemblance and probable connection of the two tales serves to bolster what is already known on the topic.

Far weaker is Hébert's argument that three Sakalava tales owe their origin to Indian folklore by way of Malaysia. As Razafintsalama found hidden relationships among the proverbs from one printed source, so Hébert finds an Indian origin for three unrelated tales written down for him by a schoolmaster, Bébé Léonard of Soalala.

In one of the tales, the hero disguises himself by smearing himself with mud; he is chosen for the princess by the king's throwing a *lamba* that chances to fall on him, and they marry. With the help of a lion, he supplies lion's milk, a magic remedy for the king's eye ailment, and, again in disguise, shows his prowess in battle. He brands his haughty brothers-in-law; recognized while sleeping from his missing finger, he banishes them and takes power. Citing another version of the same tale from Dandouau's collection, Hébert derives both from a Malay story in which the hero rescues a princess from captivity. He possessess a magic garment which works repeated transformations upon him. To obtain his kingdom, he searches for a magic musical instrument. To cure the princess's eye ailment, he has to find tiger's milk; when he finds some, he offers it to the princess's suitors if they all agree to be branded. They undergo the branding, but he has given them goat's milk instead, and in the end only he can cure the princess's eyes. Both tales do contain the quest for a magic remedy (Motif H1361) and the branding of the suitors (H55), but since these occur in many other tales both in Madagascar and elsewhere[31] the homology of the two has not been proved. Yet Hébert says there is no doubt the tales have a common origin.

In his second tale, the hero is again smeared with ashes but is exiled. He aids his brothers by capturing a while boar, stealing the horns of a wild bull, and building a silver house. Recognized by his unique ability to open the house, the exile returns and his cowardly brothers are banished. Ignoring the obvious structural parallels between this and the preceding tale, Hébert links the two only by the motif of the hero's being smeared with ashes.

In the third tale, betrayed by his faithless wife, king Tandroko-mana leaves a son who avanges his father's death after hiding outside the murderer's village and disguising in an old man's skin. He becomes a new king. Hébert asserted no connection of this tale to Hindu or Malay folklore, but the appearance of the name Tandrokomana in his first and third tales certified their common origin for him. Such arguments of analogy demand utmost cuation, more than Hébert gives to this one; Malagasy tales use the same names for characters over and over again.[32] The supposed unity of the three tales remains unproved, and our knowledge of the historical connections between Madagascar and the East is not augmented.

Although we could not reconstruct much history from Malagasy folktales, if other evidence were lost, we can learn something of the Malagasy past from their details. Especially in the realm of the settings and properties, in these libretti for folk theater, can we find archaic facts of the life of the group. The Bara tales callected by Jacques Faublée between 1938 and 1941 describe, he says, old Bara society in the south of Madagascar before royalty disappeared and society was transformed after the revolt of 1904. One tale, for instance, narrates the invention of bark for clothing; by 1938 bark clothing was nearly obsolete. The grilling of food (in "Polynesian" style) rather than boiling it, the shrouding of corpses in cow or bull hide, the levirate as a normal and expected custom all appear in Bara tales. He watched children play with a toy model of a granary supported by a single stilt, its form the same as their ancestors had used, its place shifted from adult utility into the child's realm: something nobody used any more. Faublee wisely denied that Bara narratives could furnish us any information about a supposed primitive mentality, but his granary exemplifies metataxis, the marginalzation of an object's function, and lights the way to further investigation.[33] The use and scale of the granary changed; so, probably, did its construction, but its form remained constant. What toys or other examples of present-day material culture in Madagascar preserve forms whose function has changed?

To answer the question, what works of verbal art preserve archaic cultural facts, Faublée extracted from Bara tales an equating of the violation of taboo with the destruction of family life, surely an enduring bit of ideology, and a firm belief that the children in a family belong to the father rather than the mother.[34] He also accepted as a literal statement of Bara belief the life-token motif found in folk narrative of many countries and all over Madagascar. Thompson's Motif E 761 reports from Africa, Indonesia and Europe the mystic connection of an object with someone's life, so that changes in the life-token indicate changes in the person. Tales from all parts of Madagascar employ Motif E 761.3, Life-token: tree fades. Faublée states that formerly the Bara planted trees only as a pledge of life, and that it was not until the time he was living among them that they began to imitate their Betsileo immigrants by planting trees. From the outmoded equating of folklore with fiction survives the difficulty of handling narrative motifs that are both elements of a belief system and widely known storytelling devices. Classifying tale types of central Africa, a folklorist wondered if the belief that a sorcerer can indeed remove his eyes invalidates the use of the motif "Person unusual as to his eyes."[35]

This is not the only problem facing the folklorist and historian wanting to use the Motif and Type Indexes. Some historians believe that the indexes commit their user to supporting diffusionism, an outmoded anthropological assumption. This view, however, is erroneous. The *Motif-Index of Folk Literature* and *The Types of the Folktale* are bibliographic tools that enable the user to "establish the traditional character, the family relationships, the genealogical tree, of his collected samples. In a word, is the story he had heard folklore? If so, how well known is it and in what places? To these questions the indexes provide answers."36 Diffusionism is irrelevant to the folklorist as to the anthropologist or historian, but the multiple existence of beliefs, story elements or giants is of interest to all three.

Faublée's most ambitious historical speculation is his reconstruction of the mythological figure of Zatuvu, the adversary of god. This figure, who appears in more Malagasy tales than Faublée acknowledges[37], claims to be uncreated by God; unlike Milton's Satan, he succeeds in sustaining the claim. Faublée asserts that Zatuvu is the same figure as Milaloza, the man who looks for trouble in Sakalava tale. The Zatuvu stories, in his interpretation, are the decomposed result of an ancient mythology in which Zatuvu was associated with fecundity — a thesis deserving the attention of a comparative mythologist.[38] The caution and methodological rigor Faublée displays in all his work serves him well in the glimpse through tales of 1938-1941 into the Bara society of earlier generations.

Archaic facts were also found by Louis Molet in a tale he collected in 1948 Ambohimena, Marovoay district, in the Antaimoro quarter of a Sakalava village. Conforming to its surroundings, the tale purports to show the origin of the alliance between the Antaimoro and Sakalava. According to Molet, it preserves important historical details. In former times it took three months to travel from Ambongo to Vohimasy, two-thirds the length of Madagascar. The Antaimoro believe they originated among the Arabs. They used to know a technique for killing the dwarf hippo, then still extant, at a distance: they used written books (charms) which they extended toward the hippo seven times. Molet speculates that this object may have in fact been a projectile. They had books of prayers which they knew how to read; wooden plaques with Arabico-Malagasy inscriptions, still

found among the Antaimoro, existed from early times. All these
details and others do indeed appear in Molet's tale, but wheter
they are reminiscence or fantasy remains to be proved from external
evidence. If Arabico-Malagasy inscriptions had in the past as
much potency as Antaimoro of today say they have, in their
manuscript form, Molet's interpretation of the hippo-killing weapon
as a projectile disregards how the tale affirms belief. If words
are magic, it was their power that killed the dwarf hippo.[39]

What heroes have Malagasy narrators depicted in past generations? Are these national, local, regional heroes? What potential
do they offer for revival in the present era of nation-building?
Is there such a thing as a national Malagasy hero? According
to history, the greatest hero is Andrianampoinimerina, who created
before his death in 1810 a political union of the islnand so strong
that ever since then, it can be considered a unity. Legends told
at Ambohimanga a century after his death, circulated to school-
masters for indoctrinating the young, show Andrianampoinimerina
uttering Confucious-like wisdom, using the flight of birds to divine
the most vulnerable entry for the conquest of Ambohidratrimo,
and protecting the crows who warned him of impending attack
by Andrianjafy.[40] According to the *Tantaran'ny Andriana eto
Madagascar*, this king's mother was the eldest daughter among
her royal father's children; his father came from another region;
his future greatness and rule were predicted in his youth; attempts
were made by his predecessor, king Andrianjafy, to kill him;
and he planned to leave Ambohimanga then but was persuaded to
protect himself instead by means of a sacrifice. Having been
proclaimed king, he reigned successfully and prescribed many laws.
Near the end of his life, he lost favor with some of his subjects
(the Zanakandrianato) and made an ill-omened journey away from
his royal city. After his death his body was buried at Ambohimanga; post-*Tantara* eyewitnesses saw his body moved to Tananarive, so that he had two holy sepulchres. In these particulars
the greatest of Merina rulers is an international hero resembling
Moses and Oedipus; if it were not too curious to inquire when
and how the facts of this person's life were remolded into this
Indo-European archetype.[41]

Considering his eminence in Merina history, we might expect
that Andrianampoinimerina would appear as an important figure
in the legends and tales of other groups, such as the Betsileo,

whom he annexed. In fact no tales or legends of Andrianampoini-merina are reported from the Betsileo, nor from the Betsimisaraka, nor from the Sakalava, whose folklore has been extensively collected. Nor does his son and successor, Radama I, who with the aid of the British subdued the Sakalava kingdoms beginning in 1822, make an appearance as an admired, hated, or even regarded figure in Sakalava folklore. Despite recognition, in the British treaty of 1817, of Radama as "King of Madagascar," and 160 ensuing years of acceptance by foreigners of Merina domination over other groups, folklore indicates that there was no popular acceptance of either king as a pan-Malagasy leader or hero. Radama II, born in 1829, spoke up at the age of three months and generously offered some cattle to his cousin Ramangamaso; at nine months he lifted a large ram three inches off the ground — so says Merina legend. His mother, Ranavalona I, remarked, "Ever since I conceived him, I've been seeing the most amazing things." His precocious strength (Motif F 611.3.2) continued through his childhood, when he would test his strength by lifting heavy objects and show his warlike nature by setting fire to his playmates or by wanting to tame a crocodile or a legendary *songomby*.[42] But like the fictional Iboniamasiboniamanoro,[43] Radama II is a hero only to the Merina. Remembering past heroes, according to a African political scientist, is essential to building up national consciousness in a post-colonial period. "To give the idea of a Nation warmth, it is often necessary either to personify it mataphorically, or, more effectively, to give it specific human form in national heroes" who must be recognized as common to all.[44] It appears that Malagasy folklore has provided no common heroes for a government to use in nation-building.

Historical research on Madagascar will continue to depend on extensive use of oral testimonies, but without reference to written documents, archeology, or some other corpus of evidence, there is no hope of deriving historical truth from Malagasy oral traditions. *Vazaha* (European) historians insist on objective accuracy, rigorous scrutiny of sources, and a stable and unchanging historical truth, all noble concepts representing the best of the Western cultural heritage. Their Malagasy informants, on the other hand, are more deeply committed to the enduring Malagasy world view than to a temporary cooperation with *vazaha* for short-term advantage. An indispensable component of that world view, visible through folklore, inevitable in the light of geography, assumed today to be necessary for suvival, is a bipolar orientation which arrays foreigners, especially Europeans, education, technology, money, and the power to help on one side, and Malagasy culture, rice cultivation, poverty, and helplessness on the other. Many foreign visitors to Madagascar have felt this opposition, no doubt first as a function of their foreignness, and made strenous efforts to come to grips with its meaning.[45] Among the many Malagasy spekesmen for this view, Rev. Maurice Rasamuel stands out for his thoroughgoing conservatism and clarity. A schoolmaster whose acceptance of Western religion and education brought him eminence and success in Tananarive, Rasamuel insisted, on the basis of his study of traditional Malagasy verbal art, that Malagasy and outsiders were polar opposites. Language and custom were especially important means of distinguishing Malagasy from other races and peoples. He opposed "occidental, European" things to "oriental, Asiatic" ones: counting methods, dowries, gestures of beckoning, spatial orientation, dancing, singing. In expressing so simply his profound sense of the separation between Malagasy and outsiders, Rasamuel voiced an attitude met throughout Malagasy culture, an attitude that determines the performance of informants when they are interviewed.[46] Rather than push the opposition to an embarrassing or tactless extreme, Rasamuel concluded by saying "Certain things that offer real value for the occidental have none, sometimes, for the oriental; and vice-versa."[47] Among these would appear to be fashions of thought, cognitive patterns, what have been called "folk ideas";[48] moreover, the bipolar orientation is itself a fact of history. Can the historian understand the thinking of those who speak oral testimonies without acknowledging these "certain things"?

Malagasy people, like people everywhere, have their characteristic ways of structuring the remote and recent past so as to make it and themselves comprehensible. Without such patterns, life would be intolerable. Cognitive patterns visible through folklore constitute the Malagasy perception of the past. The folklorist's main contribution to Malagasy history may be to insist on the reality of recurrent images, symbols, "archetypes," which make the past comprehensible an the present livable. Proverbs are often the most memorable statements of such ideology. A European ethnographer in Imerina in the 1960's often heard the proverb, "Those who live in one house should be buried in one tomb" (Velona iray trano, maty iray fasana). Studying the context of performance of the proverb, he realized it was an ideal statement about how things used to be, how they ought to be, but not a real statement of what people were doing.

> Nowadays, as likely as not, the people who will be buried together probably never lived together. Instead of the tomb being a continuation of the state of affairs of the living it is an ideal of corporateness and family unity which is striven for during life, but is never achieved. The return *famadihana* is therefore a ritual regrouping...the *making* of a group which ... is an ideal model for the living.[49]

The proverb as much as the ceremony is a ritualized statement of an ideal.

A narrative may purport to be about the past but really function as ideology. According to a Merina of 1853, before the time of Ralambo cattle wandered undisturbed, but their meat was thought poisonous. When some grazing oxen were burnt in a grass fire, only the authority of Ralambo persuaded his hungry slaves to try the meat. After a week of no ill effects, Ralambo amassed a large herd and held a feast at which the new food was the main course. "At the end of the feast, when the king told them to go and collect cattle for themselves, there was no lack of eagerness to obey his command."[50] Conforming as it does to a narrative structure found in many other Malagasy tales, containing as it does Motifs A 545, Culture Hero establishes customs, and A 1455, Origin of cooking, and reinforcing as it does the authority attributed to a Merina king, shall this story contribute to history through its narrative content, its surface statement about the introduction of beef, or through its reproducing traditional patterns? Oral and written testimonies require content analysis and formal literary criticism as well as distillation and crosschecking for historical data. The seven-headed monster, slain on the east coast by the heroic Ranalivuadziri, has the same name as a Betsileo monster that issues from the decayed corpses of certain royal persons. Is the *fananimpitolahy* a pan-Malagasy symbol of magic, power, and danger, or merely an instance of linguistic conservatism? However interpreted, such cognitive patterns from the past are what create the present Malagasy self-image. Such a "Western" problem as urban crime is understood by means of folk motifs. In Tananarive in 1976, people told the legend of the well-known thief Rainivoanjo, who became a snake, a rat, or fly to effect his many jail breaks (Motifs D 191, D 117, D 185). The essence of the Malagasy view of history is contained in such images and symbols, not in atomized data.

To the extent that statements purporting to be about the past derive from such patterns of thought and feeling, their historical value lies not in the atoms that can be wrung from them but in the *Gestalten* underlying them. Oral testimonies are both statements of belief and brush-strokes of a collective self-portrait. Both ideology and actuality have their history; much remains to be written.

NOTES

1. The Clever Peasant Girl is Type 875 in Antti Aarne and Stith Thompson, *The Types of the Folktale* (FFC 184, Helsinki, 1961). One of its appearances in Madagascar is in Raymond Decary, *Contes et legendes du Sud-Quest de Madagascar* (Paris: G.-P. Maisonneuve et Larose, 1964), pp. 77-79. Research on Malagasy folklore was carried on while I was Fulbright Professor in the University of Madagascar, 1975-76. Gerald M. Berg and Gerald E. Warshaver advised me in writing this paper.

2. For a review of the folklorist's problems and methods in Africa, see Dan Ben-Amos, "The Writing of African Oral Tradition: A Folkloristic Approach," *The Conch*, 2, 2 (September 1970), 69-79. The definitive historical treatment is Jan Vansina, *Oral Tradition* (Chicago: Aldine Publishing Company, 1965). Difficulties are clarified in Richard M. Dorson, "The Debate Over the Trustworthiness of Oral Traditional History," in *Folklore: Selected Essays* (Bloomington: Indiana University Press, 1972), pp. 199-224. Dorson's observation (p.216) that this controversy was strongly compartmentalized is powerfully timely.

3. Alfred and Guillaume Grandidier, *Ethnographie de Madascar*, (Paris; P. Brodard, 1908-28). G. H. Julien, *Pages arabico-madécasses*, (Paris: Societé des Editions Géographiques, Maritimes, et Coloniales, 1929).

4. R. P. Callet, *Tantaran'ny Andriana*, 1908 (this is the modern spelling). Translated by G.-S. Chapus and E. Ratsimba as *Histoire des Rois* (Tananarive: Librairie de Madagascar, 1955-58). References to the *Tantara* are to the translation.

5. Alain Delivré, *Histoire des rois de l'merina* (Paris: Klinksieck, 1974).

6. Callet, *Histoire des Rois*, I, 21-24.

7. Motifs are drawn from Stith Thompson, *Motif-Index of Folk Literature* (Bloomington: Indiana University Press, 1955-58).

8. A. Dandouau, "Conte malgache: Darafify," *Revue de Madagascar*, 4 (October 1933), 55-57. This Europeanized version, labeled Betsimisaraka, was

doubtless synthesized from Dandouau's field work, which is more faithfully reported in *Contes populaires des sakalava et des tsimihety de la region d'Analalava* (Alger 1922), pp. 380-385.

9. Gerald M. Berg supports this point in the first chapter of his dissertation, "Historical Traditions and the Foundation of Monarchy in Imerina" (unpublished doctoral dissertation, University of California, Berkeley, 1975), and "Symbolic Aspects of Merina Historical Traditions," in *African Oral Trditions and History*, ed. J. C. Miller (forthcoming.

10. L. Dahle, rev. John Sims, *Anganon'ny Ntaolo* (Tananarive: Trano Printy Loterana, 1971) has been proceded by at least six printings. J. A. Houlder, *Ohabolana, or Malagasy Proverbs Illustrating he Wit and Wisdom of the Hova of Madagascar* (Tananarive, 1915; French Trs. by H. Noyer 1916). Houlder completed this work in 1884. Bakoly Domenichini-Ramiaramanana, Ohabohan'ny *Ntaolo* (Memoires de L'Académie Malgache, fasc. 44, 1977) is a meticulously crafted re-edition of and commentary on Cousins and Parrett which explains how Houlder absorbed their work into his own, p. xxii ff.

11. J. Parrett, *Ikotofetsy sy Imahaka* (Tananarive, 1876) gave the ticksters currency among the literate.

12. Paris: Ernest Leroux, 1893.

13. Paris: Ernest Leroux, 1910-1930.

14. Dandouau's book is referred to above.

15. Paris: Institut d'Ethnologie, 1947.

16. See, for example, Dan Ben-Amos, *Sweet Words: Storytelling Events in Benin* (Philadelphia: Institute for the Study of Human Issues, 1975); James L. Peacock, *The Rites of Modernization* (Chicago: University of Chicago Press, 1968).

17. Norma Mcleod, "The Status of Musical Specialists in Madagascar," *Ethnomusicology*, 8 (1964), 278-289.

18. G. Ramamonjy, "Essai sur la toponymie malgache," *Bulletin de l'Académie Malgache*, n. s. 32 (1954), 17-28.

19. Roger le Garreres and Flavien Ranaivo, "Terre, langue et ame malgache," *Revue de Madagascar*, April 1949, 75-91.

20. B. de Froberville, reported in Leguevel de Lacombe, *Voyage à Madagascar et aux Iles Comores* (Paris, 1840), I, 176 n. This translation and all other French are my own.

21. Flavien Ranaivo, "Les *Hain-Teny*," *Revue de Madagascar*, 7 (4e trim. 1949), 78.

22. Gideon S. Were, *Western Kenya Historical Texts* (Nairobi: East African Literature Bureau, 1967); *A History of the Abaluyia of Western Kenya* (Nairobi: East African Publishing House, 1967).

23. For example his marriage-rules speech upon hearing the pathetic drowning of the legendary lovers of Tritriva: Callet, *Histoire des Rois*, III, 502-507. Louis Michel criticizes the speeches of Andrianampoinimerina in "Essai sur la litterature malgache," *Revue de Madagascar*, 28 (3e trim. 1956), 49-50.

24. Eugene de Froberville, note in Lacombe, *Voyage a Madagascar*, I, 176-179.

25. Richard Andriamanjato, *Le tsiny et le tody dans la pensée malgache* (Paris, Présence Africaine, 1957), citing M. Colançon's translation of *Kabary ampanam-badiana*, by Maurice Rasamuel (*Bulletin de l'Académie Malgache*, 11, 1928). The quotation is from the same source. Simeon Rajaona, "Aspects de la psychologie malgache vus a travers certains traits des 'Kabary' et quelques faits de langue,"

Annales Malgaches (Tananarive: Université de Madagascar, Faculte des lettres et sciences humaines), I, 1963, 23-37.

26. Translated from Dama-Ntsoha (Razafintsalama's pen name), *La technique de la conception de la vie chez les malgaches revelée par leur proverbes* (Tananarive: Masoandro, 1955), p. 4. The thesis is amplified in *La langue malgache et les origines malgaches* (Tananarive, 1928), *Le bouddhisme malgache ou la civilisation malgache* (Tananarive: Imprimerie Antananarivo, 1938), and *Histoire politique et réligiouse de Madagascart* (Tananarive: Imprimerie de Madagascar, 1960).

27. Translated from *La technique de la conception de la vie*, p. 99.

28. Alfred Grandidier, *Histoire physique, naturelle et politique de Madagascar*, vol. IV t. 3, 119.

29. William E. Cousins, "The Ancient Theism of the Hova," *Antananarivo Annual* 1 (1875), 6.

30. J. CX. Hebert, "La légende de l'anguille à oreilles, ou le mythe de l'origine de cocotier," *Mémoires de l'Académie Malgache*, 43 (1969), 119-125.

31. Aarne-Thompson Types 314 and 551.

32. J. C. Hébert, "Le cycle légendaire de Tandrokomana," *Revue de Madagascar*, n. s. 21 (1° trim. 1963), 13-26.

33. Faublée, *Récits Bara*, pp. 484-485.

34. Faublée, *La cohesion des societés Bara* (Paris: Presses Universitaires de France, 1954), p. 133.

35. Winifred Lambrecht, *A Tale Type Index for Central Africa* (unpublished dissertation, University of California, Berkeley, 1967), pp. 12-13.

36. Richard M. Dorson, "Techniques of the Folklorist," in *Folklore: Selected Essays*, p. 20.

37. See, for example, Emile Birkeli, *Folklore sakalava receulli dans la region de Morondava*, *Bulletin de l'Académie Malgache*, n. s. 6 (1922-23), 220-224.

38. Faublée, *Récits Bara*, pp. 496-500.

39. Louis Molet, in *Bulletin de l'Académie Malgache*, 30 (1951-52), 88-90.

40. Razafindramanta, "Andrianampoinimerina, anecdotes recueillies à Ambohi-manga," *Bulletin mensuel du service de L'enseignement* (Tananarive, 1910). One anecdote appeared in each issue.

41. See Lord Raglan, "The Hero of Tradition," in *The Study of Folklore*, ed. Alan Dundes (englewood Cliffs: Prentice-Hall, 1965), pp. 142-157, and Dundes's introduction thereto.

42. L. Rigaud, translating from anecdotes collected in Tananarive by "Ra...ry," *Bulletin mensuel de l'enseignement*, 13ᵉ annee, no 9 (September 1911), 311-314.

43. The elaborate tale of Ibonia is the first item in Dahle-Sims, *Anganon'ny Ntaolo*, pp. 5-34. It was re-edited by R. Becker, *Conte d'Ibonia* (Memoires de l'Academie Malgache, fasc. 30; Tananarive, 1939).

44. Ali A. Mazrui, *On Heroes and Uhuru-Worship* (London: Longman, 1967), p. 21.

45. E. Cailliet, *Essai sur la psychologie des Hova* (Paris: Presses Universitaires de France, 1925). O. Mannoni, *Psychologie de la colonisation* (Paris: Seuil, 1950), trs. by Pamela Powesland as *Prospero and Caliban* (New York: Frederick A. Praeger, second ed., 1964).

46. Lee Haring, "Performing for the Interviewer, a Study of the Structure of Context," *Southern Folklore Quarterly*, 1972, 383-398.

47. Translated from Colançon's French, *Bull. Acadm. Malg.* n. s. 11 (1928), preface.

48. Alan Dundes, "Folk Ideas as Units of World View," *Journal of American Folklore,* 84 (1971), 93-103.

49. Maurice Bloch, *Placing the Dead* (London: Seminar Press, 1971), p. 166.

50. Mémoirs (1853) of Raombana, born about 1800, trs. T. Lord, "The Early History of Imerina Based Upon a Native Account," *Antananarivo Annual,* 24 (1900), 452-453.

Radama I,
The Unification of Madagascar and the Modernization of Imerina
(1810 - 1828)

J. VALETTE*
Archives of Aquitaine
Gironde

In a very real sense the reign of Radama I marks the start of a new era in the history of Madagascar, island that would undergo a number of upheavals so far-reaching that they would have a lasting effect on the life of its populations.

At the outset, it would be unfair to claim that the new king of Imerina in 1810 did anything other than continue the work of his father, King Andrianampoinimerina (1787-1810); yet, this was done in a different style and with far greater means at Radama's disposal, thanks to a timely and most useful alliance with Great Britain, power that would supply him at the same time with modern weapons and a variety of instructors, as well as, ultimately, help the nascent Kingdom of Madagascar to make its advent at the international level. The importance of Andrianampoinimerina, which simply cannot be minimized, is clear: the power represented within Madagascar by an Imerina unified under him, the form of government he was able to impose and the fact that this contributed a great deal to establish the royal prestige itself — all of this represents a legacy of the first order, means for action that would allow Radama to complete what had started out so well.

With Radama, so to say, this enterprise changed dimensions. Where Andrianampoinimerina had been a patient collector of lands who acted, with an occasional exception, within the boundaries of Imerina, the succeeding monarch set out to extend his power far beyond, to transcend deliberately the traditional

*Translated from French by R. Kent.

ethnic isolation and — for the first time in local history — to think and act in terms of Madagascar as a whole. It may well be that the often-quoted expression "let the sea be the limit of my ricefield" was coined by Andrianampoinimerina but it was up to Radama to make the concept of unification work. One can hardly avoid comparing the respective roles of Andrianampoinimerina and Radama with those of the French Kings Louis VI and Philippe-Auguste, since the former had amassed lands and people around Ile-de-France and the second used the forces so grouped to extend the royal authority.

In the early years of his rule Radama's most pressing task was to consolidate the achievement of his father. Populations outside Imerina that had been partly subjected to Merina authority — the Betsileo, Sihanaka, Bezanozano — sought to exploit the change in monarchs by way of rebellions and the incoming ruler of Imerina had to mount a number of military campaigns against them which resulted in renewals of fealty. As order returned and the Merina royal authority acquired a more secure base among the three neighboring populations by 1815, a novel development was already on the way. It consisted of aims of cardinal importance for Madagascar held by the new British Governor of Mauritius, Sir Robert Farquhar.

In 1810-1811, the British took the Mascarene Islands now called Mauritius (former Ile de France) and Reunion (ex-Bourbon) as well as the establishment for factors and merchants at Tamatave, all of which had been French possessions at the time. Although it restored Reunion to France, the peace treaty of May 1814 formalized the permanent hold by Great Britain over Mauritius and "its dependencies," an expression that would soon produce a rather heated diplomatic struggle. As Sir Robert was claiming Madagascar to be only a "dependency" of Mauritius and hence that it was now a British possession, the French Governor of Bourbon (Reunion) argued, in writing, that such an interpretation was unfounded since Madagascar had always been considered as an independent land. The dispute reached the chanceries of Europe and the English government agreed that the thesis sustained by its representative at Mauritius was without any factual merit and accepted that France should recover the footholds in Madagascar extant on 1 January 1972. There followed an amusing *chassé-croisé:* the Governor of Mauritius was asserting

that the French did not have a single establishment in Madagascar
in 1792 while Bourbon's Governor (whose position, let us say for
the sake of equity, had also changed in the meantime) proclaimed
that all of Madagascar was a French possession.

There is no doubt that political considerations account in part
for the acrimony enveloping the two claims regarding Madagascar
but primacy must be given by far to economic reasons: both
Reunion and Mauritius were plantation economies concentrating
on the sugar cane and both required, in order to feed their
populations, the Malagasy rice, cattle and some other imports
from the Great Island; now that the two lesser islands belonged
to two different European powers each wanted to preempt the
other in Madagascar, acquire a monopoly over the Malagasy
exports and thus maximize the profits by selling directly to its
competitor. It is thus hardly surprising that the heads of two
plantation colonies sought to gain an advantage in Madagascar.

From the moment he became the Governor at Mauritius,
Farquhar developed an active interest in Madagascar. Astute
organizer, methodical, tenacious, he undertook a rigorous study
of conditions in Madagascar, researching all the archives for information that could furnish the grounds for a policy he had wished
to follow. He was not remiss in bringing together the knowledge
and the views of all those —slave traders, merchants, colons,
administrators— who had actually lived in Madagascar. Of no
small help was his consultation of an extraordinary collection
about Madagascar, put together by an unusually curious mind,
Barthélemy Huet de Froberville, who had compiled just about
everything that had been written on the subject during the
Sixteenth and Seventeenth centuries.[1] From the mass of sources
he had thus examined, Farquhar was struck by one particular
aspect: the Merina, who according to the few Europeans that
managed to visit them (above all Nicolas Mayeur and Berthélemy
Hugon)*, surpassed by far all the other Malagasy "tribes" through
their organization —political, social, economic— and by the activities correctly attributed to them.

Now, Farquhar found himself without the support of his own
government in London in respect to his territorial claims for

*Hugon had been in Madagascar since 1790 and would continue for more than
three decades there; he is also the only European who had actually seen Andrian-
nampoinimerina in person. Mayeur visited Imerina in 1777 and 1785, (Ed.).

Madagascar; but, this did not deter him at all to work out an extremely able policy that would, at the same time, oppose the French aims which claimed Madagascar for France, and ensure for Great Britain the degree of influence that would allow it a dominant role within Madagascar. In a word, since the English had not taken Madagascar he wanted to deny it to the French. He then based his arguments on the fact that Madagascar had been an independent land, factor that automatically eliminated the French; and, to provide this juridical argument with a factual basis, he had the idea to help create in Madagascar an authority of sufficient strength to be able to defend the independence of Madagascar, even by force of arms if necessary. He picked Radama as the only Malagasy ruler who could provide this authority and he sought to win the friendship of Radama as of 1816. Quite astutely, he entrusted the initial contacts and feelers to a man named Chardenoux, trader of French origins, who had been many times on the Tamatave-Antananarivo road and who had links of friendship with both Andrianampoinimerina and Radama. This was a most rewarding choice since the young monarch, who knew the messenger and in whom he had complete trust, listened with close attention to Chardenoux who spoke highly of the benefits of Western civilization, of British power, and of the increase in Radama's own power to result from an alliance. Without reservations, thus, Radama welcomed the idea that another British envoy would be on the way, this time with greater official powers. As a sign of confidence, he decided to send two of his younger brothers to Mauritius to begin their education.

Emboldened by initial success and wasting no time, Farquhar sent his *aide-de-camp*, Captain Lesage, who had the misfortune to travel during the rainy season's high point and who reached Antananarivo after a most painful journey only to become gravely ill. Still, Lesage was able to enter into lengthy conversations with Radama, report the views of Farquhar and present a draft-treaty which gave the projected alliance its concreteness. It was here that one of Sir Robert's master-ideas, *abolition of slave trade*, was made known to the Merina king for the first time as an indispensible condition of alliance.

The export of Malagasy slaves toward Mauritius and Reunion grew by leaps in the Eighteenth century as the two Mascarenes became plantation islands, following the introduction of the coffee bean and the sugar cane, islands in need of abundant labor and more precisely slave labor. This phenomenon was so widespread, from the Indian Ocean to the Americas, that it came to cause deep emotion in Europe and particularly in Great Britain. This is where some of the religious circles were able to secure in 1807, after a long campaing against slavery by the so-called Abolitionists, a law ordering the suppression of traffic in human beings. At the Congress of Vienna in 1815 the British delegate was able to persuade the whole group of European states to issue an energetic condemnation of slave trade and to assign to the maritime nations (hence to Great Britain) the task of enforcing this decision. After 1815, no British colony could import slaves but this only led to a clandestine and illegal commerce in humans. Farquhar, who was not only anxious to carry out the orders of his government but who was also an ardent and sincere anti-slaver, felt that the best way to attack this problem would be to dry-up the sources of supply by obtaining from Radama himself a ban on the export of Malagasy slaves.

Yet, Radama could only come to accept such a measure with difficulty because it would go distinctly against the locally established practices and it would also deprive him of a good part of his income, derived from the taxing of slave-trade transactions, an income with which he could buy the firearms and ammunition needed to maintain his own defense. This was a weighty consideration when placed against the British envoy's argument that one would make greater economic sense by keeping slaves in Madagascar, make them work there, and then sell what they produce abroad. In truth, the entire problem was of such magnitude that the adoption of proposed measure would require too many major adjustments. As such, too, it did not lend itself to a point-blank resolution, something that Lesage had understood quite well. The gist of his function, as Farquhar saw it, was to pose the problem while other envoys would come to continue where he had left-off.

An opportunity came about in the month of June 1817. It was then that Radama decided to descend from the highlands to Tamatave for the ostensible reason of welcoming his two brothers upon their return from Mauritius, buttressed no doubt by a desire to actually reach the sea, the marvel of which he had heard so much and one never seen before by a reigning Merina monarch.

But, given that he crossed from the interior to the eastern littoral in the company of 25,000 men, there was hardly any doubt that political purposes were present as well. The foremost among these was to show his strenght and, in a related way, to ensure free passage all the way to Tamatave and across some hostile areas as this was a condition he could not do without and still hope to establish the permanent security of trade with the external world, trade that he wanted to augment at the same time. The road was certainly not secure. The Bezanozano were as yet not under his complete control and some of the lesser chiefs of the great forest areas were pillaging travellers at will, depending upon whims of the moment. In turn, this led to reprisals by way of punitive expeditions inspired by the locally-based Englishmen but headed by the rulers of Tamatave and Ivondro, namely Jean René and Fisa.* It would seem that the two rulers, in the heat of pursuit, followed the pillagers all the way into areas under Merina control running against and defeating some of the Merina detachments in the process. One could hence assume that Radama, angry over the punitive raids, would also use the opportunity of his journey to avenge this transgression and especially to show his fist to Fisa who had treated him —it was rumored— as a "beardless young man."[2]

The arrival of Radama with an army far greater than any seen until then threw the eastern littoral into a state of consternation. No one could possibly have stood in the way of such a force. As soon as it attained the coast it was announced that Fisa, the most powerful and determined of Betanimena** chiefs had fled to the islet of Prunes (plums) in the open sea off the Tamatave Bay. Farquhar's agents led by T.R. Pye did not fail to intervene by helping to develop an area of agreement between Radama and Jean René who concluded a formal treaty of friendship. According to its signed text, they would recognize one another reciprocally as brothers while guaranteeing the integrity of their respective territorial domains, despite an ambiguous formula through which each had also become master of all possessions of the other.***

*Jean René, of French and noble Betsimisaraka parents, came from Fort-Dauphin in southeastern Madagascar to Tamatave as a businessman in 1798 to become its ruler with considerable British (and Farquhar's own) help; Fisa was at the time the most centralized ruler among the Southern Betsimisaraka, (Ed.).

**Name for the southern Betsimisaraka relating to an incident in local history with red clay *(tanimena)*, (Ed.).

But, in clear language of the text, Radama, with forces far superior to those of Jean René, remained the real master of Tamatave while allowing Jean René to remain as its hereditary ruler. In this manner the Merina monarchy secured its first foothold on the Indian Ocean and gained a port as well.

Radama's two brothers reached Tamatave roughly at the same time aboard the British warship *Phaeton* with a tutor assigned them by Sir Robert. His name was James Hastie, a curious personality. An Irish sergeant who had come to Farquhar's attention for his bravery in a huge and uncontrolled fire that ravaged Port-Louis in 1816, Hastie would come to play, from 1817 until his death in 1826, a most important role in Malagasy history.

Hastie was nominated as British Agent in Madagascar shortly after the incumbent Pye had fallen ill. In this new capacity he made the journey back to Antananarivo with Radama and spent much of his time in trying to iron out the hard questions that had arisen in respect to the proposed treaty. He also acted under Farquhar's very precise instructions. As the arguments advanced by Radama at the time of Lesage's visit were too serious to be disregarded and as compensation of the loss of revenue that would certainly ensue should the traffic in human beings come to a halt, Farquhar agreed *a priori* to give Radama annually an unspecified amount which was called *"Equivalence."* On that basis but also thanks to his own abilities and the important fact that Radama had come to like him, Hastie could persuade the Merina king who now spoke for Madagascar to accept the treaty, signed on 23 October 1817. Friendship and brotherhood between Madagascar and Great Britain, the ending of "all sales and all transfers of slaves or any persons whatsoever for the purpose of transporting them from Madagascar to another country," the annual payments of 2,000 piasters in silver or gold, and delivery of firearms and ammunition, constituted the core of this diplomatic act,[3] the first that involved Madagascar as an international entity and one that would have far-reaching consequences for its evolution.

Once the treaty was signed and even before it could be confirmed by Farquhar, Radama showed his determination to carry

***There were two aspects of the treaty, one with written and signed text and the other following Malagasy traditions. The formula was related to their blood-covenant *(fatidra)* in a merely symbolic sense as traditional ritual left no doubt that Radama was the older brother, the *zoky*, and hence superior to Jean René, (Ed.).

out his part of the bargain. He even went as far as to order the return to Imerina of a large contingent of slaves awaiting shipment at Tamatave, reimbursing the taxes already collected on them as well. Unfortunately, Mauritius failed to reciprocate. After seven years overseas in the colonial service Farquhar went on a visit home just as Radama began to act on behalf of the treaty; and his interim successor, General Hall (soon to be relieved of gubernatorial duties as his administration lacked a sense of purpose), refused to honor the treaty on the pretext, with legally valid grounds, that it had not been ratified by England's king. As could be expected, Radama ordered an immediate resumption of slave trade, gaining the impression that he had been tricked. The difficulties had an even more serious dimension since Radama used his own authority as monarch and undisputed leader to impose an unpopular measure, going as far as to execute several close associates and thus end the last enclave of opposition. From all this, both Radama and the Merina retained some bitter memories reflected in the expression "as false as an Englishman."

The situation became increasingly prejudicial to Farquhar's policies when the French government began to make efforts to recover its lost rights in Madagascar. After much tergiversating and several studies and reports seeking to determine just where in Madagascar it would be oppurtune to seek a reentry, the French government settled for an exploratory mission under the command of Sylvain Roux. Between August and December 1818 the mission visited the eastern littoral between Tamatave and Tintingue as well as the island of Sainte-Marie. Although differences of opinion were considerable (going even to the possibility of opening anew the old French outpost at Fort-Dauphin), it was finally decided that the ensuing mission should have its permanent seat at the Sainte-Marie island. With numerous delays, the mission reached Madagascar only in October 1821, right in the middle of the rainy season, the worst possible moment. As illness and death played havoc with the detachment as it landed at the Sainte-Marie island, nothing of importance could be undertaken and the mission was reduced into insignificance requiring no elaboration.

In the meantime, his vacation over, Farquhar had returned to Mauritius (in July 1820) and applied himself fully to efforts that would lead to a renewal of relations with Radama I. Farquhar had no illusions about the very real difficulties of this enterprise and he sent —not without some apprehension— his agent Hastie again to Madagascar to have Radama re-confirm the treaty of 23 October 1817 which had been ratified in its original form by England's king. The assignment strained the circumstances and Hastie had to have courage to pursue it since he learned at Tamatave of an existing and solemn promise by Radama that he would cut-off the head of any Englishman who came to see him. Staking everything on the personal friendship extended him by the King of Imerina, Hastie announced his visit and promptly went into the interior. His reasoning proved correct. At half-point of the journey, Hastie received a letter from Radama urging him to hurry and expressing the monarch's joy of seeing Hastie again. Indeed, upon his arrival in Antananarivo, Hastie was the guest of honor at an imposing reception and he presented to an enchanted Radama the gifts sent him by Sir Robert.

When Hastie began, however, to act on his mission things were not going as well as he had hoped. Radama complained to him about the unilateral abrogation of the treaty by the English (using the term "duplicity") and he let Hastie know that there was no question of renewing the 1817 treaty as his people, he said, would never accept it. Hastie came-up with a rather able answer: the temporary non-observance of the treaty had been due to an interim official, the treaty was now ratified by the King of England, and the treaty as such could no longer be violated by an English official. He expressed surprise moreover that a ruler as powerful as Radama I could not impose his will on the people and he reiterated the benefits Radama would derive from the alliance — school teachers, artisans, military instructors and the like. He also assured Radama that Great Britain and other European powers were determined to suppress slave trade, whether Radama wished it or not, and had the means to make this measure work. Thus, in proposing the "Equivalence," the British were making him a real gift, one that would not be forthcoming if force was to be used in accomplishing what they had already decided to do. As a group, the related arguments which Hastie developed, appeared decidedly convincing and Radama's support for them came despite the opposition of his own advisers. To either minimize this opposition or, more likely, to obtain something this perceptive ruler saw as an advantage, Radama asked for an additional article through which the English would undertake, from start to finish, the education of 20 Malagasy youngsters,* ten of whom were to go to England and the other ten to Mauritius. Although he did not have the authority, Hastie accepted without hesitation this new clause and the treaty was confirmed on 11 October 1820.[4]

This is an extremely important date in local history since through the treaty-renewal Radama really entered Madagascar into the international life of nations and, what is even more important, he was about to start receiving the aid needed to undertake the great reforms he had in mind and to introduce into Madagascar the instruments of modernization.

From the very beginning of his reign in 1810 Radama was preoccupied with ways through which he could —to the extent possible in each case— bring an entire serie of improvements to Imerina. Radama had kept, since 1817, a non-commissioned officer from Lesage's party, Sergeant Brady, whom he elevated subsequently to the highest Merina military ranks and to whom he had entrusted the task of instructing the royal army in European military methods. Around 1819, Radama also welcomed to Antananarivo another, this time French non-commissioned officer named Robin, deserter from Reunion, whom he employed as his secretary while covering him with honors. But, this import from outside —as much in men as in physical means— did not become really systematic and on an organized scale until after 11 October 1820, when its consequences began to came out at several levels.

Keen to attain military glories** and fully aware of what the possession of an army trained in and organized along European ways could do to enhance his power and to accomplish his plans for internal conquests, Radama concentrated first in this direction. Until then, the Merina army —and the same could be said of those in the Sakalava and Betsimisaraka areas— presented the aspect of a mob composed of all the able-bodied men who had temporarily abandoned their normal occupations to engage in war. Such a system, known by virtually all the peoples at one time or another, was adequate for intergroup warfare demanding

*One of them was Raombana, the first modern historian in Madagascar, see below the essay by Simon Ayache, (Ed.).

**Since his youth and by express wishes of his father, Radama had been in the Merina armies and was recalled to Antanarivo just before 1810, (Ed.).

slight displacements of the armies. It was a system that Andrianam-poinimerina found sufficient to conquer Imerina in earlier years; but, the moment that the Merina looked beyond their own confines, the system proved to be rather imperfect and very quickly at that; it was, in fact, catastrophic. If we only stick to facts established beyond dispute, the simple military walk taken by Radama in June 1817 from Antananarivo to Tamatave with about 25,000 men all told cost some 10,000 dead (none from combat). In the campaigns against the Sakalava of Menabé (southwestern Madagascar) the Merina losses were as high. In the first Merina incursion into western Madagascar, (among the northern Sakalava), in 1815, one-third of the total personnel was lost, not through any deaths exacted by the enemy in combat but through sheer hunger; and the results were not better at all in 1820 and in 1821.[5]

It could not have been otherwise. The soldiers themselves, who constituted only a fraction of the total personnel, were not amenable to discipline; the rest was made up of a mass of non-combatants, carriers and others who followed the freemen (commoners) who alone could be subjected to the levy. In the absence of any intendatcy, the army was forced to live off the land a few days after leaving Imerina where its initial food supplies had been assured at departure. But, such portable supplies were rather quickly depleted and the expeditions would feed off cultivators in other lands, mostly by looting. This was, however, extremely difficult to do in western Madagascar, among the Sakalava, where the land was poorly cultivated and sparsely inhabited in peace time. In wartime, the Sakalava would always evacuate their people and practice a policy of scorched earth against the invaders. From it came very fast the cruel famine which used to decimate the Merina armies. During the expedition of 1815, matters were so bad and the rice* so scarce that a couple of its handfuls went for as much as 25 gold francs (5 piasters)! In 1821, the disaster was just as great as the mortality even went up through the eating excesses of the survivors that had reached their homes in Imerina.[6]

These failures — which taxed Radama's imagination and hurt cruelly his pride — made up the young monarch's mind to

---

*Rice is a Malagasy staple and when the traditional sign is made for food it consits of bundling the fingers of one hand as if it held rice and making motions toward the mouth, (Ed.).

initiate some fundamental reforms as soon as the means became available. With his source of supply in modern weaponry assured as of 1820, Radama concentrated on recruitment. Heeding the advice of Hastie and Brady — who patterned themselves on the British model composed at the time of volunteers serving for long periods of time and revolving around a hierarchy of ranks which constituted one of its mainstays — Radama began by creating a small military corps which was to become the model for his future army. "Lahidama,* thus created soldiers; there were 50 at the start, then 100, then 200, then 400, then 1000, and they were all rich."[7] In point of fact, initial recruits did come from among the wealthy segments in Imerina. The military service thus conceived entailed lasting obligations without provisions for even the slightest indemnification (in accordance with the Merina corvée system or *Fanompoana*) and it followed that only those who could live off the labor of their own slaves could afford to enter into it; equally, there was no remuneration for the military obligations, except when there was booty to be divided. Since Radama knew that the obligations were extremely heavy he sought to offset some of the burden by conferring prestige on his new soldiers. The uniform, red tunics, epées and braids were all slated to contribute substantially to it. As Radama had said himself to the Merina when signing the treaty: "they will not only bring us rifles and cannons, but also all the pretty novelties, the red garments they had shown us, and black ones, too, the braids, the imposing sabres that are worn in such a portly manner in Europe, and I say to you o my people, this will beautify our own land."[8]

The other important military innovation was the division of soldiers into different ranks with the institution of "Honors" or "*Voninahitra*" terms with the root-meaning of "flower of grass." A paragon of logic and simplicity the system pointed to distinction and honor as the essential features of all future combatants. "The simple soldier was the 1st Honor and this entitled him to the respect of civilian population whom he could also subject to his privilege of requisition and to the corvée. The general or principal commander of a thousand men had ten Honors while the other eight intermediary ranks separated the general from the simple soldier. The 9th Honor was the lieutenant (in the sense of deputy-

---

Lahidama, more commonly used in Imerina than Radama, (Ed.).

officer, Ed.) of the 10th, the 8th the lieutenant of the 9th and so on until the 6th Honor, equivalent to the captain who commanded a hundred men. Then came the (actual) lieutenant with 5 Honors, two sergeants with 4 and 3 Honors, and the corporal with 2 Honors." While an imitation of European ranks is evident there was also an original feature, namely the replacement of a complex and possibly confusing terminology with one that was immediately accessible to the Merina at large at the time. This system, which survives today in a somewhat deformed state, used to have great elasticity. If, as it would seem, it was put into operation when the regular army had 1,000 men, it was easily adaptable to larger units through the additional Honors, that came somewhat later, all the way up to the 16th.

Acting with much wisdom, Radama started out with a small unit of 400 and later 1,000 men, closely matching the numbers of men with the means he had on hand at the moment; and, for a few years, the new recruitment system co-existed with the old one. In 1821, during the Menabe campaign which involved some 70,000, only 1,000 men came from the new army; but, in 1823, their number went up to 6,000 and 1,000 of these were artillerymen manning 14 pieces of ordnance. The reform was completed in 1824. The army, which now merited the name, had 14,210 men subdivided into 600 artillerymen, 600 engineer sappers, and six infantry brigades of 2,160 men each having four battalions.[10] The progress to-date was quite visible. The army marched behind its scouts, whose numbers went up and down according to circumstances; it had its intendantcy now and it followed principles of military art in its manoeuvres. Above all, the army discipline was severe. Soldiers were forbidden to pick-up anything in an occupied area without authorization from the commanders and any desertion in face of an enemy or any flight in combat was punishable by burning at the stake.

This was the instrument that Radama had fashioned. It would now permit him to implement his ambitious policy of territorial expansion and hence to attempt to bring all of Madagascar under his domination.

The eastern coast of Madagascar had been reached in 1817 and the port of Tamatave had submitted to the Merina since the Radama-Jean René treaty. This early result had opened a route to the sea for what the highlands could produce for export. It was in full commercial use in 1822, time when the Merina suzerainty was being threatened at some points by the French expedition sent to the Sainte-Marie island under Sylvain Roux. Through the combination of British advice and his own initiative Radama declared, on 13 April 1822, as void any concession of Malagasy territory that he had not personally ratified; this was directed mainly, as a response, at some underhanded French activities in the areas of Tintingue and Pointe à Larrée.* At the same time, 3,000 soldiers commanded by General Rafaralahy-Andriantiana and guided by Hastie were dispatched to Foulpointe, something of a gathering point for the French, as much to establish an agricultural enterprise as to occupy a region contested and claimed by the French. The French, small in number, had to incline themselves before the force and renounce any lasting residence on the Great Island.

A year later, in May 1823, Radama took a large number of men into eastern Madagascar to extend his influence and station more of his soldiers along a growing number of posts on the eastern littoral. Coming from the interior route, he sent a part of the army under Prince Ratefy toward th Bay of Antongil while he went toward Ivondro with Hastie and from there he reached Tamatave amid a huge deployment of forces. He then went to Foulpointe to meet an awaiting British frigate. As the coastal regions claimed by the French were being occupied on his orders and while his army progressed on foot toward Antongil without encountering serious resistance, Radama went by sea —the first sea voyage for a reigning monarch of Imerina— to the meeting-point at Maroantsetra; from there he went all the way north to Vohemar and subjected it to his authority. On his way back to Antananarivo Radama went through the lands of the Tsimihety, where he left a post at Mandritsara, and then entered the Sihanaka province (situated around the great lake Alaotra) where his conquest drive encountered the first serious opposition on the western side of the lake; but, an assault against the islet of Anosimboahangy, refuge of the Sihanaka who would not surrender, gave him the needed victory. While Radama was conquering the northern-central interior, Jean René and Prince Ratefy took an expeditionary force into the southernmost reaches of Betsimisaraka coast, all

*Tintingue, Pointe à Larrée were in northern Betsimisaraka-land, above the northern tip of the island of Sainte-Marie (its Malagasy name had been Nosy Ibrahim), (Ed.).

the way to Mananjary. Lastly, in 1825, the Merina took Fort-Dauphin (the eastern Madagascar's southernmost tip) although it was occupied by a small French garrison. Thus, the Merina were in control, as of 1825, of the entire eastern littoral with the exception of its extreme north (around Diego-Suarez). This rapid conquest, which at times involved nothing more than the passage of troops, is in sharp contrast to the stubborn resistance of the Sakalava of western Madagascar.

As mentioned earlier in the text, Radama had organized expeditions into Menabé (the southern Sakalava Kingdom) almost at the beginning of his monarchy, enterprise which ended in costly, blood-letting failures. The need to break away from similar defeats —and also the desire to crush the Sakalava power which had for a long time humiliated the Merina monarchy and which now stood as the sole obstacle to Radama's control over Madagascar— made Radama persevere in his plans. In truth, despite repeated invasions in 1815, 1820, 1821 and 1822, the Merina army could not defeat Ramitraho, the King of Menabé. The Sakalava tactics of avoiding mass combat, of burning everything as they retreated, of falling upon the Merina soldiers in an irregular way thanks to their thorough knowledge of the terrain, account for a great deal in this half-failure experienced by Radama in his policy against Menabé. One should also add here the valor of Sakalava warriors and the relative solidity of Sakalava belief in the sacral quality of their Maroserana dynasty* made it easy for Ramitraho to preserve his prestige as well as enjoy the real support of his people. In turn, the unyielding nature of the southern Sakalava opposition forced Radama to improvise. Instead of seeking victory through war he tried diplomacy and married Ramitraho's daughter Rasalimo. He could thus have at least the benevolent neutrality of his father-in-law which was sufficient to stop any further incursions of the Sakalava into the lands of the Merina; and he also gained a group of relay stations (consisting of solidly fortified posts) which gave him access to the Mozambique Channel by way of Morondava, a valuable port. Nonetheless, the situation of Merina soldiers stationed in Menabé remained always precarious, the concessions accepted by Ramitraho were constantly questioned and because Radama could not undertake any major military campaigns in Menabé, as his attention was elsewhere at the time,

*On this point, see the editor's essay above.

he had to send on several occasions, in 1824, 1826 and 1827, strong detachments just to negotiate with his father-in-law and persuade him not to come out openly against Radama.

However, Radama was more fortunate in Iboina, land of the northern Sakalava. The last great monarch of the Boina-Sakalava, Queen Ravahiny, was succeeded by her nephew Tsimalona who died in June 1822, leaving the throne to his brother Tsolovola, man of slight wisdom for the affairs of state. Having converted to Islam and assuming the name of Andriantsoli, he favored openly his new coreligionists, both Antalaotra and Arab,* thus alienating the traditional Sakalava chiefs and depriving himself of the potentially most faithful supporters. For these reasons, Radama's campaign against Boina in June 1824 resulted in an almost painless conquest and Andriantsoli, abandoned by everyone, had to accept a protectorate which placed Iboina, now divided into four provinces, under Merina domination. Yet, this was an illusory success for Andriantsoli did not bow to Merina control with good will by any stretch of imagination. Accustomed to have his way on the most trivial matters among his retinue he could hardly stand the control over all of his acts exercised by the Merina Prince Ramanetaka who had remained in Boina as Governor of Majunga. Moreover, Merina soldiers posted in the conquered territory began to forget the harsh discipline that had been instilled in them and started to oppress its inhabitants in all sorts of ways. The Sakalava, who in this case did not make the effort to defend their liberty and did not wish to as a result of distrusting their new king now turned to Andriantsoli, inciting him to take up the struggle. Here, Andriantsoli did show some wisdom as he refused to act immediately in order to firm the discontent up by allowing an accumulation of grievances and of hatered toward the invader. He did not emerge from his cautious wait until after an unnecessary act of violence against him by Ramanetaka. Encouraged by emissaries from King Ramitraho who promised a simultaneous rebellion against the Merina in Menabe, Andriantsoli decided, on 1st May 1825, to order the northern Sakalava revolt; and, as Radama's garrisons in Boina became hard-pressed, he was forced to send at once some strong reinforcements and extricate an encircled Governor Ramanetaka from Majunga. The military

---

*The Antalaotra were Malagasy Muslims in Boina while the term "Arab/Arabo" designated Muslims who were not Malagasy but who came to trade, especially at Majunga, at this time the major port of western Madagascar, (Ed.).

action went this time according to the book and the troops sent
from Antananarivo to Majunga were able to implement the junc-
tion with Ramanateka's garrison, which had broken out of
Majunga on its own. There was a bloody battle under the ramparts
of Majunga and it ended in a Sakalava rout. Andriantsoli, who
observed the fight from far away, escaped into the northern
regions, chased by Merina troops and, just about abandoned
by the Sakalava, he took refuge at the far-northern town of
Anorontsangana in the hope that he could gain time and come
to control his warriors again. This hope was in vain since Radama
had decided to end with Andriantsoli and he was sending troops
by land and sea to capture the exiled king. Finally, on 15th May,
Andriantsoli fled to the Comoro Islands. Apart from a few rather
limited attempts at restoration, this was for all intents the end
of the Boina Kingdom.[11]

Within a few years thus Radama was able to neutralize politically
the Sakalava power, if not crush it completely given that the
Kingdom of Menabé remained largely independent. This was an
event of extreme importance in the history of Madagascar and
one of the main stages in Madagascar's road toward national
unity. It was a result obtained thanks to the resolve of Radama
and to the modernization of his army. Yet, it was also one
secured in large measure because of an unbelievable inertia among
the Sakalava princes who neither knew how nor seemed to wish
—except for a brief and timid moment in 1825— to unite against
the Merina Kingdom. This allowed Radama to subdue them one
after another when they could have taken advantage of the fact
that he was unable to disperse his army and attack on every
front at the same time. It would have been indeed most difficult
to fight simultaneously in Menabé and Boina and all the more
so since at that point the other regions Radama had conquered
would have arisen against him in their turn.

Whatever the circumstances, Radama continued brilliantly the
conquests of his father Andrianampoinimerina and, during a
relatively brief reign, managed to bring under Merina control and
domination a large part of Madagascar, some three-fifths of its
landmass. Only the areas of south, southwest, center-south and
the extreme north were still independent.* As great as it was at

---

*The areas correspond respectively to those occupied by the Antandroy, Maha-
faly, Menabé-Sakalava, Bara, Tanala and Antankarana (extreme north), (Ed.).

the military level the work of Radama has, still, some aspects that are even more important and which left a strong imprint on the future of Madagascar.

II

Going beyond the military domain, Radama had hoped to find in his alliance with the English a way to push his land into modernization in the manner of Europe. He had been strongly impressed in his youth by the accounts of traders visiting Antananrivo relating to the wealth and prosperity of Europe; and he had been enchanted with the novelty of objects the traders carried with them as well as of the gifts sent him in 1816-1817 by the governor of Mauritius. This was the prelude to the young monarch's decision to have his land benefit from every conceivable advantage to follow in the wake of newly-introduced learning and techniques. In this area his hope was not disappointed and he found, as much in James Hastie as in the English missionaries who came after the military instructors, men who would aid him in the undertaking.

One of the major events that marked the reign of Radama was the arrival in Antananarivo, in October 1820, of the first representative of the *London Missionary Society* (LMS), Reverend David Jones, soon joined by the Reverends Griffiths, Jeffreys, Johns and Freeman. What they would come to achieve, with the total support of Radama, would form the basis —as much in the immediate sense as in the distant consequences— of the most fundamental transformation known to Madagascar. It should be pointed out at once that Radama did not even consider that missionaries might have a religious role in his land. Radama was a complete agnostic, a rather rare occurance among the Malagasy of his time, quite detached from all the beliefs and superstitions flourishing around him, something he used to laugh at occasionally. He never felt any need to introduce Christianity among his people. The missionaries whom he wanted to have around were to be the ecucators and teachers and nothing beyond that. Again, it is worth noting that they accepted the "game" (with some mental reservations to be sure) and that they devoted themselves to the secular tasks with a success that does them honor.

The difficulties encountered at the very beginning were quite enormous. The first —and hardly the least— was the need the missionaries had to learn the Malagasy language. Until then, this language had never been codified or even written in Latin characters posing thus the problem of fundamental but complex importance, namely the concordance of letters with the sounds. Jones, joined by Griffiths and Jeffreys was passionately involved with the problem, helped also by James Hastie and by the Frenchman Robin, the personal secretary of Radama I. Matters were, however, not evolving by themselves. Being of diverse origins (Jones was Welsh, Jeffreys was English), the missionaries and those who worked with them started to defend phonetic concepts at times quite contradictory and there were clashes and disagreements which —from a distance— could seem to have been "a storm in a teacup." It got to be so bad that Radama, apparently on Hastie's urging, decided in March 1824 to cut the discussion short himself by decreeing with wisdom that each letter was to have forever the same sound and that the consonants will be English and the vowels French. This phonetic system, with us still today, lent itself to a particularly fortunate use, thanks to its simplicity, and it must be admitted that the Malagasy school children have in it a considerable advantage over their little French or English classmates.

Even before the phonetic problem had been resolved, the missionaries were trying, well and badly, to acquire an oral knowledge of Malagasy as great as possible, collecting in an imperfect script the words with which to form lists, dialogues and short phrases. They had already attained very rapidly a strong knowledge of the Merina dialect; Jones and Griffiths were capable in February 1824, to preach in it; while a few weeks later, in April, they felt sufficiently advanced in their linguistic studies to undertake what would become their major work: translation of the Bible. "We are about to translate the Genesis, the Exodus, the Gospels according to Matthew and Luke, and we hope that the four Books will be ready before the end of the year."[12] In something that must have taken an admirable amount of labor, the translation of the Book of Books was almost complete in March 1828 and the problem of its printing was on the verge of solution at this time.

In the event of a future evangelism it was important to ensure ahead of time the Bible's diffusion. Although this was strictly a physical problem it created enormous difficulties for the missionaries who managed to surmount it with their characteristic tenacity, thanks to the Bible Society of London which provided 150 reams of paper and to the LMS which sent a printing press and its printer Hovenden who had previously worked for the Bible Society at Saint-Petersburg. Hovenden arrived in Antananarivo with his precious materials on 20 November 1826 but, as fate would have it, he died of fever a few weeks later (15 December). What was most fortunate, another artisan, Cameron, who found in Hovenden's luggage a printing manual, was able to feel his way through, set-up the press and become familiar with its operation. On 4 December 1827, he printed a few single-page copies of the Ten Commandments, posters that marked the birth of Malagasy printing art.[13] By the end of 1828 some 1,500 copies of the Gospels according to Saint Luke were available. By June 1830, at the latest, the entire New Testament had been printed in 3,000 copies. The establishment of a printing press was an event of great importance and it also was a response to a pressing need.

From the moment he came to Antananarivo and with direct encouragement from Radama, Jones concentrated on starting the local schools. The first to open (8 December 1820) had very modest beginnings since it only had three pupils on the day of opening; this number went up rapidly, however, and soon the school area, close to the Palace of Andafiavaratra, became too small. Radama then gave Jones a new building and to show his subjects in public that he was concerned with the undertaking he came to the inauguration of the school with members of his family. When Griffiths arrived in Antananarivo at the end of March 1821, the school and twenty-two pupils, with girls accounting for about a third of the total. As one learns from Ellis,[14] the "pupils had been selecting from among the family of the King and his favorites and among children of the nobility. In particular, there was Rakotobe, son of Prince Ratefy, and four young princesses." Some of them could read passages of the Bible and had made considerable progress in other subjects they were taught. Radama, who sometimes came to hear the children sing, wanted this school to be known as the Royal School.

Griffiths' own arrival led to the opening of a new school, reserved this time for children of the commoners. As for the missionary wives they taught mainly a class of girls which had a clearly feminine character, with sewing and embroidering. The annual exam at the two schools of Jones and Griffiths, on 17

June 1822, led also to an impressive ceremony that Radama did not wish to miss. The eighty-five pupils responded with clarity and precision to the questions posed and this delighted the King who publicly expressed his thanks to the missionaries for the progress attained by their pupils.

Undoubtedly, all of this may seem modest to us today, yet it diminishes none of the work's real importance, against the early difficulties that one can recall, both physical and psychological. Missionary schools were suspect among the people who saw in them creations of foreign provenance where children were taught a religion that was not the ancestral one. People were afraid to send their children to missionary foreigners they feared as much as they did the slave traders, foreigners they even suspected of cannibalism. There was yet another snag not to be eliminated until the end of the Merina monarchy itself: going to school was considered by his subjects and by Radama as a form of service to the state. The ruler saw an opportunity to develop state officials whom he could use later without pay by virtue of the traditional *fanompoana* (corvée); and the parents sought to avoid sending their progeny to school by resorting to excuses and subterfuges. There was even a case of hiding children in covered rice-trenches where some of them died of suffocation. Parents would also get around the difficulty by purchasing little slaves and by sending them to school in the place of their own sons and daughters; acts that would subsequently lead to a ban on teaching such subjects as reading and writing to the servile part of Imerina's population. It is not to be doubted that only the authority of Radama I and, after 1828, of Ranavalona I assured the presence of a good number of pupils. On this subject, Ellis has preserved a passage of a speech Radama had made to a group of chiefs who would not entrust their children to European teachers: "if you hope to become wise and to be happy and to please me, send your children to schools and let them learn because good pupils, who work hard and who behave, will be honored by me."[15]

With Radama's help, the missionary activities bore fruit with considerable speed. If in 1823 there was only a moderate growth this was no longer true of 1824, year of the pivotal point in scholastic policy. In Antananarivo itself, which had three schools attended by 268 pupils, a fusion of the schools took place to create a Royal College which would train *Malagasy* instructors who would, in turn, help the missionaries to diffuse education into the countryside. At the same time, the best pupils in Antananarivo were sent out around the capital to set-up rural shcools and the "results of this attempt," noted Griffiths in September 1824, "are even more gratifying than we would have dared hope, thanks to the pedagogical aptitudes of these improvised teachers whose zeal to learn and to teach others only needs to be tapped to guarantee the future." At the end of 1824, thanks to the new system, some two thousand children were enrolled in schools and one could foresee already a rapid growth in education which would involve directly both the Malagasy and the Europeans.[16]

To give this collaboration a concrete form, a Missionary-school Society was established in November 1824. Its mission was to encourage the construction of schoolgrounds in all of the principal villages of Imerina and to find the necessary funds. Noting that "the children's education costs are often too heavy to be supported by the inhabitants at large, who are thus forced to keep them home, the Society called upon the generosity of the Christian world to secure aid, private and public, that would remunerate the Malagasy instructors sent among their compatriots to carry out the mission with which they are entrusted and to buy clothing for the children who could not dress properly to go to school."[17] This appeal obtained a wide response: Radama, his ministers and his officers, the Governor of Mauritius, and the *London Missionary Society*, lastly, contributed generously. But, inspite of all, and precisely because of the growth it was undergoing, this enterprise remained always in the red.

In a report prepared at the end of 1827, Jones, in making the balance-sheet point, estimated that about 4,000 inhabitants of Imerina could read and write in the place of 6 that he had found upon his arrival. In July 1828, at Radama's death, there were in Imerina 38 schools with 2,309 pupils enrolled, and 42 teachers. Behind this was also a Radama who never tired in helping to the limits of his power, often paying personally for the magnificent work the missionaries were doing in education; and the results themselves reflected to a very large degree his own solicitude. It would seem nonetheless that his real preoccupations were far closer to a technical education than to one we could call "general." One of the points Radama had insisted upon to convince his subjects to accept the October 1820 Treaty with Great Britain was precisely that this alliance would bring to Madagascar artisans and workers who would carry out together a certain number of undertakings in material creations and who could pass on their skills to the young Malagasy apprentices. This clause of the Treaty was scrupulously adhered to by Sir Robert who did everything he could to induce artisans from Mauritius to go to Madagascar and to whom he accorded (apart from various types of immediate assistance) small pensions to allow them to be protected at the start of their installation in Madagascar. At least three artisans responsed to Farquhar's offers and they would gain an importance visible even today, especially in architecture.

The first of the three artisans to reach Imerina was a métis from Reunion named Carvaille who brought to Tananarive the ironmonger's art. Fine worker, to whom Radama gave many youngsters, he had done well (according to some) to teach them the physical side of the needed items but he kept to himself the models employed and some of his apprentices were forced to purchase the fabricated objects, dismantle them and flatten them in order to be able to attain their reproductions. However, this can be countered with the testimony of Hastie who contradicts such claims since he lets us know that a certain number of workers had been indeed initiated into the ironmonger's art through the lessons and models of Carvaille.[18]

There is another Frenchman who deserves to be mentioned, Mario, the first European who had taught the art of tailoring in Imerina. His pupils were mature men who did extremely well as the earliest tailored suits and frock coats exposed at Antananarivo were of their own making. They were also introduced to embroidery work. But the best known of artisans, also a Frenchman, the one whose influence was by far the more interesting and more durable, was Louis Gros, by trade a builder. Arriving on his own in 1819, he soon had trained his own carpenters, joiners and cabinet makers. Coppalle,* who visited Antananarivo in 1825 and who describes the workshops installed at Andohalo, was struck by the knowledge already acquired by his workers and noted on the occasion of his visit the various useful manual abilities of the young Merina.[19] But, what really gave Gros his

*André Coppalle was an artist from Mauritius who came to Antananarivo in 1825 to paint the now-famous portrait of Radama I, completed in 1826, (Ed.).

celebrity, was the construction in which another of his compatriots took part, the designer (Casimir) of the Soanierana Palace, south of Antananarivo, ordered by Radama I.* This building, the most imposing one ever seen in the area was regarded as a marvel of architecture and its influence was considerable. Constructed in wood (and let us remember that building in stone was not authoriz-ed in Antananarivo until 1867 for religious and spiritual reasons) it struck the imagination of the contemporaries by its unusual breadth of style and by its interesting arrangements. Long after the death of Radama I it was found that he would not allow access to it to those who did not know how to read and write, an aspect which —whether real or apocryphal— reveals the young monarch's penchant for a mixture of naive romanticism and moments of intolerance. This palace, commenced in 1824, con-sisted of a dwelling section, forming the main corpus, and flanked by two wings, surmounted by the first floor, itself sustained by pillars. It certainly transcended the type of A-frame dwelling that can still be seen in Andrianampoinimerina's home at Ambo-himanga.

Another construction, the *Tranovola*,** also developed by Gros was as influential as the Soanierana Palace. Both were encircled on the outside by the so-called *varangue* or verandas which came from the Mascarene Islands (and French India) and which ran the entire spans of their first floors. The *varangue* which Gros had brought over became a typical element of Malagasy architec-ture, implanted so deeply that some of our own contemporaries believe that it had always existed in Madagascar.

As valuable to Imerina's modernization as these individual roles were an even greater contribution in the domain of technical instruction came from the *LMS* artisans. It was the constant desire of Radama I —in October 1820, in demands made to Jones or sent in a letter to London— that the Mission to arrive in Madagascar under his protection must have "persons capable of teaching my people...in the various crafts, such as weaving, carpentry, etc..."[20] The request did not go unheeded and in June 1821 there arrived (together with Griffiths) four missionary artisans — a carpenter, smith, weaver and shoemaker-tanner. Welcomed by Radama

*A mile south of the capital, it was Radama's country palace, (Ed.).

**Or "Silver Palace," adjacent to the Palace of the Queen in Antananarivo and deriving its name from some silver ornaments nailed at angles of the facade, along the roof, (Ed.).

with honors due to important persons, they were immediately given the sites appropriate to individual endeavors and each one received his own domestic servant. In return, each artisan had to train eight young men selected most likely from among the free population since skilled labor was associated at the time with status of nobility. One of the four, a carpenter named Brooks, died soon thereafter of malarial fever, but the smith, named Chick, was thriving. With his workshop in the ward called Amparibe, he trained several hundred Malagasy in a variety of manufactures involving iron and other metals as well as in the construction of machinery. Chick's Malagasy associates started, in Antananarivo and in the village of Ilafy, their guild for smiths of all metals which would experience a soaring growth with Jean Laborde* as well as continue, under different forms, into our own time.

Rowland, the weaver, set-up his shop on top of a hill near Antananarivo, at Antsahadinta, ready to produce a variety of fabrics, but he ran into several difficulties, especially since weaving was only one aspect of the textile industry. He could not, for example, find a sufficient quantity of cotton thread to justify a major commitment of his labor to weaving and, instead, he began a school at Antsahadinta. For this reason, the *LMS* sent to Madagascar in 1826 a spinning machine along with its attendant Cummins who lost no time in passing on to several young Malagasy (selected by Radama) his art. He was also asked to develop locally the mulberry and the silk-worm. But, he, too, experienced such difficulties as inadequate quantities of cotton, lack of returns on his machine and the like, and he became quickly discouraged. After a brief attempt at the cultivation of hemp in an area east of Mount Angavo, he left Madagascar in 1828. Another reason for his failure to remain in Madagascar was the fact that the Malagasy had known the weaving art from antiquity and while their products mey have been less fine their prices were also far below those demanded by Cummins. As for the fourth *LMS* artisan, Canham, he had his own tannery and shoe factory at Fenoarivo, west of Antananarivo, where he also trained a good number of apprentices without doing too well

*One could say that large-scale modern industry, from the manufacture of cannon to soap, really began in Imerina with Jean Laborde (d.1878), the first Ranavalona's "universal engineer" and intimate friend, (Ed.).

financially since the wearing of shoes did not as yet become a widespread practice in Imerina.

It was, however, James Cameron, a Scott of 26 who came to Madagascar in 1826, who became the most important artisan of his time. Gifted with multiple talents and with a rare tenacity, he was able to overcome the many difficulties and to learn the techniques with which he was not initially familiar. He was a carpenter-joiner and he built a workshop in wood (in the ward of Ambatonakanga) that could house as many as 600 apprentices, it was said. He also attempted to introduce an important innovation, the wood-saw, since the method of getting planks from a tree by axe was extremely wasteful, allowing only one per tree-trunk. The result was rather disappointing since the new tool was not received with enthusiasm by his apprentices. Cameron was also well-versed in mechanics and it was he who set-up the spinning-machine for Cummins and sought afterwards to improve it by making some new pieces himself. As will be recalled, it was also Cameron who made the printing press work after the death of Hovenden and who kept it working thereafter. The activities of Cameron, who remained in Madagascar until 1835, extended also into such crafts as tannery, pottery, glassworks, soap manufacturing, the making of lime and of brick, which permitted —together with the *varangue* of Gros— the modification of architecture in Imerina. He did not go as far as to make gun-powder but it is undeniable that the contribution of Cameron to Imerina was only surpassed by Jean Laborde's, whose own work would leave a wide technological mark on the entire reign of Ranavalona I.

III

Considerable territorial expansion in the pursuit of deliberate unification of Madagascar under his royal authority, introduction and sustained support of multiple and highly influential innovations —writing, printing, modern techniques, regular army— such was the enormous achievement of a young ruler who left in just a few short years and indelible stamp on his country and committed its future. But, this attractive list of achievements contains shadows which require some circumspection if one is not to be simply dazzled by a success so brilliant in all appearance.

The conquered populations, as has been noted, had no power to eject the Merina troops from their territories. They bore, however, their loss of independence and a Pax Merina that could not be overturned only under duress. Hence, revolts were continuously fomented by chiefs who had not been removed from office after the conquests, chiefs ill at ease without being able to engage in the traditional way of wealth-redistribution through raiding that followed more or less regular patterns. It was this general state of insecurity that produced the never-ending military campaigns so costly in men and money, condition hardly favorable to the policy of developing Madagascar pursued by Radama I at the same time. Indeed, in the event of diluting his royal power by being spread out too thinly, Radama risked a general insurrection as well.

Radama did everything he could to improve the economy of Madagascar. After the loss of slave-trade income he set out to augment the export of Malagasy products, for example. He took a number of liberal measures in 1822 and in 1824: customs duties remained at fixed rate, anchorage fee was reduced, captains of commercial vessels were given a number of guarantees, etc.; and, to link the efforts, he went on to encourage the growth of production itself assisted undoubtedly by the peace he could maintain in some of the regions. Under the pressure of need and perhaps also with the advice of parties with vested interests, Radama annulled in 1827 most of the benefits that his earlier policy was yielding. He set the customs-duty rights at such a high rate that it made virtually impossible to sell Malagasy products for export.

Fundamentally an even more serious matter, Radama was an extremely advanced individual in comparison with most of his subjects and the innovations he had introduced and imposed could simply not avoid coming into sharp clash with the still-vital traditions, even within his own retinue. His scepticism in regard to the religion of Ancestors, his unconcealed disdain for the diviners and protector-dieties and the aid he gave —in consequence— to the Christian missionaries created deep discontent in Imerina but one that did not dare surface while he was still alive. To this should be added that Radama reigned, more or less, by leaning on the support of his close kin, like the Generals Ratefy, Rafaralahy and Ramanetaka, and on some major noble families of Imerina while neglecting and belittling the former advisers of his father Andrianampoinimerina, factor which led to some bitterness.

It is this conjunction of discontents that explains why the death of Radama I was followed by a reaction with consequences that would place a heavy burden on the future of Madagascar.

NOTES

1. An Indian Army officer who retired at the Ile de France around 1780, he spent the rest of his days in accumulating everything extant about Madagascar, from books in print to first-hand accounts of travellers and merchants. He sold his manuscript collection, and especially his *Grand Dictionnaire de Madagascar*, to Robert Farquhar. This collection is now at the British Museum, *Additional Manuscripts* nos. 18117 to 18129, *cf.* Jean Valette, *Catalogue du Fonds malgache du British Museum*, Tananarive, 1967 (pamplet of 56 pages in-Octavo).

2. G. Grandidier, *Histoire Politique de Merina*, Tome I, Paris, 1942, pp.163-164.

3. Text of the treaty of 23 October 1817 will be found in the *Bulletin de Madagascar*, no. 222 (November 1964), pp. 881-901.

4. On the question of the resumption of Anglo-Merina relations and on the confirmation of the treaty, *cf.* the *Journal* of David Jones in the *LMS Archives*, Madagascar, section 1A; Wm. Ellis, *History of Madagascar*, II, London, 1838, p. 223 *et sequitur*; and, Jean Valette, "Documents pour servir a l'histoire des relations entre la Grande-Bretagne et Madagascar sous Radama Ier," in *Revue de Madagascr*, no. 26(2nd quarter, 1964),pp. 39-50.

5. On the campaign of 1820, *cf.* G.S. Chapus, "Le journal d'une campagne de Radama Ier," *Bulletin de l'Académie Malgache*, new serie, XXII(1839),pp. 41-54; on the campaign of 1821, *cf.* Ellis, *History*, II, 1838, p. 255.

6. Same references.

7. G.S. Chapus, "Quatre-vingts années d'ifluences européennes en Imerina," *BAM*, n.s., VIII(1925), p. 88.

8. Chapus, "Quatre-vingts années," 1925, p. 89.

9. Chapus, "Quatre-vingts années," 1925, p. 89.

10. *Cf.* J. Hastie, "Journal," *BAM* n.s., IV(1918-1919), pp. 143-196.

11. *Cf.* J. Valette, *Etude sur le regne de Radama Ier*, pp. 61-69; his *Madagascar sous Radama Ier*, Tananarive, 1965, pp. 7-8; and Hastie (*cf.* note *supra*).

12. *Cf.* Ludvig Munthe, *Les origines des deux premières traductions du Nouveau Testament malgache* (thesis typescript, Sorbonne), pp. 112-114; see also W.E. Cousin's *Translation of the Malagasy Bible*, pamphlet, s.d., pp. 5 *et seq.*; and the letter, *Jones to Hankey*, 28 April 1824 (from which the citation) in the *LMS Archives* in Madagascar, Box 12, Folder 1, Jacket A).

13. Munthe, *Origines*, 112-114.

14. Ellis, *History*, II, 1838, 265-281.

15. Ellis, *History*, II, 1838, 322.

16. *Cf.* for 1822, J. Valette, "L'état de la scolarisation à Tananarive en 1822," *Bulletin de Madagascar*, no.285(february 1970), pp. 182-186; for 1824, *cf.* Coppalle, "Voyage dans l'intérieur de Madagascar," *BAM*, old serie, VII (1909), pp. 17-46 and VIII(1910), pp. 25-64 (but mainly VIII, pp. 44-46).

17. *Cf. Letters* (varia), Mauritius Archives, HB 4, pieces 72-74.

18. Chapus, "Quatre-vingts-années," 1925, p. 200.

19. *Cf.* Coppalle, "Voyage" (1825-6), 1909, pp. 17-46, and 1910, pp. 25-64.

20. Letter edited, in H.E. Clark, *Tantaran'ny Fiangonana eto Madagaskara hatramy ny niandohany ka hatramy ny taona 1887* (History of the Protestant Church in Madagascar from its origins to 1887), Tananarive, 1887, p. 22.

Beyond Oral Tradition
and into Written History:
The Work of Raombana (1809 - 1855)[*]

S. AYACHE[**]
University of Madagascar

In the privacy of his princely residence which clung to the sacred hillside housing the Manjakamiadana Palace an officer of the Merina Royal Court prepared, around 1850, a voluminous written history of his land. Its eight or nine thousand pages were filled with an elegant and refined "English script" which thus came to mark the very first internal literary and historical work of Madagascar. This was about a quarter of a century ahead of the better-known *Tantaran'ny Madagaskar* (History of Madagascar), penned by the Merina Governor of Tamatave (1885-1895) and Evangelical missionary Rainandriamampandry, as well as before the most widely-known *Tantaran'ny Andriana* (History of Kings) put together by the Jesuit Father Callet. Going beyond the oral traditions which Merina historians at the court of Queen Ranavalona I were accustomed to transcribe Raombana was composing a general history, impelled by an acute internal logic, to adhere to the canons of Western historiography. In so doing Raombana is the originator of the earliest "rationalistic and critical construct" of the national past, written in English but entirely Malagasy otherwise. Neither in its texture nor form, and even less in its spirit,

[*]CF. S. Ayache, *Raombana - l'Historien (1809-1855)*, Fianarantsoa, 1976, 509 pp. and its review by R. Kent in the *American Historical Review*, LXXXIII/4 (Oct. 1978), pp. 1069-1070. An elaboration of some ideas from the book will be found in my article devoted to the intellectual and moral culture of Raombana, "Un intellectuel malgache devant la culture europeene; l'historien Raombana," in *Archipel*, Etudes Interdisciplinaires sur le Monde Insulindien, no. 12, pp. 95-119. It is the intent of the present article to return more specifically to Raombana's historical work.

[**]Translated from French by R. Kent.

does his history have anything in common with recitations of
legends on which the collective Malagasy memory had been weaned.
In comparison with other Third-World cultures the Malagasy one
thus has, through Raombana, an exceptional endowment as
"peoples without writing" would have to await the school of the
colonial period, missionary or lay, to produce in their turn
similar works and enter with them into the "global play" which
has been, in this sector of the humanistic sciences, "for the most
part the West's play."[1] This does not mean at all that the Queen's
Secretary was, in his own time, a *deraciné*, an "alienated spirit."
Very far from ignoring the oral texts of his people, Raombana
studies them, subjects them to criticism, and integrates them into
the body of his work. Above all, however, in the course of his
duties, he explores an already vast repository of Malagasy
archives to which he has continuous access as personal Secretary
of the Queen.

As a Malagasy intellectual who was trained in methods of
Western science and who lived among the local potentates
without ignoring the other components of society, Raombana
secures a unique document for the history of Malagascar. He
confronts foreign texts with an authentic Malagasy source with
which to control and interpret them. He responds to a historiography wich is external and mainly colonialist in inspiration with
a work of history adhering to the same scientific principles but
through a Malagasy point of view. To the rather recently compiled
local traditions he adds an account recalling the earlier times, one
that gives context to other social milieux, like the high nobility,
and allows for a critical evaluation of the widely circulated commoner (Hova) texts. The task he had set forth is more than matched
by the richness of his work as Raombana goes into the customs
and mentalities, events and their causes, kings and peasants and
their everchanging relations. As a Malagasy who became a historian
Raombana has the fundamental merit of correcting at once the
optic of a purely European historical literature about Madagascar.
The "missionary" or colonialist writings about the past of the Great
Island suddenly found anew the modest place to which they were
entitled — the "lights" were no longer shining without the presence
of shadows and of miseries; a people about to be colonized was
not, after all, without a civilization; and, within the Nineteenth
century's global context, in the face of an all-powerful Europe,
the "Hova" (commoners) who became royalty lacked neither

some of the power nor yet some of the prestige.

The man to whom Madagascar owes its first native historical *tableau* came from a family of Imerina's earliest monarchs —the most legitimate ones— since Raombana was a direct descendant of King Andriamasinavalona (d. ±1710). Raombana had a happy childhood in a household presided over by his father at the noble domain of Anosimiarinimerina, near Ilafy. His father had been a companion-in-arms of King Radama I (1810-1828), one of his "bravest officers," while Raombana's upright mother must have been the "finest woman of Madagascar." It may well be that Raombana played with the poorer children at his parental estates, running after cattle or encircling the village butchers with a swarm of *mpanomy-kena.*[2] It was King Radama I, of whom Raombana has a precise recollection, who not only accepted the future historian at his royal table but who also selected him and his twin-brother Rahaniraka, in 1820, along with seven other companions, to "go study in Europe." Raombana would remain eight years in Great Britain in care of the London Missionary Society (LMS) and under the patronage of the celebrated anti-slavery leader Wilberforce. He received the elementary education in London from 1821 to 1823 in the classrooms of the British and Foreign School Society. Manchester was the site of Raombana's secondary education between 1824 and 1828 at the "Academy" founded by W. Roby, pedagogue of considerable reputation. To be sure, Raombana excelled in history but he was equally strong in philosophy and in religious studies. He returned to Tananarive in 1829. A few years later, as Officer of the Royal Palace, he became private Secretary of Queen Ranavalona I. His own family became quite large (the English missionaries had not been able to convince him that polygamy was immoral) and he led the rather comfortable life of a cultivated high official in a home decorated in the European fashion.

His life did not remain undisturbed for long either in the moral or temporal sense. If the uncomplicated and pleasing family duties were easy to cope with the situation at the Palace went into a completely different direction. Raombana was made an active participant in all the affairs of the Merina Kingdom and even had to lead, with its other commanders, the armies into war. He was the main commander of Merina forces in Southwestern Madagascar in 1863 and he returned home from Vangaindrano distressed by the cruelties of struggle between the Merina and provincial Malagasy whom he also perceived as compatriots and all the more so because of his stay abroad. In moments of even greater distress Raombana witnessed the martyrdom of Merina Christians whose convictions he shared even while submitting to the wishes of his Queen. The first history of Madagascar to be written from within the land was thus born in the troubled conscience of a man who considered himself at the same time a heir of the "Great Lords of Anosy," disciple of English missionaries, and servant of Ranavalona I. Raombana's royal descent and his patriotism gave him a deep sense of national unity centered around the government in Tananarive. Through his British teachers he had acquired the tools needed —a language and a doctrine— to chart for his land a new type of history. Moreover, spiritual distress in the face of increasingly narrow traditionalist policies imposed, in his view, the urgency of a liberating action. It is hence the aim of his work to prevent tyranny from turning the future of Madagascar into the caricature of itself; and, under the gaze of the outside world, his worry turned into shame. It is certain that Raombana had no illusions about the would-be "virtues" of foreigners whom he accused of introducing into Madagascar a thousand plagues; but he also knew that Madagascar's own reputation would necessarily have to be assessed by the best among them. His work is thus addressed first, to them. The work of history reassures and avenges him; it exorcises all the demons of blame and still more of contempt stemming from abroad. Without resorting to lies Raombana condemns with a Malagasy pen everything that could tarnish the dignity of his land, and he is the first one to do so. This sense of dignity, born and nurtured within his own life, is also an argument, a gesture of personal and national defense against a tyranny of the moment as well as against a false assessment of the future; and, fortunately, his history of Madagascar remains authentic because the process it selects is that of truth itself.[3]

Raombana thus perceived his task as one of allowing his land to be known and appreciated by the foreigners, just as he had learned to appreciate and love England. It is for this uppermost reason that he selected the English language as wehicle for his written work. A preface written to it around 1862 (and which remained secret along with the work for a long time) by Rahaniraka confirms this wish of Raombana: "the book contains many things worthy of being read — it narrates the history of Madagascar, its customs and beliefs...I hope that readers will be indulgent and not critical of it; this is a book written by a Malagasy who had lived but seven years only in England..."[4] We are, however, not dealing with a scholarly exercise meant to be read by former teachers alone. Raombana is as concerned about his future Malagasy readers and he bets in favor of an English culture called upon to cross-fertilize, as Radama I had desired it, the Merina thought; it is to be an evolution of Malagasy concepts regarding history and time-perspective. His adoption of English is spontaneous as an instrument of his personal culture. He did not foresee any difficulties of principle regarding the translation into English of the views and sentiments of a Malagasy historian and he wanted to create a "modern" history as an occasion for re-thinking the traditional culture and for entering into an exchange of knowledge with Europe. Indeed it seemed quite difficult to him to bring such a project to fruition in his maternal tongue. As a novel intellectual enterprise, the work he undertook also called for a mode of expression appropriate to it. Raombana still did not and could not come to believe in the *literary* dignity of a language like Malagasy, which started to be written-down only in recent times, even structured and codified by foreign missionaries. Far from being contemptous, however, of the huge amount of labor attained by the English reverends Raombana offers them eulogies but only because of their aim, namely the translation of Holy Scriptures.[5] The Malagasy language employed by the missionaries was only a humble instrument of this work of translation, a Malagasy of the primary school for catechism, psalms, Sunday prayers.[6]

The choice of English in his work sets Raombana clearly apart in the cultural history of Madagascar and gives him an exceptional place; all by himself, Raombana constitutes a literary current that would not appear anew until our own century when it would flourish, in the colonial period and under entirely new conditions, as Malagasy literature in French. Nor did Raombana forget about the other extant literary and non-literary currents, taking note of and compiling this legacy as well. From its inception, the civilization of Madagascar was an oral one. As much in Imerina as on the coast of Madagascar, the power of the oral text, on the decline since written literature came into its own thanks to the work of missionary linguists,[7] has not disappeared even today; and it stands to reason that it was quite lively in the Nineteenth century. Its historical treasures were harvested by Raombana[8] as is underscored by Rahaniraka's *Preface* for "this book contains also the beautiful passages on the history of ancient monarchs." This traditional current would reiterate its vitality and attain its greatest unfolding with the classis work of Father Callet. On the other hand, within the "traditional" civilization, the writing itself had been hardly absent altogether; it already had a place thanks to the *Sora-bé*, the Arabico-Malagasy manuscripts which represent the religious, Islamic antecedents that had not had the time to evolve into the profane literature, as a "lay" endeavor. The more cultivated segments of society both in the Southeast and in Imerina had undoubtedly assimilated this literary aspect into the Malagasy culture as well; and this had nothing to do with the simply transcribed oral texts. The language of the *Sora-bé* had served nonetheless the purpose of supporting history (at times elaborately) and of fostering especially commercial and diplomatic exchanges with the exterior. Indeed, around 1820, the Arabico-Malagasy writing knew a usage far more widespread than the English missionaries could assess in the beginning of their own presence in Madagascar. Between the world of strictly oral texts and one of vested-purpose writing, such as the missionaries had conceived it, the *Sora-bé*, either sceptical of an oral culture or frankly hostile to it, established a rich transition through their double character, sacred and profane, of oral style and rationalized thought; a transition which established itself without coming into a collision to pave the way (itself extremely slow-going) toward a written civilization marked by European influence.[9]

Through their work on the Malagasy language, to which they were inexorably drawn by their own missionary teachings (*leçons de Bogue* in the LMS Academies) the English reverends inaugurated in Madagascar a third cultural current in which writing is king. But, their monumental effort, so highly praised by Raombana, would not give birth until 1861 and more solidly until the end of the 1800's to a really new scribal culture. By the time they were forced to leave Madagascar in 1835, amid the general persecution of Christians, the missionaries had already translated and printed the Bible in Malagasy, their great Anglo-Malagasy and Malagasy-English dictionary was accomplished, and they had elaborated the grammar having submitted —as L. Munthe has stressed— the Merina dialect to the first scientific treatment. With all this they had sunk the foundation for a pervasive evolution but one in need of considerable time in which to produce its lasting intellectual and psychological effects. The reading of and reflection upon the Holy Scriptures should have, at least in the missionary eyes, not only converted the Malagasy to the Christian religion; they were also to be helped to transcend a stage of "primitive thought" to which they had been condemned for a long time by the lasting categories of Malagasy oral texts. The missionaries were able to succeed within a small elite, urban and rural, peasant and aristocratic; but, they succeeded in conversions to Chiristianity, not in any passage of one language into another. In fact, their absence from Madagascar (1835-1861), even more the closing of their schools, led to the adoption of Christianity among the Merina but within the mold of the old language, not the new one. Undoubtedly, Bible-reading would continue in secret, hymns written before 1835 would continue to be chanted, translations of the Gospels or the Old Testament would continue to be cited. Only, all of the clandestine preachings could be done in the ordinary, every-day language, as Christians gathered in the fields or in the houses of worship that managed to subsist. The language of the oral tradition, enriched with Biblical sayings, remained the instrument of direct communication between the Christian preacher and the children of God. This must have been true even before 1835, we are convinced, from the moment the English missionaries allowed the Malagasy Evangelists to preach as well. Raombana's own testimony on this point is, for us, a decisive factor.[10] The "pure" Christian religion found that it could accomodate itself extremely well with the oratorical talents that the Merina culture had fostered both spontaneously and traditionally.

The new ways of thinking acquired by the historian in England, through the disciplined use of English, strenghtened the vehicle itself not only in religious instruction but also as one bringing to Raombana all sorts of knowledge that excited his intellectual curiosity. It was through the English language that Raombana left behind at the same time the oral culture of his land and the narrowly religious culture of the missionary writings. Without reservations he was preparing a deliberate work of history in the secular mold and even his written language has scientific pretensions. From the oral traditions he extracted such knowledge as seemed important to him, divorcing it entirely from an incantatory matrix. Raombana imposed his own style on everything taken out of the books he could read and from the archives he could consult daily, for both the ideas to be considered and for the substance of events. He also adopted from the Biblical texts in English or Malagasy some of the images, formulas and rhythmical forms which went into expressions of his sentiments and beliefs but which did not determine them. One should not confuse the categories of reason and of conviction (or ideology), especially after some hundred years of "Enlightenment," and Raombana's adherence to the Western Christian morality hardly impeded him from perceiving the oldest and most profound Malagasy realities. His language, in the manner of the Eighteenth-century philosophers (whom Raombana knew well), is an instrument of knowledge for all contingent realities. His openly rationalistic thought virtually upheld Queen Ranavalona's desire to see the teaching of English severed from the Christian religion to become a language placed strictly at the disposal of her diplomatic endeavors and applied to the material advancement of Madagascar.[11] Although the cultural strand developed through Raombana's historical work would have no real posterity until much later, its advent was facilitated by the fact that his compatriots in general *wanted* to associate the resources of their old oral culture with the new science.

Raombana gave no title to his work.[12] Like Tacitus, one could call its first section *Histories* (from the Merina origins to the death of Radama in 1828) and give the name of *Annals* to the ensuing one (reign of Ranavalona I to which he was a witness and to which he applied a simple chronological approach). The third part is his *Journal* in which the author entered both events and his own reflections daily. The whole has some 8,000 pages of which we have located some 6,000. Raombana wrote on long sheets of white or blue paper imported from England and generally composed "books" of some 400 pages each (*recto-verso*, 100 double-sheets, numbered).[13] We have verified the authenticity of the text and all of it has gone into our critical edition which classifies the different *fonds* (basic collections)* in the text's chronological sequence. These *fonds* have been constituted in accordance with their own provenance, to the extent that it could be determined in each case. Despite their dispersal since 1855, countless pages found,

---

Fonds will be retained henceforth in the translation.

indeed most of them, happen to be in a fine state conservation. Moreover, the disciplined, uniform writing of Raombana is legible most of the time.

Raombana's manuscript had a rather unsettling history of its own. First Rahaniraka and later Razanakombana (the author's eldest son) were almost certainly able to preserve it in mint condition as well as complete until 1895, date of Razanakombana's exile in the early days of French colonization. After 1895, the document's integrity experienced its ups and downs, following the random game of inheritances, loans, gifts, purchases. Already around 1890, officials at the French Residency were translating several hundred of its pages into their language (*Fonds B*, conserved in the Archives of the Malagasy Democratic Republic, 24 notebooks for which the originals have not been located so far). Between 1900 and 1903, Alfred Grandidier found the largest segment of the Raombana manuscript, which remained in his private library until his son Guillaume donated it ti the Académie Malgache in 1954 (*Fonds A*, the most uninterrupted and best-ordered portion). A private collector, Mr. Mithridate, passed on to the Académie at an imprecise date a second batch of texts which are less homogeneous and which had been acquired under unknown circumstances (*Fonds D*). Another fervent collector and amateur who devoted his time to old Malagasy souvenirs and memorabilia, Mr. Razafimandimby, came up with two complete "books" of Raombana in 1938 from his treasures and gave them to Dr. Raoely James (*Fonds C*). Lastly, Mr. E. Ratsisalovanina, direct descendant of Raombana, was kind enough to communicate to us the last text still in family possession (*Fonds E*, copy, a school notebook, the original having been unfortunately loaned out and lost). Table I gives an initial idea of the general content for the different *fonds*.

The definitive writing of *Histories* and *Annals* dates to 1853-1854, for the essentials as this is when Raombana put in order and transcribed anew the notes he had taken most of his life. It is possible that he would have done the same type of restructuring into a continuous account for the pages we are calling his *Journal* but a premature death left him no time. Like Tacitus, still, Raombana wrote first the *Annals* of the reign of Ranavalona I going, nonetheless, back to year 1827 to describe in his preface the circumstances of Radama's death. He then decided to complete

ORIGIN	Vols.	Books	Desi-gnation	No. of pages	CONTENTS
					Tradition and History
Fonds Grandidier Académie Malgache	I	1-3	A1	1,406	Origins to 1828/9[1]
	II	4-6	A2	1,200	1829/30 - 1833/34
	III	7-9	A3	1,329	1834 - 1838
Fonds Residency General of France Archives of the Malagasy Democratic Republic	I	10	B1	400[2]	1837/1838 - 1841
	II	13	B2	400[2]	1846/47 - 1849/53
Fonds (Private) Dr. Raoěly James	I	12	C1	398	1844 - 1846
				5,133	Total pp. - History
					Journal
	II	19	C2	400	25 Dec.1854-15 Apr.[3] 1855
Fonds Mithridate Académie Malgache	I	16[4]	D1	184	14 Nov.1853-25 Jan. 1854
	II	17[4]	D2	16	19 Jul.1854-22 Jul. 1854
Fonds (Private) Mr. Ratsisalovanina	I	17[4]	E	188	25 Apr.1854-19 Jun.1854
				788	Total pp. Journal
				5,921	Grand Total

(1) The Chronological cut-offs were never entirely rigorous here.

(2) Evaluation is probable, not definitive.

(3) The sign, preceding the first legible date recalls that some of the earlier pages could not be absolutely dated.

(4) Fragments only.

TABLE I - ORIGIN OF FRAGMENTS FOUND

the work by going to the earlier periods. Impelled by the logic of historical explanation Raombana went back into the past of his land since the very origins of the peopling of Imerina. There is an uninterrupted line from the most ancient of kings until 1853. From November 1853 (or Alahatsy 1854 within the Malagasy Calendar) to April 1855 (Adalo 1855), and even to the day of his death, Raombana returned to the daily, piecemeal progress of events within his *Journal*. The intentions of a historian, reflected in the chronology of his work, explain the principal nature of the composition of the whole, namely the inequality of its parts. Yet, it would be unjust to label his history as "disproportionate." Despite the single-pagination the manuscript consists, in effect, of three texts — one should say three different works; and while the historian gives them a clear continuum each one preserves still its own unity and harmony, (Table II).

1	A1 ; 1 - 496	496	Introductory <u>Tableau</u> Traditional History to 19th Ruling Span (start)
2	A1 ; 497 - 1006	510	End of the 19th Ruling Span (Andrianampoinimerina) Start of the 20th (Radama Ist)
3	A1 ; 1007 -1406	400	End of the 20th Ruling Span (Radama Ist) Start of the 21st Ruling Span (Ranavalona Ist)
4	A2 ; 1 - 400	400	21st Ruling Span (Ranavalona I) Cont. 1828/29 - 1830
5	A2 ; 401 - 800	400	Ranavalona Ist (Cont.) 1830 - 1832/33
6	A2 ; 801 - 1200	400	id 1832/33 - 1833/34
7	A3 ; 1 - 400	400	id 1834 - 1835
8	A3 ; 401 - 929	529	id 1835 - 1836/37
9	A3 ; 930 - 1329	400	id 1837 - 1838
10	B1 ; 1 - 172	400	id 1838 - 1841
11	Lacunae	400?	id 1841 - 1844(?)
12	C1 ; 1 - 398	398	id 1844 - 1846
13	B2 ; 1 - 209	400	id 1846/47 - 1849/53
14-15	Lacunae	800?	End of the History of the Reign of Ranavalona Ist Start of the Journal : 1849/53 - November 1853(?)
16	D1 ; 1 - 184	184	Journal : 14 November 1853 - 25 January 1854
16	Lacunae	212	id 26 January 1854 - 24 April 1854(?)
17	E ; 1 - 134	188	id 25 April 1854 - 19 June 1854
17	Lacunae	108(?)	id 20 June 1854 - 18 July 1854(?)
17	D2 ; 1 - 16	16	id 19 July 1854 - 22 July 1854
Fin 17-18	Lacunae	488(?)	id 23 July 1854 - 24 December 1854(?)
19	C2 ; 1 - 400	400	id 25 December 1854 - 15 April 1855
20 etc?	Lacunae(probable)	?	?

(1) Pagination established by us.

(2) Evaluation here is probable.

(3) +2pp., some torn at the book's beginning (counted in Raombana's own pagination, but not in ours).

(4) Fragments only.

(5) +4pp., some also torn (and counted by Raombana but not by us).

TABLE II - COMPOSITION (RECONSTRUCTED)

The huge *opus* of Raombana opens on a vast geographical canvass, both physical and human, of Madagascar. In some hundred pages he traverses the "provinces" of the Great Island, enumerates the products of each and presents men in their larger social groupings, through their beliefs, customs and modes of life; he then embarks on the history of kings and his perspective is, in fact, that of dynastic history. The sovereign —of Tananarive— is always the central personage and all the life of the people, Merina first and other Malagasy after, revolves around the throne. One could say that Raombana succeeds in presenting a chronicle of the court which is at the same time a history of a people as he does not ignore or belittle his less elevated compatriots.

The *Merina High Epoch* includes the *History of Ancient Kings* and the *Reign of King Andrianampoinimerina* (d. 1810), going back in time to the Merina origins and until the accession of Radama I to the throne. There is the idyll of the first man and first woman, in the beginning, as God places them on the peaks of Andringitra and Ankaratra. At the terminal point, there is the violence of a civil war and the crimes of an "usurper." The initial episode, period of peopling and growth of traditional civilization, is largely dominated by the king most dear to Raombana —Andriamasinavalona— noble king, kind and good, foe of discord, man who takes his duties seriously. Alas, his reign is at end! The Golden Age of Imerina is rapidly corrupted and done away with through the incursion of European influences (Text I). The second episode is not without its greatness both because the Merina civilization is evolving through constant reformation and because at least the idea of national unity is born in it; but he brings into view of history a violent prince, the brutal and bloodthirsty Andrianampoinimerina. In this connection, the aristocratic tradition of Raombana conforms to the antipodes of the "Hova" tradition which Father Callet would collect some three decades later (Text II).

From 1810 to 1828, period of Merina conquests, *Madagascar under Radama First* found itself at a time of a very different monarch. Son of an usurper, not much less cruel, but more aware of the future needs of the Malagasy, a strong and free spirit, Radama led his country into political unity and toward a novel civilization. For Raombana, the year 1820, year of formalized alliance with England, is a monumental turning point marking the course of Merina and general Malagasy history. As European techniques and Christian beliefs penetrated Madagascar, Radama established with the aid of missionaries and British agents a new written language, new schools, a modern army and, above all, a sense of national unity. These profound changes had, unfortunately, violence as their companion. If Christian influence freed the spirit, European techniques, and especially the military ones, subjected men and doomed the defeated (Text III).

The "revolution of 1828," which carried Ranavalona I to the throne, sounded the death knell of this liberty to experiment and it unleashed an even greater violence. As there was a ban on Christianity since 1835 the Merina armies comb and ravage the land in search of its clandestine adherents. As Raombana sees it, the Queen's own "superstition" and cupidity of powerful men are at the root of the many misfortunes engulfing Madagascar at the time. Madagascar was not only isolating itself from the rest of the world. It was becoming evermore divided within itself while the external war fanned the civil one. Raombana's last remaining and great hope is the future king, his pupil, Radama II. *Under the Reign of Ranavalona I* the historian sees his homeland sliding into a deeper and deeper crisis of civilization; and he understands all the more the disarray of his compatriots because he had undergone within himself *already* some of the agonies of reconciling tradition with new ideas, even if his own specific choice in favor of the West cannot be questioned (Text IV).

When it concerns the remote period of his land's origins, Raombana offers an outline. In dealing with the Nineteenth century, when written texts gained ground, his work is a continuous narrative of events. Alternately, he applies the two methods of documentation to the whole, one consisting of compiling oral texts through the chain of traditions and eye-witness accounts, and the other of using written sources. In fact, his temperament as well as his conscientious historical approach lead him to intermix, as much as it was possible, both of them. The object is mutual enrichment for historical criticism does not spare at all the traditions while history does not deprive itself of resources secured from individual as well as collective memories. It is precisely through a constant search for the sources, immediately subjected to the critical method, that Raombana qualifies as a historian. He also accords high value to the *Lovantsofina*, traditions fixed in "heritage of the ears," and to the generally-held opinions of his contemporaries, which often contain judgements justified by facts. He cites an identifies his oral sources, such as a descendant of ruler named Ralaitokana, or one of the wives of Ramanetaka (former Merina Governor of Majunga and potential rival of Ranavalona I for the throne) who had told him personally of her husband's flight into exile to the Comoro Islands; sometimes Raombana cites Ranavalona herself. He cites all the texts conserved at the Royal Chancery —a speech, a law, a statistic— and he assesses their relative value before making use of them.[14] Raombana, however, does not refer to a single written work like his own, for example the books published about Madagascar in Europe. Instead, he assimilates such materials without copying and he extracts this wealth without specific indications and very much on his own terms. It would be, indeed, in vain to search in his text for a determined "model," one or more, reproduced with some precision. But, it is quite likely that he was influenced both by the traditions collected and written down by the literate officers of the Merina Royal Court and by the historical literature in English to which missionaries had contributed, most of it appearing outside Madagascar. Still, he retained an individuality in the face of all the possible models. To the immutable texts of the oral tradition he opposes the technique and style of a Western historian and especially the judgements independent in spirit; and he is equally in opposition to the ways in which foreigners had depicted Madagascar, from a Malagasy point of view, one that is frequently "nationalistic." But, Raombana does not elaborate upon any theoretical concepts regarding the historian's craft as he adopts the modest scheme of school textbooks, without aiming higher. As chance would have it, this was just at the time when the English "Academies," guided by teachers like J. Priestley, were diffusing new textbooks seeking to grasp —beyond the mere events— all aspects of civilization.

Until Raombana, the "historical *genre*" in Imerina was confined to the memorization and faithful transmission of oral traditions inherited from the ancestors: the royal traditions, traditions "national" in character and particular traditions reflecting the family. In contrast to the impersonal mode of the earlier *genre* Raombana prepares his own personal book in which oral traditions are treated as a method of history,[15] and he deprives oral tradition itself of all the sacred prestige in relation to his own design.

The epochs most distant in time, the "legendary" ones, he depicts through novel imagery, laicized so that rational explanation asserts its rights.[16] What really excites him about the "Dark Centuries" is the progress of Merina civilization and its various stages, each one attached to the name of a monarch, name which only has symbolic value. These kings alternately assume roles which incarnate one or more events in history: the peopling of Imerina, the establishment of principal towns, rules of succession to the throne, introduction of firearms, large works to make the soil productive. The flavor of the past as a whole does not, however, disappear at all as the historian gives a holistic "idea" of the earlier times.

For the recent history, Raombana's is a more "classic" reconstuction. His general plan, a relatively simple one, respects the chronological division of ruling spans. He is far more subtle in the exposition of details. In fact he presents a vast *tableu* of Madagascar in the Nineteenth century. If he devotes the essentials to the development of diplomatic relations and to the vicissitudes of internal affairs (from the deeds and gesta of sovereign to military operations), his canvass of a general political history also describes, in minute ways, an entire civilization, with attention to demography, economy, society and culture. Raombana's spirit is haunted by a depopulation of Madagascar, an effect of modern warfare, area in which he sees the European influence as nothing less than ruin and death.[17] The sole equivalent of the pernicious aspect of European influence is to be found in the new oligarchy which has a cynical monopoly over the means of production and of exchange.[18] Himself educated in England, Raombana observes passionately the changes taking place in Imerina since the implantation of missionary schools. Lastly, he did not shy away from an alert depiction of the daily life in Imerina, especially around the Queen and in respect to the life at the Court which reflected an extremely rapid evolution in mores.[19] Even more valuable is his logical explanation of the events he describes. There are some rather fine pages of historical analysis dealing with such aspects as the circumstances of the "Madagascar Policy" of the Mauritius' English Governor Farquhar or the depth of the movement of nationalistic reaction which embarked Ranavalona I upon the persecutions directed against Christians.[20] The historian keeps a sharp eye, a rarely indulgent one at that, on the play of interests, ambitions and selfishness. His explanations are particularly incisive through the use of psychology as an aid, both collective and individual. Indeed, the Malagasy psychological context clarifies the general behavior which is ill-understood by foreigners; there are descriptions, reasonings underpinned by judgements, measured appreciations of individuals and of peoples, of the political situations. The English missionaries (especially the craftsmen among them), convinced that their teachings were spreading good works and happiness, would have been painfully surprised to learn what Raombana had written about them. There was, in the popular opinion, a kind of sullen hostility to the presence of English missionaries, justified on the whole because they were inadvertently expanding the older corveé servitude across all walks of life in Imerina.[21]

Raombana could also cross with ease the fragile borderline between the severity of judgement and the passion of activism. He writes a history in the "humanistic" vein, caring for the general progress of his land, but his generous morality could not make him forget either his aristocratic rank or a patriotism shaped by a long stay abroad.[22] Literature was hardly a relief for the moral commitment as Raombana suffers deeply the miseries of his time, miseries which are to be explained by human baseness alone. Mass-inertia, too, especially in the "revolution of 1828," could induce genuine pessimism in Raombana, for "what a dark shadow is cast upon human nature so laden with meanness and ingratitude," he writes. It is also a pessimism accentuated by the continuous decline of the Andriana (aristocracy) in Imerina. To the question as to why so many mediocrities, so many "mean men," occupy the highest position in the Merina state he answers, in a supreme reproach to Ranavalona I, because "none of the lovers of the Queen belong to the aristocracy."[23] But, Raombana is absolutely one with his monarch in the love of *patria* Malagasy as they both share an unflinching nationalism. Admiration of Europe on the one hand and Malagasy patriotism on the other account for an extreme complexity of Raombana's sentiments but without pushing him into contradictions. While he detests the European and creole merchants who trade with Madagascar from the Mascarene Islands, Raombana hopes for support of Paris and London to bring RakotondRadama (Radama II) to the throne, in all independence and sovereignty. Raombana makes no concessions in respect to the territorial integrity of Madagascar and is a firm supporter of the Queen's analogous stand.[24] Once more, however, he parts company with Ranavalona as an enlightened patriotism suggests to him a policy of genuine internal unity and equality of the Island's populations in place of unification by force of arms which is to Raombana an aberration, an absurdity not to be forgiven.[25] The liveliness of triple engagement as moralist, aristocrat and patriot poses no real danger to the objectivity of his work, especially since it was its apparent intent to allow posterity to form an accurate —if its own— perception ot the first half of the Malagasy Nineteenth century. He was a historian and a witness at the same time and the scruples of historian won continuously over the passion of man. His portraits are indeed nuanced and that of Radama I is a telling proof.

Raomba's book, written in English for the future, was thrown like a bottle into the sea to reach his own compatriots and other peoples beyond Madagascar at some future point in time; and his account did not come to life until today. He may have exercised considerable influence on his pupils and disciples but his book had no immediate issue and one can ask whether or not this was the consequence of the secret which enveloped it for a long time. Undoubtedly, such a secret could not have remained total after 1861 and any explanation must therefore go further. In the second half of the 1800's, the Malagasy literature in general took a road quite different from Raombana's. First and foremost, it is a literature in Malagasy —or more accurately in the Merina dialect— developed by the English Protestant missionaries and assisted by the French Catholics as well. It is a literature of religious inspiration, not secular, addressed to a public that wishes to read in Malagasy, not in English. The great Protestant reviews like *Mpanolo-Tsaina* (The Adviser) and *Teny Soa* (The Good Word), which were attracting the Merina intelligentsia in the 1860's and later, manifest above all the contemporary moral preoccupations which searched into the past for the noble Christian antecedents. Later, under French colonial rule, the Malagasy Protestant writers would demand of local history to conform to the needs of their national self-awareness. Curiously enough, the English or Malagasy authors concerned with the daily life of ancestors in Madagascar were into an outlook far more foreign and replete with self-astonishment than anything attributable to Raombana; and their written style was spontaneously, if not deliberately, ethnographic rather than historical. There is, for example, Rainandriamampandry, student of Raombana, far more Malagasy in culture than his former teacher

of English, even more respectful of tradition as such, who developed
a pronounced taste for ethnographic descriptions of old customs.
In fact, in his time, the profound transformation of spiritual life
in Imerina was a direct and rapidly-evolving threat to an older
reality still dear to the people. In contrast, Raombana accords
to traditions and manuscripts alike the role of documents placed
at the disposal of historical study. The greatest literary momument
at the end of the 1800's, Callet's *Tantaran'ny Andriana,* is also
radically at odds with the *genre* of history cultivated by Raombana.
As a foreigner with a need to respect to the hilt the oral traditions
which he had made his duty to collect *in situ* Father Callet did
not allow himself liberties with the texts furnished by his informants.
As an "archivist" he could not co-mingle them with other,
kindered traditions and even less *select* what was to be ultimately
pointed from *opposing* traditions. Because of his deep respect
for a foreign but progressively assimilated culture Father Callet
presented the Merina, in a language far closer to their actual way
of speaking than what the English missionaries were able to offer,
with a text so faithful to what he had been told that it was appreciated spontaneously and at once. Raombana's motivation was
quite different as he wanted to have an internal history of the
whole Great Island presented in posterity not only to the Merina
and the other Malagasy compatriots but also to the world beyond.

The sheer value of Raombana's work is apparent to us today
and the impact that it should and could have had in the Nineteenth
century is apt to be a greater one now. If there is one major lesson
to be extracted for ourselves from the body of Raombana's work
it must surely be that he has given us an example of controlled
acculturation. All acculturative proceses conceal a degree of
aggression of an outer upon an inner force. In the colonial period
aggression had primacy in this process; it even defined it completely
and was not a simple matter of degree. In Raombana's time, during
a period of Malagasy independence, acculturation was decidedly
less brutal, allowing one to gain and hold on to an equilibrium
with greater ease. The Malagasy who live in the period of contemporary independence are also living in an open world that has
eliminated physical distances, a world in which acculturation is
inevitable, if more subtle in texture. In this context, the Malagasy
of today is much closer to Raombana than either to the intellectuals of the colonial era or of the last years of the Merina monarchy.
He can therefore discover in the history of his land, as presented

by Raombana, the best instrument for what every generation does and indeed must do for itself: reconstruct the past, as an ongoing, legitimate quest for self-definition and for truth. This past, which the Malagasy of today are recapturing as a nation, had been belittled and even negated by the Christian religious and colonialist historiography. It was, equally, idealized beyond measure by a nostalgia for roots uncontaminated by any external influences. We can do no better than to turn to Raombana for the proper weight of things. He hides nothing of the harshness of his epoch or of the inner tensions that tore him apart. Indeed, his philosophy of the human condition, derived from experiences of his own time, is not very optimistic. Yet, he also reveals to us all of the living forces which provide the dynamics of political and social behavior as well as spiritual life, whether "pagan" or Christian. He is a precursor of a national Malagasy consciousness, one that does not suffer the limits reachable through an exclusively Merina literature. Raombana is the first intellectual who feels and communicates a patriotism that abandons the narrow regionalism and is pan-Malagasy instead. His work will serve no one to fan any real polimics. It is, historically, too sound.

NOTES

1. Following the expression of H. Brunschwig in his "Histoire, passé et frustration," *Annales E.S.C.*, September-October 1962, p. 875.

2. *Cf.* Father Paul Camboué's description of Hova children, guardians of cattle and "catchers of bits of meat," in his article, "Les Dix premiers ans de l'enfance chez les Malgaches — circoncision, nom, éducation," *Anthropes*, IV(1909), pp. 275-386.

3. Thanks to the rather famous visit to England, the person of Raombana was already known but not his work. Reverend T. Lord gave a segmented outline, mostly in his own words, in "The Early History of Imerina based upon a Native Account," *Antananarivo Annual*, VI/24(1900), pp. 451-475; J.F. Radley translated some fragments into French in "Manuscrit écrit à Tananarive (1853-1854) par Raombana," *Bulletin de l'Academie Malgache* (new serie), XIII(1930), pp. 1-26; this was followed by more fragments in French in A. Siegriest, "Manuscrit de Raombana et Rahaniraka," *BAM*, (n.s.), XIX(1936), pp. 49-76; lastly, Edouard Ralaimihoatra used more directly some of the Raombana texts in two articles: "Page d'Histoire Hova," *Revue de Madagascar*, no.10(1952), pp. 19-20,

and "L'Affaire Croft et Heppick," *BAM*, (n.s.), XL(1962), pp. 33-35 (both article titles being abbreviated here). Owners of the major part of Raombana's manuscript before they made a gift of it to the Académie Malgache, Alfred and Guillaume Grandidier had not used it at all. The critical edition, now complete (with French translation), which we have prepared is now being printed by the Editions Ambozontany, Fianarantsoa.

4. We have published this precious document, kindly passed on to us by our colleague Professor Raymond Ranjeva, direct descendant of Raombana, in the *Annex V* of the work cited earlier. Herewith is a side remark by the author himself which alluded to the description of circumcision ceremonies and which brings us the confirmation looked for: "To repeat all the ceremonies which take place that afternoon and that night will take sheets of paper... and were they written down, the reading of them would not be much liked by the Europeans; and consequenty I will say nothing more about it..." (*Introduction*, AI, p. 80). An argument for secrecy might have had a role too (as the Queen and the potentates in government would not have forgiven Raombana the portraits he traced out for each one or, indeed, his opinions in general), but only a secondary one since many at the Court knew English.

5. *CF.* the letter of Rahaniraka and Raombana to W.A. Hanquey (of the L.M.S.) dated 20 August 1831: "Your missionaries of which we are very glad to inform you are indefatigable in their duties both to God and man. By their efforts, thousands here can read the word of God in their own language... There are no less than 7 prayer-Meeting houses here and it is really affecting to hear the Natives read the word of God and sing his praises in their own language", *L.M.S. — Letters*, B.3, F.4, J-C.

6. The English of Raombana was it not all too often a primary-school English? Undoubtedly. But, his developed pages, replete with insights and reasoning worked out with much subtelty, abound. We have already given a study of "La langue et le style of Raombana," pp. 158-169, *op.cit.*1976; let us now turn in passing to his vocabulary and the movement of phrases. The missionaries could easily be accused of impoverishing the Merina tongue by selecting a "dignified" vocabulary. Raombana gets even by a rather tart English: "Oh", said Mr. HASTIE to RADAMA, one day, as He (the King) was telling him the immemse number of soldiers which had died in one of the campaigns taken by one (-975-) of His Generals, and that if such deaths were to occur often, the extinction of the men of IMERINA may soon be expected. "Oh" said He to the King "the women of IMERINA who are numerous in number, will sure to be pregnant, and deliver male children, who will sure to arrive soon to be big men, and thus Imerina will never be without men, for the bottoms of women will supply the waste of wars". Such were the words of Mr. HASTIE which made RADAMA laugh..." *Histories*, AI, p. 975. What follows is a fine page on the death of King Radama I in which the historian's style finds itself carried away by lofty reflection: "As RADAMA's end approached he grew very peevish and cruel — He rather suspected that he was bewitched which was the cause of his illness; and ordered that some of his TSIMANDOS should undergo the test of the Tangena ordeal for to discover whether they have bewitched (-1041-) him or not; but happily they survived. He ordered a mpisikidy or diviner also to work his sikidy or divinition, for to discover out, what will cure him and bring him to life and activity again — He gave strict command, that these two latter circumstances are not to be made known to the resident Europeans of ANTANANARIVO, and that he will murder him or them, who should ever communicate it to them; for that he is ashamed

of the Europeans, if they were to know, that he in his sickness, has believed and performed again the (-1042-) barbarous custom of his ancestors, which he in the presence of Europeans had denounced and laughed at as much as themselves.

Thus RADAMA "the Great" (as he is styled by the missionaries), was still the slave of the customs of his country when on the point of death his great spirit could not calmly survey the other side of eternity without fear; and he had the barbarous customs revived in the fond and sweet hope, that he would be cured when they are performed; some great man in Europe, I suppose, has failings when on the point of death as (-1043-) RADAMA did." *Histories*, A1, pp. 1040-1042.

7. Cf. L. MUNTHE *La Bible à Madagascar*, Oslo 1969, 244 pp. and (o. Chr DAHL), *Les débuts de l'orthographe malgache*, Oslo 1966, 42 pp.

8. During Raombana's time Ranavalona 1st did actually encourage the compilation and the transcription of the ancient oral traditions, and the praise-singers of those in power consolidated the legends or the royal traditions of her predecessors, especially Andrianampoinimerina, but also of Radama, cf. the first inventory of such "texts" in A. Delivre, *L'Histoire des roi d'Imerina — Interpretation d'une Tradition Orale*, Paris, 1974. We have taken anew this inventory in the sense of our study on Raombana (1976), in *Annex VI*: "Models and sources: documents of Malagasy origins."

9. A large work of L. Munthe will soon make this point fully regarding *La Tradition Arabico-Malgache*; for the time being see L. Munthe, Ch. Ravoajanahary et S. Ayache, "Radama I and the English: The Negotiations of 1817 according to the Malagasy sources — The Unpublished Sora-bé," *Omaly sy Anio*, Revue d'Etudes Historiques, Université de Madagascar, Antananarivo, nos. 3-4, 1976, pp. 9-104 (the secular, diplomatic and commercial uses of the Arabico-Malagasy).

10. "The missionaries now and then attended some of those meetings; but (-147-) it is the native Christians who took the leading hand in them, and benefited their countrymen and countrywomen by their fine preachings. The Malagasy people, especially the people of IMERINA possesses fine and graceful actions whilst speaking; and they are very seldom indeed puzzled in delivering kabary or speeches however great the number of people they speak to and what they deliver was never thought before, but deli- (-148-) vered without premeditation — Judge therefore of my astonishment the first time I was at one of these meetings, to hear persuasive eloquence flowing from the mouth of one native Christian whose words I can almost say were irresistible — The Christian religion was preached in its purest state, and this by the mouth of one whom at first sight I thought was not much acquainted with it..."

11. Cf. our "Introduction to the work of Rainandriamampandry," in *Annales de l'Université de Madagascar*, Lettres, Antananarivo, 1969, no. 10, pp. 11-50 and our *Raombana*, 1976, pp. 105-107.

11. The title inscribed by Grandidier on the volumes offered to the Académie Malgache, "History of Madagascar by a Native," is a pure invention.

13. We have completed this pagination, which is quite lax, by numbering each page within each of the *fonds*.

14. An example of textual criticism:

"The proclamation which is said to be written by Radama, and issued out to the people of Madagascar, is all false, for at that time, not a Malagasy can read, and write in the English character; and moreover the King had no control over any part of Madagascar, except IMERINA, and TAMATAVE as already stated, so how can He issue out such a proclamation to them.

The above proclamation is quite different from the style of the King, or any Malagasy, and I could never find in any (-715-) of the King's paper, such a proclamation or speech, so that it is certain that Mr. HASTIE and ROBIN had between themselves composed the above letter for to astonish the people of Europe, by wanting them to suppose that the King is an enlightened and good King—" *Histories*, A1, pp. 714-715.

15. "Tradition or history states that..." (*Histories*, A1, p. 248). The historian clearly understood the "functionalist" character of the traditions, which eliminates events and people that do not come alive in the memories deemed "necessary" by the posterior generations: I must relate that Andriamasinavalona had four other wives, but as they had no children, for they were barren, their names are now forgotten, for they had no children to transmit their names to posterity." (*Histories*, A1, p. 218).

16. We have already noted a Raombana reacting against the recent tradition, minted for the glory of Andrianampoinimerina. Even more interesting is his analysis of the religious sentiments, that have been so powerful among his compatriots, ones that he places into their time-contexts and explains without emotion through the profane, political intentions of the kings:

"and it is also worthy of being inserted here, that the above celebrated King was the author or Founder of the idols RAMANJAKATSIROA, RAKELIMA-LAZA, RAFANTAKA and RAMAHAVALY, for to answer some political measures that is, that the people (-280-) may suppose that He has gods with Him and so make the people be more afraid of Him, as well as respect and love Him more —" *Histories*, A1, p. 280.

17. "The Exportations of slaves caused the miseries of comparatively few unhappy captives; but the fatal Treaty for the non-exportations of slaves has caused the miseries of millions, for almost all have suffered through it; and from the year 1820, to this present year 1853, which is now 33 long years, soldiers and provincials have both (-833-) suffered; and it is certain that during the above 33 years, more than a million has been killed, and carried away as slaves, and sold in different parts of the country particularly in IMERINA; and that to effect the above, more than 150,000 soldiers have been killed in the campaigns and by residing in military stations, and it is painful to state here, that I have lately seen two provinces, which were formerly very populous, now utterly depopulated through wars, and the rapacity of the officers of the garrisons who commands these provinces; and in these provinces I (-834-) have seen the corpses of more than a thousand persons laying on the open grounds, without any relations or persons to bury them and therefore devoured by the Dogs, and crows etc. etc. —

Nothing is seen fat in these provinces except the Dogs, who eat these corpses, and thus get fat, and it is certain that these two provinces will be "Tany maty" or dead Land, according to the emphatic expression commonly used by the Malagasy —" *Histories*, A1, pp. 832-834.

18. "By the written instructions of Her Majesty to the officers of TAMATAVE, they were ordered not to allow any people's cattle to be exported till the cattle of her son RAKOTOSEHENO, RAMBOASALAMA, RAMONJA, the princess RABODO; RAINIJOHARY, RAHARO, the Commander in Chief, RAINILA-IARIVONY his brother, RAINIMAHARAVO, and the two daughters of her deceased paramour RAINIHIARO and some of their children have been sold and exported away by the Europeans— Now the above persons has not many cattle of their own now fit for exportation; but Her Majesty gave them (-84-) the following

ideas in order to enrich them, namely, that they can buy people's cattle at the coast and sell them...

As nobody can sell cattle to the Europeans on pain of being confiscated, people are obliged to sell their cattle cheap to the messengers or agents of the above personages at the price of 4 or 5 dollars a head, and which are sold 15 dollars a head to the Europeans, for Her Majesty had ordered (-85-) that no cattle are to be sold for less than the above sum each to the Europeans; and formerly the cattle were sold ten dollars a head to the Europeans, but she has now raised their prices—

By the above atrocious act of Her Majesty, the above twelve persons are getting immense sums of money, for they by the above had engrossed to themselves the whole commerce of TAMATAVE to themselves, which (-86-) has displeased the people very much."

Journal, D1, pp.82-86.

19. "After she had breakfasted a grand dance was performed in the palace in which many of the officers and ladies were dressed in the European style, and they danced in the European fashions...Excellent Malagasy dances were also performed by first rate dancers, to the admiration of a vast multitude of people...

It is to be observed that European monthly dances etc were used to be performed in the times of RADAMA, and in Her Majesty's and at the present time, it will be performed oftener, for Her Majesty has said, that she (-333-) will have it oftener, for that she wants to enjoy herself more, as age is creeping upon her...

These monthly dances were first introduced by Monsieur ROBIN (always on Sundays) that the people being attracted by its novelty, may go to see it, and not listen to the preachings of the missionaries on those Sundays...

King RADAMA was not at all aware that this was the intention of the Frenchman; but notwithstanding this trick, the hearers (-334-) of the missionaries were always in vast number..."

Journal, C2, pp.332-334.

20. Causes which are political, social and psychological are exemined here, one by one and then combined:

"The zeal of the native Christians had in some manner a hand in putting down the propagations of the Christian religion, although I have a good authority in stating that Her Majesty has had it (-221-) in cotemplation several years ago as I have already stated— They were always declaiming against the idols, and the foolishness of those who believed in them— The native Christians were introduced to do so in order that they may procure more converts to the true faith... But their over-zeal and the plan of Her Majesty which has been laid some times before procured the abolishment of Christianity already stated— And no wonder that it should be so, when (-222-) we consider that RAINIHIARO, his brother RAINI-MAHARO, and the people of their tribe, are reckoned amongst the ministers or keepers (VADIN-TANY) of the idol RAKELIMALAZA; and RAINIJOHARY and his family those of RAFANTAKA. No wonder that these principal officers who are the first paramours of Her Majesty would try their influence with Her Majesty for the abolishment of Christianity as the object of the teaching of Christianity was directed against their (-223-) idols— The stoppage of Christianity would have taken place before, perhaps before, perhaps even at the commencement of her reign, but the thought that if she was to do so too soon the people would grumble and say that she changes the plan that has been adopted by RADAMA, deterred her from pursuing that plan which it was her ardent wish to perform;

but as seven years had nearly expired since the death of RADAMA, she proceeded by the instigations of her (-224-) officers to put an end to the teachings of the Christian religion, and consequently the driving away from ANTANANARIVO the English missionaries and artisans. For from the observations which I have made a long time, it had always appeared to me, that she was more prejudiced against the English than the French people, which appeared very strange to me, as it was the English people who tried to benefit the Malagasy people than (-225-) the French. But Her Majesty during the whole of her reign was subjected to deceits and infatuations—"

Annals, A3, pp. 220-225.

21. "But the several Arts introduced by these artisans has been the greatest scourge to the people of IMERINA, in-as-much as through them, the feudal services of the people were increased to the highest degree, which before their arrival were mild, but now it is increased to an almost intolerable degree, that they curse the Europeans in the most violent manner, and they think (-1001-) that every European who comes to ANTANANARIVO, comes to render their yoke heavy, and insupportable which is truely the case for the services which the Malagasy are compelled to perform through the Arts which they introduce, are un-paid services, and so they are miserable..."

Histories, A1, pp.1000-1001.

22. In this fine text, where Raombana dreams of his own destiny (Rahaniraka and himself are the two exceptional descendants of Prince Rafondrazaka), come together all at once the origins of chosen morality, aristocratic pride, and partiotic love (which is not in contradiction with "acculturation" to Europe — quite the contrary) on which his activism is based:

"The prince RAFONDRAZAKA has given descendants to a set of nobles or Dukes whose principal residence is at ANOSIMIARINIMERINA, and who are famous for their bravery and warlike exploits, and who performed conspicuous parts in the civil wars of IMERINA; but his most famous descendants are two brothers who have been to England, and who in all likelihood will make a prominent figures in the future gate and History of their native (-318-) country, for their good educations in Europe, and their high exalted ranks in society promise such a thing, and it is fully expected by all ranks of people, that if any persons will benefit Madagascar and free them from slavery and bondage, it will be through their means and instrumentality. These two men are the Grand-sons of a son of the prince "RAFONDRAZAKA"

Histories, A1, pp.317-318.

23. *Histories*, A1, p. 1056 et A2, p. 787.

24. After the confrontation of 1845, the Queen wrote to the two admirals (French and British) responsible for the shelling of the port of Tamatave as a way of demanding reparations. Her letter contains also a resounding proclamation of sovereignty. Herewith is Raombana's personal opinion:

"The above letter of Her Majesty in my opinion is full of sense and wisdom for it is on the basis of equality for certainly Her Majesty (-191-) has a right to make laws without asking for the approbations of any foreign powers, and the French and English commanders have no business to fire and fight against TAMA-TAVE, because its officer is putting into execution the order of their sovereign."

Annals, C1, p.191.

25. "Thus streams of blood flowed from a people who tried to raise the banner of liberty and regain the rights which they have lost" — (*Histories*, A1, p.1023). Conclusion, after the account of a Betsimisaraka Revolt.

APPENDICES

TEXT ONE*

Under Andriamasinavalona:
The Golden Age of Imerina

From King ANDRIAMASINAVALONA to the first sovereign who reigned, may be called or reckoned as the Golden Age of IMERINA, for during those Reigns, war and its dreadful consequences (-306-) were unknown amongst the inhabitants of IMERINA — No wars took place also between King ANDRIANTSIMITOVIAMINANDRIANA and His contemporaries except the two which we have just mentioned, and so their reigns may also be reckoned as a "Golden age" of IMERINA —

During the reign of the above sovereigns more muskets were added to those which had been before acquired, so that almost every able-bodied men had muskets in their possessions — From the reign of the first sovereign who reigned in IMERINA to that of King ANDRI-ANTSIMITOVIAMINANDRIANA and his contemporary brother sovereigns, no robberies and murders were ever committed — It is stated that during those reigns, the people never bolted or locked their houses during the night times or when they undertake any distant journeys, for nobody ever thinks of stealing or telling any falsehoods, for that such things were totally unknown to them — That rice, sheep, garments, spades, and other things (-308-) of value were left in the yards during the night times, and none has ever been known to be stolen away or lost; and as the above is known to posterity by Traditions, it is now a common saying amongst the people of IMERINA; to say when they wish for a plentiful or a pro-ductive year, "May the good and fruitful times of the Kings ANDRIA-MASINAVALONA, ANDRIANTSIMITOVIAMINANDRIANA and the other sovereigns of IMERINA who formerly reigned, return upon us, that no robberies and murders may be (-309-) committed, and that peace and plenty may reign in the Land." The above is a common expression in IMERINA —

78

---

* Actual extracts from Raombana's English text as it was established for the critical edition reported in note 3 above. The writing of original *mss.* has been rigorously respected, but the critical edition has sought to avoid the numerous faults of vocabulary, orthography and in syntax, especially so as not to mislead the Malagasy student-readers who are learning English as a third language.

Letters *A* and *D* designate the Grandidier and Mithridate *fonds*. The italicized numbers (*78, 85*) represent the only numbering provided by Raombana at the start of the double sheets on which he wrote. The numbers which are included in the body of the text represent the actual pages (definitive pagination in the interior of each volume within each of extant *fonds*).

.... These Europeans brought into IMERINA also, the vices of their own countries, and which corrupted the morals of the people of IMERINA very much, for formerly they were almost strangers to Lying, but by these Europeans, they soon got (-551-) addicted to it, and it is certain that the more they had connexions with Europeans, the more they increased in the above vice; and it is also certain that the venereal diseases was formerly unknown in IMERINA, but spread very much when the Europeans got to be more numerous in the Time of King Andrianampoinimerina —

Histories A1; pp. 305-309, 550-551.

TEXT TWO

Portrait of Andrianampoinimerina:
An Account Against the Legend

A man of very conspicuous figure and Talent, lived at that Time, and it was this Man who overthrew the King ANDRIANJAFINANDRI-AMANITRA from his Throne, and seized it for Himself —

The name of this Man is "RAMBOASALAMARAZAKA"; and he is said to be a nephew of the deceased sovereign ANDRIAMBELO-MASINA, and that the above deceased sovereign had in a "will" appointed Him to succeed ANDRIANJAFINANDRIAMANITRA in the Kingdom after his Death (-335-) even if he had children of his own —

It is certain however that his above relationship with the King ANDRIAMBELOMASINA is not true, for the above King had no sister who was his mother; and it is also certain that the King had never appointd Him to succeed ANDRIANJAFINANDRIAMANITRA, for ANDRIANJAFINANDRIAMANITRA is the son of King ANDRIAM-BELOMASINA, and it is probable that the King ANDRIAMBELO-MASINA would wish His son ANDRIANJAFINANDRIAMANITRA to be succeeded by his own (-336-) son or children — As to the relationship between them, it is not so near, but they are related to one another, as all the Great nobles of IMERINA are, they being all descended from King "ANDRIAMASINAVALONA." But the near relationship of King ANDRIAMBELOMASINA and RAMBOASALA-MARAZAKA, and that he was appointed by Him to succeed ANDRIANJAFINANDRIAMANITRA, was after the overthrow of the last mentioned King largely promulgated and circulated amongst the people for to make them relish much their new usurper and to 85 (-337-) be reconciled to His Government, for all usurpers are generally shrewd and very cunning.

It is also stated after He had ascended the Throne, that the King ANDRIANJAFINANDRIAMANITRA wished to have him privately killed or murdered, that He may not succeed Him, and that the Throne may descend to his son "RALAITOKANA" or the "only son", that often times, the King sends for Him, and taking Him to a place called "AMBATOMIENTENDRO", wished to roll him down that Rock, which is extremely High, but that through (-338-) the protection of God, somethings very extraordinary take place every times that he wants to push him down privately, and which happily prevents Him from putting his intentions into execution; and that often during the night Times, he sends men to spear Him in His House, but that some supernatural spectres show themselves to these Men, which frighten them, and prevents them from murdering Him — The above foolish Reports were largely spread amongst the people; after He had seized on the Throne, and which were firmly believed by (-339-) all classes of people.....

As a King, He administered justice with an impartial hand, which drew upon Him the applause of His subjects, for in all their Law-suits, He heard their cases with coolness; weighed them thoroughly in his mind (-522-) and gave his decisions with impartiality — Often He goes to hear their cases himself when they plead against one another; and when He does not go, he sends some of his wives, and great nobles to hear them; and then the above persons report faith-fully to Him the cases which has been pleaded before them — In cases which are very difficult to decide upon there being no proper witnesses to give evidences; it is decided by the Tangena ordeal being admini-stered on dogs, or on the persons themselves; and those whose dogs survive the Tangena ordeal, win the Cases —

Some years after He had got all IMERINA for himself, it was disco-vered that he had some cruelties in his temper which began to burst out, now and then upon his subjects — These cruelties aided by extreme superstitions was the cause of the death of a few thousands of his subjects during his life-time —

Generally he treated his wives in the most brutal manner, for He but seldom lays with the most part of them; and on the mere suspicion of any of them being unfaithful to his bed, He (-525-) orders them to be killed by the spears, or orders them to be sunk in marshes that they may die there; and it is worthy of being stated here for to show the cruelties of his mind, that in giving orders to have some of his wives killed, He never make any enquiry to discover whether they had been really unfaithful to his bed, but in the mere hearing that they have been so, He orders them to be killed.

8

(-549-) To be short, if we extract from the conduct of King ANDRIA-NAMPOINIMERINA, the failings which we have already mentioned, we will see that generally upon the whole, He was a good king; that he wished for the welfare of his subjects in general; and that it was through his ambition and exertion that IMERINA was consolidated into one powerful kingdom as in the time of King ANDRIAMASINA-VALONA.

(-562-) King ANDRIANAMPOINIMERINA was rather tall, and was bony and sinewy. He is said to be an excellent shooter with the muskets, and is brave even to madness, and to possess IMERINA, he showed a great deal of personal Bravery, and was several times wounded with musket balls.........

Histories A1; pp. 334-339; 521-526; 549; 562.

TEXT THREE

Portrait of Radama I:
A "Strong Spirit"

Thus died and was buried RADAMA, whom the missionaries and artisans called "Great". He was indeed' "Great" in several of His characters; but in others He does not deserve so great a name —

One of His greatest aim was the subjugation of the whole Island for Himself — For the obtaining of this object, He bent the whole energies of his mind which may be called (-1176-) "uncommonly powerful". To obtain this, He did not sluggishly remain in His Capital, but often went Himself, for to sustain the toils of war and all its fatigues. He did not like other sovereigns, send only their Generals and officers for to fulfil the accomplishment of their ambitions; but Himself went, regardless of the fevers and unhealthiness of the low provincial countries, for He in these campaigns had caught the Fever and suffered a great deal through it. (-1177-) Sword in Hand, He was seen scaling precipices and precipitating himself amongst His inveterate enemies, for to murder and to subdue them more quickly. The above was witnessed by thousands of his soldiers, at MIDONGY who being animated by the bravery of their King, soon took the place and reduced it to ruin and desolation. Even in the time of his Father ANDRIANAMPO-INIMERINA, when He was a mere boy, His father sent him to a part of the Betsileo country, with a great number of warriors for to (-1178-) conquer it. In this campaign, RADAMA was seen (attended by two or three persons only) at the gate of the enemies who whirls at him from above, stones and spears, which instead of frightening Him, animates His courage and makes Him fire unerring shots at them; and the warriors seeing Him thus exposed were ashamed and returns to the charges which soon terminates the war — Numerous deeds of bravery and skill could be told of Him, but the above is sufficient
44 (-1179-) for to prove His bravery and contempt of Death —

One of the greatest object of Radama also, was His great desire for the improvement and instruction of His people under the Tuitions of the Missionaries and the Artisans...For this purpose He ordered great number of children to be put in the schools; and young men to be with the Artisans for to be instructed in their professions —

By the frequent intercourse which RADAMA had with the British Agent Mr. HASTIE, and the Missionaries, much of the superstitions of the country were driven away from His mind, but they were not wholly eradicated; and the administration of the Tangena ordeal which had destroyed thousands of people during His Father's Reign, and Reigns of the former Sov- (-1004-) ereigns of IMERINA, were almost put a stop to; for in ordering people to drink the Tangena ordeal during the latter part of his Reign, He orders the administrators to do it secretly and privately, lest the Europeans should hear of it, and so laugh at Him, for still adhering to the customs of his country — The Europeans hearing no more of people drinking the Tangena Ordeal, because for fear of the King's mandate, that it is not to be made known to them, no body dare inform them of it, verily believed that the

Drinking (-1005-) of the Terrible Tangena ordeal is banished from Madagascar for ever; but to the glory and honor of RADAMA, it is to be stated that RADAMA disbelieved in most of the superstition of his country, and also encouraged the scholars to believe all what the Missionaries teach them, for that the missionaries are good men and never utter or tell Lies —

Even pigs which during the Reigns of the former sovereigns were never allowed to come up to ANTANANARIVO, AMBOHIMANGA etc etc, and not allowed to come within 20 or 40 moles distance (-1006-) from these Towns, were ordered by Him to be taken and eaten up in these Towns, which is a great proof that superstition is banished from His mind, for those animals are reckoned unclean beasts, and not loved by the Idols RAKELIMALAZA etc etc which is the reason that they were not allowed to approach within a certain distance of ANTANANARIVO —

The following is another incest of the King which nearly costed him his life — His sister RABODOSAHONDRA had a daughter of the name of RASOANAMAHARY, who promised to be a good looking girl when she is a little older — The King put Her under the Tuition of the Rev. D. Jones; and gave a strict order to Her nurse and other woman slaves that they are to watch carefully over Her and never allow (-1258-) Her to lay with any male, till He has first lain with Her; and that if the above order is disobeyed, He will kill them — Accordingly after sme times had expired, when the Girl was a little bigger, the King intended to put into execution what he intended to do with Her, and took Her with Him to MAHAZOARIVO, for that purpose —

But before they got to MAHAZOARIVO, the rain suddenly came, unexpected by anybody and a lightning fell just before the King which nearly killed Him —

64   This astonished him and he considered that (-1259-) it was a warning to Him from God to desist from such a nefarious act —

He accordingly returned back to ANTANANARIVO without having accomplished His evil intention at that time; but after some times, forgetting what had happened to Him, His former intention returned, which He accordingly put into execution — RABODOSAHONDRA, RATSIMANOMPO, RATSIADAIA and RAMARIVELO are the four sisters of the King, being of the same Father and Mother with Him; but he has a great number of other sisters also by the same Father, but of different Mothers — These He lay with, especially RATAVY and RAVAOZOKINY who were very fine looking young women — The latter was one of the wives of RAFARALAHINDRIANTIANA the Governor of FOULEPOINTE; and when the King arrives at TAMATAVE and FOULEPOINTE He retains Her with Him night and day for the purpose of laying with Her.

The above are the principal Faults of the King, and has disgraced His Memory. Yet upon the whole, He was reckoned a good Sovereign and beloved by His subjects —

Histories A1; pp. 1175-1179; 1003-1006; 1257-1260.

TEXT FOUR

Portrait of Ranavalona I:
The Terror of Dying

— I do not perfectly know what her sickness was but it has been frequently reported to me that it was giddiness, and diseases of the nerves which often makes her tremble very much, and when she is
40 seized by the above sickness, she shakes and rolls about her eyes (-957-) wildly, without uttering a single word till the fit is over. .

Even at this present time which is nearly 25 years since the commencement of her reign her sickness has never yet completely left her to the great annoyance of her female slave attendants. .

At the period of which I am now speaking, her sickness had returned with double fury, and it was judged necessary by her and her paramours that some skilful doctors should be sought for to doctor her... And after some considerations (-960-) it was settled that TANOSY doctors should be sent for, for to doctor her. The Sikidy was consulted who said that no doctors in the world except the Tanosy can cure her. Indeed the Tanosy people of the province of MATITANANA to the north of FORT DAUPHIN are famous for their skill in medicines. They are also supposed to be skilful or possesses witchcrafts and magics. At first, Her Majesty was rather reluctant for to be doctored by people
41 whom she (-961-) supposed possessed witchcrafts and enchantments but finding her case to be desperate she determined to send for some of them from MATITANANA...

Immediately on their arrival they commence to doctor her majesty and it must be confessed that they did her a great deal of good for she soon got to be rather better, though they were never able to cure her perfectly, so inveterate is her disease — Their principal operations consists in (-971-) bleeding her on the backs of her hands, and on her breast and back of her shoulders; also in frequently washing her well mixing some species of vegetables with the water. They themselves rubbed her when she washed —

In the year 1830, Her Majesty was very ill, and it was often thought
99 that she will die as well as her son RAKOTOSEHENO. (-393-) She suspected that she was bewitched by some persons. The divination or sikidy also stated that she was, and that if she remains much longer at ANTANANARIVO, she will die, and therefore leave ANTANANARIVO for a time.

However dearly she loved her paramours she was so afraid of being bewitchcrafted that she consented that they are to undergo the tests of the tan- (-394-) gena ordeal.

ANDRIAMIHIAJA, RAINIHIARO, RAINIMAHARO, RAINIJOHARY and RAINISEHENO etc who were her paramours drank the tangena ordeal and survived to her inexpressible delight.

In the midst of her greatest sickness, when the news was announced to her that they had survived the ordeal, she arose from her sick bed, although in a state of the greatest weakness, and danced about the room, held by two persons lest (-395-) she should fall down.

She wept and cried for joy, calling them her beloved friends and companions, and that she will certainly recover for joy as none of them had died by the Tangena ordeal.

10 Adimazana — 8 January 1854. Sunday
This morning we courtiers of Her Majesty, by her orders went into the House of the Idol RAFANTAKA and there sprinkled with consecrated water of the above Idol for to drive away magics and enchantments which wicked people might have put upon us. Such is the notion of Her Majesty — A bay coloured cow was also killed by Her Majesty at the front of the House Masoandro, as a ceremony of the Idol RAKELIMALAZA (-142-) because a bird of the name of takatra had flew over the palace, and it is supposed that if no such ceremony is performed whenever a bird of that kind flies over the palace a conflagration of the houses of the palace will sure to take place — and of course the greatest part of the meat goes to the keepers of the above Idol...

Her Majesty has been ill and is still ill of the gonorrhea (-143-) for some times past, and yesterday she nearly made some of her courtiers undergo the test of the tangena ordeal, for she thinks that some of them might have bewitched Her and caused Her above sickness.

Annals A2; pp. 956-971; 392-395.
Journal D1; pp. 141-143.

Rainilaiarivony and the Defense of Malagasy Independence at the End of the Nineteenth Century

F.V. ESOAVELAMANDROSO*
University of Madagascar

"A transaction between opposing claims,"[1] end-result of long and trying negotiations between representatives of a French government bent on establishing a protectorate over Madagascar and Malagasy plenipotentiaries with the task of preserving their land's independence, the Treaty of 17 December 1885 put an end to the first Franco-Merina War (1883-1885). Nonetheless, a day after the formal agreement and despite a reassuring speach by the Prime Minister, who congratulated himself on having reestablished cordial relations with the "Great Republic,"[2] the rulers of the "Kingdom of Madagascar" well knew that a difficult period in local history was about to begin.[3] Having made the decision to defend the Kingdom's territorial integrity as well as its own dominant position at home, the Merina oligarchy would now have to ward-off French expansionistic aims increasingly precise in nature. Through successive Residents General, posted to Madagascar in accordance with article 2 of the Treaty, there would be a clear tendency to put into effect a protectorate that had not been mentioned explicitly in any clause of the agreement and even less so in the *"appendix"* of January 1886, an explanatory letter** prepared by the French toward the ratification of the Treaty by the government at Antananarivo.

*Translated from French by R. Kent.

**This is sometimes referred to as the "lettre Miot-Patrimonio" (or Patrimonio-Miot) after the Minister Plenipotentiary S. Patrimonio and Rear-Admiral E. Miot. Its text is accessible at the end of A. Martineau's *Madagacer en 1894* (see notes 4 and 26 below); see also "Appendix L," pp. 547-559, of Samuel Pasfield Oliver's *Madagascar: An Historical and Descriptive Account of the Island and its former Dependencies*, Vol. II, London, 1886, (Ed.).

The stakes' importance was hardly lost on Rainilaiarivony, statesman and an old hand at politics. He had been Prime Minister already for two decades, since the age of 36, after Queen Rasoherina expelled his own brother Ravoninahitriniony from the office in July 1864. In the course of those long years Rainilaiarivony became rich in experience as it fell upon him to define the positions of the royal government. "Treaties of Friendship and Commerce," concluded respectively in 1865, 1867 and 1868 with England, the United States and France, reveal him as an able diplomat, a skillful player of the politics of balancing between nations that were often competing among themselves. His twenty years of accumulated experience also coincide with the maturing of a Prime Minister, feared and obeyed, if contested at times, within his own entourage, of a ruler who sought to modernize his land through a serie of reforms, of a *Manamboninahitra** uncowed by the perspective of war when it came to repel the French pretensions.

His third decade in office, following the initial conflict, went however in a very different way for Rainilaiarivony, man of great experience but also one aging rapidly through political and personal preoccupations, man increasingly authoritarian and isolated just when the Kingdom needed most to face-up to the danger of an imminent imperialist aggression. The balancing act between the French and the British was no longer apt since the facts of international life had evolved; and internal difficulties were not favoring the implementation of a goal he had pursued relentlessly — independence of the "Kingdom of Madagascar." Even some of the French contemporaries who could not be accused of being partial to him gave Rainilaiarivony due credit. "The Prime Minister," wrote Martineau," can hence claim before history to great honor of having upheld for thirty years the independence of his country, against multiple ambitions, some of which had been well-disguised indeed."[4] Actually, the policies of Rainilaiarivony were bound *not* to succeed and he must bear,

*Officer(s) of the Merina Army; from "having honors" (*manana+voninahitra*) or ranks which started with 5 "honors" (sub-lieutenant) and upward to form the hierarchy. In a more precise as well as idiomatic sense, the *manamboninahitra* (as distinct from other, non-paid, officers) formed the Queen's bodyguard as well as the Prime Minister's; they bore rifles like common soldiers and were commanded by the most loyal of Rainilaiarivony's men. In 1870, for example, in the military garrison at Tananarive of some 6,000 a sixth or 1,000 consisted of the *manamboninahitra*, (Ed.).

along with those who worked with him, the historical responsibility for the failure.

I

The attitudes of some pressure groups and of the French representatives in Madagascar, from 1886 to 1894, posed a serious threat that Rainilaiarivony was to have deflected for a variety of reasons.

Worried by the influence acquired by Protestantism —"and consequently by England"— among the *manamboninahitra*, who had for the most part converted to the religion of their Queen and Prime Minister, the Catholic missionaries accused the Malagasy rulers of partiality. It seems, however, that Rainilaiarivony did wish to make everyone respect the principle of neutrality and religious tolerance that had been inscribed into every treaty signed by his government, as is attested by recommendations addressed to his subordinates.[5] Moreover, concerned with a full exercise of his authority and with directing a state free of commitments to the missions, the Prime Minister controlled their activities rather tightly, including those of the London Missionary Society (LMS). With political interests ahead of all other considerations, Rainilaiarivony took his time to reflect before issuing ordinances on the petitions and complaints made by the Protestant missionaries themselves.[6]

Still, the fact that two missionaries did have sustained contact with the Prime Minister was sufficient to strengthen the French fears. The first was Reverend W. Clayton Pickersgill who became accredited in 1883 as Vice-Consul of Her Britannic Majesty to the government of Ranavalona III; the other was a printer, John Parrett, whom Piolet[7] had accused of being Rainilaiarivony's "evil genius." The Prime Minister's *Journal* mentions many interviews with Pickersgill; in addition, a fairly large volume of correspondence was exchanged between them.[8] It is most likely that political questions did come up in the interviews quite often and one can be permitted to assume that the Vice-Consul lavished his advice on how to side-step France and preserve the Kingdom's integrity. Yet, Rainilaiarivony's own competence suggests that he did not always follow blindly the "directives issued" by Pickersgill, as Boudou has written.[9] French accusations leveled at him were refuted and protested in a stiff but energetic manner; as either because of pride or a will to impose himself, Rainilaiarivony let it be understood that the government headed by him acts in a serious and completely independent way.

At any rate, at least until the signing of the Zanzibar Convention in 1890, and despite his general distrust of foreigners, Rainilaiarivony did listen to some of the advice given, quite pleased to have found ears that were attentive to the problems of his land. It is simply not possible to avoid some allusion to an Anglo-Merina entente against the French when a journal edited in Antananarivo by an Englishman named Tacchi could state, some months after the Treaty, that there would be the "same politics, war yesterday, peace today. The defense of Madagascar's independence will be our political programme."[10] Such remarks could only render the French worries even more intense. Some of the Catholics, represented in the Chamber of Deputies by the Bishop of Angers, Monseigneur Freppel, joined the voices of deputies from Réunion —Francois de Mahy et Brunet— on behalf of Madagascar's colonization and had no qualms for the possibility of an armed intervention.

The Europeans in Madagascar, especially creoles concentrated in the rich and commercially active east-coast province of Tamatave as clerks or settlers, were victimized by their own "persecution complex" and, in consequence, pushed for the conquest of the Great Island.[11] A victory over a government undefeated in 1883-1884 would lead to a revision of terms in a treaty regarded as unsatisfactory by the creoles. Their activities were a source of immediate concern for Rainandriampandry, Governor of Tamatave, but Rainilaiarivony, too, in Antananarivo, found himself confronted daily with the French Resident General. Spokesmen for their government as Residents General, first Le Myre de Vilers and later Bompard and Larrouy, taking advantage of the equivocal nature of the 1885 agreement, made it a point to interpret it in a sense favoring the French interests. According to their lights, the Treaty established a French protectorate over the Island even if it did not actually use the word itself in order to avoid a break in negotiations and to satisfy the Malagasy plenipotentiaries, acting under severely restricting instructions from the Prime Minister.

The French representatives would cite the first two articles of the Treaty[12] while attempting to supplant the Malagasy minister for Foreign Affairs; they would refuse, for example, to recognize those consuls whose exequaturs were transmitted by the royal government; and events of this type were dangerously compromising to the Kingdom's independence. Moreover, the end of the Nineteenth century saw a leap in the advance of Europe's imperialism on a global scale, yet another problem to worry about for Rainilaiarivony. Being a leader of a land coveted for a long time by Europeans, whose pressures grew progressively stronger, the Prime Minister had to face a movement that led ineluctably to the loss of independence.

During some dozen years that elapsed between the two armed conflicts with France, the economic dependence of the "Kingdom of Madagascar" vis-à-vis the countries of Europe or the United States became greater; thus, the problem of independence posed itself not only in political terms but even more in economic ones. Commercial houses from abroad were importing massively at ports of the Kingdom a host of manufactured goods —linen, hardware, spirits and others— valued highly at the Merina court. Rainilaiarivony wrote often to his provincial governors to order these products from *an-dafy**: hair-dyes, clothing, beverages... These goods were of low quality as well as overvalued leading also to the ruin of local craftsmen. While analyzing this fact, Guy Jacob poses quite aptly the following question: "The disastrous economic policy of Rainilaiarivony (was it not) his own weakness, even impotence."[13]

A war indeminity of some 10,000,000 francs that had to be paid to France forced Rainilaiarivony to borrow from foreigners. Well-aware of the types of opposition he would face from the French side with his selection and after hesitating a long time to avert financial expropriation by France, he turned to the English businessman and former missionary Abraham Kingdon. But, the remonsterances of the Resident General and the financial constraints (lower lending-rates than those proposed by Kingdon were available at the Comptoir National d'Escompte de Paris and, moreover, Kingdon had difficulties in amassing funds on short notice*) forced him to accept the proposals of Le Myre de Vilers,

---

*From abroad; from overseas, (Ed.).

*The term *"vola kandonina"* ("Kingdom's money") entered the Merina idiom in a lasting way to designate all false currencies, (Ed.).

his main political adversary. The CNEP, a French organism, advanced the needed moneys for the debt pay-off but at the price of being in control of customs receipts at the principal ports of Madagascar, to oversee the financial operation. This measure served to strangle Rainilaiarivony's government as its treasury was being largely replenished through the customs duties.

To this economic dependence one must add the fact that the imperial powers, while ignoring all of the remarks and protests of the Antananarivo government, agreed among themselves to seal the fate of Madagascar. In August 1890, through the Zanzibar Convention, England recognized the French protectorate over the Great Island. Confronted with the open French ambition to dominate Madagascar, now accepted by the former British allies, Rainilaiarivony —as Head of Government, representative of the clan of Andafiavaratra,* a high Merina *manamboninahitra* and a proud Tsimiamboholahy** — had all the reasons to struggle for the Kingdom's integrity. For him, as well as for his land, the stakes were indeed high.

II

It was the Prime Minister's ambition to run a "modern" state, in the image of "civilized" nations, one being hence worthy of their recognition and respect. The internal reforms he undertook, such as the publication of laws, reorganization of the army or of the administration, were largely reflecting this general direction. In the manner of other statesmen, Rainilaiarivony penned a manual entitled *Fampianarana Fitondram-panjakana* (Instructions on the Art of Governing).[14] In 1882, while presenting to the Queen the "councilors" entering into the new governmental organization, Rainilaiarivony declared that had taken as model the "civilized lands" where sovereigns were not politically responsible. The

*The Andafiavaratra were descendants ultimately of the head of Tsimiamboholahy (see just below), Andriantsilavo, who became the first minister and most powerful man under King Andrianampoinimerina, founder of the modern Merina state; but, more immediately, the Andafiavaratra as a family, started to become important when Andriantsilavo's son Rainiharo became Prime Minister of the first Ranavalona. It could be said that the post of first minister of Merina state had gone to the successive generations of Andafiavaratra, an extremely interesting non-dynastic case, (Ed.). See also note 16 below.

**The Tsimiamboholahy are one of the 28 Hova clans without which the Merina monarchy could not have been successful; the name itself means literally "those who do not turn their backs on an enemy," (Ed.).

new councilors were alone to carry such responsibility. The forming of a Cabinet, the nomination of councilors at the Queen's court, the concern of the Commander-in-Chief to direct a well-trained army — all of these converged into the single goal, to give the Western powers an image of man of state open to the idea of progress[15] and ready to enter the modernized and well-structured Kingdom of Madagascar into the international family of nations. This is the core element of Rainilaiarivony's policies. Effectively, the "Kingdom of Madagascar" derived the legitimacy of its existence from international agreements and not from the internal political situation.

In point of fact, while quite a few regions of the Island had escaped a real or theoretical domination of the government at Antananarivo, all of the treaties concluded between it and the foreign powers granted implicitly its authority throughout Madagascar in declaring Ranavalona III as ruler of the "Kingdom of Madagascar." Rainilaiarivony wanted this international recognition as it played in his favor. Being the Prime Minister, key to the Kingdom's affairs, he was the spokesman to whom the representatives of all foreign nations wishing to enter into relations with Madagascar had to come first. In return, he was invested with a heavy burden, namely to defend his land's interests and above all its integrity; and it is this role that justified to a large extent his place in the Kingdom. To be sure, by force and pressure, his own clan of Andafiavaratra[16] succeeded in imposing its own politics, its *manamboninahitra*, and even its queens. But, as Hova, Rainilaiarivony was keenly aware that such a situation could only last to the extent that he could continue to satisfy the ambitions of Merina oligarchy and as long as he could be accepted by the people as a statesman concerned with the Kingdom's independence from external control.

The turning of Madagascar into a foreign power's fiefdom risked to bring in its wake the elimination of Rainilaiarivony's own clan from the political stage and there was no lack of competitors. It will be enough to recall, for instance, that at the origin of Rainilaiarivony's convesion to Protestantism in 1869 —which also determined the Queen's conversion— one could find a variety of reasons, including the plotting of his cousin and minister for Foreign Affairs, Rainimaharavo, who sought to use the Merina Protestants to oust the Prime Minister. In converting himself to Protestantism he deflected the threat and came to control a party that was quite coherent and deemed dangerous.[17] Moreover, from the moment they became established in Antananarivo, the French had no difficulties in finding collaborators selected from lines of descent that were the rivals of Andriantsilavo's own.[18]

To be able to govern, besides, Rainilaiarivony needed the support of the Merina oligarchy; and the defence of the Kingdom's independence, which ensured its domination, also conditioned the support which the *manamboninahitra* gave the Prime Minister. The group of officers-merchants who had accumulated wealth in the provinces or in the capital had no choice but to view the French aims with some degree of concern. Remunerative governmental posts, monopoly over some branches of commerce (for example, in cattle), possession of an entire mass of *dekana* (aides-de-camp) who spent their time in making the affairs of masters prosperous — all of these were privileges attached to the existence of an independent Merina monarchy that was tightly bound to the local "bourgeoisie."

Rainilaiarivony, the statesman, represented well this class of society, main supporter of the regime in power. Holding the highest rank in the hierarchy of honors, with 16 *Voninahitra*, the Prime Minister enjoyed a host of advantages commesurate with his rank and title. In Antananarivo itself and at all of the important provincial posts one could find the Prime Minister's *dekana*, even after Rainilaiarivony himself had decreed, in 1876, a limiation on the number of aides-de-camp that could be mustered into the personal service of each *manamboninahitra*. Clients of Rainilaiarivony and confidential agents, these *dekana* supplied him with information regarding the activities of foreigners and of governors — denounciacion being one of the most common governmental practices. The same *dekana* were given the task of managing his personal possessions and resources. Properties inherited from his father or torn away from his older brother when shorn of power, domains purchased from inhabitants of the provinces or ceded by the Queen (herself a conspicuous owner of land) made-up the bulk of Rainilaiarivony's fortune. This is the way in which he pretended, for example, to have obtained from Ranavalona II "all the lands of Ivondrona" at some dozen miles south of the port of Tamatave. A rich area, the valley of Ivondro had developed cattle-rising and sugar cane plantations; and the Prime Minister had in it as well some large herds of cattle, dispersed along the pastures surrounding the governmental forts of Tsarasaotrinitompony, Soamandrakizay, Mahavelona. His *dekana* and slaves provided the guardianship and assured that his cattle would be exported toward the Mascarene Islands.[19] A large land owner, Rainilaiarivony also revealed himself as a rather enterprising businessmen for his time.

Committed resolutely to the road of "progress," he plunged into modern activities. He was interested personally and participated himself in the workings of small factories, dealt directly with foreigners to charter their commercial ships; but, it was not always clear where the line was drawn between his personal dealings and those of the state.[20] The defense of the Kingdom's independence thus happens to coincide with the defence of his own interests and those of his social class.

Although he did belong to one of the most prestigious of the Hova clans since the end of the 1700's, one associated closely with the Merina monarchy, Rainilaiarivony remained aware of the weakness of his situation. As a commoner, he had neither the prestige nor the spiritual ascendancy embodied in the person of the Queen, Ranavalona III; and his conversion to Christianity reflected in part a desire to give his power a new religious under-pinning. Not a few of the royal subjects remained attached to their personal or to the royal *sampy** and continued to invoke the *"raombinifolomanjaka"*** in their prayers. The Prime Minister could not ingnore this plitico-religious context and had to present himself at all times to a public opinion in respect of traditions as champion of the Kingdom's independence. Only such a political role could continue to justify his presence at the side of the Queen.

Lastly, Rainilaiarivony's character and ambitions made him a match for the heavy burden he had sought as his authoritarian ways, noticed by all of his contemporaries, were serving a very real political consciousness. In his well-known book on the Hova,

*The best translation of *sampy* is "protector," usually of a group, whereas *ody* applied to "protector" of an individual in Imerina, see also Berg's discussion of the *ody-sampy* earlier on in this volume, (Ed.).

**Literally, "two-in-excess-of-ten-who-ruled" hence "12" national protectors of Imerina, palladium of twelve *sampy*, (Ed.).

Jean Carol gave a striking description of the former Prime Minister:[21]

"(I) would daydream*** of this man who will have a curious page in History, for having managed, by ambition and by partiotism, to become the Richelieu of a black monarchy exposed to the covetousness of the outside would and facing the internal danger of feudal dismemberment. No one was a greater patriot than he. A great man of politics too: reserving, on the one hand, the affairs (of state) for the most active caste, the most intelligent one, and the most disengaged from the traditions, creating the government along the fief, placing the official next to the noble, and reducing the royalty to little more than cosmetic role; on the othe hand, perceiving the English as the sole possible opponents of our influence in Madagascar and knowing how to use their support without being too partial to them. (I) would daydream of this patient and bold spirit who, during more than thirty years, could succeed in maintaining the independence of his land amid intrigues of every kind..; of this newcomer who amassed all power in his hands, added to his title of prime minister that of the commander-in-chief, turned the crown into a feminine bauble, and reserved the mantle of Radama for his own shoulders..."

We are confident that this passage evokes rather well the Prime Minister's personality. Chapus and Mondain insist on it: Rainilaiarivony, last mainstay of the Merina monarchy, had the true grit of a Chief of State. Yet, his authoritarianism accounts also in part for his relative isolation, especially in the last years of his government, an isolation which created an unfavorable context for the implementation of his policies.

III

In reality, Rainilaiarivony found himself particularly isolated in his actions of resistance to the French claims.

The title of "dictator" which Le Myre de Vilers awarded him

***Carol, who actually saw Rainilaiarivony for only "a few minutes" by his own admission, and who used a great deal of imagery (he had written several novels and a theater piece), was travelling to a site some 5 kilometers from Antananarivo when he began to "daydream." There is no doubt that he was exceptionally well-informed about Imerina and the Hova, (Ed.).

expresses fairly well the manner and the conditions in which the Prime Minister felt he should conduct the policies of the Kingdom. Poorly informed about the major problems of the state, the population at large did not always understand his points of view and failed to support them. Thus, during a *kabary** held at Andohalo, which was to inform the people about the signing of a peace treaty, Rainilaiarivony simply did not go into any details and contented himself by talking about the re-establishment of cordial relations with France. He mentioned neither the difficult and protracted negotiations, nor the conditions for ratification demanded by the queen, nor the ambiguities of certain treaty clauses, nor yet the risks to which the country was exposed and of which he was completely aware.[22] The population of Antananarivo, at the capital itself, knew nothing of the exact terms of the agreement. The provincial governors were delivering roughly the same speech everywhere, dwelling only on the articles regarding liberties given to the foreigners who resided in Madagascar, especially the freedom of circulation and of commerce. These official *kabary* were reflecting an optimism far removed from meetings of the Cabinet.

Under such conditions it seemed quite normal that most of the subjects failed to grasp just how crucial were the issues enveloped within the whole question of independence at the end of the Nineteenth century. On this score, the government bore the responsibility or, more aptly, Rainilaiarivony who composed the royal speeches and gave instructions to the governors. On his own, he confessed that most of the Malagasy remained   ignorant of the treaty terms.[23] Yet, he made no attempt to inform them. Given the ambiguity of some of the clauses within the treaty, was this not a ploy with which to hide a half-failure of his own and thus come to present to his compatriots and to the foreigners alike the image of a statesman with confidence in his policies and in the future of the Kingdom? To put it another way, did not such an attitude also reflect his will to rule alone, as he expected, the affairs of the land?

At any event, he could at times fail to keep informed even the notables, the councilors and the ministers of important problems at hand; and some of his collaborators complained

*The term *kabary* covers, at the same time, "public proclamation," an "assembly" convened (usually under an old and large tree, like the baobaab) for a public discussion, "public speech," or even "anything important," (Ed.).

among themselves of his methods of governing. Only a handful of the initiated could come to understand, for example, the pressures exerted by the CNEP upon the Merina monarchy. The editor of one of the volumes of the *Journal of Rainilaiarivony* could remark in this connection that apart from the Prime Minister and his secretary Rasanjy no one knew exactly the status of reimbursements of debt contracted with the CNEP. Now, the payment of debts explains to a high degree the economic crisis engulfing the country at the end of the Nineteenth century as well as the progressive alienation from France. Without knowing the details of the financial situation of the Kingdom, other members of the government and the *manamboninahitra* posted to the provinces could not always manage to justify the need to augment the corvées for extraction of gold or the control exercised by foreigners over the customs duties' receipts. More than anyone else, it is Rainilaiarivony who must bear the responsibility for the collapse of the Kingdom.

Distrust and authoritarianism led Rainilaiarivony to neglect the judicious advice of some *manamboninahitra*, certainly better-placed than he to appreciate in full measure the realities of the land and to propose effective solutions with which to thwart the French moves. By way of an example, Rainandriamampandry, Tamatave's Governor, and a *deka* named Ramena sought to persuade the Prime Minister of the necessity to open up the royal army ranks to recruitment among the Betsimisaraka, major population of eastern Madagascar. On the one hand, this would permit to satisfy some of the aspirations held by the provincial peoples wishing to obtain the status of *Ambaniandro* (another name for the Merina) and, on the other, secure their support in the face of foreign aggression. Not to be lost sight of on the strategic level, the Betsimisaraka were also providing just about all of the troops available at the fortified government posts and forts in eastern Madagascar.[24] Yet, profoundly distrustful, Rainilaiarivony rejected the proposal of his subordinates and those who were from the provinces remained confined to the traditional military activities of auxiliary troops — *mpiloka lefona* and *antily.**

Antily or sentinel, guard (usually left behind to hold the conquered areas but also men who gathered military intelligence); *mpiloka-lefona*, literally "brandishers of spears," in this case, with the army equipped with firearms, men armed with spears, (Ed.).

If the prime minister did not always act upon the views of his ablest *manamboninahitra,* he equally could not make himself obeyed at all times, despite his authoritarianism, a factor which only served to make his political solitude even more acute. The stereotyped formulas of allegiance to him, made anew at every opportunity by the governors, did not necessarily convey their real thoughts. In the quest of making their business more lucrative, the *manamboninahitra* adopted in the provinces an attitude which countermanded the sovereignty of Ranavalona III and which favored the ploys of foreigners. In overwhelming the provincial populations with the corvées, the *manamboninahitra* did not contribute to anything that could make it easier to secure the submission and integration of the west-coast Sakalava or the eastern Betsimisaraka, seething with revolt and willing to accept even the advances made by far-away France which seemed far less menacing than the Antananarivo monarchy.

From the capital, Rainilaiarivony could not control the doings of his subordinates. The achievement of his project for a centralized state depended on a network of communications; and, as a worthy "successor" of Kings Andrianampoinimerina and Radama I, the Prime Minister believed in encumbering a foreign invasion while limiting the possibilities of inland penetration. He had no desire to open up the roads that the French could eventually use to invade his Kingdom; but, then, he neither had any avenues through which to send with some ease his reinforcements from Imerina toward the coastal outposts. A Commander-in-Chief so concerned with progress and modernization held on to a very traditional concept of territorial defense. His best military strategists would continue to be the Generals *Tazo* (malarial fever) and *Ala* (forest).

Rainilaiarivony, moreover, had no contact with the coastal populations; and he practically never left Antananarivo with the exception of regular visits to nearby Ambohimanga* and an occasional vacation with the Queen at Tsinjoarivo. There are a number of reasons for his attitude. To the difficulties in communications — lack of roads, the slow journeys by palanquin (*filanjana*) with changing teams of carriers, the great distances of some provinces from the capital (such as those in the north or the

*Ambohimanga, at some 12 miles north of Atnananarivo, had been the "sacred town" of Imerina's monarchs since the time of Andrianampoinimerina, late in the 1700's, (Ed.).

southeast) which made it imperative to safeguard the journeys by shifting and the provisioning of huge numbers of the *dekana* and slaves to go with him — one must also add his centralizing concept of government. Rainilaiarivony wanted to direct all of the Kingdom's affairs from the capital itself; and he left to local governors the duty to represent him, to speak and to act in his name. At times, he would dispatch to the provinces some of the *manamboninahitra* to whom fell the duty of solving those thorny problems that could not be resolved by local authorities. Provincial populations thus did not come to know Rainilaiarivony except through such intermediaries as the governors and the *manamboninahitra* that read his *kabary* and his recommendations, who composed the speeches that were supposed to translate the thought of the Prime Minister. If such a system was to yield positive results, Rainilaiarivony had to be sure of his provincial collaborators, something that frequently was not the case as is attested by many of his remonstrances addressed to provincial governors.[25] A stricter surveillance of the *manamboninahitra* might have led him to prevent the discontent among some subjects of the Queen who were obligated to carry out a long string of works ostensibly for the state but, in fact, done for the local governors only. Crushed under the weight of multiple taxes and corvées (the usefulness of which, on behalf of the Kingdom, they did not always understand), the provincial populations at times refused to undertake the tasks which were vital for the country or at least for its rulers. This is why chiefs of the different posts along the road to the eastern littoral had difficulties in securing, when needed, the relays for transporting goods unloaded at the Betsimisaraka coast and going to Antananarivo.[26] Cut off from the provinces, informed by the governors who were not always conscientious, the Prime Minister became physically and morally isolated in the capital he did not wish to leave for other reasons of self-interest. His determination to folow closely the social and political milieux in Antananarivo was decidedly reinforced by the fear of plots. Having acceded to power himself by eliminating his own brother, Rainilaiarivony was too keenly aware of the ongoing struggles for influence among individuals and coteries not to be distrustful. The sending, at the head of an expedition into the Fiherenana Valley (southwestern Madagascar), first of the influential officer Rainimiadana (15 *Voninahitra*) in 1888 and even more, thirteen months later, of Queen

Rasoherina's nephew, Prince Ramahatra, was an expression of his desire to keep those *manamboninahitra* who seemed dangerous away from the capital. Just when he was ill, in 1893, Rainilaiarivony also had to face a plot directed against him and involving Rajoelina, one of his many sons.

What came to accentuate even more his own isolation was the fact that the Queen's subjects, so poorly informed, so rarely invited to take some part — be it a distant one — in the affairs of state, were no longer disposed to give him unquestioned support. Even the royal troops, composed almost entirely of the Merina, sometimes refused to obey the orders of their Commander-in-Chief. Despite the sentence of death which hung over those fleeing the ranks, desertions in the army became quite numerous; for example, the Betsileo soldiers recruited by force to go with the Fiherenana expeditions deserted en masse.[27] In any event, the falling back and the rout of the royal army before the French expeditionary corps in 1895, despite its very real capacity to resist and despite the injunctions of Rainilaiarivony, bear witness to the fact taht the Prime Minister was no longer in charge of a *foloalindahy** that could be counted upon. In such a context, how could the failure of 1895 have been avoided, failure which spelled the end of an independence that he had succeeded in preserving since 1864?

As a way of still holding on to the integrity of the Kingdom, now tied to a foreign power by a treaty with ambiguous clauses, the Prime Minister attempted, with considerable skill, to have his own interpretation of the agreement validated at the national and international levels. Until 1890 at least he could easily cling to this attitude, partly because of the nature of the treaty itself and partly because of the benevolent neutrality of Great Britain and other important states when it came to the Merina monarchy.

In the first place, the explanatory letter of 9 January 1886 prepared by the French plenipotentiaries at the request of the government of Ranavalona III, reduced the degree to which the French Resident General (whose presence could not be avoided) could operate. To the Malagasy, this letter represented a referential document of inestimable value; and the constant recourse to the Miot-Partimonio letter allowed Rainilaiarivony to show himself as a skilled and cunning diplomat.[28] He could, thus, express

*Literally, "the ten-ten-thousand-men" (100,000), idiomatically, "army," (Ed.).

surprise and indignation to Le Myre de Vilers, who negated any official character of this "appendix" and he could stress, in the earliest interviews with the Resident General, that this was an agreement as valid as the Treaty itself. Pushing the French representative to the wall, he told him: "if the established agreement fails to be recognized it will be equally (impossible) to recognize (all the) dealings that we have with you." Instructions issued to the provincial governors recall the validity of this appendix, only document that could persuade Ranavalona III to sign the Treaty. In the extreme, one could claim that Rainilaiarivony considered himself less bound by the Treaty than by the appendix. While commenting to his close collaborators on the contents of the Treaty of 17 December, the Prime Minister showed forcefully and in detail that the two texts complemented each other, with the second clarifying the first and giving it the true meaning. He knew how to squeeze every advantage out of such a situation since, in his own terms, the additional protocol altered everything that could constitute a danger for the Kingdom.

Given the task to make a protectorate an effective one, the Resident-General ran into the *Appendix* which provided a list (hardly an extensive one) of the affairs relating to the domain of foreign policy in which he could intervene.[29] As for Rainilaiarivony, he adhered strictly to this famous list and excluded from the competency of the Resident-General the transmission of exequaturs. A fine tactician, the Prime Minister used the services of foreigners such as the consular agent of Italy, Désiré Maigrot[30] or the English journalist Tacchi,[31] to let the external world know what his point of view was in respect to the importance of the appendix, the limits of the Resident-General's role, and his fierce determination to defend the country's independence. He could thus stir up discord between the French and other foreigners and prevent any serious French control over the Malagasy policies.

To block French ascendancy in Madagascar Rainilaiarivony also played upon the difficulties and inexactnesses of translation and upon the differences created in their wake between French and Malagasy texts, both of which had equal value at the juridical level. To a Resident-General who pretended to be "representing Madagascar" in external relations, the Prime Minister would retort that his competence was limited to simple observance (*mitandrina*), nothing more. Linguistic subtleties, interpretations based on a document not acceptable as binding by the adversary (who would then be accused of bad faith), such were the means employed by this astute diplomat to make his ideas widely known.

At times, when the fragility of his positions was apparent as he had to face the Resident-General, Rainilaiarivony would waver, refusing to make a rapid decision or even to discuss anything with the French representative. He would then latch on to any pretext to gain time while trying mightily the representative's patience. There would be those notorious headaches or sudden abdominal pains of a Rainilaiarivony concerned in reality only with how to ward-off an interview with the Resident-General. Gabriel Gravier wrote on this subject that "every time that Monsieur Bompard (successor of Le Myre de Vilers as Resident-General) wanted to discuss an exequatur or some English correspondence, Rainilaiarivony would get his *colique diplomatique* (diplomatic indigestion)."[32] Actually, all this spelled out the weakness of the position in which the Prime Minister found himself when confronted simultaneously with a host of internal problems and with the collusion of imperialist powers on the morrow of the Zanzibar Convention.

Even before this agreement was signed by France and England, in 1890, the socio-political situation within the Kingdom had been a dominant preoccupation for Rainilaiarivony, obliging him to become less intransigent toward the Resident-General. Examples are not lacking. In Vonizongo, one of the districts were workers were recruited to exploit the auriferous resources of Iboina, the inhabitants refused to go to the main town of Maevatanana and gather for their gold corvées. This was at a time when the corvée for gold was considered vital by a government hard-pressed in finances and heavily indepted vis-à-vis a power with only one aim — to colonize Madagascar. Moreover, banditry or *"fahavalism"* became rampant in western sections of the Kingdom, reaching even into the heart of Imerina, along the outskirts of Antananarivo and Ambohimanga.[33] In 1893, Rainilaiarivony sent 2,000 men to restore order at Maevatanana, town that had already been troubled for some years by the *fahavalo* bands composed of nomadic looters, soldiers who had deserted and men who had defaulted on their corvée obligations.[34] Both the attention and the energy of the Prime Minister were thus dispersed at a moment so crucial in the history of Madagascar. It can be said that during the last years of his government Rainilaiarivony was fighting just about alone.

The Queen, whose own enthronement had been arranged by Rainilaiarivony, no longer gave him automatic support even if he was not only Her Prime Minister but also Her husband; and this allowed Her own partisans to place upon his shoulders all responsibility for a possible break with France. Although Italy had come to defend the cause of Malagasy independence since 1892, following the Ethiopian Affair and the resulting tension with France,[35] Rainilaiarivony could no longer count on the more important English benevolence. Early in 1890, one could witness the disappearance of *Madagascar Times*, the fighting paper of Britons who lived in Madagascar as well as forum for the expression of the Merina government's political positions. Tacchi, its "well-informed" editor, "had undoubtedly understood even before this decision (the Zanzibar Convention) was announced that the game was up and hence abandoned the fight."[36] In these circumstances, the policy of vacillation between foreigners to which Rainilaiarivony was attached and his constant dodging were hardly appropriate to ensure the defense of a kingdom coveted by France ready to benefit henceforth from the English support. Bitterly, the Prime Minister would talk at the time about the *Vazaha mody miady"* (foreigners who pretend not to hear).

At this point, Rainilaiarivony's efforts were concentrated on setting-up a defensive military strategy, proving once again that he would go as far as armed resistance to repel French claims. A diplomatic intervention by Le Myre de Vilers in October 1894 to have the Malagasy government accept the protectorate seemed almost superfluous before the resolve of a Prime Minister bent on fighting, even if he had to go it alone. Indeed, Rainilaiarivony had been preparing, since 1893, for the eventuality of an armed conflict with France and he devoted most of his time exclusively to the activities of the Commander-in-Chief. According to His *Journal*, he went on with an intense recruitment drive and spent days in receiving volunteers, in observing the military man-oeuvres and parades. At the end of 1890, he informed, for example, Rainandriamampandry, still governor of the Betsimisaraka province, that an American named Geldart would unload some powder kegs at Tamatave. Indeed, such military deliveries were becoming quite frequent at Madagascar's eastern ports and they

were made without knowledge of the French. Also, in his instructions to provincial governors, Rainlaiarivony recommended that
they take the necessary measures and prepare for war: limit the
exporting of food articles, fortify the posts and garrisons of the
eastern littoral and at the mouth of the Betsiboka River, on the
western side.[37] But, the strategy worked out by the Prime Minister
had nonetheless a number of imperfections. The already mentioned
traditional concepts of defense that he retained —*Tazo* and
Ala— continued to impress him as the most valuable auxiliaries;
and he was even right, given the huge loss among the French
troops that were decimated by fever, after France had decided
to attack from the western side. But, there seemed to be no
real question of a victory for the Malagasy side.

Neglecting the advice of General Rainandriamampandry who
had foreseen for a long time an attack from the west rather
than the east, the Merina Commander-in-Chief remained attached,
until 1894, to a plan —that had become something of a classic—
for an attack coming from the Betsimisaraka province. More than
that, as a member of a land-owning oligarchy that believed in
a stratagy based on having a dense network of forts and not in
possessing a navy capable of waging war along the shores of
Madagascar, Rainilaiarivony did nothing innovative in matters of
defense methods. Located in the areas from which the movement
of ships could be easily followed (such as the fort of Ambohi-
trombikely that dominates the Bombetoka Bay, at Betsiboka's
mouth, or that of Vohijanahary in control of entry to the eastern
Bay of Antongil), the "batteries" for defense formed "of old
cannons coming of (the domestic production at) Mantasoa
or yet imported from Europe and the United States," were manned
by inadequate military contigents. The French counted on this
factor to secure a victory. As Martineau had written, "such a
battery, on the whole badly defended, could not resist an attack
by Europeans..."[38] A reinforcement of the Merina army units
with recruits from the provincial populations would undoubtedly
have resulted in a far better organization of resistance; yet, as
has been shown, Rainilaiarivony refused to follow this course.
Equally, his projects to build-up a navy remained in a state of
expectations.

The *Ambohimanga*, acquired in 1890, and rather pompously
baptized as a warship, was manned by some twenty Merina

hardly accustomed to life at sea and it was commanded by a foreigner (L. Perrier). When preparations for a French attack could no longer be postponed, in 1894, the *Ambohimanga* lost its 10-cm. Canet cannon so that it could be transported ashore to Manjakadrianombana[39], fort which symbolized the Malagasy resistance in 1883, as a piece deemed essential for the defense of eastern Madagascar. The lack of a coherent maritime policy was detrimental to Rainilaiarivony's defense program; and, he just could not effectively place under naval surveillance several thousand kilometers of the coast surrounding the insular kingdom he had wanted to keep free of all foreign penetration.

To the inadequacies of military strategy must be added the lack of will to fight among the royal troops, over which Rainilaiarivony had increasingly less control and hold. The routing of the army and rapid retreat before the advancing French when the attack did come (all of which left the road to Antananarivo open) reveals this with clarity. "Neither Ramasombazaha, first field commander of the Merina forces in 1894-1895, nor Andriantavy, his deputy, showed much zeal for combat."[40] The abandonment of even easily defensible strategic points like Andriba, situated in a "region bristling with numerous fortifications," is indicative of this lack of army morale, of the true *état d'esprit* among the *foloalindahi*. Rainilaiarivony, the "dictator," was no longer in command of a well-disciplined army; no longer could he give orders to be carried out unquestionably; nor did he remain as leader of a "war government." Following the surrender of Antananarivo and the signing of the protectorate Treaty in September 1895, the Prime Minister saw the collapse of everything he had struggled for in more than thirty years — the independence of the "Kingdom of Madagascar."

IV

Despite the obstinacy with which, it seems, he had defended the Kingdom's integrity, for reasons of state or his personal interests or yet both, some of his compatriots blamed the defeat of 1895 entirely on Rainilaiarivony. The day after French conquest, there was a great deal of criticism addressed against the deposed Prime Minister who had already been accused for years, by the "reactionary party," as one giving-in to the temptations of western civilization, real source of the many illis inflicted upon Madagascar.

According to the still-resisting *Menalamba*,* who were extremely attached to the old religious traditions, Rainilaiarivony had, through his conversion to Christianity, already betrayed ancestors and country, thus alienating gradually the Kingdom's independence. The defeat of 1895 was hence interpreted as manifestation of the righteous wrath of the gods.[41] Even more, a surrender, almost without a fight, of Antananarivo itself reinforced the belief of some that a greedy Rainilaiarivony had sold the country. Still, the fate prepared by the French for Rainilaiarivony leads us not to share in the broader judgement entirely. His removal from the Prime Minister's office, which was immediate, and his exile from Madagascar argue in the final analysis that the French feared him.

The fact nonetheless remains that Rainilaiarivony had a large responsibility for the Kingdom's fall. It is true that not a few *manamboninahitra* left their leader in solitude, to discuss matters with himself, in the midst of Madagascar's worst difficulties. They hardly came to important meetings which dealt with affairs of state and were eager only to receive their share of the *isampolo* (rights of customs duties which had attained 10% of the value of goods). Ranavalona III, too, drew away from Rainilaiarivony, bit by bit, and at a time when Madagascar was in serious crises. But, his increasingly authoritarian ways, his distrust of the different populations or of those *manamboninahitra* who really could have helped him to fight, his tendency to confuse the interest of state with his personal one, his over-centralizing concept of power and his long-outmoded idea of defense could only lead to the ultimate failure of Rainilaiarivony's policies. With the protectorate established in 1895, the defeat of the "Kingdom of Madagascar" was also a severe personal defeat for a statesman whose own personality had left a mark on adversaries and compatriots alike.

---

*So named after the red-cloth toga-like garment, the *Menalamba* represent a complex mixture of an early resistance movement, neo-traditionalism (religious and secular), and incohate violence. An analogous movement emerged also among the Betsimisaraka and both were a prelude to the French Annexation of Madagascar (6 August 1896), (Ed.).

NOTES

1. A. D'Anthouard and A. Ranchot, *L'Expedition de Madagascar, Journaux de route*, Paris, 1930, p. 258.

2. Archives of the Malagasy Democratic Republic, A.R.D.M./PP 14, *Journal of Rainilaiarivony*, p. 124.

3. The number of meetings of the Cabinet members devoted to the scrutiny of this treaty, the lenght of their discussions, and the variety of questions that were brought out are tell-tale signs of their apprehensions, *cf.* the *Journal of Rainilaiarivony*, A.R.D.M./PP 13, pp. 761-777, 861-892, and 933-943.

4. A. Martineau, *Madagascar en 1894, Etude de politique contemporaine*, Paris, May 1894, p. 251.

5. *Cf.* G.S. Chapus and G. Mondain, *Rainilaiarivony, Un Homme d'Etat Malgache*, Paris, 1953, p. 437; also J. Ravelomanana, La Vie Religieuse à Ambositra (1880-1895), Antananarivo, 1971, (University of Madagascar typescript, History Department, 157 pp.).

6. J. Randriamanantena, *Les missionnaires de la L.M.S. et le gouvernement malgache; contribution à une étude de leurs relations à la fin du XIXe siecle*, Antannarivo, 1971, (University of Madagascar typescript, History Department, 91 pp.).

7. See J.B. Piolet, *Madagascar et les Hova*, Paris, 1895.

8. Correspondence of individual foreigners addressed to Rainilaiarivony, A.R.D.M., Serie DD.

9. Father Adrien Boudou's comments on Pickersgill will be found in volume II of his *Les Jesuites à Madagascar au XIXe siècle*, Paris, 1942, especially pp. 306-309 and passim.

10. Cited by J. Chastainer-Atger in *Le Madagascar Times d'Anthony Tacchi (1882-1890)*, Antananarivo, 1977, (University of Madagascar typescript, 93 pp. in the History Department).

11. *Cf.* G. Jacob, thesis in progress; M. Esoavelomandroso, *Problemes de justice et de police à Tamatave, à l'époque de Rainandriamampandry, Etudes Historiques*, No. 1, University of Madagascar, 1974 (116 pp. typescript) and his *La Province maritime du "Royaume de Madagascar," à la fin du XIXe siecle*, Paris and Antananarivo, 1976 (467 pp. typescript).

12. *Article 1:* The Government of the French Republic will represent Madagascar in all of its external relations. The Malagasy abroad will be placed under the protection of France: *Article 2* -A Resident, representing the government of the Republic will preside over the external relations of Madagascar without interfering in the internal administration of states belonging to Her Majesty the Queen.

13. Guy Jacob, "Influences occidentales et déséquilibres économiques en Imerina avant la conquete francaise," Colloquium of Historians and Jurists, Académie Malgache, September 1977, (mimeo. 13 pp.), Antananarivo.

14.In respect to everyting concerning Rainilaiarivony's reforms see H. Ratrimoharinosy-Andriantsalama, *La société malgache et la crise de 1883-1885 à travers le journal de Rainilaiarivony*, Paris, 1972 (MA thesis of 240 pp.).

15. See Jacob, "Influences occidentales," 1977 (above) and Ratrimoharinosy-Andriantsalama, *La société malgache*, 1972 (above).

16. Andriantsilavo, originally a Tsimiamboholahy from Ilafy, had been an adviser to Andrianampoinimerina; his second son Rainiharo became "Prime Minister" under Ranavalona Ist; the son of Rainiharo, Rainilaiarivony took his turn in 1864 as Prime Minister, by ousting his older brother Raharo, who had occupied the post since 1852.

17. *Cf.* Phares Mutibwa, *The Malagasy and the Europeans, Madgascar's Foreign Ralations 1861-1895*, London, 1974, Chapter 6.

18. As an example, Rainitsimbazafy, who became Prime Minister after the elimination of Rainilaiarivony, was a descendant of Rainijohary, one of the political adversaries of the former Prime Minister Rainiharo and of his son Raharo; and he belonged to the clan of Tsimahafotsy, a competitor of the Tsimiamboholahy.

19. With the studies regarding other provinces of the "Kingdom of Madagascar" still in progress, we can only give here some examples taken from the Betsimisaraka province, *cf.* M. Esoavelomandroso, 1974 and 1976 (above), note 11.

20. As an example, one could site the case of the sugar-processing factory at Mahasoa in the valley of Ivondro.

21. See "Une visite a Rainilaiarivoune" in Jean Carol's *Chez les Hova (au pays rouge)*, Paris, 1898, pp. 25-26.

21. *Journal of Rainilaiarivony*, A.R.D.M./PP 14, p. 3.

22. *Journal of Rainilaiarivony*, A.R.D.M./PP 13, p. 880.

24. M. Esoavelomandroso, *Province Maritime*, 1976, passim.

25. M. Esoavelomandroso, *Province Maritime*, 1976, passim.

26. M. Esoavelomandroso, *Province Maritime*, 1976, passim.

27. See J. Rainihifina, *Tantara Betsileo* (History of Betsileo), Fianarantsoa, 1975.

28. We are extracting here some of the main aspects of our thesis, *L'attitude malgache face au traité de 1885 (d'apres le journal de Rainilaiarivony)*, *Etudes Historiques*, no. 3 Antananarivo, 1977 (mimeo. 103 pp.).

29. The letter of 9 January 1886 cites *by way of an example:* the Resident can go into opposition to any ceding of territory to any foreign country whatsoever; to all military and naval units, in so far as any aid in men or vessels is being solicited from the Queen's government by a foreign nation it cannot be accorded without the consent of the French government. No treaty, agreement or convention could be made without the approval of the French government.

30. M.A. Poisson-Giuliani, *L'Italie et Madagascar de 1878 à 1908, le consulat de Désiré Maigrot*, Antananarivo, 1973, (University of Madagascar, Department of History, mimeo. of 188 pp.).

31. See above, note 10, regarding the *Madagascar Times*.

32. See G. Gravier, *Madagascar: Les Malgaches, origines de la colonisation française, la conquete*, Paris, 1904.

33. A.R.D.M., Serie BB, cited in Faranirina Esoavelomandroso, *L'Attitude malgache face au traité de 1885* (note 28 above).

34. G. Jacob, "Troubles sociaux et fahvalisme dans le Boina," *Annales de l'Universite* (de Madagascar), serie Lettres et Sciences humaines, no. 6, 1967, pp. 21-33.

35. See Poisson-Giuliani, *L'Italie et Madagascar*, 1973 (note 30 above).

36. *Cf.* Mme Chastanier-Atger, *Le Madagascar Times*, 1977, (note 10 above).

37. See F. Esoavelomandroso, *L'Attitude Malgache* (note 28 above).

38. See Martineau, *Madagascar en 1894* (note 4 above).

39. See M. Esoavelomandroso, *Province Maritime*, 1976, (note 11 above).

40. M. Esoavelomandroso, "Le mythe d'Andriba," *Omaly sy Anio*, nos. 1-2, 1976, pp. 43-74.

41. T.T. Matthews, "Among the 'Fahavalo: 'Perils and Adventures of a Prisoner for Fourteen Months in the Rebel Camp," *Antananarivo Annual*, VI/21(1897), pp. 80-93, being a translation by Matthews.

At the Origin of
British Evangelization:
The Dream of Madagascar

V. BELROSE-HUYGHUES*
University of Madagascar

At the end of the 1700's Madagascar showed a multiplicity of faces, some quite mysterious, to those outsiders who were interested in it and as a function of what interested them about this Great Island in the first place. Far beyond what Madagascar could have been within itself at the time, it was precisely what visitors from overseas had believed to have found within its confines that turned Madagascar into an exceptional island in European literature from the 1500's and into the Eighteenth century.

There was hardly any difference between the religious and political avenues taken out of Europe by men who ventured overseas as soldiers and sailors, merchants and missionaries. Their travels away from home were impelled by a globally-oriented dynamism, pushing Europeans from the Atlantic toward Asia, with increasing intensity, from the Sixteenth to the Eighteenth centuries. First a way station, dreaded and valued at the same time, coastal Madagascar became in the 1600's a pole of French colonization, at Fort Dauphin, and of the English one, at the Bay of Saint-Augustine. But, toward the end of the Seventeenth century, the island was nothing more than a reserve pool of men and provisions for the "Franconesie," that colonial empire France had sought to carve out for herself in the Indian Ocean; and, also, a pausing point along the route to the Indies for the Dutch and the British. Thus, much of Madagascar —including its least "profitable" sections— was left

*Translated from French by R. Kent.

to pursue its traditional life while the coastal fringes were taken and interlocked into a network of foreign interests.

Paradoxically, except just once, in 1783, neither the French Indies Company nor the Crown accumulated the means with which to dominate the seas and secure the lanes opened to commercial and other shipping. What France did not lack in individual competence and determination it lacked in the scope of the general will. Neither the rulers, nor aristocracy, nor yet the middle-class merchants were willing to underwrite a long-term overseas investment at the time. In fact, Madagascar offers a good example of those contemporary French contradictions. In the 1770's, Count of Maudave* attempted to revive a French settlement in southeastern Madagascar but was sabotaged by the planters and traders at the French Mascarenes out of fear that the new colony would become their competitor. Count Benyowsky,** with direct support of the French Court, tried for yet another colony, in Madagascar's imposing Bay of Antongil. He died of a French bullet in 1785, not, however, without making a contribution to the knowledge of Madagascar's interior attained through the journeys of Mayeur and Dumaine.*** Indeed, all attempts at the documentation of Madagascar were the doings of Frenchmen — Grenier, Rochon, Commerson and Bougainville; and all of the resulting publications would serve as underpinnings of British penetration into the Western Indian Ocean in the ensuing century. The case is a clear one: a century of human and material investments profited in the end the only nation that could bring together the determination and the means, namely the United Kingdom.

Far from being strictly commercial in nature, this collective English will had a religious quality as well. David Hume was proposing the destruction of ignorance, laziness and of barbarity to allow for the advent of economic partnerships; and this

---

* Sometimes spelled Modave, he was a former officer in the French-Indian Army who acquired ultimately large holdings in the Mascarenes. His colony in southeastern Madagascar lasted from 1768 to 1771. (Ed.)

**Polish-Hungarian by family and birth, he first visited Madagascar in 1772. In 1774 he creted the colony of Louisbourg in Madagascar and declared himself independent of France. See also note 24 below. (Ed.)

***Nicolas Mayeur was Benyowsky's interpreter and the most important observer in 18th century Madagascar; Dumaine, a trader, made some important journeys as well. (Ed.)

was not as a consequence of growth in trade and in the wealth of the English nation, but, rather, under the impact of cultural shock created through the opening-up of the world by way of the latest discoveries and through the more immediate contacts with French culture.

The huge volume of literature about travels produced in that century gave overwhelming proof of the diversity in the human species, of the variety of man's physical characteristics, customs and behavior; and this was happening just as the contours of a new economy started to emerge and as the trials of ordeal by war deepened even further the gap between the wealthy and the poor, in contrast with the peaceful and happy societies existing outside of Europe. But, as France projected the dissatisfaction of her elites into exotic dreams while waiting for the dissatisfaction of her wretched to burst into a revolution, England, with the exception of a small minority of deists, became convinced that the idea of human progress, linked directly to the efforts of men, was a design of God. The efforts of enlightened men could lead, through intellectual progress, itself assured with free exercise of reason, to social changes in a direction ordained by God. In this factor lies the origin of evangelization in Madagascar by the non-Conformists of the London Missionary Society (LMS), starting in 1818.

The first observation to be made is that Madagascar with its 228,600 square miles was an island less important on the global scale than the two lesser islands to the east of it. Solidly implanted in the Mascarene Islands of Ile de France (later Mauritius) and Bourbon (later Réunion), as these islands were uninhabited until the arrival of Europeans, the French showed themselves capable of doing little more than causing serious worry among the numerous British fleets that plied the oceans between the Cape of Good Hope and India. They could not secure a foothold either in Madagascar or in the Comoro Islands despite repeated attempts. Incorporated into the mercantile system of the European East Indies companies only at its coastal rims, Madagascar had never attracted in a lasting and systematic way the lust of ship-owners and shrewd merchants of Europe. The Portuguese and the Dutch had abandoned Madagascar rather quickly except as a port of call at various points for their vessels and some cargoes of slaves. Only the French and the English came to believe in the discovery of an 'Eldorado" denied them in their westward conquests. It should also be taken into consideration that Madagascar was a source of profits for creole traders from the Mascarenes and for their associates in France. For them, Madagascar was a colony of factories, especially after the attempts at direct colonization had failed, modest as these had been in the southeast in the Seventeenth and, again, in the Eighteenth centuries. The desire of French creoles for a conquest of Madagascar was being justified on the grounds of tangible and daily realities, even if some of the more astute among them feared that this would kill off the goose that laid the golden eggs.

In contrast, Madagascar was for Great Britain a very real illusion. The English had a "golden legend" about Madagascar that, as Hubert Deschamps has written, no failure could tarnish until the Nineteenth century, something that could not be accounted for *a priori* by any important mercantile interest.[1] In times of peace, the Mascarenes gave the opportunity to English vessels to take part in an active and profiatble contraband; but, it seems that the small islands were never coveted by the British and if they did take them by conquest at the start of the 1800's this was for strategic reasons and not for any economic benefits. For them, Madagascar was a port of call on route to the Indies, used quite often "on the inside" or on the side of the Mozambique Channel because —while this was a perilous maritime route— it had the advantage of avoiding French attacks from the Ile de France.[2] From the western coast of Madagascar, too, a few slaves could be taken out as useful items of exchange in trade with the Mascarenes. Although the English had several labor outlets in the East as well as many sources of slaves in western Africa, it cannot be said that a mercantile interest was entirely absent among the English captains who put into Madagascar at the end of the Sixteenth century.[3]

As ships of England were penetrating the Mediterranean and sailing along coastal Africa, the merchant circles were learning about India. "At Antwerp, where a Portuguese factory had always been a source of inspiration, the soon-to-be author of *Utopia*, Thomas More, would have as an interlocuter a Portuguese sailor who would map out for him a canvas of oriental civilizations."[4] Since 1530, Thomas More's son both translated and printed the accounts of Portuguese voyages in eastern Africa and in Asia.[5] Madagascar was already present, out in the open or in the guise of Utopia, in the imagination of Britons, thanks to their fascination with the glorious and promised islands of Christianized legends. One could almost say that the earliest of English navigators in these parts already knew what they would find and that this knowledge, result of belief and dream, would resist all realities.

The first contacts were nonetheless unfavorable, with such rare exceptions as the visit of James Lancaster to the Bay of Antongil in 1591. It is true that he was mainly into the chase of Hispano-Iberians across all seas, as had been the practice started by Francis Drake in 1577-1580.[6] In 1591, too, William Mace, captain of the "Edward Bonaventure" was thrown against the Mahafaly (or southwestern) coast after enduring hurricane winds near the Cape of Good Hope but he could not land and was ultimately massacred in the Comoros with 32 of his sailors.[7] This, however, did not prevent Lancaster from returning to the Antongil Bay in 1600 to trade there with the Malagasy during some two months. Shortly thereafter, the ships under John Davis anchored in the Bay of Saint-Augustine before reaching southeast Asia. This Bay became rapidly known to the merchant and military vessels on the way to India; it continued to be their favorite mooring and trading area throughout the 1600's and the 1700's, without mentioning the pirates who had made it their headquarters for a time. David Middleton who had stopped at the Bay to "take water and wood" in 1610 was the first of the merchants from whom we have, up to now, a written account of his Malagasy sojourn.[8] He had it circulated among the members of the East India Company where sailors, merchants and the influential members of Parliament and government were rubbing shoulders. This trading description inaugurated a tradition of heaping praise that would come to be widespread and last until the 1820's, a tradition to which belongs the *Memoir* of Andrew Brun, deposited with the directors of the LMS in 1795.

Incontestably, the interest that England had in Madagascar since the start of the Seventeenth century was born among the merchants and sailors in England and Scotland, as the English-language bibliography about Madagascar before the Nineteenth century can show at once.[9] Here, one can discover the importance of the demand for information about the Indian world, and even more particularly about the Island of Madagascar, in the circle of the great London merchants, the best-informed at the time because London was, with Edinburgh, the center of the most advanced and prolific printing in Great Britain. On everything that concerned Madagascar, the books published in London between 1610 and 1820 or the accounts inserted in the compilations of voyages, highly esteemed at the time, were authored by eleven merchant captains, among them a Scot named Hamilton, six captains or sailors in the Royal Navy, and six geographers and compilers, one of whom was non-secular, Reverend Thomas Banks. These last, as well as one of the very first "tourists" in the regions, the Anglo-Irishman Prior, all belonged to the period between the end of the 1700's and the early years of the Nineteenth century.[10] This list, prepared at the start with the aid of the *Ouvrages Anciens* about Madagascar, a collection put together by A. and G. Grandidier, and of the British Library card-index, is far from being a full one. A lot remains yet to be done, by following the example of the brilliant thesis of Luis de Matos, before one could hope to have a complete inventory of everything in print about Madagascar. Nevertheless, the figures of the modest sample above are confirmed by studies done elsewhere.

Thus, in a work just published, Mervyn Brown* shows the permanence in Great Britain, since the end of the 1500's of a general interest with variable degrees of intensity (according to different periods) for the southeastern Indian Ocean and its islands. The region of western Madagascar between the Saint-Augustine Bay and Morondava seems to be the pole of this attraction which also took in the Comores with Anjoun. According to a study by M. Handover, one finds that all of this was an aspect of what could be called "exoticism in the British style."[11] Begun by Thomas More, this literature is much richer in reflexions upon the plurality of worlds and upon the adventures which conditioned their exploration than in the languid descriptions of tropical Edens. The geographic tale, which is not the philosophical tale of the French, belongs to an English patrimony reaching into the popular strata. Until the Eighteenth century, it is notable by absence of any exoticism as it is understood in French literature.[12]

Madagascar Rediscovered: A History from the Earliest Times to Independence, London, 1978, esp. pp. 30-91.

One is dealing, in fact, with the literature of merchant-adventurers, rigid of religion and in their mores, a literature in which the richness of lands, the functioning of societies, and the manner in which they produce retain the authors' attention.[13] It notes the arrangements of reliefs and of shallows but does not describe the landscapes; mores are observed and admired, along with the hospitality and prodigality of the "natives" but there is no praise of the beauty of their women; there is no appeal to the libido in this literature, no sensual "urge of dream." If there is a dream, it is that of the merchant. Even Drury* kept the cool and methodical eye of the merchant. In the Seventeenth century, the merchants of London, most of whom were under the spell of Puritanism, dreamed of being free. "The Puritan merchant had seen the Crown both squeeze money out of his company, and threaten its monopoly by encouraging interlopers to infringe on its charter."[14] In the person of Charles I, the British Crown gave up the idea of establishing in Madagascar a "plantation" for Prince Rupert in 1636. The way was now clear and a chartered company was now created: in 1644 a colony of 140 men, women and children under John Smart attained the Bay of Saint-Augustine. It turned into a failure, much as was the case six years later, in 1650, with the colony at the isle of Assada (Nosy-Bé), as well as later that of Port-Louquez (Lokia), in 1816. Madagascar had disappointed every hope, refusing to become the new "Isle of Saints" for those Puritans in search of the Lost Paradise and liberty of commerce. As much was said, and written, in 1650 by Powle Waldegrave,[15] one of the rare survivors of the ill-fated Puritan colony at the Bay of Saint-Augustine, but to no avail. Indeed, if no other "plantation" came about, it was because in the ensuing hundred years, and within the context of Europe, the effort went toward the Atlantic, preventing enterprise elsewhere. Pirates now took turns with the slave traders, while Robert Drury was spending some fifteen years in a captivity which the Malagasy slaves among the Whites would have envied at the time.

This episode in the history of Europeans in Madagascar would provide the master-theme for all of the writings and undertakings in the second half of the Eighteenth century. Madagascar was no longer the island rich in gold but one in which the inha-

*See note 25 below.

bitants were among the happiest in the world, an island subjected to oppression and barbaric exploitation by Europeans, that is to say by pirates and slave-traders.

Just when England began to feel anew a need for morality in every sphere, Madagascar presented a fine opportunity to make an act of sincere penitence. All of the writings at the end of the 1700's, whether by English authors or French authors translated into English (such as the Abbés Rochon and Raynal or Bernardin de Saint-Pierre) developed this theme. One of the last to appear before the turn of the 1800's, and also one that is at the start of an interest within the LMS and, later, within the Methodist Missionary Society, expounds this theme in lyrical terms: "England bears a large part of the responsibility for this dreadful commerce practiced by Europeans in this island. We are going to send messages of peace, carrying in one hand the olive branch and the benefits of Christian education in the other."[16] Madagascar could also be a revenge for the exclusions from India and America. Thus, the Scots, recently associated with the maritime and commercial privileges of the Kingdom of England, showed an activity in printing which palced Edinburgh almost on par with London for the number of publications concerning voyages. From another direction, in the area of Glasgow, Academies of the Dissenters were orienting their studies toward the overseas. After being an "Island of Saints" in the Puritan dreams of the 1500's, Madagascar became an inn of the good Samaritan in non-Conformist projects.

In the words of Max Weber,[17] the non-privileged classes fed the missionary avocations the most; and they were also the ones seeking to improve their own social and economic status through "servant imperialism," which accounts for the colonial hue of voyages printed in the later 1700's. The *Histoire des Deux Indes* of Abbé Raynal was translated and published in Edinburgh since 1776 and it attained five successive reprintings in the rest of the century.[18] The interest of Scots in a work of colonial philosophy is revealing, especially when one considers that *Paul and Virginia* went through six editions in London between 1789 and 1802. In the late Eighteenth century London, the taste of the English gentry that made this success possible, was more susceptible to the romantic exoticism in the writings of B. de Saint-Pierre[19] than to the harsh and vehement account

of Abbé Raynal. From 1720 onward there was a considerable
demand for books on voyages; and, on the heels of a lone
narrative, sometimes not larger than a booklet, there came the
huge tomes of the *Collections* and *Histories* of voyages.[20] Works
of theology alone surpassed, in the variety of titles and the
number of copies printed, this literature which apparently
struck a chord at the popular level. Defoe's *Crusoe* and the
Gulliver of Swift, classics in their own time, were constructed
around a plot quite commonly employed at this period. Yet,
the purpose of many such books went beyond entertainment
and into the commercial, even colonial promotion. They contained descriptions of new lands, of their mercantile possibilities
and of navigational difficulties along their coasts. Not a few
were sold right at the docks, to find their way into the chests
of sailors.

It would hence be wrong to regard this literature, at least in
England, as a reflection of simple curiousity at the mass level.
"The latest discoveries seem to have been the sole subject of
conversation among the most civilized as well as all the classes
of the kingdom," wrote the Reverend Thomas Banks in the
preface to his *Universal Geography*.[21] The habit of reading had
attained the artisans and small merchants alike and even the
free peasants of Wales, as is attested in biographies of the Welsh
missionaries; and the books invited all to take part in voyages
and in missionary adventures in the Indies. The preoccupation
with the moral destiny of "natives" is even more clearly pronounced in the report of 8 October 1793 relating the shipwreck
of the *Winterton* and appearing in the *Gentleman's Magazine
and Historical Chronicle:*[22]

> "We feel it our duty to declare, from the information we
> have been able to collect from the accounts of the people
> who were wrecked...that they experienced from the rude
> and uncultivated natives of Madagascar every possible
> assistance and relief which savage life was capable to afford,
> and such disinterested attention as would have done honour
> to the most civilized Christian. The poor untutored tenant
> of the shade displayed an anxious solicitude to yield them
> every succor in his power; evincing, in the strong language
> of nature, that charity, in its noblest acceptation, needs not
> the aid of philosophy or civilization to nurture it into
> practice."

The work of Rochon, printed in 1792 in its English translation by Joseph Trapp, the most important work on Madagascar at the time, was based mainly on the French accounts about Madagascar since the 1600's (Flacourt, Mahe de la Bourdonnais, Maudave, Bougainville, Commerson, Benyowsky) extracted from Abbé Prevost's *Histoire des Voyages.** Finaly, it would have been difficult for the Evangelical circles not to have known about the *Journal* of Drury after four Eighteenth century printings.[23] The English also knew ahead of the French the adventures of Benyowsky in Madagascar and elsewhere since considerable portions of his personal journal were published first in English in 1790 as *Memoirs and Travels.* The French edition came out a year later.[24]

Benyowsky's voyage leads us to consider yet another type of influence, namely through illustrations. Here, again, Drury's *Journal*, with three of them (one religious in character), was best able to find a response in the imagination of Englishmen, especially since the earlier illustrations of Flacourt seemed generally unknown in England. Because they were done either in Madagascar or at the nearby Ile de France, the illustrations in Benyowsky's work were even more precise; and they also gave a good idea of the flora and the coast of eastern Madagascar. As for the maps, they reveal that prior to the execution of mapwork in the Nineteenth century by Bory de Saint Vincent and Lislet-Geoffrey, under Robert Farquhar's patronage,** the 1661 map of Madagascar by Flacourt, with some toponymic additions in the coastal belt, remained the main reference. The map inserted, for example, into Rochon's work by a certain "Robert" is a reflection of this fact and the map in the *Journal* of Drury was directly inspired by Flacourt's own.

What could one really learn from all of the available readings about Madagascar in the Eighteenth century? The study of Drury's *Journal* by Anne Molet-Sauvaget shows that popularization of knowledge about the Great Island had just about attained the limit of satisfaction at the turn of the 1700's.[25] To the most ancient sources used by or known to Defoe, writers

*There are several editions of Prevost's *Histoire des Voyages,* the Hague and the Paris first editions being the main ones in large octavo. Information about Madagascar (obtained without citing most sources) will be generally found in the earlier volumes in the sets of 21 (see particularly vol. II of the Hague ed.). (Ed.)

**On Farquhar see the article by Valette above. (Ed.)

were adding accounts of shipwrecks and of pirate adventures, on the one hand, and an ethnographic background that went back to the 1600's, on the other.

Within this second category, Molet-Sauvaget includes the *Histoire de Madagascar* by Etienne de Flacourt (Paris, 1658 and 1661), the *Rélation* of François Cauche (Paris, 1651), and Richard Boothby's *Description of the most famous Island* (London, 1646). The novelty of the thesis resides in the finding that the English, at the start of the Eighteenth century, through the intermediary of non-Conformist Academies, were able to recover the French legacy regarding knowledge of Madagascar or at least in respect to its southern part; and this was done long before the translation of works by Raynal, Rochon and Lescallier.* No doubt, the French authors' information was dated, especially in relation to the political situation, but the aspects redistributed by Defoe and other British authors under the general heading of ethnography (mores, religion, techniques) were still largely in force and hence usable. Thus, most of the observations found in the *Journal* of Drury had already been made by other authors (circumcision, funerary customs, alliance covenants, possession cult). In fact, all of the Eighteenth-century writings about Madagascar seem to have mined the same documentary ore which went back into the preceding hundred years, swelled more or less by data somewhat more recent and coming from the personal experience of authors or their informants, the sailors and captains who had visited the western side of Madagascar. As for the tone of these works, it had been pre-set since the 1640's by the precursors Richard Bootby and Walter Hammond. More importance is to be attached to the first group of sources, reworked by Defoe himself under the pseudonym of "Captain Charles Johnson" and "revised and augmented" in 1724 as *A General History of the Pyrates*. Slight attention has been paid, until recent times, to this enormous compilation of the eye-witness accounts of men who constantly frequented the coasts of Madagascar between 1665 and 1730. Indeed, a recent and rather magnificent critical edition of this work allows us to appreciate the precise and serious knowledge that Defoe was able to acquire through his research and compilation from

*His *Mémoire* relative to Madagascar appeared in English translation in the *Monthly Magazine*, XIX (April 1805), pp. 222-225 and (July 1805), pp. 548-553. (ed.)

among retired pirates.[26] It also allows us to see that the Eighteenth century popularizers made deliberate selections from the pool of available knowledge when addressing themselves to the public, removing everything that could tarnish the image of the island of dreams. The pirate accounts are precise on the resources of Madagascar but the formulation of Defoe provided for the disappearance of the dangers and inconveniences one could run into — the mosquitoes, the fever, the crocodiles. In contrast, the maritime dangers —the currents and sand bars— were well-described. The pirates themselves appear rather strange. There is never any question of their attacks and their heavy and continuous involvement in slave trade; but, there is much about their good relations with the "natives" and about this new "race" of "Dark Mulattoes" to which they had contributed.[27] One even sees them behaving as good Christians, hardly remiss in their duty to baptize the children sired in Madagascar.[28] Subtly, the history of pirates implanted the idea that Madagascar welcomed the Whites; that it was "to the interest of the Natives to have good relations with them...because the island being divided into petty Governments and Commands, the Pyrates, settled here who are now a considerable number and have little cattle of their own, can preponderate where-ever they think fit to side."[29] The white man became accepted and respected; he was asked to arbitrate in local disputes; and how could this fail to engender among the potential preachers of the Gospel a belief that this was practically an invitation to come? If, moreover, vagabonds like the pirates were already accepted, men of the Gospel would surely come to be venerated.

To be objective, the pirates took up what the private merchants were doing between 1632 and 1690 as they sought to find a slot for themselves within the commercial maze of the Royal African or East India Companies' monopolies, including the one over slave trade in the British colonies. In attacking therefore the East Indiamen the pirates were assisting "interlopers" with whom they also had direct business contracts. Indeed, for some six decades, pirates were the dangerous but indispensable allies of the "privateers" excluded from charter privileges of the Royal Companies. The risks were considerable since pirates could just as well capture and loot vessels belonging to private merchants as they could (and did) the Companies' ships; but, the alliance itself more than made up for the risks, especially in connection with slave trade, by yielding fantastic profits for certain Puritan circles of Boston, New York, Hull, Glasgow or Liverpool.[30]

The East India Company, which began to take strong measures against this attempt at its monopoly, made slight distinctions in attacking pirates and private merchants alike: "those who left our American colonies were either old buccaneers or privateers commissioned by their different governors and making no distinction between piratry and private commerce, or else they were captains and sailors sent to trade with the pirates in Madagascar and, debauched by their company, simply joined the lot."[31] This alliance of respectable burghers of port towns and pirates of Madagascar accounts partly for the benign image of the latter in England as well as for the restraint exercised for a long time by the East India Company which had been given already in 1698 all the power it needed to reduce the nests of pirates in Madagascar. In fact, the Company made every effort to ban slave trade, starting with Madagascar, in 1700 or almost a century before Robert Farquhar, thus reducing the bulk of pirate resources with a single stroke. Still, the expedition sent by the Company in 1699 with an Edict hardly captured every pirate. They disappeared between 1720 and 1730 along with their *raisons d'être* — slave trade with America and interloper commerce with the Indies.

Although it is clear that some of the English and American circles had been associated with the pirates of Madagascar one is hard put to understand the contradiction of how could the morally righteous Puritans of those circles compromise themselves in this way, especially in their slaving activities. For this, one cannot do better than refer back to the context of the Seventeenth century England, as analyzed extremely well by Tawney more than fifty years ago: removed from economic and political power by Archbishop Laud, the Puritan merchants were "confident in their own energy and acumen, proud of their success, and regarding with profound distrust the interference of both Church and State with matters of business and property rights;" the "commercial classes" were demanding "that business affairs should be left to be settled by business men, unhampered by the intrusions of an antiquated morality or by misconceived arguments of public policy."[32] It was, in fact, religion itself that gave men of the 1600's no other solution but to separate the domains of business and religion altogether and adhere to the formula that there were no moral principles in transactions of economic life. This is why a legacy of the pirates could merge with that of the first "privateers" Boothby and Hammond in the British Eighteenth century documentation.

English books provided a nowledge of Madagascar limited to the coastal belt and oriented by a morality toward particular interests, real as well as solid. Madagascar —people used to read— was a Great Island; it was even believed that this was the largest island in the world. While the geography and topography of the coast were known fairly well no one in England knew anything about the interior of Madagascar. The largest number of first-hand accounts concerned mainly the south and southwest, especially the area around the Saint-Augustine Bay, hence the focus; yet, information about northern and eastern Madagascar, through the pirate accounts and those put together by Rochon, was neither negligible nor inaccurate. The island was presented as fertile and important to European commerce then and henceforth as a staging point on route to the Indies. Its population was estimated at some 2 million; its inhabitants —whose mores and techniques were presented with abundant and precise details— were divided into three groups in terms of religion. The majority were "pagans" who believed in two fundamental principles —God and evil spirits— and who had a variety of religious practices, some of them "spotted" with Islamic traits. There were about several hundred Catholics in the Isle of Sainte-Marie. Finally, there were some Muslims at the Comoros and in Western Madagascar. Political information was fair, if on the whole disparate in time and space.

What was missing amounts to fresh and detailed information about the eastern littoral, the very one that had the most active relations with Europe in the Eighteenth century, by way of the two Mascarenes. But, the geopolitical situation of this section excluded *a priori* all British attempts in an area largely dominated by the French. Even less fortunate was the lack of knowledge of the interior of Madagascar in Britain as much in relation to the state of culture of its inhabitants as about its political evolution —all of which were known to the Mascarene interests since the 1770's, from the travels of Mayeur and Hugon. But, this ignorance of the British was not a latent defect since the Merina were about to expand from the interior into eastern Madagascar, to reach the coast controlled by the Mascarene French. This, too, left western Madagascar more accessible to the British, whose information was best developed precisely for this area. In 1800, the London Missionary Society was well-armed for a mission into the Bay of Saint-Augustine upon which converged all the information it had and all of the proposals made to it by Burn, Aspasio and Vanderkamp.[33] For the utilitarianists and zealots of conversion Madagascar was in no real sense an imaginary island at all.

NOTES

1. H. Deschamps, *Histoire de Madagascar*, Paris, 1965 ed., p. 66, and passim.

2. On the dangers of navigation, see R. Decary, "Les satellites de Madagascar et l'ancienne navigation dans le canal de Mozambique," *Bulletin de l'Académie Malgache*, new serie , XX (1937), pp. 53-72.

3. Not to mention the Scots who went as sailors on the ships of France, England and Portugal since the early 1500's.

4. Luis de Matos, *L'Expansion portugaise dans la littérature latine de la Renaissance*, Paris, 1959 (Doctoral dissertation at the Sorbonne). The author holds that this navigator's identity corresponds to that of Duarte Barbosa; he also identifies "Utopia" with India from a number of indications: plurality of religions, funerary rites, cult of ancestors, astrology, and the similarity of descriptions when compared with those found in the *Letters* of Albuquerque.

5. Matos, *Expansion*; see also his "La littérature des découvertes" in *Les aspects internationaux de la découverte océanique aux XVe et XVIe siecles*, Fifth Colloquium of Maritime History, Paris (SEVPEN), 1966, 23 pp.

6. Personal Communication from Mervyn Brown, see his *Madagascar Rediscovered* (below).

7. Hakluyt's *Collection of Voyages*, vol. VI, pp. 383-391; the translation of this text into French given in the first volume of the *Collection des Ouvrages Anciens Concernant Madagascar* does not inspire confidence; it was used anew by J.F. Street, "Comment les Anglais ont commencé a connaitre Madagascar," *Revue de Madagascar*, no. 21 (1963), pp. 55-56.

8. See volume I of the *Collection des Ouvrages Anciens Concernant Madagascar*, under the general editorship of A. Grandidier et all, Paris, 1903, p. 472.

9. The works which proved to be most important for the formation of the "dream of Madagascar" are those of medical doctor Walter Hammond and merchant Robert Boothby, based on three month's stay in the area of the Saint-Augustine Bay in 1630: R. Boothby, *A Brief discovery or description of the most famous Island of Madagascar...*London, 1646 (76 pages); W. Hammond, *A Paradox proving that the inhabitants of Madagascar (in the temporal things) are the happiest people in the world*, London, 1640; and his *Madagascar, the richest and most fruitful island in the world*, London, 1643.

10. To these should be added two pirate accounts or those of Johnson and Thornton published by Daniel Defoe.

11. P.M. Handover, *Printing in London from 1476 to Modern Times*, London, 1960, 224 pp.

12. For this aspect see the article of Ignacy Sach, "Du Moyen Age à nos jours: Europo-centrisme et (la) découverte du Tiers-Monde," *Annales E.S.C.*, no. 3, (May-June 1966).

13. Hammond and Boothby, for example, were genuinely convinced that the English could implant a colony at the Bay of Saint-Augustine, not only to exploit the local possibilities in agriculture and other domains but also for a commerce with the East. Boothby thought that "butter and cheese could be made at Saint-Augustine and sold with profit in India, Persia, Arabia and across all the Southern Seas in hundreds of places."

14. R.H. Tawney, *Religion and the Rise of Capitalism*, New York, 1926, eleventh printing, 1961, p. 197.

15. *An Answer to Mr. Boothby's book of the description of Madagascar*, London, 1650.

16. George Buchan, *A Narrative of the Loss of the Winterton (1792)*, Edinburgh, 1820; it was Buchan who placed the account-report of this shipwreck in the *Gentleman's Magazine* in 1793/4, and, somewhat later, he applied to be a missionary of the LMS.

17. *Sociology of Religions*, London, 1965, passim.

18. Raynal, *A Philosophical and Political History of the Settlements and Trade of the Europeans in the East and West Indies*, Edinburgh, 1776, 1777, 1779, 1782 and 1783.

19. It was, after all, in England that his *A Voyage to the Island of Mauritius*, London, 1775, was printed in just one edition.

20. Among the most famous and constantly re-edited of these are Hakluyt's, Purchas, Churchill, Banks and Osborne.

21. *A New and Authentic Universal Geography*, London, 1787.

22. Volume LXIV/1 (April 1974), p. 378.

23. Original edition in 1729, the next three in 1731, 1743 and 1750 (followed by four more in the 1800's).

24. *Voyages et Memoirs contenant les details de l'Etablissement que Benyowsky fut charge par le Ministere Francais de former a Madagascar*, Paris, 1791, 2 volumes (466 and 486 pp.) The first English edition also had 2 volumes (of 422 and 399 pp.) in quarto.

25. Anne Molet-Sauvaget, "Le Journal de Robert Drury par Daniel Defoe," *Bulletin de Madagascar*, no. 286 (1970), pp. 259-265. The book itself is entitled *Madagascar or Robert Drury's Journal during Fifteen Years Captivity on that*, (London, 1729). Its price then was six shillings.

26. D. Defoe, *A General History of the Pirates*, edited by Manuel Sconitorn, London, 1972 (published by J.M. Dent & Sons).

27. This refers to the so-called Zana-Malata (mulatto children), Euro-Malagasy who came to play an important role in eastern Madagascar in the Eighteenth and Nineteenth centuries; see also Defoe, *History of the Pyrates*, p. 1303, account of Captain England.

28. Defoe, *History*, p. 492, account of Captain Howard.

29. Defoe, *History*, p. 133.

30. For more details, see J.J. Hardtman, "The Madagascar Slave Trade to the Americas," *Océan Indien et Mediterranée*, 6th Colloquium of Maritime History, Paris (SEVPEN), 1964, pp. 501-521.

31. *Piracy Destroyed* (1701) cited by Crey, *Pirates of the Eastern Seas*, London, 1933.

32. Tawney, *Religion*, (1926), 1961, 197; "for the colonial interests of Puritan members," the author refers to A.P. Newton's *The Colonising Activities of the English Puritans*, London, 1914.

33. Brun's *Memoir* of 1795. A letter by certain Aspasio of 4 May 1799 addressed to the Londom Missionary Society proposed a mission in the Saint-Augustine Bay, to be established from the isle of Anjouan in the Comoros group; his letter referred to a book by James, probably S. James' *A Narrative of a Voyage to Arabia and India*, London, 1797.

The Social Implications of Freedom for Merina and Zafimaniry Slaves

M. BLOCH
London School of Economics

The purpose of this essay is to examine the history of the descendants of slaves in two Malagasy societies. Slaves were freed in Madagascar in 1897. However, the implications of slave descent were not wiped out by manumission. Their social situation continued to develop partly as a result of their former status, partly as a result of the specific terms of manumission and partly as an aspect of the general social process of colonial and postcolonial Madagascar.

The two people chosen are firstly the Merina, probably the most well-known people in Madagascar, and secondly the Zafimaniry, one of the smallest groups in Madagascar representing a totally different form of society. These two groups therefore offer an interesting contrast. Because what happened to the descendants of slaves depends so much on what happened to them when they were slaves, some historical background to the pre-manumission situation is necessary.

Background to Merina Slavery

All the 19th century missionary books in English on Madagascar invariably begin their remarks on slavery with a statement that it was an institution present in Madagascar "from time immemorial." The missionaries had good reason to stress that point since the London Missionary Society, the missionary arm of the Congregationalist Church to which these writers belonged, became intimately involved in the growth of the Merina State during the 19th century, a state which contained a high proportion of slaves. This involvement of the missionaries was particularly awkward since the Congregationalists were foremost in the abolitionalist movement in Britain. They therefore resented inevitable accusations that their action in Madagascar encouraged slavery and even that some London Missionary Society's missionaries were actually slave owners; accusations made mainly by their rival missionaries and which even reached London. Perhaps the greatest irony of their attitude to slavery is its link with the way they justified their presence in Madagascar by an edifying story which I quote from a popular book about the founder of the Mission to Madagascar, David Jones:[1]

> "The Welsh tutor sighed as he folded up the newsheet and reached out for his well-worn Bible. As he turned over its pages his thoughts were far away. He had been reading of the slave raids in Madagascar, at that time an almost unknown island off the East Coast of Africa. It so happened that he turned to the 16th chapter of Acts for his evening reading. Little wonder, then, that in his dreams that night Paul's vision at Troes became linked with the needs of slave-stricken Madagascar and he dreamed that the men of Madagascar stood on its shore, beckoning to him and crying: 'Come over and help us.'
>
> Next morning as he walked down the street of the little village of Neuaddlwyd to his school for preachers, his thoughts were still of Madagascar...yet so real did his dream appear that the plaintive cry still rang in his ears: 'Come over into Madagascar and help us!'
>
> It soon became plain to his students that morning that Dr. Thomas Phillips had something on his mind, and before long he found himself telling them the story of his dream. Then, with that eloquence that had made him famous as a preacher, he described to these young men, training for the Ministry, the superstition and ignorance of the people of Madagascar, and the cruelties of the slave-trade there...Dr. Phillips again described his vision and repeated the call that had come in the night and added: 'Who will go out as a missionary to Madagascar?'
>
> There was a moment's pause; then from one of the desks at the back of the room, David Jones sprang to his feet. 'I will go!' he said in a ringing voice that showed clearly that he meant it."

The Madagascar to which he and his companion went had become of crucial interest to the British as the result of the fall of Mauritius and Reunion during the Napoleonic wars and this explains the prominence of the story in the newspaper which so arrested the imagination of Dr. Phillips. As a result of this war ultimately Mauritius became British, though this did not happen until after a protracted and complex diplomatic process. The connection of Madagascar on the one hand and Mauritius and Reunion on the other lay in the fact that the East Coast of the great island was sometimes inhabited by small pirate colonies and sometimes traders and adventurers who supplied the Mascarenes with rice and cattle but also, increasingly, slaves to be used on the plantations of these islands.[2] Up to 1770 the trading links between Madagascar, Mauritius and Reunion had been relatively small-scale and fluctuating over time. They had, however, been extremely significant in Madagascar in that they had supplied petty rulers with European weapons for their aggrandizement and slave raiding.[3] Towards the end of the 18th century, however, the small but growing central state that was to become Imerina, profiting from the disarray of the Betsimisaraka League, captured most of this trade, both canalizing its network and reducing rivals by an alliance with Betsimisaraka rulers/slave traders such as Jean René and Coroller and later by building a coastal fort at the Port of Tamatave. The trader Dumaine wrote in 1790 that Imerina "is the part of Madagascar which supplies most of the slaves for our islands" (Mauritius and Reunion). This process was truly momentous in the history of Madagascar because in return for slaves the Merina obtained armaments of high quality in much greater quantities than had been available to anybody else before, since they were lucky in reaching the coast precisely at the time when the demand for slaves in the Mascarenes and generally boomed and the prices soared.[4]

The war materials that they obtained were probably the major cause of the continuing expansion of the Merina and their ultimate near-total domination of the islands. This expansion, however, was itself in part necessitated by the need to supply slaves in ever greater numbers in order to obtain the armaments necessary for conquest.[5] In engaging in this sort of trade in order to get political power the Merina were following a long tradition which had dominated the political process of Madagascar perhaps since as far back as the 16th century but which we know well in the 18th century when the Sakalava and the Betsimisaraka, managed to dominate large areas of the island by exporting slaves to various European or Arab traders in return for armaments which enabled them to conquer their neighbours and get more slaves. The process in the case of the Merina, however, was even more dramatic. The reason was that they captured the trade at a time when the Mascarene economies were booming and so was the implicated need for slaves.

Once the Merina kingdom had really become established through this process, the pattern began to change in a way which was particularly significant for the history of slavery. In 1814, Mauritius, as it was renamed, became British and in taking over Mauritius the British had also gained vague but promising rights over Madagascar. Farquhar, the Governor of Mauritius, therefore encouraged the trade between his island and Madagascar, since he saw the expansion of a kingdom dependent on supplies from Britain as a first step towards conquest, a policy we are familiar with in other parts of Africa. This policy was not without difficulty as it was taking place at a time when public opinion in Britain was moving strongly against the slave trade and slavery. Farquhar at first resisted pressure for the abolition of the slave trade, since he argued that in the first place it would ruin the economy of Mauritius and make his unruly subjects even more difficult to control and, in the second place, it would end the promising connection with the Merina which he intended to use for ultimate conquest. By 1817, however, the pressure from Britain had so increased that he had to give way, although by then the two problems of ending the slave trade with Madagascar had vanished. The economy of Mauritius had been moving away from its dependence on the importation of slaves.[6]

Secondly Farquhar had discovered a way whereby he could keep his Merina contact. He signed with Radama a treaty which in return for the abolition of the slave trade would guarantee Radama a yearly supply of armaments, as well as military assistance. By this treaty the British hoped to continue their influence in Madagascar and to ensure the ever important supply of rice and cattle to Mauritius. This treaty had its ups and downs and for a significant period was abrogated altogether, but it remained the major template for British Merina relations during the 19th century. It also ensured that whenever it was in operation the Merina would be dependent on the British. For the Merina the advantage of this treaty is also obvious. Radama, the Merina king, still retained a steady supply of British armaments but gained as well, and this is probably the most significant point, a *monopoly* of European weapons in Madagascar, a monopoly which many tried to break but never completely successfully. When the treaty was in operation British frigates patrolled Madagascar to stop any signs of the slave trade. In doing this they were stopping any potential rivals of Radama from obtaining arms with which to resist him. They were, so to speak, putting Madagascar in a vacuum in which only one group had access to modern weapons. Under such circumstances it is hardly surprising that nobody could offer any significant resistance to the Merina during their greatest period of expansion.

The implications of this process for the social significance of slavery among the Merina is equally dramatic. There is no doubt, as the missionaries stressed, that an institution which European and Arabic writers before them had no hesitation in calling slavery had existed in Madagascar since the time of our earliest records. This is very clear from the 16th century onwards in any case and indeed one of the most famous early accounts of Madagascar was the so-called diary of Robert Drury, a sailor who claimed to have been captured as a slave in Western Madagascar and whose account was romanticized by Defoe. The earliest mention of this institution for the Merina goes back to Mayeur but there are several references which give us a relatively clear idea of the type of institution slavery was among the Merina before the reign of Radama. It should be stressed that much of the recent literature on slavery in Africa and Asia has emphasized the differences of these institutions from those encountered in either Greece or Rome on the one hand or New World plantation slavery on the other hand.[7] There is no doubt that these qualifications cannot be over-emphasized but since the Merina institution has normally been translated by the word slavery I shall keep to this practice, especially since the changing character of its nature through the 19th century means that it cannot be characterized without greater qualification by such words as slavery, captivity, etc.

For our early period certain facts stand out. First of all slaves were obtained in two contrasting ways. They were obtained either by warfare and raiding of enemies, or they were obtained through legal processes which disgraced individuals and their families, or even in some cases whole descent groups. The relative importance of these different ways of obtaining slaves seems to have changed for the period under examination and there is no doubt that from the time of Radama onwards most slaves were captives obtained either in wars, slave raiding or simply by kidnapping.

The slaves obtained in these two different ways were always separate from each other and did not intermarry, although further sub-divisions existed amongst the slaves of both categories. One of the most important differences seems to be that the process of manumission for descendants of disgraced Merina seems to have been much simpler than it was for captives. Some slaves were captured for export and these are the ones with which we have been concerned so far. Secondly, slaves might be used for domestic purposes, for the 19th century slaves seem to have been used for a whole range of productive tasks in a way which does not very much differ from junior members of families. They were especially used for some particularly arduous tasks such as mining and smelting and above all for transporting wood from the forests of Imerina. Slaves were also used in agriculture, as domestic servants and as concubines. This type of domestic slavery seems very similar to that which has been described for so many African societies.[8] Furthermore some slaves, or slave groups, even lived almost independently of the Merina and acted as cattle keepers for royal herds.

It is difficult to know exactly what sort of treatment the slaves might receive. There are some reports of acute ill-treatment but also many mentions of the mildness of some of the regimes to which they were submitted; many writers stress the fact that some slaves were treated very much as family members of junior status.[9] Slave families who lived in slave villages as cattle keepers must have led a fairly independent life.

There is, however, a striking difference between Merina, or indeed Malagasy, slavery and that found in other parts of Africa and this difference seems to be directly due to the nature of Malagasy kinship systems. Most writers on African slavery stress the fact that after a few generations slaves became incorporated into the free population and in all cases children of free men by slave women were free. This is the main point made by Kopitoff and Miers[10] in their typification of African slavery. Again the point is made by Terray for a much more specific West African case.[11] This integration takes place in all cases through adoption and marriage.

These two possibilities would run against the fundamental emphasis in Merina kinship on endogamy.

The Merina are divided into small endogamous descent groups carefully ranked. Normally to be a member of such a group one had to have both parents from the group. If both parents did not come from the same group then the offspring always belonged to the lower group. This meant that marriage was unlikely to occur between free and slave persons and that in any case the children would belong to the lower group, that is they would be slaves. This contrasts with the African situation where descent groups are never endogamous and nearly always strictly exogamous and where status is derived from one parent only and the status of the other parent is irrelevant. This facilitates the merging of children of slaves in the free population while the Malagasy system hinders it. Thus Merina slavery was transmitted unaltered from generation to generation; the children of slaves were slaves and so were their children and so on. Similarly, although slave women were fair play for free men, in theory at least no offspring of such unions could be considered free or were indeed thought of as related by kinship to their fathers. This characteristic of Merina slavery which marks it out so clearly from other African systems is, I believe, directly attributable to the representation of society as an agglomeration of self-reproducing endogamous groups linked to each other by their rank in a kingdom, not as is the case in Africa as a system of inter-marrying groups. Among the Malagasy the only normal legitimate union was one of two parents of equal status and the group was visualized as reproducing itself endlessly from its own stock. In such circumstances the boundary between kinsmen and outsiders is extremely sharply drawn[12] and so the half-way house model of such writers as Kopitoff and Miers for Africa is inapplicable. One was either a freeman, and if a freeman a member of a descent group, or not. Similarly, paternity was insufficient for social status and therefore children of mixed unions were outsiders. Another way in which this sharp break is represented can be seen in the critical relationships of tombs, territory and kinship in Imerina. Imerina is completely divided into the territories of descent groups where the association of people and land is symbolized by stone tombs of a permanent nature. Free Merina are, therefore, tied to a segment of their valued territory by a symbol of permanence. Unless such a tie can be established one is outside society and this is precisely the position of slaves. They had no tombs to which they had a right. They were either buried in temporary graves or they were allowed to build tombs of mud where the symbolical difference between the impermanence of earth and the permanence of stone was used to demonstrate their fundamental different relationship to the land. Slaves could also be buried as juniors in their masters' tombs but there the point to notice is that it was not because of themselves that they were buried there but because of their masters and the fact that they were buried there did not give their children the right to be buried with their fathers.[13]

In this light we can understand the position of slaves in traditional Merina society. They were junior members of families who though normally relatively well treated could be badly treated with impunity (although not killed) but they could not ever become full members of society because they had no ancestral territory and their progeny was condemned to the same fate. They were outside the social system in its ideological representation rather than an inferior part of it as was the case in other societies. The nearest parallel would probably be with the outcasts of India although without any notions of pollution.

The position of the slaves outlined above is one which may have existed for a long time. It is quite clear that the growth of the Merina State in the 19th century implied the appearance of what was really a very different type of slavery, although it was covered by the same term. The growth of the Merina kingdom is parallelled by the development of large hydraulic works at the end of the 19th century involving the draining of the large marshes which surround Tananarive and which once transformed into rice fields by immense dykes were to supply food for the administration and the army. At first the labor for these massive works was largely supplied by corvee labor but the unpopularity of corvée, taken together with the ever-increasing need for soldiers and administrators from among the free Merina, meant that the public works required more and more labor which could only be supplied by slaves.[14] We therefore find that at the time of Radama the demand for slaves was increasing from three different causes. First of all the increase in military service for the ordinary Merina meant that his families back home depended more and more on slave labor to replace those who were at the wars or in garrisons far away. Secondly, the State needed more and more labor for public works because on the one hand these were expanding and on the other hand it could draw less and less on corvee labor. Thirdly, slaves were needed in ever greater numbers for the slave trade in order to obtain the weapons on which the Merina state was dependent. It is in the light of these conflicting demands that we can understand well why Radama was so willing to agree to the end of the external slave trade, so long as he could carry on obtaining his weapons. The internal effect of the end of this slave trade therefore was a tremendous growth in the number of slaves in Imerina. This was because the supply of slaves through conquest was continuing unabated and indeed increased, while the drain on slaves, the export sales stopped.

All estimates of the proportion of slaves to free men in Imerina are very high but based on very little and it seems to me that strong evidence could be adduced that indeed slaves outnumbered significantly free men by the time of the French conquest.[15]

We therefore find in Imerina at the time of the French conquest, a society where large numbers of slaves are used, some as domestic slaves to replace men out on military service, the others as royal slaves living in settlements rather like barracks and whose life seems to resemble much more that of plantation slaves. If the usually drawn contrast between African slavery and plantation slavery is worth stressing for the beginning of the period we are talking about, it is possible that it would become misleading for the second half of the 19th century.

Social Implications of Freedom for Imerina

The situation outlined above was that found by the French at the time of their invasion of Madagascar in 1895. This invasion ultimately resulted in the Declaration of the Abolition of Slavery throughout Madagascar in 1897, a Declaration as much motivated by humanitarian motives as for the need to undermine Merina domination in the island. The effect of this measure on Imerina was inevitably dramatic when we bear in mind the central place which the different types of slavery had achieved for Merina social organization. However, the effect of this measure would have been much greater and of a totally different nature were it not for the fact that although manumission gave slaves access to their labor it did not, at the same time, give them access to land through which their labor might have directly led to freedom. The slaves were freed but no thought was given to what might happen to them after that, or how they might make a living. The ambiguity which resulted therefore could only be resolved in one of three ways which I shall discuss briefly.

The first way was for slaves to return back to the areas from which they had been captured. This possibility, of course, could only have been opened to those slaves who had been fairly recently captured and who were likely to find some relatives back home. There is no doubt that some slaves went back but how many is impossible to judge from the information at present available. James Sibree describes the reception of the Declaration of liberation of the slaves in this way:[16]

> "We had feared that there would be much disturbance from such a great social change but it passed without difficulty. In a few hours from the announcement by large posters on Sunday morning, September 27th, several hundred slaves were on their way south to the districts from which their parents and grandparents had been chiefly captured in former wars; while a good many who had been kindly treated by their owners and had been regarded as members of the families with whom they lived, remained as paid servants in Imerina.

Clearly the number which remained must have been very large, if we can judge from the very high proportion of present-day Merina who are descended from slaves, a proportion which has been variously estimated as between 45% and 50%. Furthermore, those anthropologists who have worked in areas from which the Merina obtained large numbers of slaves do not report, among the people they studied, descendants of returned Merina slaves. All this is very inconclusive evidence but the high degree of cultural absorption of Merina slaves which we find today among their descendants, and which probably already existed for many slaves in 1897, would have meant that they could only with difficulty have been reabsorbed among the peoples from which they had orginally come.

The second solution of freed Merina slaves was to stay put in the villages where they had worked as slaves. To do this they had to get the agreement of their masters so that they could have access to land in order to survive. This is the most critical element in understanding their present-day position.[17] This agreement seems to have often been given and took the form of share-cropping arrangements which still characterised the relationship of ex-slaves to ex-masters at the time of my last fieldwork in Madagascar in 1971. The share-cropping arrangement is of itself not particularly extortionate. It took the form of the owner of the land receiving a quarter of the crop if he had not contributed the seed grain and a third of the crop if he had contributed the seed grain. The reason behind such a mild arrangement was that quite simply in the areas of central Madagascar where the free Merina had always had ancestral land, the land was so poorly productive without the massive input of forced labor that it gained with the system of slavery, that it would have been very difficult to get more and by then the free Merina were obtaining income from other and more significant sources. The exploitative aspect of the situation, however, lies not so much in the actual share-cropping arrangement as in the type of obligation which continued to exist between ex-masters and ex-slaves. Most Merina of free descent left their ancestral villages, taking advantage of their better education, to become petty administrators, traders and teachers throughout Madagascar and in Tananarive, or to become farmers in newly opened lands and plantations where a high income could be obtained. They kept their ancestral lands for ideological reasons rather than for economic reasons and they kept their link with their ancestral villages by means of ancestral property, houses, churches and, above all, tombs. The most important tie of a free Merina is to the ancestral village where his tomb is found, even though he may never have lived there. This means that the descendants of free Merina need caretakers in these ancestral villages for their houses, churches, and tombs, in order to maintain their ideological status and it is to these duties that the slaves were made to answer. They were given land, therefore, less in return for the rent that they might supply than for the services they would offer. A phrase used by the Merina of free descent describes these descendants of slaves who have remained in their ancestral villages: *"Valala miandry fasana"* (the grasshoppers who guard the tombs).[18] The descendants of free men in such a village, as is described with brilliant subtlety by J. Razafindratovo for the village of Ilafy from which she originally came, still expect the descendants of their slaves to do jobs reminiscent of their previous duties and what is more they expect them to supply them with servants, usually children, who will work in the houses of descendants of the free for minimal or nil wages, wherever these happen to be: in Tananarive, in new lands, or any other parts of Madagascar. This is probably a more economically significant form of exploitation than the tasks back home. Naturally such work is greatly resented and ex-slaves bitterly refer to it by the term for forced labor *Famanpoana*, while their employers prefer to use the less loaded term for work *asa*.[19]

It seems to me, furthermore, that another element of an ideological nature comes into this relationship and that is that by maintaining people in quasi-slave status, even though no direct benefit may be obtained from these, an ideological picture of a previous domination is reproduced which is seen as the potential tool of future domination, in other words by still having slaves the ex-free demonstrate that they are the legitimate rulers of Madagascar. The resentment which the ex-slaves feel of this use of their position is not easily transformed into action since they know that in the end they can, because of the share-cropping arrangement on which they depend, be pushed out of their lands. Some ex-slaves even say that they feel their present situation is even more oppressive than when they actually were slaves and that the behavior of their masters is even more arrogant as well as hypocritical. An old man pointed out to Razafindratovo that while her grandparents, when his parents were slaves, would willingly share the same plate, her present-day relatives would not do so with him, saying that his house was dirty, that he had bad eating habits and that they might catch diseases. A new element is therefore creeping in. The fact that the ex-slaves are usually poor countrymen, while the ex-free are often richer city dwellers, more westernized and more sophisticated in terms of foreign European knowledge, has been used as a new and further justification for the continuation of an old exploitation.

Razafindratovo's facts coincide perfectly with my observation in a similar village to that of Ilafy, Andrainarivo. The only dissenting view in this picture is that of the O.R.S.T.O.M. sociologist, J. Wurtz[20] who carried out a study in a village of old Imerina. He argues on the basis of social surveys that the ex-slaves in his village, the majority, are better off then the ex-free and gives some figures to support this claim. He explains this difference by the fact, which is justified, that the descendants of free men have much greater ritual expenses involved in the upkeep of their tombs than the descendants of slaves. These figures give a completely different picture from either mine or those of J. Razafindratovo[21] but even assuming that he is right I believe such figures miss the point. The descendants of free men in such a village do not live in their ancestral villages in normal circumstances. They live in towns, or in other parts of Madagascar and have a standard of living which is incomparably higher to that of the people who actually live in the ancestral villages. The few descendants of freemen who do live in the ancestral villages are failures, or old people who have returned to their homelands, and so the comparison which needs to be made is not between the descendants of free men and the descendants of slaves *in the villages* but between all the descendants of slaves who mainly live in the villages and all the descendants of free men who mainly live in towns or new lands but who still retain lands and tombs in their ancestral village. This is the crucial fact about central Merina. It is an area which ideologically (through tombs) belongs to absentees and where a few descendants of slaves are allowed to remain cultivating the meager lands which are found there, in return for maintaining and reproducing the ancient status of their old masters in a semi-symbolical semi-material form.

Finally let us turn to the third response of the slaves to the granting of their freedom in 1897. What many of the slaves of Imerina did at that point was neither to go back to their probably largely forgotten families, or to stay put as share-croppers, but to go to the new empty lands to the north and west of Imerina to start a new life by cultivation and the building of rice terraces. In this they were doing the same as many descendants of freemen who finding that they could not any more live on their ancestral lands but who could not get administrative or trading jobs or land concessions in other parts of Madagascar decided, like the slaves, to turn to these more profitable open lands. By and large these lands were either empty or thinly populated and the ex-slaves and the ex-free formed separate villages. They therefore started on an equal footing, yet the subsequent history of their villages and their differential development is to be explained in part in terms of the pre-existing social structure which they carried to these new lands with them and this is especially so in the case of kinship. As noted above, the fundamental aspect of free Merina kinship is a division of society into groups with a high degree of endogamy. The marriage rules of the descendants of free men are contradictory. On the one hand they have an idea of incest which says that one should not marry any close relative and on the other hand they have an idea of re-grouping property within the family which says that one should marry as close a relative as possible. The leads in the case of free-men to an uncomfortable balance where one marries as close as one dares. The slaves of Merina, on the other hand, accepted their ideology without their problem. The reason is that simply because they had no property the second rule about re-grouping property did not apply and they also had no concern about maintaining descent groups. What this means, and meant, is that ex-slaves now marry anybody so long as they are not closely related, while ex-free marry close relatives within their descent group.[22] The descendants of free men in the new lands, therefore, married back along the old alliance patterns of their group, married back relatives with whom they only shared a common origin but who often lead a totally different style of life, perhaps as administrators or teachers in Tananarive, perhaps as plantation owners or traders in other parts of Madagascar. They do not, and can not, marry their neighbours, since these most probably belong to other descent groups, and are therefore ruled out, or worse, are of slave descent. The descendants of slaves, by contrast, have no such problems. They marry whoever they fall in love with and who is willing to have them. This means that the descendants rapidly form supportive kinship networks with their neighbours of slave descent irrespective of where these come from. Further more when there are non-Merina nearby the descendants of slaves will also intermarry with them. Kinship in ex-slave society becomes a continuous web, spread throughout Imerina and beyond. However, this web rapidly becomes localised in the neighborhood as neighbors intermarry amongst themselves. Ex-slaves in new lands are therefore able to form kinship networks very much more quickly than the ex-free who remain isolated by their marriage rules. They therefore can organize such things as agricultural and political cooperation much more easily. Because of this it can be argued that the ex-slaves in new lands have an initial advantage. They have the ability to quickly forge powerful new links. This initial advantage of the descendants of slaves seems however to subsequently disappear and in fact turn to a disadvantage.

The reason is linked with the changing nature of Malagasy society. While at first it is an advantage for a peasant to have a strong local base it is also important for him to have, if he can, links with administrators for his relation with the government, links with traders and people living in other parts of the island for commerce, and with school-teachers, or at least with people who live near relatively good schools where his children can board. Now the strengthening of local networks by descendants of slaves is accompanied by a correlated lack of contact with people living different types of lives in different places, precisely the kind of people needed for contact with the administration or the educational system. Some of the old relatives of slaves from the village where they came from may have gone to Tananarive and may even have become administrators, but because the ex-slaves in new lands do not marry back into the families of these relatives, the ties fade and become forgotten as they get more and more distant. This is so at a time when these contacts with towns, administration, and schools are becoming ever greater sources of power and wealth than subsistence or cash cropping activities.

The descendants of free men by contrast marry back into their original descent groups. Because of their marriage rules the members of these descent groups although originating from one place are now dispersed both throughout Madagascar and throughout the classes existing in Madagascar, and so their traditional marriage maintain these links, links which for a rural peasant are becoming more and more significant. Their relationship to other people who originate from the same village do not fade and since people have gone from these ancestral villages in all kinds of directions they are, in fact, maintaining links to a diverse and differentiated networks which often lead them to other traders in other parts. They can get administrative and legal support when this is necessary (and this is increasingly necessary) by tracing kinship to administrators whether in Tananarive or outside, and, perhaps most significant of all, they can get access to education, partly through their contacts with school-teachers and partly through the fact that they always have relatives in urban centers where they can board their children when they need to go to secondary schools. Because of these facts the descendants of free men settled in new lands are again drawing ahead socially of the descendants of slaves, while these are becoming more and more isolated in the countryside even though this was an area where it might have been thought the two groups had equal opportunities.

The Zafimaniry

When we turn from the Merina to the Zafimaniry the contrast could not be greater. We turn from a group of over a million who dominated Madagascar for almost two centuries, who evolved one of the largest states of the African continent south of the Sahara, to a group of around 15,000 people living by shifting cultivation in a particularly inaccessible part of the Island. Nonetheless, the Zafimaniry undoubtedly share a common origin with the Merina and there are good reasons to believe that the Merina evolved from very similar groups. Perhaps the most famous peculiarity of the Zafimaniry in the part of Madagascar in which they live is that rice is not the basis of their diet. This is due to their highly specific emplacement. They live below the central plateau suitable for wet rice in highly mountainous country where areas available for irrigation are restricted, at the same time the climate is still too cold for the dry rice cultivation of lower down the escarpment. They therefore depend mainly on three crops — maize, taro and beans, supplementing this with various forest products, the two most important being honey and crayfish.

One may well ask what a group like this is doing with slaves and the answer is not altogether clear to me but the first point to note is that by contrast to the Merina the 'slaves', to use the word by which the Malagasy *Andevo* is usually translated, only form (and presumably formed) somewhat less than ten per cent of the population and were not spread as a servile body throughout the population but grouped in two separate villages, closely associated with the two Zafimaniry political foci of the country. It seems that a traditional feature of the cultures to which the Zafimaniry belong is the presence of mediators (*mpifehy*, litt: binders) who had a kind of court, *Lapa*, and settled disputes. It is with the seat of these mediators that the slaves are associated. Probably towards the end of the 18th century the Zafimaniry came under the rather nominal jurisdiction of rulers to the East who used these mediators as their administrators and gave them more authority. This system of delegation was taken over by the Merina in the mid-19th century when they conquered the Kingdom of Ambohimanga Atsimo. The slaves continued to be closely associated with these administrative centres and were not, as far as I can judge, owned individually. They were in, origin partly disgraced Zafimaniry and certain foreigners and captives. They were very few and at the time of the French conquest, they most probably numbered less than 300 people over the age of 15, probably considerably less.

It is not easy to know in what consisted the task of these slaves. The only clear indication is that they had various duties such as fetching salt from the coast[23], collecting certain trees, helping in the carrying of timber back to the village, and supplying cattle for sacrifices at certain key moments and perhaps even themselves. The comparison of their situation with that of, on the one hand, the types of African slavery discussed in the books edited by Meillassoux in 1975 and Kopitoff and Miers in 1977 and on the other Merina slavery, as outlined above, is instructive. We are clearly dealing with a type of slavery which was not a major factor in the overall pattern of relations of production, also it seems that there was no great difference in the day to day life of the slaves and that of the freemen. For example, houses in slave villages and free villages antedating manumission are very much alike. We seem in this respect therefore to be dealing with a very similar pattern to that reputed for many parts of Africa.

In one respect however the same contrast that we saw between the Merina and the African case exists here also between the Zafimaniry and the African. Among the Zafimaniry too the slaves and the free did not, and do not, intermarry and produce mixed free/slave offspring who represent a halfway house between the two statuses. The reason again is thay the free marry according to relatively fixed patterns which are reproduced from generation to generation. In the case of the Zafimaniry, by contrast to the Merina, the reason behind these repeated alliances is partly political, partly in order to secure access to new virgin forest.[24] Nonetheless, the result is that, as with the Merina, the pattern of the alliance of the free is not a continually changing one as is the case so often in Africa where the repetition of alliance is almost always forbidden by the incest and exogamy rules. Furthermore, when the free Zafimaniry do marry unrelated people, which they do more easily than the Merina, it is in order to form political or economic alliances with other powerful groups. These alliances in turn will become semi-permanent. This type of arrangement between groups is something which could not be achieved by marriage with slaves. As with the Merina therefore there are no legitimate unions between free and slaves and consequently there was and there remains little blurring of the divide between them.

The main difference between the Merina and the Zafimaniry lies in the overall organization of society in the two cases. The Merina were as we saw organized in a state whose territory was entirely divided up into the "homelands" of the various descent groups. If you had no such ancestral homeland you were a non-person. The Zafimaniry by contrast had no such systematic organisation either ideologically or geographically. The slaves therefore by being other than the main alliance groups are not by this fact outside society as they would be among the Merina. Nothing illustrates this difference better than the difference of the way the Merina and the Zafimaniry site their tombs. For the Merina the place of a tomb is the ultimate symbol of social groups and territory and the slaves were not allowed to have permanent tombs of their own anywhere. For the Zafimaniry no such problem existed or exists. Tombs are placed anywhere in the forest and the slaves have always been able to have their own tombs in similar locations and built in a similar way to freemen.

This overall difference is, as we shall see, crucial in order to understand their subsequent history. It is closely linked to the nature of access to land among the Zafimaniry and the technology they use to exploit it.

Unlike Merina slaves the Zafimaniry slaves did have access to land but this was through a series of impermanent permissions given to them by free villagers. This type of permission is a traditional part of the Zafimaniry land system, and is often given to freemen as a preliminary to acceptance within the in-marrying groups. This is not so when it was given to a slave since there is no possibility of transforming them into affines or kinsmen through marriage, and this difference is reflected in the type of land that slaves were given permission to cultivate.

The Zafimaniry, as was noted above, traditionally are shifting cultivators. Not only do they change swiddens when these are exhausted but also like other shifting cultivators the whole population is slowly moving to new areas, partly as a result of over-swiddening which took place in the past and more recently because of the dramatic growth in population. This movement has been roughly from West to East which means that Zafimaniry villages have to their West better lands and virgin forest while to the East the land is more or less exhausted, most of it only usable for sweet potatoes (the last crop planted on a swidden) or even completely exhausted for swidden, when the forest land degenerates completely into thin grassland.[25] Naturally the land given for cultivation to the slaves tended to be much more of this latter type, and the siting of the traditional slave villages were significantly to the East of the two largest Zafimaniry villages largely in these semi-exhausted lands. This was the situation, when as an indirect result of French rule, the Zafimaniry slaves were freed, and this fact was to characterize their subsequent history.

The Effects of Manumission for the Zafimaniry

Nominally slavery was abolished among the Zafimaniry at the same time as anywhere else in Madagascar, but this decision really only had effect after the mid-1930s when the local administrator enforced manumission in this region. Previously the Zafimaniry slaves who wanted to benefit from the abolition of slavery had to leave the Zafimaniry area and a few in fact did so. However, in the 1930s the local administrator insisted that all traditional tasks of slaves should end and in contrast to what had happened in Imerina he insisted that free Zafimaniry grant them land. The areas which were granted were very largely those lands which the free Zafimaniry had allowed slaves to cultivate before; that is the areas of semi-exhausted land to the East of the large villages, as well as some more favoured land just near to the colonial administrative posts where some ex-slaves had moved to.

At the same time as this process was going on an equally important change took place as regards the slaves. The Zafimaniry area became intensely missionized by Catholic Jesuits. From the end of the 19th century on London Missionary Society missionaries had crossed Zafimaniry country occasionally and some villages of freemen had become more or less Protestant, others had retained the Zafimaniry religion. The Jesuits, when they came, converted some of these 'pagan' freemen but their greatest success was among the descendants of slaves. This was because they were largely excluded from the traditional religion as well as Protestantism and because Catholicism symbolized their opposition to those of free descent. Now the situation is that while ex-free may be 'Pagan', Protestants or Catholics, all ex-slaves are Catholics. Conversion to Catholicism however, meant something different from conversion to Protestantism. In true Jesuit fashion conversion was massively followed up by the building of churches and above all of primary schools. This action gave a clear educational advance to Catholic villages, an advance which has never been lost but which, as we shall see, has been particularly significant for the ex-slaves. Because of the coincidence of manumission and conversion the effect of the two need be taken together at this stage and these effects can be followed up in the economic, kinship and national spheres.

The giving of land to the ex-slaves was accompanied for the Zafimaniry by a period of increasing economic difficulty. First, it was the time when the government first began to take taxes from the Zafimaniry. This forced them to get cash somehow. Secondly, it was a period when land shortage began to be felt. This was due to three causes. Firt the Eastward movement had more or less reached its end as the Zafimaniry were coming close to the escarpment which marked the edge of the ecological zone which they had specialized in exploiting. In any case there were other people at the bottom (although a few Zafimaniry have settled there). Secondly, the government withdrew permission for the Zafimaniry to use large tracts of forest to make them into forestry reserves and generally they tried to stop swiddening, banning it at least twice but only succeding in making nuisances of themselves as they offered at first no alternative mode of livelihood and when they did, by trying to encourage irrigated rice, this turned out not to be really viable.[26] Thirdly this was a period of massive population growth throughout Madagascar, but especially there. Coulaud calculates that for the period in question the increase in population is of the order of 2.5% per year, or in other words, a doubling of the population in 28 years.

All these factors have forced the Zafimaniry to seek a number of partial solutions. The first has been temporary wage migration of a large part of the male population as woodsmen to other parts of the island. In this respect there is as far as I know no difference between the descendant of slaves and freemen. The second solution has been trade. This has taken two forms. The first has been the selling of roughly prepared timber. At first sight it would seem that the ex-free would have an advantage over the ex-slaves in this since their village lands are those with the most forest. However, the Zafimaniry have no notion of ownership as regards forest in the western sense of the term and so anybody can cut down trees anywhere. Nonetheless, the better knowledge on the part of the freemen of the forest in which they make their swiddens has probably advantaged them in this area, and they seem to dominate here, but this may also be due to the fact that since non-Catholic freemen have had much less opportunity to engage in the newer and far more profitable trade in wood carvings for tourists which has developed since the middle 1960s, they have had inevitably to concentrate on this outlet.

There is no doubt that the Zafimaniry are master carvers, their houses are famous for being carved all over in low relief. This art became widely known partly as a result of the descriptive work of P. Vérin of the Museum of Art and Archaeology in an article published in 1964 in the semi-government publication *Revue de Madagascar*. This was followed in 1966 by an exhibition-cum-sale of Zafimaniry art in Tananarive. This was a year of widespread starvation among the Zafimaniry due to a plague of rats which ate most of the crops. The money obtained was used to buy emergency food supplies. The organization of the gathering of these carvings, windows, honeypots, snuff boxes, etc. was done by the local Jesuits principally from the Catholic villages and whether consciously, or simply because they used the organization of the Catholic Church the food was also largely distributed to Catholic villages.

The exhibition/sale, however, turned out to be such a good thing that the missionary decided to put this on a permanent footing every six months, thereby producing an important income both for the carvers and for the Catholic Church which used the considerable profits for a building program so that every Catholic Zafimaniry village of 100 people has a massive cathedral-like structure of concrete and stone, as well as a school. Some money has also been coming directly to the Catholic Zafimaniry. The recent expansion of this industry has also meant that many new types of carvings have been produced often under the direct instigation of the Jesuits, which has produced a set of unimaginative figurines which have been distributed to churches all over the world.

This sale of carvings has, however, proved too lucrative a source of income for the missionaries to be able to maintain their monopoly, and several Zafimaniry, not only Catholics, soon found other outlets for their wares. By 1971 a great mass of products were being sold, bringing in very large sums of money by Zafimaniry standards. Nonetheless, the fact remains that this highly significant source of income is still very largely in the hands of the Catholics. This is probably because of their earlier introduction to this trade but also because the main outlet remains the Jesuits. Furthermore, from among the Catholics, it is the ex-slaves who have benefited most, especially for the trade which is out of the hands of the missionaries. This is to be explained by two facts — one is the range and the nature of the contacts of the ex-slaves outside Zafimaniry counrty, which is discussed below, and secondly because of the very small scale but financially highly significant growth of tourism in Zafimaniry country. This tourism, of up to 400 people in the year when it reached its peak, is to be explained by the desire to buy Zafimaniry artifacts cheap and to see the famous villages of the Zafimaniry, photographs of which appeared in the Malagasy press in 1970 and 1971. This tourism consits mainly of buying expeditions and David Coulaud has estimated that each tourist spent 5000 FM, approximately £10 in 1971 money. Nearly all this money has been spent in the largest slave village, Antetezandrotra, the reason being that the guides who the tourist finds, will come from this village. This is again because of the contacts outside the Zafimaniry country of its inhabitants and of their higher standard of education to which we shall return.

The third economic response to the worsening situation of the Zafimaniry has been perhaps even more fundamental, the turning to irrigated rice agriculture in some areas. The colonial government and even before them, the Merina, tried to stop swidden and in the end tried to suggest that irrigated rice cultivation would be an alternative which they therefore encouraged. By and large, however, for reasons tellingly discussed by Coulaud, this has been unsuccessful, not because of the cussedness of the Zafimaniry as the French believed (an administrator in the 1950s suggested that they all be put in a concentration camp until they learned better manners), but because irrigated rice cultivation involves a dramatic fall in the productivity of labor as opposed to swidden and because the mountanious terrain of Zafimaniry

country made irrigation extraordinarily difficult and highly ineffi-
cient by comparison to the plateau area. Nonetheless, in some
areas, apart from the show ricefields the administration insisted
on, economic irrigated terraced rice-fields have begun to be made.
These are found, either in the few exceptional areas where
the country is suitable or because the villages were running out
of forest for swiddens in a disastrous way. Of the latter the first
and the most affected villages in this position have been the villages
of ex-slaves, not, I believe, because as Coulaud suggests they
are more forward looking, but simply out of desperation. This
is because, as we have seen above, the ex-slaves were given land
in the last stages of exhaustion. Now one of the features of irrigated
rice agriculture is the high initial capital investment, so if you are
going to do it at all an early start is an advantage since as the
years go by you accumulate more and more rice-fields. This is
especially so here because the basically inappropriate nature of
the country means that irrigation is peculiarly complex. So complex indeed, that the Zafimaniry have not been able to make rice
terraces themselves and have had to employ experts in this, that
is Betsileo wage earners. Characteristically all the people in the
largest Zafimaniry slave villages asked by Caoulaud what would
they do if they had L500, answered that they would spend it
on having rice-fields and irrigation channels made, and that this
is what the spare cash which the ex-slaves have obtained has
gone into.

This has meant that the ex-slave villages have been the first
to turn to irrigation. Subsequently other villages of freemen
which have also run out of land for swidden have also had to
do the same. In these circumstances the ex-slave villages have
had an advantage over those latecomers and they are terefore
better off. They are, however, still worse off than those Zafimaniry
villages which still have adequate forest access for swiddens and
they are certainly worse off in terms of the amount of time they
have to devote to agriculture.

Finally, let us turn to the significance of the effect of manumission
and conversion for the kinship system. Manumission left the Merina
slave in a social limbo, having no place in society and being
indeed actually excluded from it by the symbolical system of
tombs and territories. This absence of location in the social system
itself was a source of fundamental inferiority. The situation of

the Zafimaniry was very different since, as we have seen, there
was no comprehensive social system containing a defined and
limited number of groups. Freedom for the Zafimaniry slaves
enabled them to become simply another group among the many
in-marrying groups. They were not trying to squeeze into an
already fully formed and complete order, there was no such order.
They did not intermarry with the groups of freemen but this did
not matter because they did not have to merge into these groups
to join society. The Zafimaniry slaves became just another Zafimaniry group of which there was no fixed number.

The marriage pattern of the ex-slaves among the Zafimaniry
has also been significant for their history. As we saw the Zafimaniry
slaves formed an endogamous group, not because of any particular marriage rules they had, but simply because no freeman or
descendant of freeman is normally willing to marry them.

However, on their annual wage migration or simply their journey-
ing, their lack of positive marriage rules means that they are
likely to often settle down and marry foreigners (usually ex-slaves
of other groups than those of free descent). The descendants
of freemen by contrast are caught up in long-standing alliances
which require their marrying back in the complex network of
Zafimaniry kinship. They therefore must go back home after their
migration to marry Zafimaniry girls and they therefore form no
kinship links outside Zafimaniry country. No such system of
alliance recalls the ex-slave migrant worker, he breaks no long-
standing ties by marrying a girl he meets on his travels and such
young men commonly do this. The ex-slaves therefore do form
marriage and then kinship links well beyond the confine of their
territories.

This process started at the time of the freeing of slaves throughout Madagascar when the Zafimaniry slaves could really obtain
their freedom only by going away to more administered parts
of Madagascar and settling down there, but the pattern has
carried on since. As a result, the Zafimaniry slaves by contrast
to the Zafimaniry freemen have many affines and kinsmen outside
Zafimaniry country. The Zafimaniry ex-slaves have relatives in
several of the towns outside Zafimaniry country, especially
Ambositra, the nearest town of any size, and this has had significance in a number of ways. It has not given them access to the
ruling classes, as geographically dispersed kinship ties do for the

Merina of free descent, since the people they meet are not near the sources of economico-political power, but it has given them contact with people who have some knowledge of towns, roads, post offices, etc. and even of dealings with the lowest level of the administration. This sort of knowledge is not a problem for *any* Merina but it is for many Zafimaniry and so the ex-slaves are in this sphere advantaged over their ex-masters. The fact that the descendants of Zafimaniry slaves have relatives outside Zafimaniry country is most important in the sphere of education since it means that their children can board with these relatives in towns when they have reached the top level of the local shcools and when they need to go on to school in Ambositra. Young Catholic Zafimaniry are often well able to do that, due to the high standard of many of the Catholic schools in the Zafimaniry country, but it is only easy for the possibility to be taken up by those children (usually of ex-slave descent) who have relatives with which to stay in town. It is significant that the few modern successes among the Zafimaniry have all, with one exception, been school-teachers and have all been descendants of slaves. This is because in the first instance being a Catholic gives an educational advantage because primary Catholic schools are better and all ex-slaves are Catholics, and, in the second, because among the Catholics it is to the ex-slaves who have the greater possibilities to follow up their education because of their kinship contact outside Zafimaniry country.

This higher number of educated boys among the descendants of ex-slaves and their more widespread geographical contacts has yet a further implication. It explains why the educated Zafimaniry that the free spending tourists need for guides are recruited from ex-slave ranks, they can speak French and can be contacted in Ambositra. It is not surprising that these guides take the tourists in the first place to ex-slave villages to buy carvings, thereby enriching these villages still further.

The ex-slaves, or at least some of them, have therefore in terms of the wider society been more successful than their ex-free counterparts. The question remains however whether with time these successful individuals will move to towns and sever their links with their country relatives as they will not remarry back, thus doing the same as the Merina ex-slaves. This is highly probable unless of course being brokers in carvings and tourists should develop into an ever more profitable business which is an unlikely prospect.

It is interesting to contrast this situation with that of the Merina. Among the Merina it is the descendants of freemen who have the more widespread kinship network and who have therefore benefited from access to the wider Malagasy society. This has been brought about by their marrying back with their descent groups which are in fact dispersed, while the descendants of slaves by marrying their neighbours have narrowed their networks. Among the Zafimaniry the descendants of freemen by marrying along traditional alliance lines have kept their network small and localized, because their kinship groups are in one place, and have therefore not benefited from wider contacts, while the ex-slaves by marrying on their migration have widened the geographical spread of these contacts and have gained in a similar, though more modest way, to that of descendants of Merina freemen.

Conclusions

It is inevitably difficult to conclude about the effects of the freeing of the slaves in Madagascar when, as we have seen, these can be so varied in different cases. Certain points, however, stand out.

The first and most important point is that there is no question of understanding the social implications of manumission without also considering the access given to the slaves to control over the means of production. The Merina ex-slaves who have remained in the villages of their masters are practically still slaves, in spite of manumission, because they were not given any land and were left in total dependence. By contrast those slaves who went to new lands were, in the short term at least, as well off as the freemen who went to new lands. The slaves of the Zafimaniry were given poor, exhausted land, and ultimatly their position is fairly uneviable. In the short term, however, the time advantage that they have gained in being the first to invest in irrigation has given them an advantage over those free Zafimaniry who have also found themselves on similar land. This point then is clear and could easily be documented in all cases in other parts of the world.

The second point to make is that the sources of income may be changing and so access to what were once the old means of production may not be so important as potential access to what will be the future sources of income. In this case the growing importance of towns and bureaucracy as sources of wealth is clear, and the situation in which different groups find themselves in terms of this access, is critical. There the difference between descendants of slaves and descendants of freemen is revealing. The effect of education and continuing access to education, has given descendants of freemen in Imerina an unassailable advantage both in Government fields and in trade. Similarly the fact that the geographical networks of the Zafimaniry slaves are more widespread, and that they therefore have more chance of having experienced advisers in their dealings with the administration, gives them an advantage over their old masters. Education is particularly interesting in this respect because of the time gap between the moment when it is given and when the benefits which it gives are reaped.

Finally, we can conclude more generally from these examples, and that is by stressing what might be called the presence of a process which may be called the process of entailment; a process by which the situation of one moment implies, although it does not determine, the next moment. This is in part because different aspects of society do not change in the same way and at the same speed. One crticial example of this here is the significance of endogamy. Endogamy in the pre-colonial situation can be seen as having developed for specific economic and political tasks but it was encoded in people's minds through education and therefore still affects their action long after its former foundation has gone. This is a particularly interesting example in that it is neither the ideas of the slaves themselves nor even the ideas about the slaves held by the free which was to prove so significant for their destiny but rather ideas held by the free which were concerned with matters other than slavery or labor. Another way of putting it would be to say that manumission in bringing about a change only relating to the status of slaves, but not changing in other ways the social process, has only slightly affected the logic of inequality contained in the societies discussed. There is no doubt that manumission has been much less important for the fate of the descendants of the slaves than the wider processes of colonializa- tion and embedding in the world economy but that is not to say that these processes have affected the ex-slaves in the same way as they have affected the descendants of their masters.

NOTES

1. E.H. Hayes, *David Jones: Dauntless Pioneer*, London, 1923, pp. 9-10.

2. J.-M. Filliot, *La Traite des Esclaves vers les Mascareignes au XVIIIe Siècle*, Paris, 1974, pp, 113-127. This work appeared originally as an unpublished M.A. thesis in 1971.

3. Filliot, *La Traite*, 1974, 205-208.

4. Filliot, *La Traite*, 1974, 62-65 and 216; PH.D. Curtin, *The Atlantic Slave Trade A Census*, Madison (Wisconsin), 1969, pp. 266-269.

5. M. Bloch, "The Disconnection between Rank and Power as a Process," (Imerina) in (eds.) J. Friedman and M.J. Rowlands, *The Evolution of Social Systems*, London, 1977, p. 314.

6. This was a rather slow process and large numbers of slaves were smuggled into Madagascar until quite late in the 19th century and, indeed, there were times when the slave trade with Madagascar was restarted. Nonetheless, it is quite clear from Filliot's statistics that the peak of the import of slaves had passed and the introduction of sugar in Mauritius meant there was far less need for slaves as the sugar planters preferred Indian indentured labour, *cf.* Filliot, *La Taite*, 1974, pp. 67-69.

7. C. Meillassoux, *L'Esclavage en Afrique précoloniale* (dix-sept études presentées par Claude Meillassoux), Paris, 1975, p. 18.

8. Meillassoux, *Esclavage en Afrique, passim.*

9. Wm. Ellis, *Three Visits to Madagascar*, London, 1858, pp. 146-149.

10. I. Kopytoff and S. Meyers (eds.), *Slavery in Africa: Historical and Anthropoligical Perspectives*, Madison (Wisconsin), 1977, in the "Introduction."

11. E. Terray, "La Captivité dans le Royaume abron du Gyaman," in Meillassoux, *Esclavage en Afrique*, 1975, pp. 437-448.

12. M. Bloch, "Property and the end of Affinity," in (ed.) M. Bloch, *Marxist Analyses and Social Anthropology*, London, 1975.

13. For the siginificance of all this see M. Bloch, *Placing the Dead*, (Tombs, Ancestral Villages and Kinship Organization in Madagascar), London, 1971, passim

14. A. Coppalle, "Voyage dans l'Intérieur de Madagascar et à la Capitale du Roi Radame pendant les années 1825 et 1826," reprinted from the *Bulletin de l'Académie Malgache* (old serie, vol. VII, 1909, pp. 7-46, and vol. VIII, 1910, pp. 25-64) in the *Documents Anciens sur Madagascar*, Tananarive, 1970 (Vol. I), p. 54.

15. This evidence would rely on the proportion of free men to slaves now modified by the fact that we know that some slaves went back home to their own peoples.

16. J. Sibree, *Fifty Years in Madagascar*, London, 1924, pp. 279-280.

17. J. Dez, "Les baux ruraux coutumiers à Madagascar," in J. Poirier (ed.) *Etudes de Droit Africain et de Droit Malgache*, Paris 1965, pp. 76-83.

18. J. Razafindratovo, *Hierarchie et Traditions chez les Tsimahafotsy* (Imerina), unpublished thesis, University of Paris, 1971, p. 162.

19. Razafindratovo, *Hierarchie*, 1971, p. 127.

20. J. Wurtz, "Evolution des structures foncières entre 1900 et 1968 à Ambohibo-anjo (Madagascar)," *Etudes Rurales*, nos. 37, 38 and 39, 1970 pp. 449-479.

21. Razafindratovo, *Hierarchie*, 1971, pp. 266-268.

22. M. Bloch, "The implications of Marriage rules and Descent categories for

Merina Social Structure," *American Anthropologist*, LXXIII/1(1971).

23. D. Coulaud, *Les Zafimaniry: un groupe ethnique de Madagascar`a la poursuite de la foret*, Tananarive, 1973, p. 9ln.

24. Bloch, "Property and the end of Affinity," in *Marxist Analyses*, 1975, *passim*.

25. Coulaud, *Les Zafimaniry*, 1973, pp. 168-179.

26. Coulaud, *Les Zafimaniry*, 1973, 329-338.

Bibliographical note: in addition to sources cited in the notes above the author consulted also Wm. Ellis, *History of Madagascar*, London, 1838, 2 volumes; E.C. Andre, *De l'Esclavage a Madagascar*, Paris, 1899; J.P. Dumaine de la Josserie, "Voyage fait au pays d'Ancaye dans l'ile de Madagascar en 1790," *Annales des Voyages, de la Geographie et de l'Histoire* (ed. Malte Brun), XI (1810), 146-218; and P. Verin, "Les Zafimaniry et leur art," *Revue de Madagascar*, No. 27, 1964.

The First and Second Malagasy Republics: The Difficult Road of Independence[1]

Y.-G. PAILLARD*
University of Provence
Centre D'aix

Along with the other colonies of France in Africa south of the Sahara Madagascar attained the status of independent state at the end of the 1950's. The calm in which this apparently far-reaching and rapid change took place came as no small suprrise to many who could remember the turmoil of 1947, when Madagascar underwent a major colonial revolt. Yet, not only had the two partners been transformed over the years, as much on the Malagasy as on the French side, but the very recall of 1947 came to act as an agent of prudence.[2]

The early years of an independent Malagasy Republic were untroubled as well. To be sure, discussions were widespread, the press was often bitter and opposition parties were present. With the passage of time, however, the opposition seemed far more concerned with joining the government through negotiation than in preparing itself for a contest of power. If anything, the memory of 1947 served to promote harmony, the *fihavanana* among the Malagasy ethnicities; and when 29th March, date of the 1947 revolt, started to be officially celebrated after 1967 only,[3] the stress was placed far more on national reconciliation than on anti-colonial struggle. Indeed, relations with the former colonizers remained excellent while the Malagasy government seemed to be in continuous fear of tribal competitions.

As is now generally understood, political independence does not automatically produce economic independence and cultural liberation. Although the Malagasy do not suffer any real famines they

*Translated from French by R. Kent.

are in every respect an underdeveloped people. A large gap stands between the living standards of a social elite, both foreign and domestic, and the masses. Under an apparent stability, thus, there came into being a situation of conflict which the ambiguous socialism of the government could not resolve. By 1971 in southwestern Madagascar and by 1972 in the capital of Tananarive things were falling apart. In 1972 a huge wave of youth overturned the local institutions. The military regime which inherited this movement became rapidly entangled in its own contradictions and went on for two years in a state of paralysis. By 1975 a very real drama became all-dominant as part of the army went into revolt and the new head of state was assasinated six days after a nomination which proposed a basic reshaping of both society and government. It was only after months of extreme tension that a new man and a new team took hold of the country anew. The second Malagasy Republic is now centering its efforts to achieve decolonization at last and to implement the guidelines of a different form of socialism.

I — From the French Union to the first Malagasy Republic

The French Constitution of 1946 had allowed the Malagasy to begin their modern political apprenticeship amid a multiplicity of local assemblies while three of them went to Paris as deputies. But, the framework of the French Union came to exclude for all of the colonies any possibilities for independence or even substantial autonomy just when nationalist movements began to assert themselves everywhere. As the revolt of 1947 in Madagascar showed without fail, despite its many ambiguities, nationalist resentment had real vigor. As the state of alert came to end it was the administration's aim to regain the favor of public opinion by improving the economic and social outlays thanks to the funding of FIDES.[4] And, more than ever, its tactic was to exploit the older rivalries between the highland Merina, always distrusted, and the coastal ethnicities, the *côtiers*, deemed to have been loyal to France and more trustworthy. With all the nationalist political organizations dismantled following the 1947 revolt, a new "coastal" party, the PADESM,[5] enjoyed the official protection with the idea of promoting only the indigenous spokesman who had an "understanding" attitude. Quite apart from considerations of personal careers, these men were not the dupes of anyone. They had determined that French strength was too great and that it would be a vain undertaking to seek a short-term change in the statute of Madagascar through violence and plotting; they were also playing for time so that non-Merina elites would increase in numbers, improve their training, and confront at a future point in time the highlands elites on the basis of equality.[6]

The leftward tilt of the January 1956 elections in France brought to power a government determined to be bolder overseas. The "enabling act" *(loi-cadre),* drafted by Gaston Deferre and adopted on 23rd June 1956, provided for the generalization of the universal suffrage and for a single electoral college (all the former colonial subjects became French citizens) while each territory had its elected local assemblies. Madagascar had one assembly for each province and the Representative Assembly for the Island as a shole. Provincial assemblies were given real powers in the manage-ment of local affairs. A Council of Government with eight ministerial posts was elected within the Representative Assembly; the French High Commissioner became its president while a Malagasy vice-president was mandated by law.

All of this served to revive the political life of Madagascar. Claiming the Spirit of Bandung as their own and influenced more or less by communists the "hard-line" nationalists began to regroup in such cities as Diego-Suarez, Tananarive and Tamatave. They found the *"loi-gadra"*[7] too narrow in scope and demanded the rapid granting of independence but one attained through negotiation (the French Communist Party was urging moderation, besides). In May 1958 some ten groupings coalesced at the Tamatave Congress, naming a permanent delegation to be presided over by Richard Andriamanjato, one of the most brilliant Malagasy intellectuals.[8] This was the birth of AKFM,[9] a party with the slogan of "Independence, pure and clear." Its adherents came from an as yet limited working-class force, from among the intellectuals especially, as well as from such middle-class compo-nents as employees of the administration and minor executives and managers in the various commercial and industrial enterprises. Although the AKFM did not exclude the côtiers (mainly from the eastern littoral) it was composed mainly of the Merina. A more moderate current, supported by the government as could be expected, constituted the opposing trend in Malagasy politics; and, among its groupings, the one selected for a most dazzling political future was the PSD, social-democratic party founded in

Majunga from the old PADESM at the end of 1957 by Philibert
Tsiranana, former school teacher, lycee professor and spiritual child
of the French Socialist Party (SFIO). The French High Commissioner,
Soucadaux, who was also a socialist, lost no time in noticing the virtues of Tsiranana as a political head and as a diplomat, along with
his practical sense and a decided ability to make himself popular;
and he would come to protect the career of Tsiranana in the
future. While Tsiranana was the Secretary-general of the PSD,
André Resampa became his closest collaborator and Associate-
secretary of the party. Their program also included independence
for Madagascar but a qualified one while an unquestioned
friendship with France came to be regarded as its cornerstone.[10]
The beginnings of the PSD were actually quite difficult as most
of its adherents came from the western coastal provinces of
Majunga and Tulear but in 1957 Tsiranana and Resampa were
sent by the Representative Assembly to the Council of Government, with Tsiranana as its Malagasy Vice-President. From these
commanding positions the two would transform the PSD from a
purely provincial into a national party while using it as the
battering ram of the *côtiers'* political struggle with groupings
in the highlands of Madagascar.[11]

In May 1958 a crisis born in Algerian events brought General
De Gaulle to power in France. His prestige was as enormous in
Madagascar as in Africa. The Fifth Republic's constitution
allowed the French Union to change into a "Community" of
federated autonomous states[12] while a referendum would provide
a means for the former colonies to enter and integrate into
it. In fact, De Gaulle did not envisage independence for the
"territories" but the maintenance of tight links to the metropole
after the local organisms acquired greater responsibilities than
under the enabling act (*loi-cadre*). The referendum itself
followed somewhat the style of an ultimatum, coupled with the
threat of immediate withdrawal of all French economic, financial
and administrative assistance in the event of a negative vote.
Just before the referendum De Gaulle made a grand tour of
Africa; he was in Tananarive on 22nd August 1958. Pointing
his finger at the Queen's Palace, the monument of old Merina
monarchy, he told the assembled Malagasy in a phrase which
is still quoted: "Tomorrow you will be a state!" This rather
inept allusion to the Merina monarchy did little to reassure
the *côtiers* although it was clear that the General did not

know the past of Madagascar too well. Just the same, the PSD merged with other non-Merina parties to form a "Cartel of Republicans" which urged "yes" in the referendum, the hint of republicanism being quite transparent. The AKFM, as well as MONIMA,[13] a south-western party on which more will be said later in this text, recommended to the Malagasy that they refuse an autonomy which was both conceded and limited in nature. The results of the referendum in Madagascar were comparable to those obtained in most of the Francophone Africa save Guinea: less than 400,000 votes against and 1,360,000 for Madagascar's entry into the Community. Still, the 400,000 negative votes amounted to a remarkable 22% of the total cast against the background of a colonial administration still *in situ* and hardly exempt from electoral irregularities while in control. Nonetheless, there is no doubt that the victory of "yes" did represent the general wish of the Malagasy as it did Tsiranana's and that of the PSD, party which André Resampa had by then implanted in all the regions of the Great Island.

On the heels of the referendum a congress of provincial assemblies convened at Tananarive on 14th October 1958 to proclaim with open enthusiasm the birth of the Malagasy Republic by 208 to 26 votes.[14] The new state received recognition the next day from the French High Commissioner while on the 16th Madagascar had a new national flag in which green, symbolic color of the *côtiers*, was added to white and red, official colors of the former Merina monarchy. Because of its population numbers the Malagasy Republic became the leading state of the Community leaving to the "guardian" France the domains of defense and foreign policy as well as the task of managing the general economy and finances.

When the congress turned into a constitutional assembly it was the PSD that triumphed with its own project for the constitution.[15] Its text, adopted on the 29th April 1959, affirms in the preamble that the Malagasy believe in God and in the eminent dignity of the human person, to demonstrate the will of Madagascar to remain attached to the Western Civilization. As in the French constitution of 1958, legislative power was vested in two assemblies of which the national assembly, elected through universal suffrage, was the more important one; the President of the Malagasy Republic, chosen by the assemblies, was also bound to exercise the functions of the chief of government[16] and was given very considerable powers. To no one's surprise, Philibert Tsiranana became the first President on 1st May 1959 and for a seven-year term.[17] There was only a single dissenting voice. The municipal elections, held in the same year, revealed also the strength of the PSD. If this party did not quite win the majorities in Tananarive, Tamatave and in Tuléar (where MONIMA's founder, Monja Jaona, became the new mayor only to be invalidated in 1961 for rather arguable reasons) all the other wards in the Island went to the PSD.

At best, the Community was a fragile edifice which the Africans had accepted only as a stage. The Accra conference, the survival of Guinea which had been left to fend-off for itself, its presence at the United Nations as full-fledged member state and the pressure of nationalistic parties made revisions imperative. Since the article 78 of the 1958 constitution provides for an exit from the confinement of the federation Mali demanded its independence by invoking the article at the end of September 1959. De Gaulle accepted the inevitable evolution[18] but linked all of the negotiations for independence to those for cooperation agreements which in organizing assistance to the fledgling states also limited their ability to maneuver. Having accepted this condition Mali became independent with the arrival of 1960 to provide an example hard to resist. In Madagascar, Tsiranana had asked for the transfer of all governmental competencies to the Malagasy Republic since 18th December 1959; the actual negotiations, directed from the Malagasy side by André Resampa, began on 11th February 1960; and there was a most friendly agreement that 26th June should be the date on which to proclaim independence. In this way, the PSD stole the thunder of the most nationalisticof its adversaries, the AKFM, now a party disoriented by the flow of events which left it behind. On 29th April Richard Andriamanjato even declared that he was quite ready to respond to an appeal for political union of all parties launched earlier by Tsiranana who refused, however, the offer and turned to his own advantage the internal AKFM dissensions.

The independence ceremony of 26th June at the large stadium of Mahamasina was also an occasion to affirm the permanent nature of the Franco-Malagasy friendship. The Malagasy Republic

continued as a member of the modified Community of confe-
derated states, an already hollow structure and also one that the
Entente States had refused admission to.[19] In contrast, 14 agreements and conventions of cooperation came into being at once
and were signed on 2nd April 1960. The military accords for
Madagascar turned over the defense of the island to France which
continued to station locally all of the necessary units, including
air, naval, and ground. France also agreed to help organize the
Malagasy national army with a host of French officers retaining
their commands in Malagasy uniforms; it was given bases in
Madagascar, especially the fine naval facility at Diego-Suarez;[20]
and Tananarive became the headquarters of the French forces in
the western Indian Ocean. In the realm of foreign policy there
was an agreement for mutual consultation and exchanges of
information between the two states; and, in fact, Madagascar
would adopt most of the time French positions on the major
international problems. The monetary accords stipulated that
France would back the Malagasy franc (the so-called "Fmg,"
somewhat distinct from the CFA) through fixed-parity attachment
to the French franc. But, the French remained all-dominant at the
Mint (Institute of Emissions) which had replaced the French Bank
of Madagascar. An absolutely free transfer of capital permitted
the French enterprises in Madagascar to repatriate their future
profits while a convention on establishments gave the French-
owned enterprises a status of co-equals with their Malagasy
counterparts. Economically, France was committed to aid the new
state: the FAC[21], created since 1959, had already relieved the FIDES
in several respects and continued to contribute to local investments; in France, preferential tarrifs created a privileged market
for products from Madagascar and, conversely, favored the
exporting of French manufactured goods to the Great Island. In
cultural affairs the French were pledged to provide the schools
and lycées with metropolitan teaching personnel, to make
teachers into the strongest contingent of the so-called "technical-
cooperators;" a new university would also be created and given
official birth in 1961 while regrouping the different institutes and
superior schools established in the preceding decade.[22] French
remained the official language on par with Malagasy in principle
while actually retaining the favored position since it continued
to be the language of both instruction and administration; and
one would also have to mention the many accords in such

domains as the judiciary, the merchant marine, telecommunications and the like, an entire panoply through which to demonstrate with ease and in retrospect what a fine position the former metropole had in the new state. Yet, at that time such a situation still reflected the real balance of forces.

It was believed that, as the Malagasy Republic became increasingly stronger, it could secure more or less quickly the direct control over some of the areas in the existing statute and thereby increase the reality of its independence. For the moment, however, the cooperation accords precluded the chaos a total rupture would bring about; Madagascar conserved the markets for its exports, it possessed a good currency, it was assured of advantageous credits and of gifts while French functionaries responded to the management continuum by training their Malagasy successors. Was not all of this enough to permit those in power to harness themselves to the tasks of development without wasting any time?

II — The Joys and Sorrows of the First Malagasy Republic (1960 — 1972)

Admitted into the United Nations in September 1960 under Franco-Tunisian sponsorship, the Malagasy Republic was now a state completely on its own. If in Madagascar everything seemed to go on as before this gentle accession to independence,[23] if the same team remained in power as could be expected, it would be held accountable to the future generations for the progress of Madagascar. Nonetheless, opposition groups were still around, along with the older ethnic rivalries, and it seemed to the PSD that the liquidation of such shackles should command priority. In the longer run this concern would become something of an obsession in character; and it was possible to ask earlier on if this would not be at the expense of more fundamental tasks. It would not be far-fetched to perceive the structural crumbling of 1972 as its direct result.

a) During the first four or five years Madagascar entered into direct relations with some of the major western states, mainly the common-market partners of France but especially with West Germany where its socialist party, the SPD, far wealthier than its French counterpart, was more than willing to aid the PSD in the Island. The relations with the United States were correct but far more distant as the U.S. respected in Madagascar the French zone of influence. There was a cordial dialogue with Israel, then very interested in Africa. André Resampa, who was the PSD's new Secretary-general following the election of Tsiranana to the Presidency, worked to promote closer contacts as he sought in the Israeli experience a model of "non-aligned" Socialism. Madagascar had, however, no direct relations with a single communist country — a by-product of PSD's visceral anti-communism which may have been inherited from the old French Socialist Party (SFIO), of fearing the "Asiatic Peril" or China,[24] and of a belief that the Soviet Union had managed to infiltrate the AKFM as main opposition party.[25] In contrast to such suspicions there were no clouds in relations with France: the Malagasy Republic, averred the President in press in 1961, was the sister of the French Republic; everything was being done to reassure some 60,000 French in Madagascar, regarded in Tsiranana's words as the "Nineteenth Tribe" (after the eighteen "tribes" of Madagascar, defined more or less artificially, with Comorean settlers in the Island being the 20th "tribe"). A massive exodus of the French from Madagascar was presented as a calamitous possibility of the future; but this was at a time when "Cartierism" was clamoring for credits with which to modernize the metropolitan regions rather than lands not only distant but ingrate as well.

It was still under French auspices that the Malagasy Republic inaugurated its collaboration with the "sister-republics" in Africa — the other former colonies of Paris.[26] As for its participation in the Organization of African Unity, if Madagascar went alone and did not have, for example, direct relations with South Africa and Portugal, it was also in fear of being pushed too far by the progressive states in the Continent.[27] This balance, this "wisdom" in the domain of foreign relations also came to guarantee peace within the young republic which, in turn, allowed it to concentrate all efforts on the perfection of its structures and, one would think, on its development.

As for the institutions the only notable innovation was the law of 6th June 1962 which provided for the election of president through universal suffrage, measure which in fact would give him an even greater authority.[28] In practice, too, centralization began to grow stronger, partly in reaction to the relative decentralization in the twilight of the colonial period but also out fear that regional particularisms would be exploited by ambitious men, by rivals; and there was also a will to take command in an Island left somewhat perplexed by an evolution its people did not always grasp too well.[29] A variety of administrative extensions and consolidations were completed while an ordinance of 30th October 1960 forbade strikes by public employees. Functionaries who staffed the upper echelons of government found their competencies heavier to the point that they became even more powerful than the earlier colonial officials; yet, being Malagasy, they had probably less of the spontaneous acquiessence to authority as they could not obtain in the beginning that fearful respect accorded *vazaha* (generally, "white foreigner" residing in Madagascar) chiefs; and this was all the more true of the Merina functionaries serving in the coastal regions, under a government controlled by the *côtiers.*

This vigorous taking of control over the country also came to be confounded in its essentials with the soldification of the party in power. In 1960, Madagascar still had 35 political parties even if some consisted of the sole founding member, a normal phenomenon in a country both new and facing as yet a major re-grouping of political forces. Yet, this did not appear serious when viewed from abroad or, as Tsiranana said it, "to have 35 parties in a land like ours is shameful!" In reality, the PSD apart, only the AKFM and MONIMA[30] had some strength. The AKFM perceived itself as being left or extreme left and ultra-nationalist; it proposed nationalizations, it wanted the Malagasy to collectivize, citing at times the example of the USSR; it was for the cultural Malgachisation, it wanted non-alignment in foreign relations and exit from the franc zone; and it accused the PSD of being the flunkey of neocolonialism. The AKFM had the support of a dynamic press and of the labor unions which were hardly effective in politics without a substantial labor force. To some extent the AKFM benefited from the support of FJKM[31] or the Federation of the Protestant Churches in the northern half of Madagascar. Pastor Richard Andriamanjato[32] remained as its leader while the active party workers were of rather good quality having been trained abroad, both in Western and Eastern Europe. But, the AKFM had lost out on the issue of independence; its leaders continued to have ambiguous feelings toward France. Having been brought up *a la française,* sometimes in France itself, they remained attached to French values. Moreover, De Gaulle also maintained good relations with the Soviet Union while Moscow seemed to respect the French zone of influence in this part of the

Indian Ocean. There was also a distinct fear that an elimination of France from Madagascar would most likely open its doors to the United States, perhaps the greatest fear of all. In short, the position of AKFM was rather uncomfortable as a party most coherent in criticism but one unable to come up with really constructive proposals. This party was moreover torn between the more or less orthodox Marxists and the more or less progressive liberals. As for its undeniable links with a Church these were far less compromising in terms of a political future than the AKFM's increasingly "bourgeois" recruitment, more pointedly among the middle class of Tananarive and hence Merina. Another, double, inconvenience consisted of the fact that the relatively privileged men and women who also doubled-up as the party's cadre became less and less receptive to popular demands, suspecting even that such demands were deliberately provoked. As for the AKFM adversaries they had a field day in denouncing the demagoguery of people favored by luck and especially in accusing them of wishing nothing less than a return of Merina hegemony in Madagascar. The MONIMA continued under the direction of its founder, Monja Jaona, as a party of leading citizens in the south-west (including some Lutheran fathers, small merchants, former war veterans, etc.) geared toward the villages through local and traditional hierarchies. Madagascar's attainment of formal independence took away from MONIMA as well one of its main issues so that the party began to appear immediately after independence as little more than expression of southern particularism. Although MONIMA shared with the AKFM a progressivist bent it was nonetheless quite distinct as it recruited its supporters and militants from among ethnicities far humbler than the Merina and from among the lower classes; and some of the MONIMA adherents, being preoccupied with rural problems, came to observe the Chinese revolution with far greater sympathy than the Soviet state.

With self-confidence, the PSD exploited the weaknesses of its political rivals. Nationalist in orientation but "moderate," "realistic," the PSD saw itself as the party of little people, those of the bush and of the rice-fields; and it made it a practice (not without any compromise) to recruit its partisans among all of the ethnicities in Madagascar. From some 400,000 declared in 1960 the PSD would attain one million ten years later. It thus became in effect a mass-party and multi-ethnic at the same time. It also remained highly centralized, under the tight discipline imposed by both Resampa and Tsiranana, while its activists came from the ranks of traditional leaders in every ethnicity of the Island. As it became rather difficult for the functionaries, propertied people, merchants and others not to join the PSD (its membrship card was a sort of insurance against all risks), the party's stance seemed oftentimes petty-bourgeois and it had distinct paternalism toward the humble folk, marvellously depicted in the name given by PSD women to their grouping, "Association of good-deed ladies." The party militancy was just about absent except around election time. The PSD also tried to eliminate other parties, not without astuteness and sometimes with brutality. One could cite as astute the move of Tsiranana when he took with him from Paris in July 1960 three leaders of the MDRM, party heavily implicated in the Malagasy Revolt, leaders who had been in exile since the events of 1947. Subsequently, two of them joined the PSD.[33] Another astute example would be the colloquia at Antsirabe of October and December 1961 to which the PSD had invited all other parties to hammer out a common program. Along with the other groupings the AKFM not only attended but also left the colloquia with the belief that it had obtained commitments to policies far more progressivist in nature, that some nationalizations would be carried out, that there would be an opening toward the communist nations and so on. But, the PSD soon retracted on these apparent concessions and it did so at a time when it could count on the additional support of some smaller groupings and some personalities generally listened to. There were other, deplorable, moments such as the seizure of newspapers under a variety of pretexts and despite a regime committed to freedom of the press; MONIMA was intimidated at times; the radio was used as a strictly one-way instrument of communication (when an "operation transistor" multiplied the number of sets in Madagascar). In a similar vein there was much talk of the "Cyclone Ramahavita" so named on the east coast of Madagascar after a PSD deputy bent on intimidating his opposition: bands of youths over-excited through inibriation ravaged the huts and crops of AKFM sympathizers in the eastern region; and the hudreds of depositions of complaint received by the authorities did not lead to a single follow-up. The elections were hardly free except in the larger towns as the old colonial practice of "advising the electorate" turned out to be far from dead. In truth, because of the *fihavavana*, not a few people conceived the elections as a way of showing their support of the state, of the collective organization, and made it a matter of personal duty to vote for men in power no matter who they were. At the same time, the electorate did not frequently get to see during elections anything except the PSD voting slips, not to mention other types of manipulation and pressure. In addition, Resampa was by then Minister of Interior, head of all the functionaries best placed to follow elections at close range. In such conditions the MONIMA did not have a single deputy in the National Assembly while the AKFM never had more than three altogether, all from Tananarive where it was most difficult to meddle in the electoral process; and these are the figures for the total of over 100 deputies to the National Assembly.[34]

Officially, thus, Madagascar did not have a one-party system. It was the wish of Tsiranana to impress upon the outside world an image of pluralistic regime, similar to those in the West, and he never tired of repeating his regrets over the absence of a really constructive opposition with which the President could have a dialogue. Still, what was left of an oppolition did have its value for a democratic alibi or as a convenient scapegoat. In effect, the state was confounded with the PSD which the administration used as receiver-amplifier to get words of official policy out and mobilize the people. This was clearly visible at the level of rural communes and the *fokonolona*.* A traditional institution, its achievements mainly in the past, and now noted for the conservative spirit of its *rayamandreny* (elders regarded as collective parents), the *fokonolona* at each village were assigned in 1962 by ordinance a host of tasks deemed important for the grass-roots development. While these village mini-democracies were thus made to enter the present as an expression of confidence in their maturity the truth was that everything had already been grouped into vast rural communes back in 1960, communes in real control of rural life but with a machinery completely penetrated by the party in power, with our without elections.

This very particular state construct was equally animated by a prolongation of the *côtier*-Merina disputes, an aspect which gave the state its harshness. But, the problem was not all that simple. The advancement of *côtiers* suited well those who were directing the simultaneous extension of state control and party power;

Fokonolona: village council(s). (Ed.)

and the PSD became rightly the high instrument of both recruitment into and the initial formation of the coastal elites. In some
of the ministries the cabinets were composed almost entirely from
the same ethnic group as the minister in charge. To the detriment
of younger functionaries who were mostly Merina and graduates
of the university-level School of Public Administration in Tananarive, the government multiplied the positions for those holding
diplomas of the Institute of Advanced Overseas Studies in Paris;
men who were above all *côtiers* on government fellowships and
who found themselves exempted from the tough competitive
examinations at home in the field of public administration. Even
more numerous than the ladder-functionaries were the so-called
NENA (Neither Enabled Nor Auxiliaries) who were given a
variety of tasks and most of whom came from the coastal areas.
It has also often been claimed that the government used to retain
far longer than necessary the technical assistants from France
at the most elevated positions in order to deny them to the
Merina functionaries quite competent to fill them at once. And,
yet, the Merina functionaries came in the greatest numbers since
the highlands of Madagascar continued to reap benefits from their
cultural advance over the rest of the Island (schools in Imerina
were commonplace for at least a century). The expansion of public
services after independence allowed the Merina to fill a large
number of "technical" posts which were devoid of any political
responsibilities and which had spread even in those provinces
least thouched by cultural influences of the once-dominant
Merina empire. We thus have an outline of an ethnic distribution
of both functions and functionaries issuing from contingencies
most likely beyond the vision of any pre-determined schema.
In the long run such a development would not materialize without
creating a sense of solidarity among the different ethnic elites,
among the social segments of "tribes" most prone to competition.
For the time being, however, the idea of prevention had won
the day, fed by policies from the top. One should not fail to
add here that the absence of a polulist threat upon those assured
at least of a decent standard of living also precluded a play on
the reflexes of class-solidarity; and when the Merina functionaries
joined the PSD they did not do so without some mental reservations.

It goes without saying that such quarrels and grudges also put
the brakes on a mobilization for development with a great deal

yet to he done. Although as yet not too large (some 6,000,000 in 1963) the population was increasing rapidly, with a 4.5% birthrate and an increase of 3% per annum and about forty-five percent of the population under the age of 15. It therefore required a most vigorous effort in promoting production just to insure that the average standard of living —which was quite mediocre—[35] would be on the slight increase or would not at least decline. The soils, too, were exhausted without much wealth available under the ground. Internal transportation was extremely insufficient and hence expensive, forcing a compartmentalization of regions when unity was being sought.[36] And the remoteness of external markets did not work in favor of Madagascar's exports in comparison, for example, with competing exports from an Africa bordering on the Atlantic. It was not easy at all, equally, to animate an overwhelmingly rural population (over four-fifths of the total), accustomed to a subsistence economy and rooted in its habits — for example in starting brush fires during the dry season, fires which could make the grass retreat slightly while depleting the soil even further. There was little honor to be found in manual labor as well, trait carried-over from the slave-holding days which also goes a long way to explain the esteem for schools that allowed one to enter into "intellectual" functions, at least in principle; but, would the evolution of structures really produce jobs for all of the candidates? Even more serious was, from some points of view, the paucity of capital in Madagascar; and when some of it was generated locally it fell to the temptation to give it shelter in Europe since the transfers of capital were unrestricted; even when invested locally, the capital went into real estate where returns were most rapid. In point of fact, after independence some 80% of all the modern-production equipment was still owned by foreigners, "heirs" of the colonial period. The exchanges, too, remained in all essential respects under the control of three French import-export conglomerates (best symbolized by the Compagnie Marseillaise) on which came to depend a complex network of resellers and collectors, mostly Indians and Chinese. The companies also financed the vast majority of the small local factories as well.[37]

In the face of the sheer scope of the task one could understand the hesitations. The very conditions for the accession to independence, the protection which the former metropole extended to the team in power, no less than the options still available to the French tutorial power, could not lead to any visions of rupturing the old economic links without instituting at the same time a more auto-centered system. Most probably, a choice of this type would lead into a more authoritarian organization of production, into nationalizations and fundamental restructuring, in short to an economic and ultimately social revolution. Now, the Malagasy society in 1960, especially the rural part, was rather far from being ripe for such upheavals. The small cultivators (there were about 1,000,000 of this type) were also quite often proprietors and the concept of private property was very entrenched. When they were sharecroppers tied to city-dwelling owners this reproduced an older situation in that the urban owners were often members of former slave-holding families while the sharecroppers were descendants of slaves; and, in this context, their relations continued to be defined by the old ideas of service exchanges (like protection for supplies in kind). But, this particular situation was confined to the central highlands of Madagascar. In contrast, around the coastal provinces there were as yet many concessions, granted during colonial rule, and often not fully developed, which had not been the object of protests as vigorous as those in some other former colonies; indeed, along the East Coast for example, such concessions (often reduced in size) as were once given to creoles from the Mascarene Islands of Réunion and Mauritius (who produced vanilla and especially coffee) passed-on progressively into Malagasy hands. It was a trend that had started long before independence and it went on with a momentum of its own.

The Malagasy Republic simply confirmed the option which imposed itself — an economy that was liberal in character and integrated into the world market, one leading implicitly into the development of commercial yields within the rural setting. If the government proclaimed itself able to nationalize some of the industries (producing primary materials, for example), the large commercial houses and transportation enterprises were in a "reserved sector;" and even the principle of nationalization never came to be applied.[38] In the same way, if a 1962 ordinance sanctioned incursions into the private property rights to augur a transfer to the state of any large but unexploited concessions this came attached to long probationary periods before the state would come to intervene.

In a world which moved rapidly on its own it was not possible to wait for the game of supply-and-demand to improve the local production and the local standard of living. There was also the risk of allowing the foreign enterprise to gain possession of the country and thus aggravate the existing inequalities. Developed countries, which Madagascar took as potential models, were themselves giving examples of an "organization" of production by the state (via management, through plans for guided development and in the mixed economies). The Malagasy state, by need, made itself intervene as well, for instance, by limiting the number rice factories and thus avoid the problems of over-equipment and poor management.[39] In the countryside, where so much remained to be done,[40] some operations concentrated on commercial production, especially where private investors were hesitant to act; and the large rural-management societies like the SAMANGOKY[41] had as their aim the development of new areas for profitable cash crops through the use of large technical means. But the official vision in the early years of the Republic was a participatory one, seeking to transform the producer through the production. This was the case in "grass-roots" operations assigned to the *fokonolona* and the rural communes such as the maintaining of nearby roads, construction of schools, reforestation, drainage and the like.[42] Partly under the Israeli inspiration a vast cooperative movement was launched charging the Tananarive-based General Commissariat for Cooperation to prepare the enabling personnel and to develop a spirit of cooperation.[43] In fact, "rural animation" since 1962/1963 and the "civic service" created to mobilize a section of the needed conscripts were going in the same direction. This should be at once qualified by the fact that these efforts were partly as well as rapidly compromised by various abuses of power and illicit trading, notably within the cooperatives. It can thus be seen that an intervention of state, inevitable if the ever-increasing organisms were to be coordinated, became an occasion for the politization which only froze all enthusiasms. Local conditions in the industrial domain were crying for moderation but the problem remained as to how to impose a particular policy on the foreign enterprises the plight of which would constitute economic loss and cause urban unemployment. There was the urge to produce more, to transform an increasing number of local products before these are exported, to manufacture at home a part of the finished goods which were normally imported (such as automobile assemblies). A stress was placed logically on the light industries (shoes, cloth, plastics); and to encourage them (and the foreign capital within these enterprises), an Investment Code gave in 1962 a variety and multiplicity of advantages in fiscal matters, in customs and elsewhere. All enterprises with major investments in Madagascar could also benefit from one or more conventions on establishments ratified by the Malagasy Parliament, sort of power-to-power accords. Nonetheless, the National Society for Investments practiced, through its own interpretation, a certain amount of state intervention, since the state could participate in industrial enterprises and induce local savings, including forced savings since all the functionalries had to subscribe to it. Let us note also in the financial setor a rather orthodox type of management, one of great prudence and of great concern with balanced budgets. The state had few debts overseas as loans had been granted to enterprises managed independently of the state or else funds were invested directly into the enterprises pure and simple. On the other hand, the state received gifts in material and, directly, in money — occasion for many ceremonies at which Tsiranana used to say that there were "not enough words to say thank-you!"

Under such circumstances the "Malagasy Socialism," advertised by the party in power, was rather difficult to define. It perceived itself as "practical and humane," especially pragmatic: as according to Tsiranana one should not spend time on the "grand theories which are often bypassed by events." It was a socialism rather marked by refusals, as much of the laissez-faire capitalism as of class-struggle. It was, in the words of Roger Pascal, a "socialism in the hollow." With its imprecision, it translated the incertitudes of a group "wedged" between the powerful interests (most often foreign ones that went along with conditions of independence) and the masses, as yet not well-organized, masses for whose wellbeing there existed a concern but also masses which represented a body of clients. "Socialism," said Tsiranana, is "for me a bit like religion," putting thus the stress on the moral aspect. There was, on the way, a wish for a grand fraternal nation, much like the vast and idealized *fokonolona* in which every individual would work for the good of all.[44]

Against such intentions, one must confess, the Republic's early years were disappointing. It was to be hoped, staring with 1964/ 1965, with the PSD well in control of the land, that the dynamism of its leaders might come to be applied more effectively to development and the mobilizing of public opinion so as to resolve some real problems. Additionally, the year 1964 saw the birth of the first five-year plan. Its aims were undoubtedly modest but designed to speed-up production and meet the basic needs of the population as a whole.

b) Philibert Tsiranana was reelected President on 30th March 1965 with 97.7% of the total votes cast. Elections for the Legislature in August gave more that 95% of the votes to PSD candidates who triumphed everywhere except in Tananarive, as usual. The PSD power was now quite safe and the AKFM soon seemed ready to join it. Its leaders related that they were 80% behind policies of a government they had criticised mainly on the conditions of policy-applications; it was an attitude said "hand-in-hand." But, the PSD repulsed this outstretched hand; it was one representing a "cameleon-party" of poorly disguised crypto-communists. There was a distinct preference in the high circles of government for the type of political commodities offered for instance by Her Majesty's Loyal Opposition. The AKFM was, moreover, being abandoned by the young attending the University of Madagascar as they did not appreciate what had seemed to them simple recanting.

As France remained the main external spokesman[45] Madagascar was harboring the largest group of French residents in Africa, right after Morocco and Algeria, with some 50,000 French nationals in 1968/1969. But, relations were also developed with other countries of Western Europe and through the framework of CEE-EAMA.[46] Emerging from the Yaounde convention of 1963, this association held a session in Tananarive early in 1969. The activities of FAC were completed by the European Development Fund (FED) while the United States obtained an authorization to build a large NASA base at Imerintsiatosika, in the highlands. Some melting occured toward Eastern Europe early in 1968 but there was no question of any accords except commercial ones with lands not too subservient to Moscow, mainly Yugoslavia and Roumania. However, some negotiations were started with the USSR but were broken-off at the time of the Prague events; indeed, the numerical strength of the mission which the Soviets were proposing to install in Tananarive caused a lot of fears. As for Mao's "little red book," its distribution was banned.[47]

With a continuity hence at home and abroad, had not the moment arrived for a government that no one contested seriously any longer to give some impetus to the fight for the "take-off" constantly mentioned? Well, not yet at all: although the national unity was

at hand, as was recognized at the top, it had as yet to be consolidated. With so many pledges made to the côtiers the ethnic
rivalries were now being fanned instead of appeased. The
"Republican Security Forces" (FRS) which André Resampa had
created in 1966 and which were attached directly to his Ministry
of the Interior, represented basically a paramilitary police force
recruited from within the peripheral provinces and intensively
trained by the Israelis. This force was infused with an anti-Merina
spirit. Since the Army's officers were for the most part Merina,
the government gave its support and encouragement to the gendarmerie, more populist in orientation. Under the direct responsibility of its Headquarters Chief attached to the Presidency itself,
a Chief who was French, the gendarmerie was directed operationally
by Colonel Ratsimandrava who was from Imerina but who belonged to the former class of slaves(andevo). Even in the Malagasy
Army itself, the government tried to "push" some of the raking
officers from the coastal areas, officers like Brechard Rajaonarison.
One can thus perceive the setting for some of the elements
and actors of as yet forthcoming dramas.

The implementation of the five-year plan lacked sufficient vigor
and even its original conception was being debated: there was
an excessive dribbling of investments too feeble to profit too many
operations; and, yet, it was a necessity that all of the regions
and all of the socio-economic sectors gain from the incepted plan.
As for the modalities of its application, these were susceptible
to corrections in practice. It was thus with the ushering of 1966
that governmental policies became even more oriented than before
toward the capitalist models of growth and, in so far as the
direct intervention of the state was concerned, toward large-scale,
production-oriented operations. Toward the end of 1966 "state
farms" were being instituted to organize, in certain regions, both
production and commercialization within quasi-authoritarian
structures.[48] True enough, all the participatory-type initiatives
on which so much hope was placed seemed by then to have completely misfired. The Commissariat for Cooperation was completely
recast in 1967 as a matter of necessary priority; while the "communes syndicates," which had been extended into all the prefectures
of Madagascar came once more under direct management. Work
of André Resampa who had the initial experience at his "fief"
of Morondava, on the west-central coast, the communes syndicate
had as its principal duties the loaning of large agricultural equip-

ment (supplied by the state) to communes and to individuals; in turn, it secured local monopoly of the commercialization of agricultural productions for crops like peanuts, maize, rice and cassava; through it, the state still controlled, assisted and suggested.

Generally speaking, the peasant standard of living was rather on the decline. While the price of rice was fixed the cost of living went up, even if moderately so. This increase resulted in the swelling of money in circulation tied to public investments within the five-year plan. In 1969, there was a devaluation of national currency following the pattern of the French franc devaluation. As in all of the Third-World lands' cases Madagascar suffered also a deterioration in terms of exchange. On one particular point the producers of sugar in Madagascar became the victims of the end in preferential French trade imposed by the Common Market agreements; and all the propaganda to promote a growth in local consumption of sugar propaganda to promote the growth in local consumption of sugar could hardly provide a compensation to offset the export losses. The Malagasy government was quite aware that local discontent could, one day, manifest itself dangerously and it had the courage to re-examine its options: the so-called "Days of Development" in April and May of 1967 made it possible for all of the tendencies to express themselves; and even views of major international experts were being solicited. Yet, no fundamental revisions could emerge in the face of the many divergences among the participants. In effect, the larger operations of 1968 called for such types of investments that foreign support became even more indispensible than ever.

c) One verdict would be that ten years after the Republic had been proclaimed it was a sense of gloom that came to characterize Madagascar. The dependence upon foreign trade and foreign capital was almost total. The three giant French import-export companies still controlled through their network almost one half of the total value of commercialized agricultural production and just about three-fourths of all exports while some two-thirds of all investments came from abroad.[49] On top, these investments were quite inferior to what had been anticipated; private investments, notably, did not represent more than 33% of what the plan had counted on as foreign capital found a field for more lucrative activities elsewhere. As in other under-developed countries with virtually identical options, the overseas remission of profits became often larger than the sums obtained under a variety of headings on a government-to-government basis; yet, Madagascar was one of the Third-World countries where the sum obtained per capita happened to have been the highest! All along, one could add, key-positions in the banks and in the private corporations were held, for the most part, by Europeans.

The foreign capital created undoubtedly in Madagascar, at least for some time, considerable employment for Malagasy workers but the internal transportation failed to improve one whit. While the International Airport at Ivato was a thing of beauty most of the roads in Madagascar were in a deplorable condition.[50] The modernization of agricultural equipment was quite limited in scope and the few light industries that had been founded in recent years attained rather quickly their production ceilings so tight was the local market. The commercial balance showed continuous deficit, something which is of course not confined to Madagascar but if, in the importations, one could note some increases in hard goods, primary materials and the energy products there was also a large increase of rice imports, reflecting the demographic growth in Madagascar (once exporter of rice), several poor harvests as well as the fact that the country was stagnant. The out-of-the way position of Madagascar was even more aggravated with the closing of the Suez Canal in 1967. There was one favorable aspect in the exchanges: if France continued as the leading partner (and notably as the main provider), other states, mostly in the Common Market,[51] also developed their economic relations with Madagascar. This would logically lead to the multiplication of the chances of providing some guarantees in the event of a crisis in the internal economy of the former metropole.

At the moment, growth continued to be limited. The United Nations' statistics revealed Madagascar as one of the worlds least dynamic lands. The provisions of the five-year plan, modest as they were, had not been realized; and the agricultural production had barely increased at 1% per year. Society, too, seemed to evolve at a snail's pace while the pauperization of the countryside caused some exodus into towns where a sub-proletariat swelled especially among the youngest generations auguring a future full of potential problems. This is even more so because of the discrepancy in the standard of living which tended to improve for the petty and middle bourgeoisie of functionaries, free professions and merchants and still more among the highest-ranking officials and the national partners in the foreign corporations. There was, among the young in school, an increasing apprehension, a feeling of dismal job prospects, an ever greater scepticism toward the traditional authority of the elders, and the growth in contestatory spirit which was readily noticed by teachers in the lycées and at the University of Madagascar.

Still, for those who made no effort to pay close attention everything seemed unchanged. Behavior toward the *vazaha* was often of the dependency type which Octave Mannoni had described in 1950.[52] Taboos of castes and ethnicities were still in vigor among the Malagasy.[53] Such old impediments could be regarded as sufficiently strong to prevent for a long time to come any real changes at the base; and Tsiranana was convinced that he could fill the role of grand mediator among the factions for years to come, too.

d) The crisis which would overtake the regime in 1972 began at least four years earlier and it came about gradually as an accumulation of grievances. It was the absence of coordination among the contesting groups that accounts for the crisis' complexity and for the difficulties of its resolution. Madagascar did not possess either a coherent social class nor a dynamic political party which could lead, as in other parts of the globe, into a sweeping and ultimately successful revolution.

Bit by bit, a malaise permeated the Malagasy country-side. Brush fires, for example, damaged more and more acres of land each year, but, by burning far beyond the immediate planting needs and habits, the cultivators wanted to show their disapproval of the *fanjakana* (government) which precisely urged against such practices and did not hesitate to suppress them as well. In 1969/1970 Malagasy city-dwellers were badly hurt by the first instance of soaring prices since independence in 1960[54] and extremely violent tracts came into circulation now and then. A clandestine pamphlet was being passed around at the time of the Republic's tenth anniversary, for example, its title being the exact replica of the occasion, "Ten Years of the Republic;" and its contents revealed that there were two authors, one a Malagasy and the other a French "technical cooperator."[55] It was clearly the Malagasy youth that became "unhinged" preceded by the university students who had been more or less infected with the fever of the French May 1968 despite the difference of contexts.[56] Although most of the men in power were Catholics, the Catholic Church in Madagascar began to take its distance from them. *Lumière*, the important French-language weekly published by Jesuit fathers at Fianarantsoa (fourth largest town in Madagascar), did not gloss over a general sense of disorientation, as much in the rural world as among all those who could be called thoughtful. If the AFKM seemed content with a formalistic opposition, in the southernmost area of Madagascar, a section starved out for years by the droughts, MONIMA was in a state of political revival as it began to integrate better with the villagers. A congress at Amboasary in July 1970 revealed just how influential the youth had become in the south as the younger men did not hesitate to propose the adoption of violent methods to remove the inequalities and lift the yoke of the PSD, methods which were repugnant to the older generations; and, in contesting local hierarchies, the young were seeking new ways to give power to the base. The MONIMA also had contacts with Malagasy students (as at the Tamatave Congress in 1969 of the FAEM, the main student organization in the Island) and there were now apparently some contestatory tendencies within the PSD itself. This was perhaps inevitable since the PSD had been virtually the sole pan-islandic party and as such had absorbed through amalgamation too many political families which continued to subsist as factions within the PSD. A left-wing, under A. Besy, demanded in 1969 a fundamental agrarian reform; others proposed nationalizations and the stepping-up of Malgachisation among the upper echelons of government and of private enterprise; and André Resampa had the reputation of listening to such calls with considerable attention. For their part, students belonging to the PSD were denouncing — in the name of more orthodox socialism — the submission of Malagasy state to capitalism and the progressive impoverishment of rural Malagasy.

Tsiranana remained undaunted and he gave much the same speeches. There was a feeling that those closest to him concealed part of the truth as the President's health left much to be desired since 1966. It became indeed a matter of priority to find new inspirations. In 1969 the government abandoned the principle of strict budget-balancing. This was deemed necessary because of the expenses incurred directly by the state and, as fiscal burdens became heavier, it seemed convenient to seek confidence at home by novel means, including a diversification of

Madagascar's external partners. On the last point there was even a sense of urgency since France appeared no longer able or willing to do more for Madagascar just as the cooperation credits began to be nibbled away through price increases in the Island.

The opening of Madagascar toward other financial backers, although well-intended in design, ended up by provoking the indignation of many African states as well as reprobation of very many Malagasy since their government had, in effect, negotiated a rapprochement with South Africa. A movement in such a direction began some years earlier indirectly, through excellent relations with Malawi, a state itself linked by geographical position, and by choice, to South Africa. In 1967 an airline was inaugurated from Tananarive to Johannesburg and the new orientation of Madagascar came into the open in 1968. Tsiranana, while reminding everyone that he formally opposed apartheid and had never ceased to do so, also argued that h would not be trapped by demagoguery; it seemed to him rather astute to attract to Madagascar many South Africans so that they could see a place where race-relations are at their fraternal best and return home rather shaken.[57] The real issue, of course, was economic — to get the South African rand through the tourists, especially since the ever-succeeding programs at home had overestimated continuously the tourist numbers from Europe and the United States. It was also a case of taking advantage of simple geographical proximity to develop exchanges and visiting commercial delegations became more and more frequent. There was no question of full-fledged diplomatic relations but one could easily suspect these to be just around the corner and no one doubted that South African intentions in Madagascar were far more political than commercial.

Inside Madagascar, it seemed as something was about to happen in the last few weeks of 1969. Indeed, on 2nd December the government was abruptly dismissed by Tsiranana. Two ultra-secret meetings with the Director of National Security and cryptic declarations (like "no one is irreplaceable" or the "real reasons are too serious to be mentioned") fed as much the curiousity as the hopes of many. Even Richard Andriamanjato was called in for consultations. Then, one day after another, all of the personalities from the previous cabinet were reinstated (and this lasted for some three weeks). Apparently, Tsiranana either wished only to instill some fears around him or else had to renounce a clean sweep in the face of unforeseen difficulties. The opposition was beginning to talk about the engine that misfires. Vive-President Calvin Tsiebo was given the power to sign all acts and decrees of government, an act pointing to him as successor should misfortune strike. Tsiebo, an aged good man, was symbolic of the idea of continuity. But was there any need to change at all: the municipal elections of 21st December underscored again the strength of PSD, party which even gained some new wards (as in Antsirabe for example). Still, the PSD lost the absolute majority in the major eastern port of Tamatave and it had to retreat still more in favor of the AKFM in Tananarive.

At the end of January 1970, while attending an OCAM conference at Yaounde, President Tsiranana fell victim to a grave health accident (diabetic coma?); he was transported to Paris and did not regain Madagascar until four months later. This period of absence might have been the moment to infuse some new blood into the guiding team and to revise some of the options set a decade earler; yet, no one wanted to run the risk of being blamed for profiting from such delicate circumstances. After all, Tsiranana remained the "father of Independence." It was published that there could be no need for a Presidential vacancy and the caretaker government busied itself mainly with expediting the day-to-day business. When Tsiranana returned home so well-recovered that even his doctors were astonished he had even more authority than just prior to departure for Yaounde; this type of resurrection had the fel of a miracle. Indeed, in his "Blue Notebook," started at the hospital in France and to be published somewhat later, the Malagasy President erected something of a monument to himself: if God had kept him alive it was because He wanted Tsiranana to achieve his prophetic mission; God had chosen him, the Tsimihety shepherd-boy,[58] as He had once selected David for the Chosen People; had not prophecies accompanied his birth? Some were saying at the time that the President had not recovered as well in mind as in body.

Elections for the Legislature, held in September 1970, returned again to the PSD the totality of seats, excluding the usual three in Tananarive. As a new government reshuffle was announced just after the election, Tsiranana again took back the very same men. A law of 9th October, authorizing the nomination of four Vice-Presidents of the Republic, seemed destined to relieve the President of some duties. What was noted at once, however,

André Resampa became the First Vice-President and, as such, the designated dauphin. On the 19th and 21st November accords of cooperation were signed with South Africa as the new partner gave Madagascar a substantial loan on favorable terms and engaged itself to contribute to a tourist infrastructure at the resort isle of Nosy-bé, off the northwestern coast of Madagascar. Above all, the South African capital would get off the ground a project very dear to Tsiranana personally, namely the improvement of the Narinda Bay located also in this area of Madagascar. There would be a deep-water port and repair-dock for the giant petro-tankers going through the Mozambique Channel and an industrial zone. One year later, after intense negotiations, the Narinda Bay program became operational; in the meantime, De Beers Consolidated was able to secure vast prospecting rights in Madagascar.

In 1971 events began to move at an even faster pace. At the end of 1970 and the start of 1971 Tsiranana made a grand tour of the south and the north, noting a great deal of local insolvency; and there was a new dissolution of government on 17th February, following his return to the capital. Again, the same men were recalled to duty but André Resampa, relieved of the FRS direction immediately upon becoming the First-Vice-President,[59] was now only in the second position, after Calvin Tsiebo; and Resampa lost his portfolio for the Interior Minister for the one in Agriculture. It was Tsiranana himself who held the Ministry of Interior, assisted by a personal ministerial delegate. The President had never accumulated so many responsibilities before and it was generally understood that he had found himself amid both opposing tendencies and personal quarrels.

In March and April Tananarive was awaiting some major international meetings — a conference of Finance Ministers from the Franc Zone, the colloquia of francophone universities, and the meeting of the Council of the CEE-EAMA association. But in March, too, began a protest movement of students at the Faculty of Medicine (University of Madagascar) against an automatic application in Madagascar of the French exams regime; and, now, the whole University went on strike as well for the first time. The students (somewhere over 6,000 in various establishments) were beginning to question the entire system of studies, copied directly from the French model, along with the insufficient Malgachisation of educational programs, lack of adaptations to national realities,[60] and absence of student participation in the responsibilities of university administration and organization.[61] The government closed the university on 25th March *sine die* to reopen it a few days later, during the colloquia of francophone universities. The students came back, however, only to organize demonstrations and the crisis did not abate until April, with the appointment of a 30-member Commission (with 15 students in it) wich was to review the status of the university. In July, the mixed Franco-Malagasy committee which still managed the university (since it was essentially a French university still) accepted the progressive Malgachisation, at least in the juridical sense, with France continuing to furnish funds and teaching personnel. There was to be a study of possible reform through which to attain a basic transformation of the system of study but this could also be regarded as a delaying tactic.

Much more serious but apparently unrelated to the student movement in Tananarive[62] was a rebellion in the south which began on 1st April and of which the MONIMA was the organizer. In this region of Madagascar, always on the threshhold of poverty, the fiscal oppression and administrative arbitrariness became, in effect, insupportable. The MONIMA, implanted as was seen deeply into the rural masses, could not avoid articulating this deep-seated discontent. Neither the strike against the fiscal powers of the government[63] nor yet emergency supplies brought to help through certain sectors of the party were enough to alleviate the problem. Rumors of a major movement were circulating in March and, during the night of 1st-2nd April, bands of some dozens or possibly hundreds of men armed with spears and axes began to attack the police outposts, the sub-prefectures and the prisons throughout most of the large Tuléar Province in what amounted the first use of violance against the Malagasy Republic. Still, the village leaders were able to retain a part of their authority and, while accepting the movement demanded by the young, they also gained positions of leadership within it. Thanks to these men, many lives were spared, especially among foreigners in the area since the numerous Indians and Frenchmen were not seriously harmed. Even the Merina were protected as well, with the MONIMA claiming to have transcended the old ethnic rivalries and wishing to preserve nationaly unity. A revolutionary power was installed nowhere to replace the *fanjakana*. In sum, the movement, after easily gaining control of some moderately

important aglommerations, went no further. There were claims
that it was waiting for foreign weapons and reinforcements,
slated to arrive by sea; the MONIMA militants believed in
this and announced the collaboration with Communist China
but the wait itself proved to have been in vain. The MONIMA
leaders knew quite well that there was no one to be counted upon
and were resigned from the start to defeat, factor which made
the repression by local gendarmerie quite easy. There were some
one thousand dead in its wake. Arrested with the MONIMA
leaders, including Monja Jaona, were some 5,000 of which 600 were
deported to the convict prison on Nosy-Lava. To this should
be added also the settlement of old scores *in situ*, summary
justice which was swift — an abuse against which even the
President was warning on the national radio.[64] As could have
been expected, the MONIMA was dissolved; and the leading
official thesis (stated in the earliest of Tsiranana's declarations)
claimed an extensive communist plot predicated on widespread
killings. During the so-called "Days of Planning" instituted between
19th-25th April, however, the government acknowledged that the
southern discontent did have its valid excuses and that the
local exactions had been committed by an administration un-
deserving of the land.

This rebellion served to weaken the PSD's political power since
the party could no longer brandish the unity of all *cotiers*, now
something of a scare-crow; and the very harshness of repression
excesses in the south resulted in the transformation of those
hesitant into decided opponents. Bishops, Catholic newspapers, FJKM pastors, all expressed disapproval in public.
The atmosphere was poisoned. Some weeks after repressions in
the south there came to light in Tananarive a "Maoist" plot
at ORSTOM, the main French scientific-research organization
in Madagascar; and the two main culprits were a Malagasy and
a Frenchman.[65] Within the PSD itself, factionalism was on the upswing. On the one hand, much of the mutual friendship seems
to linger in Resampa and Tsiranana as they tour together the
areas of rebellion in the south, wielding the threat and the pardon,
directing ceremonies of reconciliation with fraternal elders and
notables. On the other, on 25th May, Resampa submits to
Tsirarana the collective resignation of PSD's ruling Bureau. On
1st June, following the meeting of the Council of Ministers,
Tsiranana had Resampa arrested while accusing him of plotting

with a foreign embassy. Other supporters of Resampa —the "Resampists"— all high officers of the PSD and its Bureau were arrested with him as well. The conjured accusation would never be supported by the slightest proof.[66] The real reason for the rupture with Resampa was Resampa's own impatient irritation with a land that had sunk into a state of stagnation and with the rapprochement with Pretoria, now fully confirmed; nor did Resampa hide at all his intention to solicit support for his own succession to the incumbent President and the Office. But, Resampa could not be accused of trying to precipitate a presidential downfall. More and more touchy, Tsiranana could not tolerate premature preparation for an eventuality that was not apparent in the immediate future.

Thus called to order at its 14th Congress, the PSD gave Tsiranana a *carte blanche* to seek the renewal of his national mandate in 1972; and, during the Presidential elections on 30th January 1972, Tsiranana was the sole candidate in what amounted to a veritable plebiscite. Even in Tananarive, where the AKFM was asking for abstentions, the voting was almost entirely in Tsiranana's favor. *Lumière* spoke of a sort of collective resignation.

III — The Long Crisis of 1972-1975 and the Birth of the Second Republic

Within three dramatic years, all of the solutions brought to bear on the early problems of independence were questioned anew as transient solutions that came to be regarded as permanent in error. As for the Second Republic, proclaimed just recently, one can only note its intentions at the time when this text is being written (February 1977).

1) To begin with 1972/1973 can be seen in some ways as a second phase of decolonization which is cultural, diplomatic and —to some extent— economic as well. In January 1972 and, after an intermission, at the beginning of March, student ferment began to reappear. At the old School of Medicine at Befelatana, Tananarive, students destined to become a lower category of doctors, not too-well regarded, went into strike to secure their inclusion into the structure of modern university instruction; it was their goal to unify the cycle of their studies with the one in force at the Faculty of Medecine. For reasons which were at once administrative and budgetary, the government refused this move and closed the school at Befelatana. Now, upon reflexion,

the students were denouncing the entire colonialist character of education in Madagascar and refused to return to classrooms when their school reopened on 31st March. The scenario was about the same as in 1971. At the end of April, the University of Madagascar, the lycées and colleges in the capital and later in several other towns, went on strike in turn. This intervention of all secondary-education students would give an exceptional amplification to the coming events: indeed, there are more than 100,000 of them, many in private and paid-for educational establishments the level of which was quite mediocre.[67] There were new demonstrations, the largest of which by far took place in Tananarive on April 25 as a protest against the death of a college student at Ambalavao (in Betsileo country), supposedly killed during a scuffle with police. The next day, during a huge meeting at the main stadium, the then-minister of Education, Botokeky, tried but failed to regain the confidence of university and lycée students whose program had crystallized: the voiding of cultural cooperation accords with France, Malgachisation and democ- ratization of instruction. There was an interesting fact, too. Many parents became worried over the radicalization of a move- ment in which their children were participants and began to feel that their progeny was escaping parental authority as well. It was in vain that a committee of both parents and students sought a return to the classroom. To bring matters to end, on 9th May the PSD Bureau demanded that any and all means be put to work so as to end the strike; and, during the night of 12th-13th May, the government arrested and deported to Nosy-Lava almost 400 of the student leaders. It also closed the entire edu- cational establishment and banned all further demonstrations. On 13th May it is riot in the streets of Tananarive as the security forces (FRS) start shooting at the youthful mass, swelled also by the young out of work and coming from the poorer sections of Tananarive. Tsiranana, who happened to have been in the provinces, returned with all speed, clamped a lid on the armed ripostes, decreed a state of national emergency, and ordered a curfew.[68]

The day had made some 40 deaths.[69] The next day and for days to come, the capital was criss-crossed by demonstrators who seemed in control of it. The city hall was set afire[70] as well as the printing shop of the large French-language newspaper *Courier de Madagascar*, officious organ of the government. The gendarmerie interposed itself; but, further clashes with the FRS were avoided in the process. While Minister Botokeky was resigning droves of white-collar employees and other workers abandoned their jobs on the 15th to join an immense march toward the Palace of Andafiavaratra, seat of the government.[71] A dialogue could not be established at all. Tsiranana, however, did let it be known that he was setting free and returning home at once all of the deported students; but, a militant town wanted even more now. As no coherent force seemed capable of acting as a government virtually anything could have happened during these few days of extraordinary disorder in Tananarive. It was in such conditions that the idea emerged among the demonstrators to turn to the Malagasy Army which had been kept out of all political events and which had avoided taking any of the political sides. This goes as well for 1971 when the Army did not take part in the southern repressions. On 18th May, without anything better in sight,[72] Tsiranana dissolved his government and granted full powers, under his own high authority as President, to General Gabriel Ramanantsoa, Chief of the Malagasy Army. Calm returned gradually to Tananarive but there still was an air of feverish liberty among the youth, probably unexperienced for generations in Madagascar.

Member of an important Merina family, man in his sixties who had spent most of his career in the French Army, himself very French and speaking French better than Malagasy, General Ramanantsoa was far from being a revolutionary. It is even unlikely that he harbored any political ambitions whatsoever, accepting the duties placed upon him by Tsiranana only to preserve national unity and stop the country from being engulfed by disorder. He announced the new government of national union of 25th May and it was one composed of 5 military and 6 civilian "technicians" who represented collectively most of the Island's ethnicities. It came as a considerable surprise to see thus elevated to the highest positions in the land so many new faces, young for the most part yet men whose talents came into clear view the moment they began to speak in public. The least unknown among them but surely the least popular at the time as well was Colonel Richard Ratsimandrava, Chief of the gendarmerie. It was a pressing need for him to dispel the many grudges which the instrument of power he came to command had earned for him as well, an instrument of repression used as such by the government in the country-side and most pointedly in the south just a short-while ago. Ratsimandrava was, moreover, regarded as a protégé of Tsiranana. By contrast, just about completely unknown, was Commander Didier Ratsiraka. He would soon direct at the Ministry of Foreign Affairs all the negotiations for the revision of cooperation accords with France, measure demanded by everyone in Madagascar.[73] In theory, this new multi-ethnic team could be widely accepted while Tsiranana conserved his title of President of the Republic, something the *côtiers* could see as an additional guarantee. Still, in the popular opinion of the Merina there was a feeling of historical revenge: a Merina was at long last at the helm again.[74]

The new government, vested with the special powers which the state had granted out of national necessity (an act provided for in the Constitution of 1959), wasted no time in passing spectacular measures: control of foreign exchanges, including any within the franc zone, minimum-salary relief (mostly for the urban Malagasy), elimination of capitation tax as well as of head-of-cattle tax (favoring mostly the rural Malagasy). A Malagasy was also placed at the head of the University of Madagascar. All victims of previous repression were released, staring with André Resampa and Monja Jaona.

While Malgachisation and democratization are in the air there still had to be some nuances. If everyone or nearly so had agreed to the need to review the cooperation accords with France, democratization itself was not an object of such unity of views beyond the elementary measures designed to improve the general standard of living for the masses. It seemed out of question among the majority of those now in power to undertake a fundamental uprooting of internal structures within society and economy; and the middle class —the functionaries and men of business (mainly small ones)— rallied quickly to the support of the government as it could have everything to lose if democratization led into a basic restructuring. The May interventions of populist elements and the violence had upset the "honest people." Were not, after all, the banderoles, seen on the ruins of the City Hall, claiming power for the *madinika* (the humble folk)? Moreover, the lowland and generally poorer sections of Tananarive were still in state of mobilization, especially among its young who were the prime-movers of the more or less coherent ZOAM groupings[75] which maintained liaison with both the lycée and university students. One can thus come to understand not only why the bourgeoisie of the highlands rallied at once to the government (the AKFM, surprised by events too, gave its support in the name of struggle-aganist-imperialism to avoid focus on local issues), but also why the diverse elements controlling the provinces had been just as rapid in extending their support, among them most of the PSD activists, natables and political newcomers.[76] There thus was emerging a consciousness of solidarity within a leading national class even if this change, unsettling the older particularisms, was not always accepted with a glad heart.

Against the high probability of incidents the different forces did nonetheless manage to avoid confrontations between June and October. For instance a large demonstration was to take place on 26th June in the presence of Tsiranana and Ramanantsoa; this was simply a repeat of the annual anniversaries of independence, attended by the highest authorities in the land. The street protest against a public reappearance of the President made it however necessary to annul the ceremonies. During its July congress the MONIMA, while giving its support to the government, made it known that it would remain vigilant; and not only in Tananaive but also in many other towns the so-called KIM[77] were conducting quasi-permanent seminars involving students, teachers, workers, the ZOAM and, at times, peasants, in a study of what was to be a profound political change. A sort of popular power seemed to have been emerging as the KIM announced that a massive national congress would take place to pave the ground for a new society within a second Republic. For the KIM the Ramanantsoa governemt had only a provisionary authority, granted by the people; and the government did not attempt to oppose preparations for the huge meeting (it probably could not have done so anyway) which lasted from 4th to 19th September in Tananarive, bringing together several thousand participants. As could be predicted, the principles adopted at the congress were Malgachisation of the economy and educational system, foreign policy independent of France, break with South Africa, opening of relations with Communist countries. Yet, proposals to recast society itself remained rather vague. The KIM, too, had their inner contradictions as they contained not only the populist element but also the leisured one represented by students and teachers whose own education and experience allowed them to come to direct the work of the KIM.

At any rate, the government did not recognize any constituent powers of the KIM congress. Even before the congress came about the government had decided to prepare, itself, a broad public consultation and secure through it the ratification of policies implemented since May; and, as the concern for giving a legalistic basis to governmental power is particularly remarkable in Madagascar, the Government wanted to obtain this sanction as well for its actions yet to come. Indeed, on 1st September, General Ramanantsoa confirmed this in a radio broadcast which announced a referendum for 8th October to that effect. The text, published on 4th September, on which the Malagasy were to pass judgement would accord General Ramanantsoa, and the men he would select (there no longer was a question of Tsiranana) to assist him, full powers "in order to implement within 5 years a structural transformation without which there could be no renewal" and "to bring about a climate of public life consonant with the wishes of the people." A "Populer National Council for Development" (CNPD) would advise the government and assist it. This meant the abolition of the 1959 Constitution which would be superseded by a new text at the end of proposed five years. Most likely, the parting with Tsiranana came from the recognition of the fact that his unpopularity could not be reversed and from the conviction —a bit hasty, perhaps— that the *côtier* problem did not exist any longer. A lively campaign for elections brought into play the military (as Ramanantsoa went all over Madagascar and became rather fond of his immersion into the masses); the AKFM; the Malagasy Socialist Union (USM), which Resampa and Botokeky had formed at the end of September while supporting the new governmental team from PSD cross-overs and notables who would soon become the *"Vonjy"* (helpers) favoring the government; the MONIMA and the KIM were in it also as participants with the "yes" vote, although not without some hesitations until Ramanantsoa promised progressivist policies through nationalizations and administrative cleansing. Only Tsiranana and what was left of his PSD were recommending a "no" vote on the grounds that the referendum itself was not constitutional. While there were some abstentions, about 15%, mainly from the provinces of Majunga and Diego-Suarez, Malagasy voters approved the projects presented to them to the tune of 96.43%. One could, of course, remain sceptical of such results (as well as of those expressed in earlier elections) which tended to corroborate the presence of general conformity. Nevertheless, this could not minimize the wide rejection of Tsiranana's regime. Tsiranana himself gave a farewell to the nation, not without dignity, and General Ramanantsoa assumed the functions of the sole head of state on 7th November.

In peace, a new era was about to begin. Students were returning to schools after 23rd October without a single noteworthy incident and Malgachisation was being felt as instruction resumed. All commercial accords with South Africa were abrogated. New diplomatic relations were in force with the Soviet Union, People's Republic of China,[78] and with Guinea; the talk now was of an "all-azimuth diplomacy;" and preparations were made to negotiate with France again.

The old specter of intra-tribal conflicts could not, however, be made to disappear altogether. In Tamatave and Fenerive (a smaller port north of Tamatave) lycée students went on strike at the end of November — this time against the new government and its drive for accelerated Malgachisation. As this process was predicated on the Merina version of national dialect-language at the expense of other provinces, and because most of the teachers were Merina, the student protest was against what seemed to be an unacceptable return to a policy of past hegomony. Soon, Tamatave was in the midst of violence. There were brutalities against the Merina, arsons, pillaging, and an attack on the local prison which resulted in the freeing of prisoners who had been there as common-law transgressors. Almost by any means, including a constant airlift, some 6,000 Merina fled toward Tananarive, while Tamatave, the main port of Madagascar remained in a state of paralysis. Similar incidents occured in Diego-Suarez at the end of February 1973, reflecting also the local fears, related to the probable dismantling of the long-established French Naval Base and the economic repercussions within this port-town; at Majunga somewhat later, as well as within Antsohihy and other small towns of the northwestern Madagascar. But, calm was quickly re-established and govern-mental inquiries seemed to bring to light some real discontents and worries, with the added conclusion that fallen political figures had come to exploit them quite readily at times. From this time on, however, considerable precautions were attached to the policy of Malgachisation; it was hoped that these would be the very last of the *rotaka*;[79] and the tours of Tsiranana in the provinces were deemed a qualified success at best.

A far greater threat to the new government came from the populist movement in all probability. Once affirmed by the referendum, the Ramanantsoa team found itself soon in a state of pause which earned it especially the criticism of a new political grouping, founded in December 1972, the MFM,[80] which continued to express the hard-line KIM tendencies in Tananarive, mooring itself among the least favored social strata. From a Marxist perspective, the MFM came to accuse the government of representing only the interests of national bourgeoisie which was quite satisfied with a simple transfer of power. The MFM was headed by a sociologist at the University of Madagascar, Manandafy Rakotonirina, former representative of MONIMA in Tananarive Province. The attention which the MFM was beginning to get induced the government to act fast, at the first opportunity. When the MFM sought to commemorate the events of preceding year on 13th May 1973 by a march through Tananarive, 64 of its activists, including Manandafy Rakotonirina, were arrested.[81] This could easily serve to give those arrested a halo of martyrdom and thus endanger the existing govenment; it was a possibility not to be overlooked.

It was through a success in negotiations with France and through a genuine restoration of the *fokonolona* in Madagascar that the government hoped to restore its prestige. Official talks with France started in January 1973 in Paris and the Malagasy delegation at once denounced the 1960 accords. But, normalization of relations became quite difficult as the French government made things drag first because of approaching elections at home and in the hope that deteriorations within Madagascar would induce its negotiators to become more moderate, particularly in respect to the French military bases which had assumed new importance in an Indian Ocean which had become the site of great-power competition. But, this was to count without the determination of Malagasy spokesmen led by Didier Ratsiraka. They had already obtained by 29th March French recognition of Malagasy sovereignty, a full one, over its territorial extent; yet, nothing concrete seemed to be coming out of the negotiations. Then, on 22nd May, unilaterally, and no doubt to compensate among the home public its repression of the MFM, the government announced the exit of Madagascar from the franc zone. This was something that France most likely had wished to avoid and especially because it seemed that some sort of conciliation had been reached on this issue. Although this act did not facilitate the ongoing negotiations, new accords were signed on 4th June. France accepted to return all the military bases in Madagascar allowing only a two-year delay for Diego-Suarez, with future guarantees of French-fleet receptions, and with the Arsenal of Diego-Suarez going under the management of a Franco-Malagasy society in which three-fourths of the capital would be Malagasy. Cooperation personnel from France would continue to be furnished upon the request of the Malagasy government and fellowships would remain at the disposal of those Malagasy students whom the Malagasy Republic wished to send to France for training. Also, a variety of buildings of the colonial era were placed at the disposition of Madagascar (such as the French Embassy in the middle of Tananarive, once palace of the Governor-General and the future seat of the Malagasy head of state). No new conventions came into force as yet regarding the status of French persons and properties in the Great Island, and there were no new monetary and economic accords. When all of the texts of agreements were published in Tananarive on 26th June, the agreements were celebrated as a second independence.

The policy of *fokonolona* rennovation was to give the now government a popular base in the countryside more than in towns. To this particular endeavor came to be attached the name of Colonel Ratsimandrava, new Minister of Interior in-charge of planning. Indeed, he was everywhere, criss-crossing the rural areas. His impromptu meetings with peasants were often transmitted over the radio integrally. During this type of mobile forum, Richard Ratsimandrava came to grasp guite well the magnitude of rural problems and sought to invent a new socialism at a time when this term had been devalued by earlier experiences. On 14th March 1973 the (much-abused) rural communes were abolished while the *fokonolona* were fully restored by the ordinance of 4th August; and the government committed itself not to take part in the management of their production efforts and not to interfere in the use of their revenues. This was done to give power to the people or, as the official formula would have it, to allow for the "people's control over development." A new and more complex apparatus was to be established, replacing the previous functionnaries (ward-chiefs, sub-prefects, prefects) of government with an echelon of those elected directly. The state would continue to maintain its technical services in the country-side but it would not intervene in that capacity unless requested to. While this rural revolution could not arrive in anything larger than small steps, 1973 marked the point at which elections started to be held at the lowest level, at the *fokontany* (land-area of the *fokonolona*), with the clear purpose to do away with the authority of the petty local officials who were simply acting for the central government. Self-managing in spirit, this experience created considerable criticisms, including those from the Left. The MONIMA,[82] for example, agreed to participate in the undertaking but warned against the reconversions of the elected into new officials or the former notables' (mostly PSD vassals) re-elections under the guise of reform. The MONIMA also demanded that, prior to all political reconstructions, the state abolish such socio-economic structures as share-cropping, source of inequality since the "land belongs to its cultivator." In effect, elections at the base did give back the power to over 70% of traditional notables (60% of whom were marked by PSD links). Always within the schema of "social reconstruction," the CNPD (Popular National Council for Development) was established rapidly at the opposite or highest end of the spectrum. This assembly-like organization was to assist the government in matters of "concrete development" but without being able to embarass it since it was only a consultative body and had no powers of its own. The rural *fokonolona* elected to it 93 members, 51 were elected by towns,[83] and 18 were appointed by the goverment. Elections for the CNPD came off on 21st October 1973. Although the CNPD assembly was to be "apolitical" the political parties were into the elections everywhere with supporting candidates; only the MFM urged abstentions but its influence did not extend beyond a mere fraction of the public opinion. A large voting turnout placed pro-government men in majority within the CNPD. Elected himself, Monja Jaona still denounced the arm-twisting and irregularities which had prevented the MONIMA from having as many of its representatives in the CNPD as it would otherwise send; but, it was evident that grass-roots elections were not in favor of previous local-level influences as, for example, André Resampa was badly beaten at Morondava. During its initial session (it was to have only two brief sessions per year) the CNPD concentrated discussions on the development plan for 1974-1977; it was high time to return in earnest to the effort of economic growth in Madagascar but the perspectives were not all that bad. If many French enterprises in Madagascar were playing a waiting game offers of new investments from other lands, especially Japanese investments, gave hope for the start of new activities.

2) As time went by, however, the enthusiasm began to sag as well. Adversaries of the government regrouped their forces; Tsiranana and Resampa, both disappointed with the last elections, had reconciled; the Malagasy Socialist Party (PSM) resulted from the fusion of the PSD and USM, becoming now the main party of opposition. Its program was hardly novel (defense of *côtiers*) but it got the ear of many in the provinces, including the youth, everywhere, in fact, when something did not work too well; and one could note that the government was far more attentive to the MFM initiatives than to the progress of the PSM. In what was certainly more serious in nature, towns in Madagascar were no longer being adequately supplied from the country-side. To induce the peasants to grow more rice, the government doubled the price of this staple; however, despite large imports of rice from eastern Asia, long lines of people were formed at retail shops which awaited deliveries. At the same time, consumers were complaining that the price-increase tended to favor only the rice producers. The towns were being sacrificed to the country-side; unemployment was on the upswing, too, partly a result of certain French departures from Madagascar.

The government tried hard to take hold of the economy. It limited, for instance, the import of luxury goods; it sought to control through state-capitalism at long last the commercial network of Madagascar. It formed the "Societies for National Interest," such as SONACO (for external commerce) and SIMPA (for commercialization of agricultural products). But, barely incepted, these societies were ridden by scandals (even when austerity was the order of the day). This was most prominently the case within SIMPA in which the faulty management was hardly unaware that the peasants kept in their possession a good portion of their harvests or else simply limited production. The incompetences, the embezzlements and even sabotage were beginning to harm the new *fanjakana*.

Most worrisome was also the fact that there developed now some antagonistic tendencies within Ramanantsoa's team. Against the progressivists like Ratsimandrava, who were convinced of the urgency of the need to associate the people directly with the management of the economy and with political decisions, who were also ready for nationalization, were grouped those who came to be known as "Club of the 48," formed presumably in secret. Such a "club" probably never existed. What did exist was a network of lasting friendships, of kinship involving the most socially-prominent families; old networks to be sure, but ones with members who went into the highest positions and thus accumulated enormous influence in both the army and in administration. A state capitalism did not repel this oligarchy, at least for the time being and in so far as it could assist in the development and facilitate economic control. Indeed, this minority would find a place to put its abilities into play within the state enterprises in a decidedly technical and technocratic sense, something clearly incompatible with the populism of men like Ratsimandrava. On the other hand, both by training and by liberal convictions, these men were hardly averse to the preservation of an important private sector which General Ramanantsoa endowed with an "eminent role"[84] since July 1972. Nor were there links with the private enterprise lacking (including foreign-owned), from a perspective of associations created for the greatest benefit to the land and the sharing of benefits; it was regarded as enough for the enterprises, and particularly the foreign ones, to renounce their total independence and accept a certain amount of enabling by the state. Politically, it was also this tendency within government which sought to promote "normalization," that is to say reconciliations from which came after some months, for example, the freeing of the main demonstration organizers at Majunga and Diego-Suarez.

After some two years of military government, in 1974, Madagascar seemed to be leaderless. There had never been so many indiscretions, "news from unimpeachable sources," and plain gossip. There were unkind remarks about the incompatibility of Ratsimandrava himself and Colonel Rabetafika, Director General of the Government, who held without any publicity the heaviest responsibilities and who would become the most valued of General Ramanantsoa's counselors. Rabetafika belonged to one of the noblest families in Imerina and the rumor made him into one of the members —if not creators— of the "48 Club!" As for Didier Ratsiraka, known to be "of the Left," it was said that he would rather side with Ratsimandrava but that Ratsiraka had started a long "treatment of silence."

On 31st December 1974, General Ramanantsoa presented his whishes to the nation while congratulating its political maturity and calling for national unity. But, on 3rd January, there was a sudden arrest of three managers of the famous Compagnie Marsellaise on order from Colonel Ratsimandrava. He made rather menacing allusions against those seeking to impede his policy of *fokonolona* rennovation, those who were sabotaging efforts in economic reconstruction; and this was an undisguised warning to an entire segment of the government, perhaps even to the head of state himself. In mid-January, the *Madagascar-Matin* (which had replaced the *Courrier de Madagascar*) brought out the news of deep cleavage that was ripping the army apart. On 31st December several *côtiers* officers were arrested for plotting to overthrow the extant government; they wanted to replace General Ramanatsoa with Colonel Brechard Rajaonarison. This officer with an official title of Military Counselor to the Head of State, was about to be arrested when he disappeared only to take refuge on January 22nd at the camp of the Mobile Police Group (GMP, the former FRS) at Antanimora, on Tananarive's periphery. The GMP would not deliver him and it so happened that virtually all of the members of the GMP had been dispatched close to the capital from other regions months before the incident. Soon, Rajaonarison let it be known that despite having been the senior and highest-ranking officer of the Malagasy Army he had been kept down as everything was being decided among the Merina; and he was a *côtier*. It was clear that Rajaonarison was guilty, not perhaps of fomenting the plot but of not denoucing it, and he was now in a state of open rebellion as were the men of GMP with him, holding a flank of Tananarive and auguring a possible return to earlier alarming situations. Moreover, the Malagasy Socialist Party, PSM, did not hide its support, at least the moral one, for the Mobile Police Group; and Rajaonarison gave an ultimatum; liberation of all officers under arrest and the parcelling out of posts in proportion to the ethnicities of Madagascar. Without reversing its decisions, the government could simply not give in.

In an impasse, General Ramanantsoa dissolved his government on 25th January. He had wanted at that point to bring together a new and more united team. But, while the General did surround himself with all points of view (perhaps he had even consulted Tsiranana), the task he had set for himself proved an impossible one. Ramanantsoa found himself facing a coalition which included, among oterhs, two of the most popular ministers, Ratsimandrava and Ratsiraka, together with the most influential members of the Left parties, MONIMA and AKFM, as well as the members of CNDP's permanent committee. While the General wanted to include Rabetafika in the new team, the CNPD spokesmen turned his departure into a matter of principle. Colonel Ratsimandrava, or members of the CNPD, threatened to publish several documents which would reveal illegal activities of some high officials; and, on 5th February, General Ramanantsoa capitulated and turned all powers over to Colonel Ratsimandrava,[85] man whom he had, surely, never foreseen as his own successor.[86]

With the coming to power of Ratsimandrava it was also the triumph of his own perspective of basic national reconstruction, starting with the rural and, later, urban *fokonolona* (the urban ones were to be set-up as well). His is also a perspective of great austerity and tension-building. If parties of the Left were generally in its favor the Tananarive bourgeoisie was extremely bitter. Moreover, the government which Ratsimandrava had put together at once gave numerical preponderance to the *côtier* elements with a notable absence of Ratsiraka. The foreign observers were in a state of excitement. On 11th February, in the evening, at the crossroads of the high town's old cobblestone streets, Colonel Ratsimandrava was shot to death.

There immediately came into being a Military Directorate of 19 members, presided over by General Andriamahazo[87] and including Didier Ratsiraka. Martial law was proclaimed and all the political parties were dissolved. Since the actual shooting had been done apparently by members of the GMP, who had thus assassinated the head of state, the Directorate first gave an ultimatum to the Antanimora camp then ordered an attack. The camp surrendered on the 13th, with all those inside; there had been some 15 dead among the GMP and 20 among the attacking forces of order. Some of the GMP men had also taken refuge at the center of the Malagasy Socialist Party, building located itself in the center of Tananarive, besieged on the 14th and taken on the same day in turn. André Resampa was among those who had surrendered. With a hinderance thus out of the way the Directorate was constituted in full now and it announced the pursuit of work started since 1972. But, the public opinion is at a total loss.[88]

The "Trial of the Century," held from 21st March to 12th June, was to clear-up the horizon. Regarded as guilty from the start were essentially Colonel Brechard Rajaonarison, members of the Mobile Police Group, Resampa as well as Tsiranana and their friends.[89] As the radio broadcasted the trial sessions it became progressively perceived that matters were not quite as simple as it was generally believed. There would have been two plots at the same time, perhaps even a third, more or less converging. The côtiers, the GMP, and Colonel Rajaonarison had perhaps only planned to kidnap the Chief of State for a few moments to have him agree on a division of responsibilities among the various ethnicities. Only some of the GMP men, those who had prepared the ambush, would have been involved but as a secret party of yet other interests. Was it, moreover, really the GMP men that had fired the actual shots; or were they not seeking in fact to protect their Chief of State upon learning that other conspirators were waiting at a suitable spot? In fact, a reconstruction of the assassination itself revealed absolutely nothing and it seemed that judges (all military and all close to the Directorate) had no desire to have the whole truth divulged. Put to task were other suspects; and they were given hearings in turn, among them Colonel Rabetafika who was at the assassination site very shortly after the shots were fired. His enigmatic declarations made things look even worse. The "Affair of the Marseillaise" Company was also revived during the trial; all in all some 302 appeared before the court. Of these 270 were released on 20th May on Directorate's orders (most of the GMP men being little more than supernumeraries).[90] On 12th June all were acquitted, except the three survivors of the 11th-February commando who were given five years of forced ·labor. The conclusion of the trial was thus openly political. Without any crushing proofs against this group or that man, or because no proof was to be given, the jury —and hence the government— found it preferable to adopt a solution which really did not satisfy anyone but which did avoid an aggravation of existing quarrels. Still, many of the personalities of the two preceding regimes would remain tarnished by the scandal.

3) Such an end to the trial made it easier to establish at least, behind closed doors, a new government in power. In effect, the government dissolved itself at the end of the trial by Directorate's announcement and on 15th June powers were to be turned over to a new Head of State. While it was not announced who he

would be everyone believed that it could be none other than Didier Ratsiraka; and it was certainly he who became elected by the Directorate with a two-thirds majority arrived through a secret ballot to save the nation.

Born in 1936 this naval officer could impose himself on the opinion through the vigor with which he had regenerated the image of Madagascar abroad while still under General Ramanantsoa. The candor of his intentions and the quality of his interventions at the United Nations and the Organization of African Unity were his assets. A cõtier, Betsimisaraka, he is very representative of a new generation for which the ethnic problems no longer matter. He also enjoys some links with the Merina bourgeoisie. He is an intellectual, a theoretician and not a man of the field. His career as naval man and later diplomat was greatly enhanced when he learned (less concretely than Ratsimandrava) to assess in 1975 the internal problems of Madagascar, especially the problems of peasants. It was General Ramanantsoa who should have wanted him to be the successor and the "treatment of silence" in 1974 permitted the Commander to preserve his image outside the rivalries and conspiracies. His support of Ratsimandrava *in extremis* of a crisis situation could be explained by a desire to resolve the impasse without giving up the benefits of the two preceding years. If he did not enter the Ratsimandrava government this was partly out of personal incompatibility and far more because of fundamental divergence of concepts regarding the type of socialist state to be constructed.[91] But, parties of the Left and most notably the MFM would continue to be predisposed against him. His assent came discretely within the military Directorate but he also seemed to be the only leader of national stature and the only one capable of presenting a program. Indeed, since 12th April, the Directorate had made his main ideas of reform as its own: promote changes within the army in a democratic direction, pursue a non-aligned foreign policy, reform the rural structures as well as society as a whole in the spirit of Ratsimandrava's projects, and decentralize to reassure the cõtiers.

Didier Ratsiraka became the Head of State on 15th June as the Directorate turned all the powers over to him. A "Supreme Council of the Revolution" was set up (CSR) with nine members, all of them military. It was presided over by Ratsiraka himself and its main task was to assist him to control the government itself. As of 16th June, there were 14 ministries and 12 of them were headed by civilian appointees. Ratsiraka's new team was composed predominantly of men close to him but there were some followers of Ratsimandrava (the "Ratsimandravists") as an embodiment of continuity. General Andriamahazo, excluded from the CSR, presided instead over the "Military Council for Development" which was to prepare a reform of the armed forces and make them participate much more actively in the work of national rennovation.[92] The CNDP would not hold more than a single session by the year's end; and it was really the Supreme Council of Revolution, along with the Chief of State, that assumed all the real responsibilities.

Martial law was lifted on 26th June, as spirits had calmed down somewhat. Already, Ratsiraka was taking measures which appeared to be spectacular and which would confirm that a new era was being inaugurated, leaving no doubts about his conception of socialism. Starting with 17th June, there came the nationalization of all banks, insurance companies as well as of all production and diffusion of films. On the last day of June the state took a controlling interest in some petroleum-refining and maritime-transport enterprises. On 1st August it was the turn of the great Marseillaise Company to be nationalized. In fact, within weeks, the most pressing demands of the Malagasy nationalists were met. Also, the NASA was shut-down on 15th July while friendships with socialist countries were reinforced.

Ratsiraka went on the national radio at the end of August to present to the people his "Charter of the Malagasy Socialist Revolution" (its text was his little Red Book in Malagasy, the *Boky Mena*). There was to be a genuinely revolutionary government, a control of administration by the people, decentralization and so on; this was basically a continuous systematization of principles stated on 12th April. There would be committees to oversee the enterprises and industry, new cooperatives for agricultural production, and revolutionary associations which would include the women and the young, and which would function everywhere in the Island. The greatest concentration of activities would continue, of course, in agriculture which was basic to all efforts. The rennovation of the *fokonolona* would go on as well but with the "support of structures which are both ideological and technological." The concern with ideology permeates everything. The provinces would obtain, gradually, institutions already integrated into the general reform of society, and of the state, institutions which would confer real autonomy on each province. In the armed forces, the Navy and the Air Force would be developed at the expense of the army, step justified in the light of more intense big-power rivalries in the Indian Ocean. The Civic Service, expanded into a People's Army of Development, would get most of the state funds that had previously gone to the regular army, and would see to it that people in the rural sector are helped to help themselves as well as formed ideologically. The Chinese model is evident.

These institutions were stabilized by the end of the year. On 7th November Ratsiraka announced a referendum for the establishment of the Second Republic which would be called the "Democratic Republic of Madagascar." Later, the object of popular consultation would be much broader: a popular verdict was not to be given only on the principles of the Red Book, itself the ideological basis of the Democratic Republic, but also on the new constitution and on the choice of Didier Ratsiraka as the new President. All of this formed an idivisible package. The Constitution took on the main traits of the regime in power since June, adding that the President would be elected through universal suffrage for a 7-year term and that two-thirds of the Supreme Council of the Revolution would be chosen by the President. There was one innovation in that the government would be directed by a prime minister responsible directly to the President and appointed by him. A new National Popular Assembly would be in the place of the CNPD, with members elected by universal suffrage for a term of 5 years. Its powers would be limited: there would be no more than four months of sessions per year and a two-thirds majority would be required to place the government in a minority position.[93]

In the electoral campaign before the referendum Ratsiraka and his friends were extremely active in the number of meetings, speeches and tours of the provinces; and, on 21st December, out of 3,394,000 votes cast, 3,216,000 approved all of the proposals made. The new Republic was proclaimed on the 30th; on 4th January Ratsiraka became the President officially; and, on the 11th he designated Joel Rakotomalala as his prime minister.[94] The Supreme Council of the Revolution was reshaped to include 6 military and 6 civilian members.

1976 was the year of stabilization and of preparation for yet another lap during the first semester of 1977 and consisting of elections for the national assembly and the institution of popular committees that would relieve the administrative structures of authority at every echelon. A few incidents did trouble the end of 1976, the most disquieting of which (for the new government in power) was undoubtedly a strike by students at the Technical College, strike which was *really* repressed. Accused of having inconsiderately provoked the strike movement was the MFM, which seemed favorable to Ratsiraka early in 1976 but which rapidly drew away from him; the party was dissolved and its directors were placed under house arrest.[95] It seemed hence that an opposition on the Left was being critical of the government for going neither fast enough nor too far. It was equally apparent that, on the Right, the various bourgeoisie groupings were practicing at the very least a wait-and-see policy. This made it necessary for the government to strengthen its base among the public, reason behind the large number of ideological seminars that had to be attended by the military and civilian personnel from all the responsible agencies.[96] With much the same intentions, an "Avant-Garde of the Malagasy Revolution" or AREMA sought to regroup a revolutionary elite under Ratsiraka's high directions. However, the beginnings of this unit, which was to spear-head a socialist revolution *a la Malagasy* ran into considerable scepticism; and when its adherents began to multiply, doubts came to the organizers as well when they guessed that the rallying was merely complacent, just as it had once been the practice to rally to the PSD by convenience.[97] There was the great danger that when the new structures are put in place in 1977 the country could scatter into small and discordant units, providing a fine opportunity for the enemies of the regime. It thus became indispensable to attain a coherent assembly of all those who were in support of the Ratsiraka experience but who nonetnheless regarded themselves as different groupings. A "National Front for the Defense of the Revolution" was formed on 18th December 1976, after long and numerous negotiations. It alone would present candidates in the different elections to come; and it regrouped now the AREMA, the *Vonjy*, the AKFM (now known as KDRSM), a Christian-Left party, and the MONIMA (which had become *KAMIVIOMBO*); only the MONIMA's own adherence was lukewarm as it, too, had sought a radicalization of reforms at its congress of November 1976.

The economic situation of Madagascar in 1976 could not be

regarded as bad. Against a very steep increase in prices at the end of 1975, the 1976 rate of inflation was somewhere between 6 and 7 percent only. Madagascar had a plus in the balance-of-payments thanks to a drastic reduction of imports and a fortunate combination of circumstances for its coffee and chromium exports. As against a figure of only 13 percent two years earlier, the state now controlled 61 percent of the national commercial turnover and it could re-invest in Madagascar the profits of the older but now nationalized commercial establishments. Still to be tackled as a most serious problem was the lack of rice for a population in continuous expansion (8,500,000 now); and the "battle for rice" tended to enlist everyone.

Although only a prophet could predict the Second Malagasy Republic's future it is clear that the pace of history in Madagascar had accelerated within the last four or five years; that in just a few months' time decolonization had progressed more than during the dozen preceding years. From the colonial past and beyond, from a coplex evolution which is at times contradictory, there subsist in Madagascar both social structures and mental molds that will take a long time to regenerate. The international convergence in the Indian Ocean also risks to provoke internal tendencies to which Madagascar could not remain indifferent. But, the team in-charge has confidence in its ideology and seeks to prove the reality of revolution through action, not words. Only the near future will tell if the Malagasy people as a whole intend to follow.

NOTES

(1) The information employed to prepare this study came mainly from the following works (other than the studies devoted to the more general histories of Madagascar or Africa, to decolonization, to the Third-World, etc.):

Roger Pascal, *La République Malgache*, Paris, 1965; Charles Cadoux, *La République Malgache*, 1969, Paris; Alain Spacensky, *Madagascar, 50 ans de vie politique, de Ralaimongo à Tsiranana*, Paris, 1970; V. Thompson and R. Adloff, *The Malagasy Republic, Madagascar Today*, Stanford 1965; Raymonde Litalien, *Madagascar 1956-1960, une étape vers la décolonisation, étude d'opinion à travers la presse malgache francophone* (Thesis, University of Paris, EPHE-6eme section, 1975); Pierre Lupo, *Englise et décolonisation à Madagascar*, Fianarantsoa, 1974; *Annuaire des Pays de l'Océan Indien*, I, 1974, Centre d'études et de recherches sur les sociétés de l'Océan Indien, Aix-en-Provence, 1976; Gerard Althabe, *Oppression et libération dans l'imaginaire, les communautés villageoises de la côte orientale de Madagascar*, Paris, 1969; Jean de Gaudusson, *L'Administration malgache,*

Paris, 1976.

Two studies deserve special mention, namely those of Francois Partant, *La Guerilla économique, les conditions du développement*, Paris, 1976, a highly *engagé* work which presents original points of view with passion; and, above all, the work of Robert Archer, *Madagascar depuis 1972, la marche d'une révolution*, Paris, 1976; this work by an English university student had certainly profited from confidences imparted by those who participated or who were the privileged witnesses in the events he reports. It is possible that these confidences were made so that their publication would influence the course of events to come in a certain desired direction; but this renders the reading of this volume all the more tittilating.

There are also sources, to be regarded in the strict sense of this term such as: Philibert Tsiranana's *Le Cahier bleu, pensées, souvenirs*, Tananarive, 1971; Didier Ratsiraka's *Charte de la revolution malagasy*, 1975; as well as the different publications which are official, such as those of the Commissariat General au Plan, *Economie Malgache, Evolution, 1950-1960* or *Plan Quinquennal, 1964-1968*.

Among the newspapers and reviews published in Madagascar, one should mention, apart from the daily press in French and/or Malagasy, the weekly *Lumière* (which did not appear in March 1975), and also the weekly *Lakroan'i Madagasikara*; and such reviews as the *Bulletin de Madagascar* (published by the Ministry of Information, last issue of December 1974), the *Madagascar Renouveau* (which is the successor of the preceding one, its no.1 came in the fourth quarter of 1976), as well as several reviews published by the University of Madagascar, such as the *Revue économique de Madagascar*.

For publications in France, one should retain *Le Monde, Le Monde Diplomatique, Jeune Afrique, Afrique-Asie, Africasia*; and among the reviews *Esprit, Etudes, Les Temps Modernes, Tiers Monde*, and especially *Afrique contemporaine* and the *Revue Française d'Etudes politiques africaines* (ex-*Le mois en Afrique*). Much interesting information can be found also in the mimeographed bulletin (with a limited distribution) of GIMOI, *Groupe Madagascar-Océan Indien* (January 1972 — July 1974).

Lastly, the author was inspired, as could be expected, by his own recollections and notes, after having lived in Madagascar during a good part of the period under discussion.

(2) It goes without saying that the global environment had undergone change as well. If in the text of this study no allusions are made on the whole to the great world events it is nonetheless convenient to keep them in mind. It would be easy to reconstruct a chronology of the great problems of our time, starting with general texts which deal with contemporary history, with diplomatic relations and the like.

(3) This was made possible through the use of a law dated 19th December 1966. The commemoration of the revolt freed the local spirits a bit as, until then it was *fady* (taboo) to talk about 1947, especially with foreigners.

(4) *FIDES* - Fonds d'Investissement et de Développement Economique et Social (established by a French law of 30 April 1946). PADESM - Parti des Deshérités de Madagascar, founded in June 1946.

(6) To the reporters from the *Courrier de Madagascar* who came to interview him in 1968 on the Republic's anniversary Tsiranana declared : "I have never been against independence. But, if it had been demanded since 1946 this would lead definitely to a civil war since the *côtiers* were not in agreement...The populations of the highlands wanted an immediate independence. The *côtiers* were against because they were not ready at the time, they did not have enough of

the trained people..," *Courrier de Madagascar*, special number, 12th October 1968.

(7) This was a play of words since *gadra* means "chains" in Malagasy.

(8) Author of the Penetrating study entitled *Le Tsiny et Le Tody dans la pensée Malgache*, Paris, 1957.

(9) *Ankoton'ny Kongresin'ny Fahaleovantenan'i Madagasikara*, party of the congress of the independence of Madagascar.

(10) To show that the PSD was not less nationalistic than the other parties, not withstanding the differences of tactics, Tsiranana had demanded the abolition of the Law of Annexation (of Madagascar) of 1896 at least since December 1957.

(11) Tsiranana had also been elected as Madagascar's deputy to the French National Assembly in January 1956.

(12) Tsiranana also participated at Paris in the work of the committee which prepared the constitution. It was he who proposed the term "community." Again, it was Tsiranana, together with Leopold Sedar Senghor, to be credited with persuading an initially reticent De Gaulle to accept the Article 78. As will be seen below, first Mali, and later most of the other member-states, would profit from it very quickly to become legally independent.

(13) *MONIMA* meant at the time in French "MOuvement National pour l'Independence de Madagascar," (National Movement for Madagascar's Independence).

(14) It was Tsiranana who insisted that this congress meet since members of the provincial assemblies had been elected via universal suffrage in contrast to those of the Representative Assembly who were simply delegated by the provincial assemblies. Virtually all of the deputies who came to the capital were PSD or UDSM —this "Union of the Social Democrats of Madagascar," itself issuing forth from the PADESM as well— the leader of which, Norbert Zafimahova, president over the Representative Assembly.

(15) The UDSM only proposed a regime dominated by the assemblies and with a rather weak executive.

(16) On this point, the Malagasy text diverges from its French counterpart, in which the functions of the Head of State and the Chief of Government are separated.

(17) In July, Tsiranana was also chosen as one of the four ministers-counselors from Africa delegated to the joint ministers of the Community in Paris.

(18) There was rightly some talk about "preventive" independence.

(19) Ivory Coast, Niger, Upper Volta, Dahomey; grouping which was the stepchiled of Felix Houphouet-Boigny.

(20) The AKFM, concentrating henceforth its attacks on the accords of cooperation, talked about a "Malagasy Bizerte."

(21) Fonds d'Aide et de Cooperation (Aid and Cooperation Funds).

(22) It would take the name of "Foundation Charles de Gaulle."

(23) It passage was supple to the extent that a certain amount of confusion lingered among the Malagasy, at the popular level. For example, some six years later, a Besileo peasant women asked one of my European colleagues who visited her village to tell her for sure if, as she believed to have understood, De Gaulle is still Tsiranana's boss.

(24) Madagascar would refuse to follow France, for example, when she extended recognition to the People's Republic of China; for Tananarive only the Nationalist China was in existence. This was one of the rare instances of independence in

Malagasy diplomacy in respect to Paris before 1972.

(25) The journeys of Richard Andriamanjato in Eastern Europe, several articles in the AKFM paper *Imongo Vaovao*, seemed to give credence to this conviction. On the position of the party, see below.

(26) Madagascar took part in the founding of the *Organisation Africaine et Malgache de Cooperation Economique*, the OAMCE, in March 1961. From September 1961 the OAMCE became the *Union Africaine et Malgache* the charter of which was elaborated upon during an international get-together in Tananarive; and this organization was clearly political in character. As this did not seem compatible with the adherence to the OUA (Organization of African Unity), when it was founded in turn, the UAM changed itself into UAMCE in March 1964; but after 1965, the OCAM (Organisation Commune Africaine et Malgache) rediscovered its purely political character.

(27) There was a great deal of criticism of the attitudes which marked certain members of the OUA during the Congolese crises; and Tsiranana was delighted that the OCAM became once more a political outfit.

(28) To some extent, the model is still a French one even if it was not until 12th September that the referendum project, on this point, was presented to the Council of French ministers. But, the idea was "in the air" in Paris for a long time.

(29) The period of transition underwent an increase in the number of the *dinampokon'olona*, associative conventions among villages; and some of them did not only provide for a common preservation of public order, as had been a custom once, but also for solidarity in defense against governmental authority, going as far as to prevent agents of the state's public forces to cross into land areas of the associated villages.

(30) After 1960 MONIMA retained only a Malagasy name (*Madagasikara otronin'ny Malagasy* or Madagascar embraced by the Malagasy). There was talk at the time about the emergence of a "third force" between the PSD and parties of opposition in the Left. Such a movement could only be Catholic-Socialist in inspiration and to have a chance for success it would have to be wedged between two rival blocks of equal power, which was not the case.

(31) *Fiangonan'i Jeso-Kristy eto Madagasicara*. This federation was not in force before 1968 but a pro-AKFM tendency was already clear among some of the pastors and within the many parochial associations of churches hitherto autonomous. The Lutheran churches to 1968 and the one Lutheran Church afterwards for the southern half of Madagascar had much more respect generally for the governmental power.

(32) He was accumulating some prestigious titles: President of the Council of Churches of Africa and of the World Conference for Peace, Vice-President of the World Federation of sister-towns.

(33) They are: Jacques Rabemananjara, the poet, who would become Minister of the National Economy; and Joseph Ravoahangy-Andrianavalona, future Minister of Public Health. The third, Joseph Raseta, refused to come over to the PSD and he would become the unlucky adversary of Tsiranana in the presidential elections of 1965.

(34) The Municipal Council of Tananarive, overwhelmingly AKFM, received in 1961 an overseer delegate general from the government who held all of the essential powers (regime inspired by the Parisian statutory example). Thus, instead of being the Mayor of Tananarive, Richard Andriamanjato was only the President of the Municipal Council.

(35) At the beginning of the 1960's the average per-capita income was only $80 in Madagascar while it went over $150 in Senegal, Ivory Coast, etc.

(36) One still travels mainly by plane for an easy access to the various provinces of Madagascar; hence the number of airfields is far superior to that of railroad stations. Air travel is, however, quite expensive and most of those who avail themselves of this type of transportation do so on government vouchers.

(37) A detailed sketch of Madagascar's economy during this period is to be found in René Gendarme's *L'Economie de Madagascar, diagnostic et perspectives de dévemoppement*, Paris, 1963. This work contained a number of proposals which were considered subversive by the authorities.

(38) "Nationalization is theft," Tsiranana would declare in 1969. Another time he said that there was, besides, nothing to nationalize in the Island.

(39) The yield being rapid, capital investments found their way more than willingly into this type of enterprise.

(40) The average income of a peasant family represented barely one-fifth of income attained by a modest urban family. It is true that peasants lived basically in auto-subsistance but the comparison does show that their conditions were miserable.

(41) Which was developing the lower valley of the Mangoky, major river of the southwest, located slightly north of Tuléar. See Paul Ottino's *Les Economies paysannes malgaches du Bas-Mangoky*, Paris, 1963. This work deals with traditional society at the start of its transformation.

(42) Already in 1959 Philibert Tsiranana was saying "it is not so much a question of growing rice as it is of creating cultivators, not of producing meat but of turning out breeders of stock."

(43) The Institute of Social Improvement, which was the brain-child of the University of Madagascar, also took part in training the enabling personnel.

(44) Besides, the Republic equipped itself with the legislation against idleness in 1962. For the President, "a patriot is someone who works."

(45) At the conference held durig October 1967 at Algiers within the "Group of 77," Jacques Rabemananjara, then Minister of Foreign Affairs, was able to declare: "Whether accepted or not, and whatever term is used to depict our attitude, we are forced in the present conditions to recognize that we still have quite a long road to traverse with our colonizers of yesterday who are now our partners."

(46) *Communauté Economique Européenne* (Common Market) — *Etats Africains et Malgache Associés*.

(47) It is also necessary to note that in the field of foreign policy Tsiranana took violent stands against the Biafran secession in 1967 (another rare instance of non-alignment with French positions). What seemed ominous in Madagascar was the provincial separatism in a new state; and the Congolese experience was transposed as a threat to Malagasy national unity. This was also a time of talk in Madagascar about discords between the northern *côtiers* (including Tsiranana and a large number of his closest collaborators) and those of the south.

(48) Their advent would be a frequent object of criticism. In order to allot to vast herds of cattle an analogous tract of grazing lands, a certain large "ranch" of the middle-western interior expelled the peasant settlers from the highlands who had created enterprises for intense rice cultivation. In fact, several of the state farms used the old lands exploited once by the European *colons* who had abandoned them as hardly profitable.

(49) A Malagasy professor told a group of French students at the end of 1969: "One could not say that the Malagasy (citizen) (really) participates in the con-

struction of a modern economy (in Madagascar)...of all the African lands, Madagascar is the one in which there is the largest number of foreign companies in action (and) all that can be called modern in production is managed by them... Curiously, the large firms developed even more *after* independence because they can profit from a (very) liberal code which governs investments; and the revenues from their activities assist the development of former colonial enter- prises" (cited by *Africasia*, no. of 16th March 1970).

(50) Not a single important track of the railroad was in the making. There was talk about an Antsirabe-Fianarantsoa line that would link two networks which dated back to the colonial period. But construction difficulties and the rather dubious prospects of viability repelled the possible financial backers from outside the Island. Disappointed, the President declared that Madagascar itself would construct it but nothing came out of all this.

(51) West Germany became the second-ranking commercial partner of Mada- gascar. One should also note a vigorous Italian commercial offensive at the end of the 1960's.

(52) Octave Mannoni, *Psychologie de la Colonisation*, Paris, 1950.

(53) Even in 1972, after the start of local revolution, I could hear some reve- lations of a young girl from the most prominent stratum of Tananarive's society to the effect that when the most terrible things would come about at the time of her marriage, "all in all," she said, "I would rather marry a *côtier* than a *mainty*" (the *mainty* or Blacks are the descendants of former slaves in Imerina).

(54) In addition to the causes mentioned earlier, one should cite the strong increase in the "transaction" (sales) tax by an administration hungry for new sources of revenue.

(55) Following the first generation of cooperating personnel (composed mainly of reconverted former functionaries of the colonial administration) the new- arrivals are far more to the "Left;" among them a good number of Christian progessivists. The authors of the pamphlet were denouncing, among a variety of scandals, the one of the "Large Mills" in Dakar. This firm (Grands Moulins de Dakar) had a government contract in 1964 to exploit Malagasy forests on a large scale, and it had also obtained a monopoly on providing flour to the Malagasy. But, as time went by, no enabling investments came from abroad while the director of the firm demanded additional favors, including a large loan guaranteed by the state. He was suspected of having corrupted a number of Malagasy functionaries and politicians. In Madagascar, accusations of coruption were becoming more ans more frequent as well; indeed, the frequently deficit- ridden balance-sheets of the state farms and the communal syndicates were attributed to embezzlements. A scandal would tarnish André Resampa at Moron- dava: he would give the endorsement of the state for a huge loan contracted by an "Americano-Greco-Malagasy" firm (the AGM) which consisted of some rather questionable people. There was to be a huge slaughter-house, applying the modern industrial techniques, but one with a capacity far in excess of the availability of cattle in the area; and, when the scandal came into public view, the slaughter-house had already been constructed.

(56) The government was so frightened to see a reproduction of events in Paris that it forbade the University to adopt the Faure reforms which stemmed from the French May events.

(57) The young Malagasy were being urged at the time to adopt the "non- violent"comportment of Mahatma Gandhi.

(58) The Tsimihety are an ethnicity of north-northwestern Madagascar and Philibert Tsiranana is their native-son.

(59) The FRS are attached directly to the Presidency at this moment.

(60) 'And who is going to define the 'national realities?' No one," said Minister Botokeky, in charge of National Education and one of the oldest followers of Tsiranana, since the foundation of PSD.

(61) The official point of view was stated as follows: "We have decided that student-participation should simply be confined to what they had been trained for."

(62) At the time the FAEM had a majority of moderates.

(63) On some occasions, instead of giving tax-collectors the amounts due, southerners gave them the PSD membership cards.

(64) Andriamanjato approved the repression: "Had I been the President I would have done the same thing."

(65) The Catholic Church became increasingly suspect and the ORSTOM plot was sometimes labelled as a "Catholic conspiracy." Leaders of Catholic organizations were also harassed at times.

(66) Suggested by the rather cryptic turn of phrases, the foreign embassy was that of the United States. Herewith is one version of the affair to come out subsequently: Resampa did not (really) conspire with anyone; but, confronted with an obvious decline of the extant President, the different Ambassadors in Madagascar were advising their respective governments of Tsiranana's possible successors; without any regrets, the American diplomats anticipated the coming of Resampa into the Office as he was a strong man and one of solid anti-communist convictions; but, the French Intelligence services intercepted an American telegram to that efect and passed it on to Tsiranana, c.f. A.-M. Coguel, "La Diplomatie Malgache," *Revue Française d'Etudes Politiques*, June 1972.

(67) Shortly after its establishment the government did away with the competitive national exam for entry into the upper-lycée classes (the so-called "second-cycle" of studies). But, the second-cycle classes were available earlier only within a few of the main educational establishments in the Island (all of them in the largest towns) where they were free and where there was no room for more than one-tenth of the available candidates. Moreover, the second-cycle was pre-reserved for those who had completed their first lycée cycle with success in the same schools, namely children of the most Gallicized families, that is, the richest and most influential families in Madagascar. An extension of the competitive exam to the national level seemed therefore to have been a democratizing measure. In fact this was a bit illusory since the very French nature of the second-cycle and hence of the exam itself would end up by favoring the same social stratum. Demands for the return of a *national* exam turned out to have been nonetheless a mobilizing force that went hand-in-hand with the extension of the student movement beyond Tananarive.

(68) "Now we have the dead here. Who are the killers? They are the strike leaders, for if they had not pulled this strike off there would be no dead. *Voila!* Let me give you a piece of advice, parents, workers, pupils: if you value your lives take no part in the strike...If it is necesary, even to the tune of 2,000 dead, we will have that many in a single sweep! 2,000, even 3,000 dead. In a single action! Tsak! Tsak! Here are the dead. Tsak! More of the dead. After that, if there are 5,000, 6,000, 100,000 of you we are going to get you! Tsak! Tsak! But, of course, that is not going to happen. Be good, what!? Get out of this fishy affair." It is easy to understand after such an upsetting speech, diffused by radio in the evening of the 13th, that the break with those who had already had difficulties in even supporting the regime was not to be remedied.

(69) Most of them among the demonstrators. There were a few deaths in Majunga, site of analogous incidents.

(70) This was a popular condemnation of the AKFM ambiguities.

(71) That was the Palace of the Prime Minister during the Merina Monarchy period.

(72) Tsiranana was to have asked for the French Army's help which had been refused. He was only offered an escort to take him to a safe place.

(73) The French had, at no time, been really worried by the riots.

(74) The red and white flag of the old Monarchy could be seen at times on the streets of Tananarive during the days of 13th to 15th May.

(75) *ZOAM - Zatova Orin'asa Anivon'ny madagasikara:* the young unemployed of central Madagascar.

(76) Considerable fortunes were made through politics and examples were not lacking at the very top either, see the cases cited by Robert Archer, *Madagascar depuis 1972*, p. 86.

(77) *Komity Iombonan'ny Mpitolona* or Committee of the fighters' assemblies.

(78) China would give a loan to Madagascar allowing it to pay an indemnity to South Africa for the termination of accords contracted in the past.

(79) Meaning "violent manifestation(s);" this word is probably of coastal origin and it came to notice during this period. In fact, the Malagasy vocabulary began to enrich itself through a bevy of popular expressions and terms, something which dismayed and scandalized a bit the traditionalists.

(80) *Mpitolona ho amin'ny Fanjakan'ny Madinika* or those who sutrggle for the power of the little people.

(81) Condemned to terms of 6 months to two years in prison, they were freed after the *appel* in September.

(82) The party was able to capture the rural areas around Tuléar and it began to experiment with a new type of cooperatives.

(83) A manifest case of inequality as 93 were elected for 80 percent of the (rural) population and 51 for the other 20 percent.

(84) The 1974-1977 plan had as its principles the development of state capitalism and collaboration with the private sector. An ordinance facilitated the absorption of foreign into national enterprises: any proprietor who wishes to sell must announce the sale six months in advance and the Malagasy have a right to acquire the property before-hand.

(85) According to the terms of Article 3 of the Referendum Law of 1972. The Superior Council for Institutions rubber-stamped this interpretation of the text.

(86) On all of these events and the ones which follow, future histotians will bring to bear other and fuller information. A am following here that of R. Archer who seems to me to be quite acceptable at this time.

(87) One of the three existing Malagasy generals, with Ramananatsoa and Philibert Ramarolahy (who never had as important a role). The recall of General Ramanantsoa, soon to retire from the Army, was not envisaged at all.

(88) News came of the formation of a provisional government in exile in Paris, work of the 1972-Secretary-General of the PSD. But, this attempt was not taken seriously by anyone and no foreign power offered it any support in all probability. The German Ambassador talked about a hoax....

(89) Tsiranana remained in Tananarive until 8th February, then he went to Majunga escorted all the way to the aeroport by men of the GMP in FRS uniforms; he was to have been kept informed of projects for the coup d'etat, as well as André Resampa who was at the Antanimora camp some hours before the actual

assassination. As for Rajaonarison, he was the most likely suspect because of the unsettling nature of his claims: for him, the coming of Ratsimandrava to power as Head of State was illegal; on the 7th he demanded the formation of a Government of Public Health.

(90) Following this intermixing of the executive and judiciary, the Ratsimandrava family withdrew its complaint. The trial, naturally, continued since the state itself had been the victim of conspiracy against its security.

(91) On the rivalries and secret negotiations among the various tendencies, see again the work of R. Archer, chapter 9.

(92) It goes without saying that Colonel Rabetafika was not included in this team.

(93) There was no longer any reference to God in the preamable but rather the condemnation of the exploitation of man by man as "well as of all forms of domination, oppression and alienation that might ensue."

(94) Joel Rakotomalala was in all of the governments since 1972 and was member of the military Directorate. He would die in a helicopter accident on 30th July 1976 and would be replaced by Justin Rakotoniaina, a civilian.

(95) For the President, the MFM had been manipulated by reactionary instigators; it was just after the measures were taken against the MFM that the Palace of Andafiavaratra was gutted by fire. Was it a coincidence? At any rate, the damage is irreparable for the historians since the flames consumed all of the documents on the events of 1975 which had been housed at the Palace. It seems rather farfetched that if the MFM partisans had set fire to it according to rumors this was done precisely to make the documents disappear.

(96) The culminating point of this ideological reconstruction was, in September, the Malagasy-North Korean seminar on the ideas of Djoutche (North Korean Socialist Revolution).

(97) Testimony of Charles Ravoajanahary, historian, professor at the Department of Malagasy Studies, University of Madagascar, personal counselor of the President, in-charge of animating the AREMA; cf. *Le Monde*, 30 and 31 December 1976 and 1st January 1977.